SCHOOL
FINANCE

D0914067

DEBATING ISSUES
in American Education

SCHOOL FINANCE

VOLUME EDITOR

WILLIAM E. THRO

CHRISTOPHER NEWPORT UNIVERSITY

6

VOLUME

DEBATING ISSUES
in American Education

SERIES
EDITORS

CHARLES J. RUSSO
ALLAN G. OSBORNE, JR.

⑤SAGE reference

Los Angeles | London | New Delhi
Singapore | Washington DC

Los Angeles | London | New Delhi
Singapore | Washington DC

FOR INFORMATION:

SAGE Publications, Inc.

2455 Teller Road

Thousand Oaks, California 91320

E-mail: order@sagepub.com

SAGE Publications Ltd.

1 Oliver's Yard

55 City Road

London EC1Y 1SP

United Kingdom

SAGE Publications India Pvt. Ltd.

B 1/I 1 Mohan Cooperative Industrial Area

Mathura Road, New Delhi 110 044

India

SAGE Publications Asia-Pacific Pte. Ltd.

3 Church Street

#10-04 Samsung Hub

Singapore 048763 049483

Copyright © 2012 by SAGE Publications, Inc.

Printed in the United States of America.

Library of Congress Cataloging-in-Publication Data

School finance/volume editor, William E. Thro.

p. cm. — (Debating Issues in American Education ; v. 6)

A Sage reference publication
Includes bibliographical references and index.

1. Education—United States—Finance. I. Thro, William E.

LB2825.S33595 2012
371.2'06—dc23   2011031311

Publisher: Rolf A. Janke

Acquisitions Editor: Jim Brace-Thompson

Assistant to the Publisher: Michele Thompson

Developmental Editors: Diana E. Axelsen, Carole Maurer

Production Editor: Tracy Buyan

Reference Systems Manager: Leticia Gutierrez

Reference Systems Coordinator: Laura Notton

Copy Editor: Robin Gold

Typesetter: C&M Digitals (P) Ltd.

Proofreader: Jennifer Thompson

Indexer: Mary Mortensen

Cover Designer: Janet Kiesel

Marketing Manager: Carmel Schrire

SUSTAINABLE FORESTRY INITIATIVE   Certified Sourcing
www.sfiprogram.org
Label applies to the text stock   SFI-00341

12 13 14 15 16 10 9 8 7 6 5 4 3 2 1

CONTENTS

ABOUT THE EDITORS-IN-CHIEF

Charles J. Russo, JD, EdD, is the Joseph Panzer Chair in Education in the School of Education and Allied Professions and adjunct professor in the School of Law at the University of Dayton. He was the 1998–1999 president of the Education Law Association and 2002 recipient of its McGhehey (Achievement) Award. He has authored or coauthored more than 200 articles in peer-reviewed journals; has authored, coauthored, edited, or coedited 40 books; and has in excess of 800 publications. Russo also speaks extensively on issues in education law in the United States and abroad.

Along with having spoken in 33 states and 25 nations on 6 continents, Russo has taught summer courses in England, Spain, and Thailand; he also has served as a visiting professor at Queensland University of Technology in Brisbane and the University of Newcastle, Australia; the University of Sarajevo, Bosnia and Herzegovina; South East European University, Macedonia; the Potchefstroom Campus of North-West University in Potchefstroom, South Africa; the University of Malaya in Kuala Lumpur, Malaysia; and the University of São Paulo, Brazil. He regularly serves as a visiting professor at the Potchefstroom Campus of North-West University.

Before joining the faculty at the University of Dayton as professor and chair of the Department of Educational Administration in July 1996, Russo taught at the University of Kentucky in Lexington from August 1992 to July 1996 and at Fordham University in his native New York City from September 1989 to July 1992. He taught high school for 8½ years before and after graduation from law school. He received a BA (classical civilization) in 1972, a JD in 1983, and an EdD (educational administration and supervision) in 1989 from St. John's University in New York City. He also received a master of divinity degree from the Seminary of the Immaculate Conception in Huntington, New York, in 1978, as well as a PhD Honoris Causa from the Potchefstroom Campus of North-West University, South Africa, in May 2004 for his contributions to the field of education law.

Russo and his wife, a preschool teacher who provides invaluable assistance proofreading and editing, travel regularly both nationally and internationally to Russo's many speaking and teaching engagements.

Allan G. Osborne, Jr. is the retired principal of the Snug Harbor Community School in Quincy, Massachusetts, a nationally recognized Blue Ribbon School of Excellence. During his 34 years in public education, he served as a special education teacher, a director of special education, an assistant principal, and a principal. He has also served as an adjunct professor of special education and education law at several colleges, including Bridgewater State University and American International University.

Osborne earned an EdD in educational leadership from Boston College and an MEd in special education from Fitchburg State College (now Fitchburg State University) in Massachusetts. He received a BA in psychology from the University of Massachusetts.

Osborne has authored or coauthored numerous peer-reviewed journal articles, book chapters, monographs, and textbooks on legal issues in education, along with textbooks on other aspects of education. Although he writes and presents in several areas of educational law, he specializes in legal and policy issues in special education. He is the coauthor, with Charles J. Russo, of five texts published by Corwin, a SAGE company.

A past president of the Education Law Association (ELA), Osborne has been an attendee and presenter at most ELA conferences since 1991. He has also written a chapter now titled "Students With Disabilities" for the *Yearbook of Education Law*, published by ELA, since 1990. He is on the editorial advisory committee of *West's Education Law Reporter* and is coeditor of the "Education Law Into Practice" section of that journal, which is sponsored by ELA. He is also on the editorial boards of several other education journals.

In recognition of his contributions to the field of education law, Osborne was presented with the McGhehey Award by ELA in 2008, the highest award given by the organization. He is also the recipient of the City of Quincy Human Rights Award, the Financial Executives Institute of Massachusetts Principals Award, the Junior Achievement of Massachusetts Principals Award, and several community service awards.

Osborne spends his time in retirement writing, editing, and working on his hobbies, genealogy and photography. He and his wife Debbie, a retired elementary school teacher, enjoy gardening, traveling, attending theater and musical performances, and volunteering at the Dana Farber Cancer Institute in Boston.

ABOUT THE
VOLUME EDITOR

William E. Thro is university counsel and associate professor of constitutional studies at Christopher Newport University, a public liberal arts university in Newport News, Virginia. He is an accomplished appellate advocate, constitutional scholar, and education lawyer.

As solicitor general of Virginia from 2004 to 2008, he was responsible for the Virginia state government's U.S. Supreme Court litigation (except capital cases) as well as lower court appeals involving the constitutionality of statutes or politically sensitive issues. He argued 2 cases in the U.S. Supreme Court and 33 cases in the lower appellate courts. He was on brief for 7 cases in the U.S. Supreme Court and 70 cases in the lower appellate courts.

His scholarship focuses on constitutional law in educational contexts in both the United States and South Africa. He has authored or coauthored more than 50 articles in peer-reviewed publications and has written extensively on the subject of school finance litigation.

ABOUT THE CONTRIBUTORS

Nicola A. Alexander is an associate professor in the Department of Organizational Leadership, Policy, and Development at the University of Minnesota. Alexander is a board member of the National Education Finance Association and has published in *American Educational Research Journal, Educational Policy, Journal of School Business Management,* and *Journal of Education Finance.*

Dana K. Bagwell is a doctoral candidate in the Department of Health Education at D'Youville College in Buffalo, New York. For more than a decade, Bagwell has conducted research centered on health promotion and conducted numerous educational seminars and interventions designed to increase the health and wellness of the aging population.

Scott R. Bauries teaches education law and state constitutional law at the University of Kentucky College of Law. Before entering academia, he served as an associate with McGuireWoods, LLP, and as a clerk to Judge Emmett Ripley Cox of the U.S. Court of Appeals for the Eleventh Circuit.

Victoria Carr is an associate professor in early childhood education and director of the Arlitt Child and Family Research and Education Center at the University of Cincinnati. She is an experienced administrator and teacher of children in preschool, special education, and gifted programs.

Luke M. Cornelius is an associate professor of educational leadership at the University of North Florida. He teaches and researches in the areas of education law, school finance, educational policy and politics, and sports law.

Betty Cox is an associate professor, educational studies, University of Tennessee at Martin, and former superintendent of three successive school districts. She is also a member of the Louisiana State Bar Association.

Janet R. Decker is an assistant professor in the School of Education at the University of Cincinnati where she teaches education law and personnel courses. Decker received both her JD and her PhD in education leadership and policy studies from Indiana University.

Barbara M. De Luca is currently an associate professor at the University of Dayton, where she teaches school finance, research design, and statistics. She has published research on school finance in a variety of journals from the more scholarly, such as the *Journal of Education Finance,* to the more practical, such as *Journal of School Business Management,* and has contributed to several other publications.

Lisa G. Driscoll is an associate professor in the Department of Educational Leadership at the University of North Carolina at Charlotte. Her research is in the fields of educational finance, law, and policy. Driscoll serves on the editorial board of the *Journal of Education Finance* and on the advisory board of the National Education Finance Conference.

Carlee Poston Escue is an assistant professor in the Educational Leadership Program at the University of Cincinnati. She holds a PhD from the University of Florida, where she focused on education finance with a minor in research and evaluation methodology. Her research interests are the adequacy and equity of funding for public school students.

Shana Goldwyn is an assistant professor in the College of Education, Criminal Justice, and Human Services at the University of Cincinnati. She earned a PhD in educational leadership and policy studies from Florida State University in 2008. She is a former special education teacher at the elementary school level. Her research interests include instructional and urban educational leadership, as well as data analysis and progress monitoring.

Michael Hazelkorn is a professor of special education at the University of West Georgia. His background as assistant superintendent for personnel and pupil services provided him with insight into the law and financial issues as they apply to special education. He teaches special education supervision and law.

Steven A. Hinshaw is the finance director at the City of Centerville, Ohio. Previously, he worked as a chief financial officer for more than 17 years in Ohio public school districts. He also serves as an adjunct professor teaching school finance classes at the University of Dayton and Miami University.

Christine Kiracofe is an associate professor at Northern Illinois University where she teaches education law and finance.

William S. Koski is the Eric & Nancy Wright Professor of Clinical Education, professor of law, and professor of education (by courtesy), Stanford University. He directs a legal clinic that advocates for equality of educational opportunity for disadvantaged children and serves as plaintiffs' counsel in pathbreaking school finance litigation in California. Koski has published articles on educational equity and adequacy, the politics of judicial decision making, and teacher assignment policies.

Steven K. Million is a retired professor of education from Winthrop University and has served both as senior national lecturer for finance and law at Nova

Southeastern University and founding faculty in doctoral studies at St. John Fisher College in New York. He holds a PhD from the University of Florida with graduate and undergraduate degrees from the University of Kansas and the University of Missouri. He is a former National Accreditation of Teacher Education (NCATE) accreditation team chair and American Association of Colleges for Teacher Education (AACTE) national consultant.

C. Daniel Raisch is associate professor and associate dean in the School of Education and Allied Professions at the University of Dayton. His research interests include school finance, school law, and educational leadership. His consulting interests include strategic planning and administrator/board member relationships. He has published several journal articles and is coeditor of *The Encyclopedia of Educational Reform and Dissent.* He was a public school educator for 30 years, 25 of those as an administrator including 18 years as a superintendent.

Anthony Rolle is professor and chair of the Department of Educational Leadership and Policy Studies at University of South Florida's College of Education. His education finance and economic research is published in books, journals, and monographs such as *To What Ends and By What Means? The Social Justice Implications of Contemporary School Finance Theory and Policy, Modern Education Finance and Policy, Measuring School Performance and Efficiency,* and *Journal of Education Finance.*

Robert J. Safransky is an adjunct professor of school law and American government, Nova Southeastern University. He received a BA from St. Francis College, an MA from Stetson University, and a PhD from Florida State University. He has worked as a high school teacher, junior high school and adult vocational school principal, and a central office administrator.

Jennifer A. Sughrue is an associate professor in the College of Education at Old Dominion University. Her areas of specialization and research include education law, policy, ethics and leadership, finance, special education law, and comparative international education. She earned a PhD in educational leadership and policy studies at Virginia Polytechnic Institute and State University (Virginia Tech) in 1997. Before that, Sughrue was in K–12 international education for nearly 20 years. She began her higher education career as an assistant professor of educational leadership and policy studies at Virginia Tech, then joined the faculty in the Department of Educational Leadership at Florida Atlantic University in 2004 and became an associate professor. She has been primary investigator and project evaluator on Association Liaison Office for University Cooperation in Development (ALO) and U.S. Agency for

International Development (USAID) grants for educational development work in Malawi and continues to seek funding opportunities to sustain this work. She has served on the executive board of the Education Law Association as well as chaired its national conference.

Lenford C. Sutton is an associate professor and program coordinator of the doctoral program in educational leadership, policy, and law at Alabama State University. His teaching and scholarly focuses are in the areas of school finance, education law, and the distribution of education resources.

Spencer C. Weiler is an assistant professor in educational leadership and policy studies at the University of Northern Colorado. His research focuses on equal access to knowledge for all children. Specifically, he explores access issues from a school law, school finance, and leadership perspective.

R. Craig Wood is professor of educational administration and policy at the University of Florida in Gainesville, Florida, and chair of the National Education Finance Conference.

Korrin M. Ziswiler earned an MBA from Wright State University and is a doctoral student in the education leadership program at the University of Dayton in Dayton, Ohio. She has extensive experience with the Ohio Department of Education's Autism Scholarship Program (ASP).

INTRODUCTION

State school financing systems have been subject to legal challenges for several decades. Many of these challenges have their roots in the inequalities that exist from one school district to the next within the same state. These inequalities exist because school districts rely largely on the property tax to finance their public schools. To the extent that the wealth of various communities within a state varies, the quality of education from one school district to another, within the same state, will not be equal. The quality of education depends on each district's ability to raise revenue through the property tax. Wealthier districts can better support a higher quality of education than can poorer districts.

Few would argue that education is one of the most important undertakings of state and local government entities. The U.S. Constitution does not mention education. Thus, the establishment of school systems and the determination of how they will be financed have been left to the states. All states have included provisions in their own constitutions requiring the establishment of a system of public education.

Yet, that constitutional value is expensive. If all children are to have the opportunity for an education at taxpayer expense, then the government must find a way to raise the necessary revenue and must determine the most efficient and effective way of spending the money. Although these tasks appear simple, they are actually quite complex. Moreover, decisions about how to raise revenue or spend money inevitably implicate various other constitutional, political, policy, and even cultural issues. In effect, every educational issue discussed in the other nine volumes in this set is, at least indirectly, a finance issue. To debate issues of school finance is to debate whether the local school board or government at the state and federal level controls the community's schools. It is to discuss whether the judiciary will intervene to ensure equity and adequacy in a state's public school system. It is to consider whether government should use public funds to empower parents to choose a private or nontraditional public school. It is to ponder whether funding the unique needs of children with disabilities or children with high intelligence is the responsibility of the local school district or of the state and federal government. It is to dispute whether public schools must be free or whether students must pay for some services.

The 18 debates contained in this volume are actually different ways of framing five broad questions. First, what is the proper role of local school boards? Put another way, should local officials have discretion to do what they believe is best or should the state and federal government impose controls as a means of ensuring equal education? Second, what is the proper role of the judiciary in ensuring educational equity and adequacy? Phrased differently, when the state constitution contains a provision stating that the legislature will create a system of free public schools of a particular quality, should the courts determine whether the legislature has met its obligations? Third, should taxpayer money be used to promote parental choice? In other words, should the government, directly or indirectly, subsidize private schools or allow the creation of public charter schools that operate much like private schools? Fourth, what is the proper role of the state and federal government in financing special education and gifted education? To restate, if Congress or the state legislature requires local school districts to provide extraordinary services, should those entities also provide all or at least most of the funding? Finally, what is the obligation of the public schools with respect to providing elite programs or activities? To state this in different terms, must all programs or activities be provided free of charge?

The remainder of this introductory essay provides a brief overview of the constitutional, legal, and political framework for each of these broad questions and the specific debates that fall within the broader questions. Within each individual debate chapter in this volume, there is a lengthier introduction.

THE PROPER ROLE OF LOCAL SCHOOL BOARDS

In the United States, questions of educational finance often involve two competing state constitutional values. On the one hand, there is a state constitutional value of equality. All public schools should be equal. On the other hand, there is the constitutional value of local control. Local school boards have broad discretion to determine who will teach, what subjects are covered, and how education will be delivered. In some situations, the vindication of one value necessarily means the subordination of another value.

The constitutional value of equality is reflected in the education clauses of the state constitutions, which mandate the establishment of a system of public schools. In many states, the constitutional text specifies a level of quality. Implicit, if not explicit, in this constitutional command is the notion that the public schools throughout the state will be of similar, if not virtually identical, quality. The system of financing the schools typically embodies this belief. The state mandates that local school districts impose property taxes, but also provides additional money for those districts where property values are low. Thus, every school district, regardless of its socioeconomic makeup, has a minimum level of funding. This level should be sufficient to enable the school district to meet the state standards of competency and to ensure that the public schools are broadly equal. Put another way, the state designs its finance system to ensure educational equality.

In contrast, the method that all states except Hawaii provide for the delivery of educational services reflects the constitutional value of local control. The states created smaller political units—typically called school districts—that are responsible for the public schools in a given geographic area. A school board, which generally is elected by the voters of the school district, oversees the operations of each local school district. The local board typically has broad discretion over hiring, financial, and curriculum decisions. For example, as long as the board hires certified teachers, the board may hire whomever it wants. Similarly, subject to certain state mandates, the board may spend the available money as it sees fit. Finally, although the state may mandate particular subjects, the choice of textbooks and the choice of curriculum approach are left entirely to the school board. In sum, the quality of the local public schools is very much the result of decisions made by the local school board.

The great discretion given to local school boards almost inevitably leads to some inequality among school districts. Because some local school districts are better at making decisions than others, some local districts become better than others even where the school districts have approximately the same level of funding. It is inevitable that some teachers will be better, some principals will be superior administrators, some curriculum approaches will be more effective, and some textbooks will be of a higher quality. Although these differences in educational quality are problematic, local boards presumably can eliminate these disparities simply by altering their hiring and curriculum approaches. In other words, local boards must make better use of the resources available to them.

THE PROPER ROLE OF THE JUDICIARY IN ENSURING EQUAL AND ADEQUATE EDUCATION

Although local school districts receive funds from both federal and state sources, all local school districts except those in Hawaii raise much of the money necessary for operations through a percentage tax, on the value of the real property in the district, with the tax rate set by the local residents. Because of differences in rates and in the value of real property, this system results in vast disparities in the amount of funds available. As a result, some districts have trouble providing even the basics, but others are able to offer educational luxuries. Given the probable relationship between level of expenditures and the quality of the education received by the students, disparities in funding will often lead to disparities in educational achievement. Although state legislatures and executives have adopted various mechanisms to correct this financial inequality, the disparities remain.

Yet, every state constitution has a provision mandating, at a minimum, that the state provide a system of free public schools. The constitutional text of these clauses varies a great deal. At one end of the spectrum are the 21 "establishment provisions" that simply mandate that a free public school system be established and nothing more. In the middle are 18 "quality provisions" that mandate that an educational system of a specific quality be provided. Similarly, there are 6 "strong mandate" provisions that establish a level of quality and that also provide a strong mandate to achieve it. Finally, at the far end of the spectrum are 5 "high duty provisions" that seem to place the requirement to provide education above other governmental functions such as highways or welfare.

Given the apparent conflict between the state constitutional provisions and the funding disparities created by the states' school finance systems, it is not surprising that the courts have been asked to intervene and vindicate the constitutional value of free public education for all by declaring that the current system of financing the schools is unconstitutional. Indeed, during the last four decades, the high court of virtually every state has wrestled with the question of whether the state's school financing system is constitutional.

School finance litigation has relied on two distinct litigation approaches. First are "equity suits," where the plaintiffs assert that all children are entitled to have the same amount of money spent on their education or that children are entitled to equal educational opportunities. In effect, the plaintiffs in such cases believe that more money means a better education, and they have little or no tolerance for any differences in money or opportunities. In an equity suit, the plaintiffs rely on the equivalent of a state equal protection clause and assert that education is a fundamental right and that disparities in funding violate that right. The dominant legal theory during the 1970s and 1980s tended to be that found in equity suits.

Second are "adequacy suits" in which the plaintiffs argue that all children are entitled to an education of at least a certain quality and that more money is necessary to bring the worst school districts up to the minimum level mandated by the state constitution. The emphasis is on differences in the quality of education delivered rather than on the resources available to the districts. The systems are struck down not because some districts have more money than others do, but because the quality of education in some schools, not necessarily the poorest in financial terms, is inadequate. In an adequacy suit, the plaintiffs assert that the state constitution establishes a particular standard for educational quality and that the schools do not measure up to that standard. The plaintiffs assume that the reason for this failure is inadequate funds. Although many contemporary cases have equity suit arguments, the adequacy suit has been the dominant strategy of the 1990s and the early 21st century.

The history of school finance litigation comprises three waves. During the first wave, which lasted from the late 1960s until the Supreme Court's decision in *San Antonio Independent School District v. Rodriguez* (1973), this litigation relied on the Equal Protection Clause of the U.S. Constitution. Essentially, the plaintiffs asserted that all children were entitled to have the same amount of money spent on their education or that children were entitled to equal educational opportunities ("equity suit"). In effect, the plaintiffs believed that more money meant a better education and had little or no tolerance for any differences in money or opportunities. To prevail under this equality theory, the plaintiffs had to persuade the court that education was a fundamental right, that wealth was a suspect class, or that the finance system was irrational.

Similarly, during the second wave, which lasted from the New Jersey Supreme Court's decision in *Robinson v. Cahill* (1973) until early 1989, the emphasis continued to be on equity suits. However, because *Rodriguez* had foreclosed the use of the federal constitution, the plaintiffs were forced to rely on state constitutional provisions, particularly education clauses. Although the plaintiffs were able to prevail in Arkansas, California, Connecticut, New Jersey, Washington, West Virginia, and Wyoming, the overwhelming majority of the cases resulted in victories for the state.

In contrast, the third wave, which began with the Montana, Kentucky, and Texas plaintiffs' victories in 1989 and continues, has been fundamentally different in three distinct ways. First, instead of emphasizing equality of expenditures, the plaintiffs argue that all children are entitled to an education of at least a certain quality and that more money is necessary to bring the worst school districts up to the minimum level mandated by the state education clause ("adequacy suit"). The emphasis is on the differences in the quality of the education delivered rather than on the resources available to the districts. The systems are being struck down not because some districts have more money than others do, but because the quality of education in some schools, not necessarily the poorest in financial terms, is inadequate.

Second, rather than relying on state equal protection clauses, which had been the focus of the school finance litigation or decisions before 1989, the new wave of decisions are based exclusively on the education clauses in the respective state constitutions and, thus, represent a profound shift in litigation strategy. The interpretation of the education clauses has fewer implications for other areas of the law, so this shift appears to make a plaintiff's victory more likely. Consequently, assuming that the plaintiffs can prove that some schools are below the constitutional standard and that this deficiency is caused by lack of resources, it is, theoretically, much easier for the plaintiffs to prevail.

Third, the courts have been more sweeping in their pronouncements and their willingness to take control of the finance system. Kentucky's highest court invalidated the finance system as well as every statute related to the public schools and then ordered the legislature to design a new system. When the Texas legislature attempted to correct the finance system, the Texas Supreme Court held that the legislative remedy was inadequate and ordered legislators to try again. Previously, the courts had readily accepted the legislative correction. This emphasis on quality of education rather than equality of funds, using the narrow education clauses rather than the broad equal protection provisions, and asking for sweeping reform or continued court supervision represents the future of school finance litigation.

THE ROLE OF THE STATE IN PROMOTING PARENTAL CHOICE

Even though all children in the United States are entitled to a free public education under their states' constitutions, James Peyser (1994) has observed that many schools are failing, and few will argue that U.S. schools are not in need of reform. In a landmark report issued in 1983, the National Commission on Excellence in Education warned that our educational foundations were being threatened by a rising tide of mediocrity. The commission specifically pointed to the facts that U.S. students did not fare as well as their counterparts in other industrialized countries on comparisons of student achievement, 23 million U.S. adults were functionally illiterate, functional illiteracy among minority youth was as high as 40%, and the average achievement of high school seniors at that time on standardized tests was lower than it was in 1957. The report concluded that the decline in educational performance was the result of the way education in the United States was conducted.

U.S. cities and urban areas have been particularly affected by school failure. Robin Barnes (1997) has noted that in urban schools, the dropout rate is well above 50%, truancy is rampant, violence is common, and school buildings are in poor condition. Christopher Pixley (1998) contends that minorities suffer the consequences of much of the failure in urban schools. Almost 30 years ago, Charles Murray (1984) noted that the large gap between black and white students in educational achievement threatened to defeat other attempts to narrow the economic differences separating the two groups. More recently, Clint Bolick (1998) found that minority students' mastery of basic skills was less than half that of their white counterparts.

Given this crisis in urban education, particularly among students of color, it is not surprising that some would propose revolutionary reforms. These reforms include vouchers and charter schools.

Vouchers

Vouchers are monetary certificates, typically issued by the state, that the parents of poor children can spend on their children's education at either public or private schools, including religious schools, as long as the receiving school meet certain standards. The voucher amount may not necessarily cover the full costs of tuition and fees at a private school but usually covers a substantial part of those costs. Vouchers allow some poor children to attend private schools that may be educationally superior and safer than the public schools they would otherwise attend.

Because vouchers can be used at private sectarian schools, school choice programs benefit the religious schools by making it easier for parents to send their children to religious schools. Many opponents of voucher programs as well as those who advocate for the strict separation of church and state question the constitutionality of allowing vouchers to be used at sectarian schools. As far as the federal constitution is concerned, the issue was pretty much settled in 2002, when the U.S. Supreme Court ruled in *Zelman v. Simmons-Harris* that a school choice program that included religious schools did not violate the Establishment Clause. Even so, there may be instances where state constitutional provisions preclude the use of vouchers at sectarian schools.

Constitutional issues aside, a profound policy debate remains about whether school choice programs are a good idea. Proponents of vouchers argue that urban schools are failing and that there is a moral, if not constitutional, obligation to allow children to pursue opportunities that are more likely to educate them. Moreover, forcing schools to compete with each other for students likely will cause all schools—both public and private—to improve. Conversely, opponents of school choice programs argue that vouchers undermine the public schools. Resources that would normally be spent on public schools are diverted to private schools. Moreover, children who do not wish to attend a religious school may have little or no choice. Furthermore, the solution to failing urban schools is to reform them, not to abandon them in favor of private, often religious, institutions that are not fully accountable to the public.

Charter Schools

The creation of charter schools, which are public schools with substantially more autonomy than most public schools have, has been one of the more controversial issues in education since 1991 when Minnesota enacted the first charter school law. Today, 40 states, the District of Columbia, and Puerto Rico have charter schools (WestEd, 2000a). State laws vary greatly in how they provide for the creation and accountability of charter schools. For example, Mississippi, which passed its charter school law in 1995, has only one charter school of 371 students. California, albeit a much larger state, has 280,854 students attending 733 charter schools (WestEd, 2000b). In some states, such as Colorado, charter schools have become viable competitors to the traditional public schools.

Charter schools are not accountable to local school boards and are not administered by the school district. They are governed by an independent school-based board and are exempt from many, if not most, of the regulations that normally apply to public schools. For that reason, charter schools may follow a different curriculum than the rest of the school district. Because charter schools may be exempt from the provisions of a school district's collective bargaining agreement, their teachers may have different salary schedules, benefits, working conditions, or professional qualifications than those in the regular public schools. Perhaps most significantly, the role of parents in school decision making is substantially higher than at the general public schools.

Despite the recent popularity of charter schools, they still represent a controversial experiment in educational reform. As could be expected, some charter schools are quite effective, but others struggle and do not perform as well as traditional public schools. The inconsistent quality of charter schools adds to the ongoing debate regarding their existence. As the essays on charter schools in the *Alternative Schooling and School Choice* volume in this series point out, many opponents feel that resources should not be diverted to experiments that fail. Charter schools are also controversial because they can operate outside of normal union work rules. Further, in communities where there is a history of unconstitutional racial discrimination, many believe charter schools appear reminiscent of the private, all-white academies that characterized the era of massive resistance.

THE ROLE OF THE STATE AND FEDERAL GOVERNMENT IN FINANCING SPECIAL EDUCATION AND GIFTED EDUCATION

As explained earlier, every state constitution requires the establishment of a public school system and, in many states, the constitution requires a certain level of quality. Similarly, the Equal Protection Clause of the U.S. Constitution prohibits irrational discrimination against those with disabilities. Presumably, a similar prohibition applies to discrimination against those with extraordinary abilities. Implicit, if not explicit, in these constitutional commands is the notion that the public schools should provide an education that is appropriate for every child, regardless of whether the child is disabled or exceptional. To that end, the federal government has mandated that children with disabilities receive a free appropriate public education. Similarly, many states have insisted that local school districts provide gifted education.

Yet, the existence of theses constitutional commands and accompanying policy mandates begs the question of what level of government will fund special education and gifted services. Under the Individuals with Disabilities Education Act (IDEA), school districts must provide appropriate and individualized programs and services that address the underlying physical, emotional, educational, and social impediments that limit these students' access to the educational opportunities that their nondisabled peers enjoy. For a local school district, the costs of implementing the IDEA include additional teachers, paraprofessionals, therapists, equipment, technology, transportation, diagnostic testing and evaluation, environmental and instructional modifications, instructional materials, and, in some instances, attorneys' fees.

Similarly, children who are gifted have special needs and, arguably, require special services. They may need special classes where the pupil–teacher ratio is smaller or where there is greater use of technology. At the high school level, it may be necessary to have a special curriculum that closely resembles a college curriculum. It may also be necessary for gifted students to participate in labor-intensive extracurricular activities such as Odyssey of the Mind, Future Problem Solving, debate, or science fairs. Of course, coordinating all these activities may require additional administrators.

Yet, such mandates seemingly conflict with another state constitutional value—the value of local control. All states except Hawaii provide for the delivery of educational services through smaller political units—typically called school districts—that are responsible for the public schools in a given geographic area. Each school district is controlled by a school board, which generally is elected by the voters of the school district. The local board typically has broad discretion over hiring, financial, and curriculum decisions.

The tension between the state's promotion of the state constitutional value of equality and the local district's preservation of the state constitutional value of local control is exacerbated when the state mandates the provision of services, but does not provide the money to perform the services. In essence, the state takes control away from local school boards when it mandates that school districts provide certain services. When the state also fails to provide full funding for these mandated services, school boards cannot always spend their limited revenues as they see fit when they must spend a portion on the mandated programs. This may also force boards to make policy choices that are not necessarily their own. State mandates to provide gifted education, which are motivated by a desire to see that children receive the services necessary for them to develop fully as human beings, are a classic example of the unfunded mandate.

THE OBLIGATION OF THE PUBLIC SCHOOLS TO PROVIDE ELITE PROGRAMS OR ACTIVITIES

In the United States, we expect that public education will be free. Yet, such an expectation necessarily begs the question of what constitutes a "free" public education. Certainly, basic courses in reading, composition, mathematics, and science must be free, but what about other specialized educational opportunities such as advanced placement or International Baccalaureate classes? What about extracurricular activities such as band or sports? Must they also be provided for free?

On the one hand, advanced placement and International Baccalaureate programs are an integral part of the curriculum for gifted students. Just as the parents of special education students do not have to pay for the enormously expensive educational services that are provided, the parents of gifted students should not have to pay for the specialized educational services that are available to them. Moreover, advanced placement and International Baccalaureate programs often serve as a means of promoting social mobility. They allow children from poor or lower-middle-class households to obtain the equivalent of a private school education, and they increase the likelihood that those students will attend and, ultimately, graduate from college. Such movement up the socioeconomic ladder is a deeply held value of U.S. society and is one core purpose of the public schools.

Similarly, extracurricular activities often are an important part of the educational process. Extracurricular activities teach important lessons regarding teamwork, self-discipline, hard work, courage, determination, dealing with adversity, working for long-term goals, and so forth. Those lessons can be more critical to success in our society than are some of the skills that students learn in the basic curriculum. Moreover, if athletics and band are not part of the educational curriculum, then why are the schools spending thousands of dollars employing coaches and band teachers as well as constructing facilities? If the purpose of these activities is to entertain the community rather than education, then such activities are incompatible with the schools' core mission.

On the other hand, these specialized classes involve only a small portion of the student body and require enormous additional expenditures. For example, an advanced placement class may have only 10 students, but a regular class may have 25. International Baccalaureate programs require additional teacher training and, in some instances, may require the school to restructure the curriculum sequence. In those districts where such specialized programs are offered only at one particular school—the normal practice for the International Baccalaureate programs—the school district may well incur additional transportation costs.

Similarly, extracurricular activities—particularly sports and band—involve only a small portion of the student body and require enormous additional expenditures. Only a dozen male students may play varsity basketball even though several hundred males attend the school. Band or chorus inevitably will involve less than 10% of the student body. Why should the school pay all or even most of the costs of an activity that benefits only a few?

William E. Thro
Christopher Newport University

FURTHER READINGS AND RESOURCES

Barnes, R. D. (1997). Black America and school choice: Charting a new course. *Yale Law Journal, 106,* 2375–2408.

Bolick, C. (1998). *Transformation: The promise and politics of empowerment.* Oakland, CA: ICS Press.

Murray, C. (1984). *Losing ground: American social policy, 1950–1980.* New York: Basic Books.

The National Commission on Excellence in Education. (1983). *A nation at risk: The imperative for educational reform.* Washington, DC: Author. Retrieved from http://www2.ed.gov/pubs/NatAtRisk/index.html

Peyser, J. A. (1994). School choice: When, not if. *Boston College Law Review, 35*(3), 619–632.

Pixley, C. J. (1998). The next frontier of school finance reform: A policy and constitutional analysis of school choice litigation. *Journal of Legislation, 24,* 21.

WestEd. (2000a, August). *U.S. charter schools: State information.* Retrieved July 12, 2011, from http://www.uscharterschools.org/pub/uscs_docs/sp/index.htm

WestEd. (2000b, August). *U.S. charter schools: Steps to starting a charter school.* Retrieved July 12, 2011, from http://www.uscharterschools.org/pub/uscs_docs/r/steps.htm

COURT CASES AND STATUTES

Individuals with Disabilities Education Act (IDEA) of 1990, 20 U.S.C. §§ 1400 *et seq.*

Robinson v. Cahill, 62 N.J. 473 (1973), 303 A.2d 273 (N.J. 1973).

San Antonio Independent School District v. Rodriguez, 411 U.S. 1 (1973).

Zelman v. Simmons-Harris, 536 U.S. 639 (2002).

Should local school districts be able to impose additional taxes to provide additional educational resources?

POINT: Anthony Rolle, *University of South Florida*

COUNTERPOINT: William S. Koski, *Stanford University*

OVERVIEW

In the United States, questions of educational finance often involve two competing state constitutional values. On the one hand, there is a state constitutional value of equality, according to which all public schools should be equal. On the other hand, there is the constitutional value of local control. Local school boards have broad discretion to determine who will teach, what subjects are taught, and how education will be delivered. In some situations, the vindication of one value necessarily means the subordination of another value. One such instance is the issue of local school districts being able to impose additional taxes and then using the additional money to fund better schools.

The State Constitutional Values of Equality and Local Control

The constitutional value of equality is reflected in the education clauses of state constitutions, which mandate the establishment of a system of free public schools, and in many states, the constitutional text specifies a level of quality. Implicit, if not explicit, in this constitutional command is the notion that public schools throughout the state will be of similar, if not virtually identical, quality.

The system of financing the schools typically embodies this belief. The state mandates that local school districts impose property taxes but also provides additional money for those districts where property values are low. Thus, every school district, regardless of its socioeconomic makeup, has a minimum level of funding. This level should be sufficient to enable the school district to meet the state standards of competency and to ensure that the public schools are broadly equal. Put another way, the state's finance system is designed to ensure educational equality.

In contrast, the constitutional value of local control is reflected in the way that all states except Hawaii provide for the delivery of educational services. The states created smaller political units—typically called school districts—that are responsible for the public schools in a given geographic area. Each school district is controlled by a school board, which generally is elected by the voters of the school district. The local board typically has broad discretion over hiring, financial, and curriculum decisions. For example, as long as the board hires certified teachers, the board may hire whomever it wants. Similarly, subject to certain state mandates, the board may spend the available money as it sees fit. Finally, although the state may mandate particular subjects, the choice of textbooks and the choice of curriculum approach are left entirely to the school board. In sum, the quality of the local public schools is very much the result of decisions made by the local school board.

Local Control Leads to Inequality Among School Districts

The great discretion given to local school boards almost inevitably leads to some inequality among school districts. Because some local school districts are better at making decisions than others, some local districts become better than others even where the school districts have approximately the same level of funding. It is inevitable that some teachers will be better, some principals will be superior administrators, some curriculum approaches will be more effective, and some textbooks will be of a higher quality. Although these differences in educational quality are problematic, local boards presumably can eliminate these disparities simply by altering their hiring and curriculum approaches. In other words, local boards must make better use of the resources available to them.

However, problems of inequality are exacerbated when a local school board is allowed to impose additional taxes on the local population and then use those new moneys to provide additional educational resources. For example, assume that the state finance formula provides sufficient money for every school district to have a 20-to-1 student–teacher ratio in the elementary grades. If one school district imposes additional taxes, it may suddenly have enough money to have a 15-to-1 student–teacher ratio in the elementary grades. Similarly, the school district may be able to offer more specialized classes or dramatically improve its facilities. Perhaps most importantly, the district with greater resources will be able to offer financial incentives to attract the best teachers and administrators. Consequently, the district with the new resources will offer a superior education. Short of raising taxes to match their competitor, the other districts will be unable to compete. Boards cure managerial inefficiencies through adopting better practices, but financial disparities simply require more money.

Summary of the Debate

This debate asks whether local school boards should be able to create inequality among school districts by imposing additional local taxes and then using the proceeds to improve the local schools. Those who favor the constitutional value of local control answer in the affirmative. School boards should have the discretion to do what they believe is best for the schools in their districts. If the voters of a school district favor higher taxes, higher spending, and, presumably, better schools, then they should be allowed to pursue those objectives. Conversely, those who favor the constitutional value of equality answer in the negative. Disparities caused by managerial inefficiencies are already great enough. The states should not allow the rich to become even richer, nor should they allow the quality of education to depend on the willingness or ability of local citizens to tax themselves.

Anthony Rolle, a professor of education at the University of South Florida, takes the affirmative view. He argues that increasing local control, whether financial or otherwise, leads to greater efficiency and higher student outcomes. William S. Koski, a professor of law at Stanford University and a leading advocate in school finance litigation, takes the negative view. He contends that, in an increasingly global society, local control is simply incompatible with the values of liberty, equality, efficiency, and social cohesion.

William E. Thro
Christopher Newport University

POINT: Anthony Rolle
University of Southern Florida

School districts are expected to provide high quality curricula, fully equipped classrooms, highly qualified teachers, a wide range of extracurricular activities, as well as new computer- and web-based technologies. In addition to these expectations, public schools also are expected to provide all students with academic counseling, health and psychological services, library media services, and a whole host of additional noninstructional services. Yet, despite a long history of education finance and policy reform efforts developed since the "Sputnik spook" of the 1950s, claims that costs for a world-class education should not increase without commensurate increases in educational outcomes are common. However, two companion questions require discussion as well: *Why?* and *How?* Researchers, policymakers, and administrators across the United States have spent considerable energy developing student school finance formulas and achievement standards—as well as quantitative measures associated with those standards and formulas—designed to create cost efficiencies for public schools. Despite these efforts, it seems that as federal and state pecuniary—and nonpecuniary—resources diffuse into districts, concomitant local increases based on voter-approved supplementing tax revenues should be allowed.

BACKGROUND: PURSUING EFFICIENT SCHOOLS

In *A Nation at Risk,* the 1983 National Commission on Excellence in Education reported that school districts and their personnel should pursue fiscal equity and economic efficiency simultaneously:

> We cannot permit [efficiency] to yield to [equity] either in principle or practice . . . To do so would deny young people their chance to learn and live according to their aspirations and abilities. [Granting preference to equity] also would lead to a generalized accommodation to mediocrity in our society on one hand or to the creation of an undemocratic elitism on the other. (National Commission on Excellence in Education, 1983)

Further, the commission charged that within the educational equity movement, traditional measures of academic success (e.g., grade point average, high school graduation, and college admission) came to be seen as compensation to which all students were entitled regardless of their academic performance rather than as rewards to be earned through persistence and achievement:

> The educational foundations of our society are presently being eroded by a rising tide of mediocrity that threatens our very future as a nation and as a people. (National Commission on Excellence in Education, 1983)

As disturbing as these findings seemed for students, the commission and the media focused the nation's attention on the negative economic consequences of a low quality education system:

> If only to keep our competitive edge in world markets, we must rededicate ourselves to the reform of our educational system for the benefit of all.... Learning is the indispensable investment required for success in the emerging information age. (National Commission on Excellence in Education, 1983)

Ultimately, the politics and publicity surrounding *A Nation at Risk* shifted the focus of school finance researchers away from the issues of fiscal equity. Instead, these researchers began to explore new avenues of research designed to support the development of a more demanding curriculum, improving levels of economic efficiency in education, and increasing local control of spending decisions.

Later, the ensuing "educational excellence movement" used *A Nation at Risk* as the sociopolitical basis for its liberty- and market-based educational reform efforts. This movement repopularized the notion that high quality superintendents, principals, and teachers know how to educate students well, but the "slow to innovate and improve" educational bureaucracy reduces their effectiveness. Concomitantly, educational excellence researchers sought to spread the idea that what works in schools does not necessarily require additional educational revenues. What might be needed, they argued, is more effective and efficient uses of existing resources as well as local decision-making control over additional revenues. Put simply, educational excellence researchers proclaimed that greater effectiveness in the educational process can be achieved through increasing efficiencies in the organization, management, and operation of districts and schools.

Nearly 30 years after the release of *A Nation at Risk*, research detailing the low levels of educational productivity generated by federal- and state-controlled combinations of students, their families, teachers, and school administrations is plentiful and accepted. Fittingly, the original education excellence reformers revisited the inequities of public education in the United

States in *Education Manifesto: A Nation Still at Risk* (Center for Education Reform, 1998). They claimed that the United States no longer faces a global danger of economic decline or technological inferiority. Yet, primarily because of the "unchanging educational bureaucracy," reformers assert the state of our children's futures still is at risk in terms of providing equitable academic opportunities for all students.

Currently, educational excellence reformers claim that issues at the center of fiscal equity and educational efficiency reforms still have to do with demanding high academic standards for all children and teachers, as well as effectiveness and efficiency from the system as a whole. Changing the public's perception of the education system was their success in the 1980s and early 1990s. Early in the 21st century, the challenge for these reformers is to build on their successes by attempting to increase the popularity of educational liberty—that is, more local control of the educational process—through the creation of educational service markets in the form of vouchers, charter schools, and tuition tax credits—and by implementing successfully the federal No Child Left Behind Act of 2001. All these policy options are designed to support increased local control of educational processes and the fiscal resources that support it.

Ironically, *A Nation at Risk*'s conclusions that public schools exert little influence on the achievement of children spawned educational excellence research; it also created what now is known as *effective schools research*. Effective schools research usually focuses on one of three concepts: educational leadership, effectiveness, and equity—all policy values that typically limit local control of tax revenues. Typically, the issues of effective, efficient, and locally controlled schools are embedded in the seminal educational finance research conducted by giants such as Ellwood Cubberley, George Strayer, Robert Haig, and Paul Mort who discuss the issues of educational efficiency in terms of minimum dollar inputs that generate desired outcomes.

Moreover, effective schools researchers often assert that fiscal equity and economic efficiency research no longer should imply that spending more money on schools will generate increases in educational outcomes. Determining how current revenue levels are spent best to improve student learning would be more useful. In economic terms, educational revenues are necessary—but not sufficient—to increasing student achievement. In support of these ideas, effective schools researchers also have asserted that even increasing funds for low-achieving students—a form of vertical equity—will help only some students in some districts because of inefficiencies in organizational and management structures. Therefore, the argument goes, because a few districts may not be successful, all districts should not be allowed fiscal flexibility over local tax revenues (Rolle, 2003).

PROVIDING THEORETICAL EVIDENCE
FOR INCREASING LOCAL CONTROL

Normative economic models applied to the behavior of private enterprises seem to be inappropriate for public schools. Using a budget-maximizing framework challenges cost minimization assumptions and allows a discussion on the structure of educational bureaucracies as well as ideas of efficiency and accountability in education. This alternative economic model describes public schools as budget-maximizing agencies—as opposed to cost-minimizing organizations—whose costs are determined by the amount of revenue available. Such a model follows from economic theories of bureaucratic behavior. In this context, administrators are viewed as maximizing personal utility across such variables as salary, perquisites, public reputation, power, patronage, and organizational size rather than the interests that support organizational goals specifically. In other words, administrators of public education bureaus may place considerable value on keeping employees responsive, cooperative, and effective to maintain agency reputation and to prevent employees from understanding the administration fully. If this is the case, local control of revenue sources for educational agencies becomes imperative for communities.

Budget-maximizing educational bureaus—detailed in *Bureaucracy and Representative Government* (Niskanen, 1971)—are organizations that have the following characteristics:

1. The managers and employees of these organizations do not receive any part of the difference between revenues and costs of services as personal income.

2. Some part of the organization's recurring revenues is derived from something other than the sale of output at a per unit rate.

More specifically, bureaus are nonprofit organizations that are financed— in part or in whole—by a periodic appropriation or grant (i.e., local revenues). The first organizational characteristic includes nonprofit organizations such as county hospitals, governmental agencies, and public educational institutions. This "nonprofit" characteristic clearly excludes corporate businesses, partnerships, and sole proprietorships. The second organizational characteristic includes all nonprofit organizations that receive a recurring appropriation or grant. Some government enterprises and private nonprofit organizations that were established initially by a government appropriation or grant—such as the post office or toll road authorities—are excluded by this characteristic. Budget–maximization theory claims that the exclusion of these organizations is warranted because their recurrent operations are financed entirely by the sale of output at a per unit rate.

Common stereotypes portray bureaucrats either as disinterested and slow-moving workers or as altruists maximizing some concept of general welfare. Private business managers, conversely, are represented commonly as being self-interested profit maximizers. Of course, other elements may contribute to a business manager's personal utility function other than income. Still, there are no a priori assumptions supporting the existence of any personal interest in efficiency or profit maximization. Some of these conditions are consequences of purposive behavior, though they all are not the objectives of the behavior: The central motivational assumption for a business manager is that when profits of the firm are maximized, personal utility can be maximized in a variety of pecuniary and nonpecuniary ways.

Similarly, budget–maximization theory holds that bureaucrats also need to be recognized as individuals who maximize personal utility and are not devoted solely to promoting the general welfare or the interests of the state. Consequently, several variables may enter a bureaucrat's personal utility function: salary, perquisites of the office, public reputation, power, patronage, output of the bureau, ease of making changes, and ease of managing the bureau. As a result, budget maximization becomes an adequate proxy even for those bureaucrats with relatively low pecuniary motivations and relatively high motivations for attending to the public interest.

Ultimately, the theory of budget-maximizing bureaucratic behavior claims that public bureaus produce output inefficiently. The theory states that subject to a budget constraint greater than or equal to the costs of supplying the output expected by a bureau's sponsors, bureaucrats attempt to maximize an agency's total budget during their tenure. This budget-maximizing behavior produces

1. budgets that are larger than optimal,

2. output that may be too low when compared with expenditure levels, and

3. output that is produced inefficiently.

In both normative and "positive" economic frameworks, local control seems to be desirable and necessary to advance the needs of the communities closest to the educational organizations.

PROVIDING ANALYTICAL EVIDENCE
FOR INCREASING LOCAL CONTROL

Major challenges still complicate the study of increasing local taxing authority to improve levels of economic efficiency for public districts and schools. These issues range from accurately measuring inputs to defining outcomes to selecting the proper mathematical models to determining the role of student effort. Moreover, public school spending is conducted in a sociopolitical environment where both organizations and individuals struggle for legitimacy and the capacity to distribute scarce resources. As a result of this conflict over differences with respect to perceptions of reality, values, and preferences, the ability to negotiate and compromise becomes an important asset for all actors in the system. The resulting compromises generate a multiplicity of objectives—many in opposition to one another—that emerge as political, organizational, and personal goals. Therefore, when these nonmarket influences on educational processes are acknowledged, exploring the possibility of increasing local control of district-level taxation becomes imperative.

All of the aforementioned research studies that conclude spending on public education should increase or remain constant sustain these arguments using complex statistical analyses. The evidence provided by these works shows that statistically significant fiscal equity and economic relationships do not exist between educational expenditures and the outcomes generated. Concurrently, research studies that conclude spending on public education should increase also sustain their arguments using similarly complex statistical analyses. The evidence provided by these works shows that statistically significant economic relationships do exist between educational expenditures and the outcomes generated. Regardless of perspective, educational efficiency debate was summarized most appropriately in *Private Wealth and Public Education* (1970):

> Whatever it is that money may be thought to contribute to the education of children, that commodity is something highly prized by those who enjoy the greatest measure of it. If money is inadequate to improve education, the residents of poor districts should at least have an equal opportunity to be disappointed by its failure. (Coons, Clune, & Sugarman, p. 30)

Almost 40 years later, the same message is being reiterated, claiming that reasonable and intelligent people almost always will agree that the generation, distribution, and management of resources available to public schools affects their level of performance. And, despite controversies about research results, economic efficiency analyses have led to generalizations about what resources consistently improve educational outcomes in addition to local control over tax revenues:

- *Administrative policies:* Appropriate levels of collaborative management, low student–teacher ratios, and small class sizes

- *Classroom and curriculum content:* Appropriate preschool preparation, student ability groupings, and instructional interventions for students at risk of failure

- *Teacher characteristics:* Appropriate levels and types of teacher training, verbal ability, years of experience, and cultural diversity

If these views are correct, research studies should be conducted to investigate the optimal levels of financial and human resources equity, economic efficiency, and educational achievement. And yet, despite the breadth of research available, there has not been a concerted empirical effort to examine these relationships across the United States. As such, for both empirical and practical purposes, it is necessary to conduct these types of analyses before deciding if the current usage, a reallocation, or an increase in resources is appropriate to achieve desired student performance levels (Rolle, 2004).

CONCLUSION

Two concepts important to the generation, distribution, and management of education resources in policy discussions are concerns for fiscal equity and economic efficiency. Quite simply, the term *equity* means "being fair." We all want to be sure that public education resources are distributed in such a manner that no district or school is given preference over another. But being fair, or equitable, is not always easy because there are two primary perspectives to consider: (1) the pursuit of horizontal equity—the act of treating districts or schools with similar qualities in similar manners—and (2) the pursuit of vertical equity—the act of treating districts or schools with different characteristics in different manners.

Efficiency, by contrast, is concerned with how much knowledge or service is delivered to—and acquired by—students based on their costs. In the private sector, being "more efficient" means one of two things when discussing school finance and economic issues: (1) increasing output levels while using the same amounts of input or (2) maintaining output levels while using lesser amounts of input. However, the standard used to define *efficiency* in public schools is not the same standard often used to measure efficiency in the business community. Public school spending generally is conducted Pareto efficiently; that is, no district's or school's educational situation is made worse in order to improve the situation of another.

Given the primacy of the two aforementioned resource allocation principles critical to successful student achievement policy, there is a need to investigate the veracity of the underlying assumptions supporting the linkages between them:

Assumption 1—*Pursue equity first:* Distributing financial and human resources equitably among public districts and schools reduces differences in student outcomes based on wealth, ethnicity or race, or geographic location

Assumption 2—*Pursue efficiency second:* Managing financial and human resources efficiently by public districts reduces differences in student outcomes based on wealth, ethnicity or race, or geographic location

Assumption 3—*Pursue accountability third:* Defining, measuring, and reporting progress toward meeting student achievement standards across public districts promotes equitable distributions and efficient management of financial and human resources

Accordingly, there must be efforts to trace and analyze the use of expenditures from state legislatures down to state departments of education down to district financial offices, and when possible, down to individual schools and classrooms. Legislators, superintendents, principals, teachers, parents, and the public need to know where and how money is spent in attempts to improve the quality of education provided to students. And, when these constituents find components in the educational system that can be improved, the local district should be allowed to supplement—not supplant—its expenditures to pursue educational achievement successes.

The abundant equity, efficiency, and achievement research pays little attention to the linkages between the assumptions underlying resource allocation principles—or the strength of their interrelationships, and no rigorous nationally comparative analyses have been conducted on the success of local enhancements. To improve expenditure practices crucial to obtaining desired educational and organizational outcomes, research and policy debates first must recognize and focus on investigating the nature of the three principles. Simply suggesting the provision of more revenues to each state's public education system—as simple adequacy and costing-out studies are prone to do—will not be enough to address appropriately the student achievement, fiscal equity, or economic efficiency relationships associated with education spending.

COUNTERPOINT: William S. Koski
Stanford University

I t is beyond argument that parents possess the basic liberty to provide their children with an education of the kind and quality that is consistent with their values and goals. Moreover, local control over public schooling is a hallowed U.S. tradition. As a result of these two precepts, it seems viscerally evident that parents and taxpayers should have the ability to approve additional local taxes to provide additional educational resources to local schools.

But such liberty and local control are illusory for many families and ignore, or even contravene, other important values that are at stake for the state and citizenry in educational finance policy making. This counterpoint essay argues that notwithstanding the legitimate parental choice concerns, local taxation for and funding of schools undermine other important goals and values embedded in school finance policy. The argument proceeds as follows: First, the essay briefly reviews the history of educational finance and governance arguing that the historical rational for local control cannot be squared with modern educational policy and governance. Next, the essay provides a normative argument—with empirical evidence to support the argument—why local communities should not be able to raise more than modest school revenues locally. That section provides a framework of values—liberty, equality, efficiency, and social cohesion—for evaluating proposals for the distribution of public school resources and evaluates local finance control through that framework, concluding that local funding does not necessarily advance the values of liberty and efficiency but undermines the values of equality and social cohesion. The essay concludes with principles for a local school funding proposal that strikes a balance among the competing values.

FROM LOCAL CONTROL TO A GLOBALIZED SOCIETY: THE HISTORICAL ARGUMENT AGAINST ADDITIONAL LOCAL FUNDING

Given that the United States is unusual among modern industrialized nations in the degree to which it has historically permitted local political control over public school governance and funding, it is worth tracing the history of educational funding to better understand why this chapter even asks the question about raising additional school funds locally. The argument here is that local control is an historical anachronism and cannot be squared with modern demands on U.S. children and schools.

The Establishment of Public Schools and Compulsory Education

Although the founding fathers recognized the value of education in creating a unified nation and enhancing economic progress, the U.S. Constitution says nothing about education and implicitly cedes authority over public schooling to the states. The federal government, however, facilitated the expansion of public schooling by requiring states that receive federal land grants to set aside certain parcels of that land for the support of public schools. The states, for their part, devolved authority over the governance and support of schools to local school districts, cities, or towns, most of which were vested with taxing authority to raise revenues to support the schools. Perhaps this devolution of authority was rooted in the belief that self-interested local communities were best situated to protect individual and community liberty, but the result is that the United States now has approximately 14,000 public school districts.

Although control of public education was largely placed in the hands of school districts, by the latter half of the 19th century, state legislatures, responding to the demands of industrialization and concerns about assimilating new immigrants, began to require all children of certain ages to attend school. The implementation of compulsory education laws worked to constrain parental choices for their children, and it further solidified the state's interest in ensuring that all children are educated and, equally important, created an implicit and reciprocal state obligation to ensure the well-being and fair treatment of students.

State Funding of Local Schools

During the Industrial Revolution, revenues for schools were generated locally through taxation, particularly property taxes. Even today, local school districts provide some 42% of all public school funds with 79% of that revenue raised through local property taxes. Beginning in the early part of the 20th century, however, states began to recognize that many school districts, particularly low-property-wealth rural districts, could not provide sufficient resources to ensure a basic education. As a result, states began to supplement local revenues through flat grants and foundation grants, typically based on the number of students in the district, in an effort to ensure a basic educational resource floor below which districts could not fall. Recognizing the difficulty in setting that floor and concerned about creating fairness and proper incentives for local taxpayers, states in the latter half of the 20th century began to adopt percentage equalizing plans that ensured through state subsidy that up to a certain level, equal tax effort (i.e., equal tax rates) resulted in relatively equal school revenues, irrespective of local property wealth. Regardless of the specific formula for state contribution to local funding, school funding has become more centralized at the state level such that states now contribute almost 49% of overall education funding.

School Finance Litigation, Standards-Based Reform, and the Growing Influence of the Federal Government

Despite state funding programs aimed at creating equity among districts, advocates for poor children began in the 1960s to highlight the dramatic spending differences between wealthy and poor communities. Those advocates initially took their claims to federal court and asked the courts to strike down the inequitable, local property tax–based school funding schemes. In the landmark *San Antonio Independent School District v. Rodriguez* decision in 1973, the Supreme Court refused to find a fundamental interest in education under the federal constitution and refused to deem children in property-poor school districts a suspect class worthy of heightened constitutional protection. Undaunted, advocates turned to state courts and state constitutions and pressed their claims for more equalized—and, later, more adequate—school funding as an obligation of the state. The state courts were much more receptive to those claims, and some 27 state supreme courts have struck down school funding schemes. The result has been further centralization of school funding at the state level and more equality in per student spending.

Beyond finance, there has been a steady march toward the centralization of educational policy making, as all states have embraced standards-based reform (SBR). SBR centers on establishing challenging content standards for what all children should know and be able to do, assessments tied to those standards, and, more recently, accountability schemes that ensure students meet performance goals on those assessments. This movement has further intensified as the federal government's No Child Left Behind Act has tied Title I funding to the states' adoption of content standards, assessment, and accountability schemes. More recently, as a condition of competing for federal grant moneys, the U.S. Department of Education has persuaded most states to adopt the so-called Common Core State Standards that effectively nationalize curricula in certain content areas. The rapid and ubiquitous adoption of SBR demonstrates that the United States has come a long way from locally controlled one room schoolhouses to highly standardized and centralized curricula and funding in an effort to ensure equity and excellence in public education.

The point of reviewing this brief history is to emphasize two things. First, the roots of local control over public school finance run deep, and such local control made much sense when the United States was a largely agrarian society with relatively little geographic mobility or interstate (let alone international) trade, and much autonomy was given to families regarding the education of their children (even the autonomy to keep their children out of school). But, second, that historical argument for localized funding has been eroded to the point of irrelevance. Americans now live in a highly mobile, globalized society and must be able to engage socially and compete economically in that society. Equally important, because all children must attend school and do not get to choose the families and communities into which they are born, there has been a clear recognition that all children require relatively equal educational opportunities to participate in civic institutions, be economically productive, and realize the American dream of personal success. The federal government, state legislatures, and state courts have recognized these developments and now play a central role in funding education and, more recently, delineating the content of that education. Put simply, local control over education is neither appropriate nor a reality.

THE NORMATIVE ARGUMENT AGAINST LOCAL SCHOOL FUNDING

Turning from history to theory and norms, this section sets forth a framework for evaluating school funding proposals and considers how additional local funding stacks up against those values. As Henry Levin (2002) has argued, these values are animated by the choices made in organizing and governing public schools, financing those schools, and selecting the educational content and curricula for those schools.

Liberty and Choice: The Illusion of Local Control

Liberty and choice are central to furthering parents' rights and obligations to direct the upbringing and education of their children. Although such liberty is not unconstrained (e.g., parents cannot refuse to educate their children), parents ought to have the ability to choose an educational setting for their children that best comports with their values and goals for their children.

At first glance, it seems an easy case that the value of liberty—that is, parental choice—is furthered by, if not dependent on, the ability of parents and communities to raise additional funds. Indeed, one must concede the point that parental and community liberty is enhanced by the ability to raise funds locally and such liberty will further local interest in, support of, and perhaps monitoring of local public schools. Moreover, the mere liberty to make the choice to raise or not raise additional funds will enhance the psychic well-being of parents.

But the analysis does not end there because such liberty extends only to *parents (not children)* and, even then, *not all parents* enjoy such liberty.

Children do not control where and to whom they are born, yet parents and localities under a local school funding scheme control the educational opportunities children receive and, ultimately, their social and economic well-being. To allow some children lesser educational opportunities based on an accident of birth effectively strips them of autonomy and liberty in both the short run (because they cannot choose where to live as children) and the long run (because an inferior education will lead to worse socioeconomic outcomes and life choices for children in lesser resourced schools).

Moreover, for low income parents, the liberty to raise additional revenues locally is illusory. Indeed, low income families may exert greater tax effort by willingly giving a greater percentage of their personal incomes to their local public schools, yet they still might not be able to raise as much in additional funding as their wealthier peers who do not exert such effort.

That said, one must acknowledge the ultimate liberty that parents possess: the liberty to remove their children from public schools and the consequent erosion of support for public schools. Although it is beyond the scope of this essay to consider the question of whether parents should have the right to exit public schools, it cannot be ignored that given that right and given the fact that middle-class and wealthier interests exert greater political control both locally and at the state level, one must be concerned about the potential for diminished support for public schools if there is no liberty for parents to enhance their own children's public school education.

Equality: Local Control and the Exacerbation of Inequality

Liberty's classic adversary, *equality* means that educational resources, opportunities, and, perhaps, outcomes should be distributed relatively fairly among children. Although the meaning of equality of educational opportunity is hotly debated, there is much consensus that there should be no inequality of opportunity based on arbitrary characteristics (such as race, ethnicity, or gender) and, to the extent there is inequality, additional resources ought to be directed to children who require more support (such as economically disadvantaged children or English learners).

In *Brown v. Board of Education* (1954), the Supreme Court famously stated that the opportunity for an education, "where the state has undertaken to provide it, is a right which must be made available to all on equal terms" (p. 493). Beyond the legal force of this principle, the Court was articulating an ethical principle to which the state must adhere. Education is a good that is essential to the success and well-being of the individual, and it is a good with significant "positional" aspects, that is, one's position or relative standing in the distribution of education, rather than one's absolute attainment of education, matters a great deal. One person's possession of more education necessarily decreases the value of another's education. Because the state requires all children to be educated and because the state provides that education at public expense, it is incumbent on the state to at least not exacerbate existing inequality through the provision of unequal education that will allow those of greater means to further enhance their standing at the expense of others.

But that is precisely what government-sponsored additional funding of public education would allow. It would permit some—already wealthy—individuals and communities to provide a higher quality education to their children, thus enhancing their relative standing compared with those who cannot provide such add-ons. It is one thing to allow parents to enhance their children's education privately (and many do by reading their children bedtime stories, monitoring the completion of homework, and providing after-school tutoring and summer academic camps to their children), but it is quite another to use the state through its public education system to exacerbate inequality.

Efficiency: Unknown Consequences of a Stratified Educational Resource System

In a world of scarce resources, communities want their schools to produce the greatest utility at the lowest cost. Any educational finance proposal must be evaluated to determine whether the additional dollar is well spent relative to the outcome it produces—whether that desired outcome is graduation, student achievement, or some other measure of effectiveness.

The effect of additional local funding on efficiency is mixed because theoretical arguments cut both ways. If academic achievement and attainment are the primary concern and if the unit of analysis is the performance of the local school district, there is empirical evidence to support the notion that local voters who face a higher tax price will engage in heightened monitoring of their local schools and thereby improve the performance of those schools. That said, it is not clear that local voters would be able to detect inefficient overinvestment in their locals schools in which the marginal academic returns cannot be justified by the additional investment.

If, however, we consider the efficiency of the overall investment in public schools, the analysis gets even more difficult. Assume that the state has a choice between allowing local taxpayers to raise additional revenues for their local schools or simply collecting additional revenue from those taxpayers to be distributed in a manner the state deems most efficient. In the former scenario, one could argue that it would be a wise investment to allocate additional resources to the already higher-performing students who tend to live in wealthier communities because maximizing their achievement and attainment (which maximizes their knowledge and skills) will redound to the benefit of all persons as they will serve in leadership, entrepreneurial, and other highly productive capacities.

But investing in wealthy communities is more likely to be inefficient for at least two reasons. First, academic ability is not *ex ante* concentrated in wealthy communities, and it would be inefficient to overinvest in wealthy communities and underinvest in poor communities when future scientists and leaders may be found in both communities. Second, it is theoretically unclear that investment in the higher-performing students is an efficient strategy in the first place. It is possible that raising the bottom performers with additional investment will ensure that those children will lead productive economic lives and not be a drain on the public treasury. It is also possible that allowing wealth-based stratification by investing in wealthy communities will cause greater social unrest and undermine civic and economic institutions in the long run. The upshot is that the decision on how to distribute educational funds is, for the most part, better made at the state (or even national) level, as efficiency concerns are broadened beyond the immediate local level.

Social Cohesion: The Balkanization of Education

Social cohesion is a broad concept that embraces the common capacities, skills, and values that schools ought to convey to children to ensure participation in social and civic life, as well as to instill tolerance and harmony among citizens in a democratic state. In a diverse society such as the United States, one cannot count on cultural traditions and norms to ensure that individuals will exercise mutual tolerance and respect. Moreover, in a democratic and capitalist society that is not governed by authoritarian regimes or religious norms, the functioning of society depends on shared norms of civic engagement and participation in the economic life of the nation. The very existence of the state, therefore, depends on a mechanism for transferring those values, and Americans have in large measure relied on public education to be the vessel of transfer.

The effect of local funding on this concept of social cohesion is a bit speculative. Although evidence indicates that students who have attended private schools (that is, students whose parents have exercised the liberty to exit public schools) are no less (and may be more) civic-minded than their public school peers, it is not clear whether the lesser liberty to raise funds locally will have a similar neutral-to-positive effect on civic engagement. Perhaps clearer, however, is the obvious sorting into residential enclaves that will result from enhanced local control over funding. Put bluntly, parents with means will choose wealthy suburban enclaves to raise their children because they can afford to do so. Such socioeconomic stratification of housing is already the norm in the United States, so it is unclear how much this stratification will be exacerbated by local school funding add-ons. But it is clear that the balkanization of communities will not be improved by permitting greater local control.

CONCLUSION

Permitting additional local school funding does not advance any of the central values that public education furthers. Even the parental liberty to spend as much as they want on their own children is muddied by the lack of liberty afforded children and families of lower income. And, more important, the deleterious consequences for equality of educational opportunity are clear. Still, one might be uneasy with a wholesale rejection of local add-ons, if there is a substantial risk of exit from public education and corresponding erosion of support for public schools.

Given that risk, perhaps an updated version of a percentage equalizing plan would strike an appropriate balance. Additional local revenues would be permitted up to a certain amount, but the state would effectively guarantee an income base from which those revenues could be drawn. In wealthy communities that can afford the add-on amount, the revenues would be drawn from taxpayers (through either an income or property tax). In low income communities, taxpayers would be required to tax themselves up to a certain percentage of the community's average income and the state would subsidize that contribution to equalize the additional investment to that of the investment in the wealthy communities. In essence, for an equal tax effort, an equal add-on would be guaranteed. That would be liberty for all.

Further Readings and Resources

Center for Education Reform. (1998). *Education manifesto: A nation still at risk.* Washington, DC: Author. Retrieved from http://www.edreform.com/published_pdf/Education_Manifesto_A_Nation_Still_At_Risk.pdf

Coons, J. E., Clune, W. H., & Sugarman, S. D. (1970). *Private wealth and public education.* Cambridge, MA: Belknap Press of Harvard University Press.

Friedman, M. (1962). *Capitalism and freedom.* Chicago: University of Chicago Press.

Guthrie, J. W., Springer, M. G., Rolle, R. A., & Houck, E. A. (2007). *Modern education finance and policy.* Boston: Allyn & Bacon.

Jencks, C. (1988). Whom must we treat equally for educational opportunity to be equal? *Ethics, 98,* 518–533.

Koski, W. S., & Reich, R. (2006). When adequate isn't: The retreat from equality in educational law and policy and why it matters. *Emory Law Journal, 56,* 545–617.

Levin, H. M. (2002). A comprehensive framework for evaluating educational vouchers. *Educational Evaluation and Policy Analysis, 24*(3), 159–174.

The National Commission on Excellence in Education. (1983). *A nation at risk: The imperative for educational reform.* Washington, DC: Author. Retrieved from http://www2.ed.gov/pubs/NatAtRisk/index.html

NEA Research. (1999). *Investing in public education: A discussion of schooling in the new global economy.* Washington, DC: National Education Association.

Niskanen, W. A. (1971). *Bureaucracy and representative government.* Chicago: Aldine-Atherton.

Rodriguez, G. M., & Rolle, R. A. (2007). *To what ends and by what means? The social justice implications of contemporary school finance theory and policy.* New York: Routledge/Taylor & Francis.

Rolle, R. A. (2003). Getting the biggest bang for the educational buck: A discussion of public school districts as budget-maximizing agencies. In W. J. Fowler, Jr. (Ed.), *Developments in school finance 2001–02* (pp. 25–52). Washington, DC: National Center for Education Statistics.

Rolle, R. A. (2004). Out with the old and in with the new: Thoughts on the future of educational productivity and efficiency. *Peabody Journal of Education, 79*(3), 31–56.

Court Cases and Statutes

Brown v. Board of Education, 347 U.S. 483 (1954).

No Child Left Behind Act of 2001, 20 U.S.C. §§ 6301 *et seq.*

San Antonio Independent School District v. Rodriguez, 411 U.S. 1 (1973).

Should states limit the indebtedness of local school districts?

POINT: Luke M. Cornelius, *University of North Florida*

COUNTERPOINT: Spencer C. Weiler, *University of Northern Colorado*

OVERVIEW

This debate asks whether the states should limit the ability of local school boards to issue debt as a means of ensuring both educational equality and long-term financial stability. Those who support the constitutional value of equality answer in the positive. They argue that disparities caused by managerial inefficiencies are already great enough. The states should not allow the rich to become even richer. Nor should the states allow the quality of education to depend on the willingness or ability of local citizens to incur debt.

Conversely, those who support the constitutional value of local control answer in the negative. School boards should have the discretion to do what they believe is best for the schools in their districts. If the voters of a school district are willing to undertake long-term debt for better facilities or better schools, then government should allow the voters to pursue those objectives.

Why School Districts Issue Bonds

School districts typically borrow money for long-term projects by issuing bonds—obligations to pay a fixed sum of money, at a definite time, with a stated interest rate. The amount of the interest rate depends on the market's assessment of the likelihood that the school district will be able to repay. If the market believes that the school district can easily repay the money, the interest rate will be low. If the market believes that the school district may have difficulty repaying the loans, then the rate will be high. After the bonds are issued, the bonds may be freely traded among individuals and institutions in the bond market. The price of the bonds will vary depending on the difference between prevailing interest rates and the rates assigned to the bond. If a bond's rate is higher than the prevailing rate, investors will want to buy the bond. If the bond's rate is lower than the prevailing rate, then investors will want to sell the bond.

School districts generally issue bonds for two purposes: (1) school construction and (2) additional resources to supplement annual budgets. Construction costs typically include renovating existing buildings, replacing outdated buildings, or adding buildings to accommodate growth in student populations. Bonds for additional resources supplement the annual budget beyond what is provided by the state and local taxes. In both instances, the district is pledging its future revenue to finance present-day expenditures.

Different Levels of Indebtedness Can Lead to Inequality

The issue of debt limits, like most questions of educational finance involves a debate about two competing state constitutional values. On one side of the debate is a state constitutional value of equality, according to which all public schools should be equal. The education clauses of state constitutions create a system of free public schools and, in many states, stipulate a level of quality. This constitutional directive makes it implicit, if not explicit, that the public schools throughout the state will be of similar, or even identical, quality. Thus, the system of financing the schools, including incurring debt, should embody the belief in equality. States require local school districts to impose property taxes, but also provide additional money to school districts where property values are low. This ensures every school district a minimum level of funding that should be sufficient for districts to meet the state standards of competency and to ensure that the public schools are broadly equal. Such a finance system is designed to bring about educational equality. Those who advocate for educational equality usually support limitations on school district indebtedness, arguing that allowing wealthier districts to incur additional debt gives them the ability to pull ahead of poorer districts.

Conversely is the state constitutional value of local control. All states, except Hawaii, provide for the delivery of educational services through smaller political units—typically called school districts—that are responsible for the public schools in a given geographic area. School districts are controlled by school boards whose members are most often elected by the voters. The local school board in most jurisdictions has broad discretion regarding matters such as hiring employees, establishing the curriculum, and financial management. Subject to state laws and regulations, boards have the authority to allocate and spend available funds. Thus, the quality of the local public schools is a consequence of decisions made by school boards. Those who advocate for local control of the public schools would argue that state debt limits should not be imposed on districts willing to spend additional money to improve the quality of their schools.

In some situations, the vindication of one state constitutional value necessarily means the subordination of another value. One such instance is the issue of whether the state should limit the indebtedness of local school districts. As might be expected, the great discretion states give to local school boards naturally leads to some inequality among school districts. Officials in some local school districts are better at making decisions than are others, so some schools become better than others even where the districts have similar levels of funding. Further, it is a fact of life that some teachers are better, some principals are more talented, some curricular approaches prove more effective, and some textbooks are of a higher quality. Although the resultant differences in educational quality are problematic, local boards presumably have the means to eliminate these disparities simply by altering their hiring and curriculum approaches. In other words, local boards can make better use of the resources available to them.

However, problems of inequality are exacerbated when local school boards are allowed to incur additional debt. Most obviously, a school district may be able to fund better facilities. Similarly, if the school district uses debt to fund additional programs, the school district may be able to offer more specialized classes or dramatically improve its facilities. Perhaps most importantly, the district with greater resources will be able to offer financial incentives to attract the best teachers and administrators. Consequently, the district with the new resources will offer a superior education. Short of incurring additional debt to match their competitor, the other districts will be unable to compete.

Summary of the Debate

Luke M. Cornelius, a professor of education at the University of North Florida, takes the affirmative view. He argues that the state constitutional value of equality mandates limitations on debt. Moreover, in the absence of strict limits, taxpayers in low wealth districts will have to bear higher taxes. Additionally, excessive debt may undermine local economic development plans. Furthermore, because of interest payments, districts with high debt levels may effectively be transferring large amounts of money to bond holders rather than spending the money locally. Finally, in Professor Cornelius's view, the financing of education is a state, not a local, function.

Spencer C. Weiler, a professor of education at the University of Northern Colorado, takes the negative view. Assuming that a state has met its state constitutional obligation to fund the schools adequately, he contends that free market forces, not statutory limits, should control the amount of state indebtedness. Specifically, he argues that limits are arbitrary, are ineffective, change frequently, are unnecessary, are frequently paternalistic, indirectly involve the state in construction, restrict economic and population growth, and ultimately undermine local control. Professor Weiler acknowledges that limits are necessary when the state has failed to meet its constitutional obligation to fund schools adequately.

William E. Thro
Christopher Newport University

POINT: Luke M. Cornelius
University of North Florida

There are numerous reasons for states to limit the indebtedness of local school districts as well as of all their other political subdivisions. It should be stated up front that, relative to other public and municipal debt, school district debt is remarkably safe and stable. The vast majority of school district debt is incurred for capital purposes, usually for facilities construction and improvement, and is backed by a dedicated property tax millage (a tax rate assessed per thousand dollars of property value) that normally cannot decrease. Indeed, many school districts would benefit from a decreasing millage rate, which is unusual, to offset increases in assessed property values that result in greater tax increments. Although recent decreases in property values in many parts of the country may defy this long-term trend, it remains a fact that school district defaults are essentially unknown in the modern era. Additionally, the very nature of the bonding process, with its reliance on notoriously conservative rating agencies and voter approval, tends to impose natural limits on school district indebtedness.

This being said, there are still numerous arguments for state limitations of local educational agencies' debts. Perhaps foremost among these are much-litigated issues of equity and adequacy. It is not unusual to see school finance pleadings that allege inequity and inadequacy of facilities caused by the heavy or exclusive reliance on local funding for school construction and repair. When states leave capital funding to local option and local resources, the result can be that districts with a relatively high property wealth are able to construct higher quality facilities with fairly modest increases in debt levels and millage rates. By contrast, property-poor districts are often unable, even with high tax and bond rates, to raise enough debt-financed funds to meet even limited capital needs. A good illustration of this would be the *DeRolph v. State* (1997, 2000, 2001, 2002) decisions in Ohio. Here, the state courts found numerous examples of great inequities in facility age and quality in a system where the construction and maintenance of school facilities were left entirely to local funding. The result, in Ohio, was that some high wealth districts were building state-of-the-art schools, replete with golf courses and indoor swimming pools, but extremely poor districts were still using facilities between 60 and 100 years old and in extremely poor condition. Although poor districts might ultimately require state intervention to provide even minimally adequate facilities, a state limitation on local borrowing authority may, at a minimum, prevent higher wealth districts from using their advantages in property wealth and bond ratings to further exacerbate these physical inequities.

Limitations on local debt may also assist states in the area of taxpayer equity. The bonding system is, to put it mildly, often considered a complex and even arcane process. As a general rule, more affluent districts are considered better risks and consequently can borrow at lower rates. By contrast, independent bond agencies may use criteria related to local property wealth and to racial demographics, resident income, and even standardized test scores to impose much higher bond rates on lower wealth communities. As a result, even modest debt in some communities may impose a dramatically higher millage burden on low wealth taxpayers than their higher wealth peers have. Left unregulated by states, these discrepancies can widen over time as tax increments allow wealthier districts to constantly issue new debt with little or no increase in millage rates, but poorer districts must continually raise debt and millage in an effort merely to keep pace with demands for new and upgraded facilities. If left unchecked, such discrepancies eventually expose states to equity litigation and taxpayer revolts. Most states currently use some form of foundation or other equalization formula for ongoing school district funding to reduce or restrict extreme discrepancies in local tax rates and per pupil funding, as well as for other purposes. Foundation formulas are mathematical equations that account for several factors, such as the overall wealth of school districts, to determine the funding that each district will receive. However, equalization for capital financing is not nearly so widespread or comprehensive. As a result, differences in local debt capacity can introduce wide disparities in facilities funding and composite millage rates that tend to work against the equitable goals of other school district funding processes.

Additionally, allowing unlimited school district debt can affect states and communities in other ways as well. A high debt school district, and its attendant high millage rates, can thwart local and state development plans. States seeking to entice business and other development may find themselves forced to compensate local districts for tax revenues lost to development tax credits or face the loss of development interest or even the possibility of school district defaults and the ensuing crisis in local school operations. Given the general prejudice of bond issuers against low wealth districts, a school district's high debt can be a barrier to development in precisely those areas where it is most needed and attractive to potential developers in actual property values. Furthermore, the status of local school districts as arms of the state varies from state to state. Constitutionally, it is possible in some cases for states themselves to be legally or politically forced into an obligation to assume or subsidize excessive school district debts.

Allowing unlimited school district debt also raises numerous policy concerns. Not the least of these is that local moneys raised for the purpose of educating children can be siphoned off in large quantities to lenders and investors. Another issue raised in the *DeRolph* litigation was a statutory provision allowing districts to pursue short-term operational debt at commercial lending rates. Although such authorizations may be convenient, they again tax all districts, and especially lower wealth districts, by diverting large amounts of interest from student needs to lenders. In Ohio, the courts expressed concern about the further inequitable effects of such policies for low wealth districts.

This concern has also appeared in ongoing debates about traditional debt funding for capital needs. Many states, such as Georgia, are increasingly turning to education special purpose local option sales taxes, or E-SPLOST, to fund major construction projects. These taxes, which are collected and distributed by state revenue authorities at little or no extra cost, allow for the funding of capital programs with 100% of the revenue going to actual construction rather than bondholders. Admittedly, there is a good policy argument for funding capital projects over a facility's anticipated life span, thus allowing all users, not just current ones, to share in the project's cost. Additionally, such long-term funding typically allows districts to take advantage of inflation and repay current spending with less valuable future dollars. Nonetheless, it must be realized that even with a reasonable interest rate, the costs of funding a 30-year bond issue may include an additional cost of 50% or more added on to the cost of a school construction project.

Nor is the sole policy issue with long-term debt merely an issue of how much additional interest payments a district must make while retiring the debt. Since the terrorist attacks of 9/11 and the growing debates about rising debt at all levels of government in the United States, increasing attention is being given to where municipal, including school district, debt is being purchased. Some reports indicate that local bond issues are being purchased largely by foreign governments and concerns, including some of the world's most notorious dictatorships, and even terrorist organizations. To some, there is an obscene irony that a bond issued to build an elementary school in Middle America may also be funding repression in places such as Myanmar or even supporting extremist groups such as al Qaeda. Because such concerns are impossible to address comprehensively at a local level, increased state limitations, or even outright prohibitions, on municipal debt are obvious solutions.

Regardless of who holds school district debt, there has been increasing pressure on states to limit local indebtedness by legislative action and ballot initiatives. California's famous Proposition 13 in 1978, which limited property taxes, was adopted largely in response to the growing pressure on local taxpayers as a result of the *Serrano v. Priest* (1971, 1976) school finance litigation. Whether taxpayer resistance to unlimited local indebtedness, and related issues such as property valuations and exemptions, represent valid policy concerns, they nonetheless indicate a demand that states limit the degree to which local governments, including school districts, may burden property owners with additional municipal debt. Nor are such concerns voiced solely by taxpayers themselves. Critics have noted that although national debt occurs largely in the open and under the harsh glare of legislators and a well-informed media, local debt issues usually receive little expert critical review, and voters are usually poorly informed about such matters as the average or typical cost of a school building or the availability of more cost-effective alternatives. Generally, when there is public reaction to very expensive projects, such as Los Angeles, California, Unified School District's new $578 million Robert F. Kennedy Community Schools campus (the most expensive U.S. public school project ever built), it usually comes after the passage of what is often a highly technical and little-read bond referendum. The inability of most local voters to fully comprehend the meaning of bond issues often leaves these voters at the mercy of board members, district administrators, and even outside bonding agencies and construction interests. Additionally, negative taxpayer reaction to excessive debt issues in some instances may cause voters to unilaterally reject later, but needed, issues. Some advocates of good government argue that capital needs are better discussed in the open, on an as-needed basis, and using limited sources such as E-SPLOST funds, rather than necessarily large and complex bond issues drafted by technical experts and administrators with limited public input and oversight.

This leads to the role of the state as protector of the public's interest. Surveys often show that voters and taxpayers place more trust in their state governments than in local ones. Although it may be true that local officials who allow or commit excessive debt-funded projects to occur can be recalled or voted out of office, this still leaves local residents with possibly decades of high millage rates to retire these long-term bonds. State imposed limits on district debt tend to force local districts to seek more manageable and cost-effective plans for their current and long-term needs, and imposing greater state oversight, possibly from the states' departments of education or revenue, could to a large extent relieve local voters of the need to read and analyze complex bond issues by allowing independent expert analysis of these issues before they can be submitted for voter approval. This would also aid states in pursuing their constitutional interest in promoting equitable educational opportunities by allowing greater oversight of overly elaborate plans for educational facilities at a time when other districts are struggling to provide even minimally adequate ones.

This leads to a final consideration. Although school districts may share many similarities with other municipal subdivisions of state government, such as counties, towns, and special districts, they remain constitutionally much more closely tied to their states than to these other jurisdictions. Education remains principally a state constitutional responsibility. For historically well-documented reasons, states initially sought to meet this need through the expedient of local property taxes and the concomitant creation of local boards of education. Regardless of this, the obligation to provide effective educational services, compared with other obligations of government such as fire protection or trash collection, remains primarily a state obligation. When a local district unwisely engages in excessive local debt that affects its overall bond rating and its ability to pass future debt referendums, or when it simply exhausts its ability to raise additional capital funding, this directly affects the ability of both the district and the state to meet the future educational needs of the district's citizens. Even with municipalities that are largely free to operate under home rule provisions, states are often required, as in the case of Miami, to intervene in local finance and debt issues. In Miami, the governor of Florida declared the city to be in a state of financial emergency in 1996 and appointed an oversight board to monitor the city's financial management. Given the much closer relationship of states and their subordinate school districts, it follows that states would exert an even greater control of local districts in a variety of areas, including local debt and finance.

In the counterpoint essay, Spencer C. Weiler notes that Adam Smith, considered the founder of modern economics, argued in favor of free market economies and limitations on governmental interference with economic trends. Weiler argues that these principles apply to state limits on the indebtedness of school districts. Poor Adam Smith. In 2 centuries, he has evolved from the father of modern economics to the last refuge of those who argue for the devolution of governance and civil society. It is beyond the scope of this series to debate the numerous criticisms of Smith and his followers' perfect market theories. Suffice it to say, even in the private sector, which was the primary focus of Smith's work, fortunately no one has yet attempted to demonstrate in a real economy the perilous premise that free markets always work perfectly. Nonetheless, there are those who are all too eager to expand loosely on Smith's pioneering work and attempt to apply his unproven market theories to the public sector. In this, policymakers and theorists alike are all to eager to use the notoriety and gravitas of Smith to promote much more modern and debatable free market public sector theories that are more properly identified with neoclassical economists such as Friedrich Hayek and Milton Friedman.

Even if one does accept Smith's free market theories as infallible in the private sector, this is still far from persuasive when applied to the public sector in general, and to local public school districts in particular. In the private sector, entrepreneurs are encouraged to match their relative advantages, including fiscal capacity as well as ingenuity, determination, muscle, and even greed, or "private vices," as Smith put it, in a competition for profits and efficiency. Inevitably, there must be winners and losers in any capitalist competition. And, aside from such concerns as combinations and monopolies, it is theoretically desirable that such outcomes result from the application of free market principles to the private sector. In such a competition, it may be both predictable and desirable that, for example, a fish retailer with better access to the ocean will supersede a rival with a less direct supply.

But does this approach even remotely make sense in the context of public services such as schooling? Nearly all issues of public debt at the district level invoke property wealth, so simple math dictates that the winners and losers of this "free market" will be predetermined before the race is run. And unlike the theoretical assumptions of the classical free market, abundant empirical evidence indicates what happens when poor school districts and students "compete" against wealthier ones. History has demonstrated, as it has for decades in general education funding, that if the unhidden hand of the state does not intervene, well-to-do school districts will use their comparative advantages in property wealth to ever increase their students' opportunities relative to their disadvantaged peers. And here, philosophically, the free market comparison falls completely apart. For unlike the positive competition of the private sector, with its promises of cheaper goods and efficient distribution of goods and services, the goal in public education is not to produce winners and losers, but to seek to maximize the personal outcomes of all learners for *both* their benefit and that of the society as a whole. And without the intervention of the state, because of the harsh realities of demographics and geography, this goal can never be achieved and local advantages will continue to exacerbate the differences. Free market advocates need to be challenged as to how an uneven competition between communities, each concerned solely with maximizing the outcomes of its own children, will ever produce a greater public good or maximize societal outcomes. And it can be doubted that even Smith would accept the proposition that it could.

But this brings about the question of the proper role of the state. The counterpoint essay suggests that the state can and should find alternatives to debt limitation to provide for equitable or adequate educational programs. As the debates about state funding for annual general education programs demonstrate, if the state cannot place some upper limit on local revenues and expenditures, as this essay suggests, then its only alternative is to use state resources to equalize the differences created by local debt capacity. Given the extreme disparities in local property values, especially within a narrow band of districts at the highest levels of property wealth, the counterpoint author's suggestion that states should raise revenues and expenditures for perhaps 98% of their districts to meet a fiscal effort level set by a small handful of affluent districts is unfair. Although local control is a noble and cherished tradition, perhaps allowing a couple of local school boards to set capital funding policies for an entire state is allowing the tradition to go too far.

The counterpoint essay author's assertion that bonded debt is naturally controlled by market forces also demands a response. The suggestion is made that at some level, the free market sets its own limitations on local debt. This is an overly general and simplistic statement. As levels of local bonded debt rise, there is the risk that a district's bond rating may fall and, eventually, it will be unable to market further issues. This may even be a case of proving the opposite argument. Bond ratings determine bond interest rates. A lower rating, which nominally indicates higher risk, also necessitates a higher interest rate and, therefore, a higher return for investors. The simple truth is that in the modern bond market, almost any product offered will be bought by someone. It can even be argued that, given the low rates of school bond default, a DDD bond offering from an affluent and well-capitalized school district, given its much higher interest rate, may actually be more attractive to investors than its original AAA issues. Again, given the inherently complicated terms of these bonds, it is unreasonable to expect average voters to fully appreciate the long-term consequences of each new issue.

Finally, it must be reiterated that the consequences of excessive bonded debt and credit down rating do not affect individual districts and their residents alone. In the modern economy, municipal bonds are almost always issued by regional bonding authorities under series of "pooling agreements." A decline in a member district's rating affects its own capacity to issue bonds, as well as that of other member local government agencies. In the end, the lack of fiscal restraint by even a few members can affect the credit worthiness of all members or force the dissolution of what are considered both highly efficient and useful market mechanisms. Simply put, a lack of local fiscal restraint, contrary to the counterpoint essay position, is not a victimless crime.

COUNTERPOINT: Spencer C. Weiler
University of Northern Colorado

The issue debated in this chapter concerns the limitations, if any, that states should place on the ability of local school boards to incur debt.

This counterpoint essay, which argues for the elimination of limits on indebtedness, begins with a discussion of school districts and debt, examines the importance of adequately funding public education, explores Adam Smith's philosophy for free markets, and concludes with an explanation of why state imposed limits are unnecessary.

ADEQUACY, FREE MARKET, AND AN ARGUMENT FOR THE ELIMINATION OF STATE IMPOSED LIMITS ON INDEBTEDNESS

In extolling the attributes of a free market economy, Adam Smith (1776/1976) penned the following, "It is not from the benevolence of the butcher, the brewer, or the baker, that we expect our dinner, but from their regard to their own interest" (p. 284). The concept of self-interest has a role in the discussion related to the need for states to impose limits on a school district's indebtedness. On the surface, it appears prudent to protect a school district from itself by restricting the amount of debt that can be assumed, but such a policy is shortsighted and fails to consider all the facts. If a school district's voters agree to additional debt in the form of an override or a bond because the electorate desires an augmented system of education, then that form of self-interest should be free from unnecessary state interference.

INDEBTEDNESS AND SCHOOL DISTRICTS

Why would school districts accrue debt? Why would states limit the amount of debt a school district can accrue? School districts typically borrow money for construction or to supplement annual budgets. School districts can ask voters to approve a bond that would address construction needs. These construction costs could include renovating existing buildings, replacing outdated buildings, or adding buildings to accommodate growth in student populations. School districts ask voters to approve overrides to finance specific projects not fully funded by the annual budget that is received from the state. Both bonds and overrides are, in effect, mortgages that the school district initiates with voter approval.

States are interested in limiting the amount of money school districts can borrow to ensure they remain financially solvent. In addition, states do not want to allow excessively expansive opportunity gaps between school districts to surface. Opportunity gaps, by definition, include the educational experiences available to students in one district versus another. Problems arise when students in one district receive access to a state-of-the-art system of education, but students in another school district are condemned to attending school in dilapidated facilities using outdated supplies. Any form of an opportunity gap could be mitigated if public education were funded at an adequate level.

ADEQUACY

The focus of school finance litigation shifted in 1989 from equity to adequacy when the *Rose v. Council for Better Education* (1989) case was adjudicated. By definition, *adequacy* requires states to ensure a minimum quality of education for all students (Rebell, 2004, pp. 218–220; Verstegen & Knoeppel, 1998, p. 560). Adequacy does not require taking money from wealthy school districts to supplement poor ones (Rebell, 2004, p. 219; Wood & Baker, 2004, pp. 143–145). The purpose of adequacy is to guarantee all students a minimum quality of education and, depending on the minimum quality of education, so that all students can have similar educational opportunities, regardless of where they live (Rebell, 2004, p. 214). In other words, adequacy might achieve what previous efforts failed to secure, namely, a higher standard of education made available to all students.

Unfortunately, not all states currently attempt to fund public education at an adequate level. In states where adequacy is the desired standard, there is a lack of uniformity concerning the definition and its measurement. The definition of *adequacy*, which is ultimately based on the education clause in each state's constitution, varies greatly from state to state (Alexander & Alexander, 2008, p. 29). A second variation in adequacy is the way it is measured. State officials could either use input or output measurements of adequacy to determine the quality of education (Odden & Picus, 2008, p. 75). An input measurement of adequacy would ensure that all students attend schools that receive comparable services, such as student–teacher ratios, textbooks, technology, and so forth. A state's legislature would predetermine the desired levels of service for each category and then fund school districts at that prescribed level. An output measurement of adequacy focuses on student achievement and the assumption is that if students are achieving academically then the funding is adequate. An input measurement of adequacy appears to better control for extraneous variables on student achievement and is, therefore, preferable.

The central question of this debate is whether state limits on indebtedness should be eliminated. If a state has failed to ensure all students have access to an adequately funded school system, then the elimination of state limits on indebtedness would only allow affluent school districts to benefit from a greater opportunity gap over the less affluent school districts. Such a position is indefensible and should never be tolerated.

For that reason, the concept of adequacy has been explored. The primary assumption in the following arguments against state imposed limits on the level of indebtedness a school district can accrue is that the state is funding all public schools at an adequate level. If that is not the case, then the state is correct in limiting indebtedness as a way of curtailing the opportunity gap between students attending property-rich school districts and those attending property-poor districts. However, if a state is only limiting indebtedness and not properly addressing the issue of adequacy, then those limits are like a small bandage for a severe laceration. Assuming states have properly addressed the issue of adequacy and ensured that all students, regardless of zip code, skin color, or parents' economic status, have access to an adequate education, the following arguments are presented to encourage states to do away with limits on indebtedness.

FREE MARKET AND EDUCATION

Smith, considered to be the founder of modern economics, argued in favor of free market economies. Smith felt excessive government interference with economic trends could "repress self-interested people" and that an economy can only expand when self-interest is viewed "as a natural resource" (Buchholz, 1989, pp. 20–21). As evidenced by the quote that started this paper, the butcher, the brewer, and the baker make dinner for people because such efforts benefit them. They act out of self-interest, not benevolence. Self-interest is a natural resource because people are born with a "desire of bettering [their] condition" (Smith, 1776/1976, p. 341). The push to improve one's condition results in three factors that allow an economy to grow and flourish: motivation, invention, and innovation (Buchholz, 1989, p. 7).

The economic principle of free market economy, or the limit of government interference on economic trends, applies to the issue of state limits on indebtedness. State legislatures must first fund a system of education that ensures all students have access to an adequate educational opportunity. In effect, states must guarantee all students have the same minimum starting point. Next, state legislatures should strive to create a climate that fosters motivation, invention, and innovation in school districts. Just as excessive tariffs hurt an economy, state imposed limits on indebtedness represent a ceiling or a cap on motivation, invention, and innovation. That cap, ultimately, hurts children and stifles competition.

Imagine, for example, a state that did not impose limits on indebtedness, in which one school district approached its voters for permission to pass a large mill levy override to augment its annual budget. If that override passed, what influence would that infusion of additional funds have on neighboring school districts? It is conceivable that the neighboring school districts would also seek similar overrides to finance a better system of schools. As a result, the application of free market concepts to the issue of eliminating limits on indebtedness could actually foster greater competition between school districts in addition to supporting motivation, invention, and innovation. In the end, children benefit from the competition, motivation, invention, and innovation that are fostered when free market concepts are applied to public education.

ARGUMENTS FOR THE ELIMINATION OF LIMITS ON INDEBTEDNESS

The framework for this argument against state imposed limits on indebtedness stresses two points: first, each state's funding formula ensures all school districts are funded at an adequate level, and second, the concepts of a free market economy should be applied to the manner in which states oversee local school districts. With the framework established, it is now time to offer specific arguments against the use of limits on indebtedness. Eight arguments against the use of limits are offered in this section.

Limits are arbitrary. Rules that limit growth through borrowing are "arbitrary and ad hoc" (Dothan & Thompson, 2009, p. 464). The state restricts the amount of additional funding school districts can obtain through the passage of an override, and the limit is typically a percentage of the total program, or the district's annual budget. For example, in Colorado, the limit is 25% of the school district's total program (Colorado Department of Education, 2010, p. 8). However, there is no justification for such a limit. Why not 30% or 20%? In effect, states are instituting a cap on motivation, invention, and innovation without a compelling rationale for the position of the cap.

Limits are ineffective. In addition to being arbitrary, limits on indebtedness appear to be ineffective. Michael Dothan and Fred Thompson (2009), while analyzing the reasons for a number of municipalities having to declare bankruptcy recently, stated, "Rules and norms do not guarantee that jurisdictions will keep out of fiscal trouble" (p. 463). Even with limits on indebtedness in place, school district personnel are still able to either manage or mismanage existing funds. The state imposed limits do not guarantee that school districts will be fiscally solvent and appropriately responsible with entrusted public funds. Rather, the desired solvency and responsibility can be achieved through a transparent budgetary process and a distributive leadership strategy at the local level. Limits on indebtedness do not ensure school districts will always remain fiscally viable, and they do restrict creativity and growth that could positively affect student achievement.

Limits change. Over time, changes have been introduced to state imposed limits on indebtedness. According to Vern Brimley, Jr., and Rulon R. Garfield (2001), state limits have included "some percentage of the assessed value of taxable property," or "a similar percentage of true value," while other states have "increased the limit by a stated dollar amount," and yet other states have "provided for additional tax rate levies" (p. 272). Why all the changes to limits on indebtedness? Clearly, the system is flawed and efforts have been made to improve it. However, it is difficult to improve a system that places a cap on growth and creativity because that cap limits motivation, invention, and innovation. Instead of working to improve a system by limiting the amount of debt a school district can accrue, states would be well advised to focus efforts and resources on clearly defining what an adequate education looks like and then funding that level of education for all school districts and students. Once an adequate education is properly funded, then limits on indebtedness no longer need to be adjusted since such limits would become obsolete.

Limits are unnecessary. The lending system already has sufficient safeguards in place to prevent an entity from excessive borrowing. This is especially true of public entities, such as school districts, because any bond or override would have to be approved by voters. If a school district has too much debt for its net assessed value, or its total taxable wealth, then it "cannot borrow on any terms" (Dothan & Thompson, 2009, p. 473). Why? "Lenders will increase their exposures no further" and, consequently, will not consider lending the school district money (Dothan & Thompson, p. 464). Far more effective than a state imposed limit on indebtedness is one imposed by the lender. When the lender imposes a limit, then there can be no borrowing.

School districts receive debt ratings based on the wealth of the district and the amount of outstanding debt (Lipka, 2005, p. A9). Typically, school districts are viewed as a safe investment by lenders because the local dollars that pay down debt are generated from property tax, historically a stable source of income. School districts, therefore, receive a high debt rating and, consequently, pay a lower interest rate. However, the debt rating for a school district will drop if the district amasses too much debt and, as a result, each subsequent loan would be offered at a higher interest rate. All borrowing has to be approved by the school district's voters and these voters would be aware of the higher interest rate. The voters could either tell the school district that it has too much debt, by voting against the proposed bond or override, or the electorate could act as an informed consumer and willingly assume additional loans at a higher interest rate by approving the bond or override. However, under the current structure, with state imposed limits on indebtedness, the option of approving the bond or override is not available to the voters.

School districts require protection from the whims of a state. David N. Figlio (1998) wrote about a "local property tax revolt" in Oregon (p. 56). A similar tax revolt could take place statewide and has already taken place in a number of states. School districts require protection from any political backlash against taxes because a district's total program is funded exclusively with federal, state, and local tax dollars. If a statewide revolt against taxes were to take place and limits on indebtedness were in place, then school districts would have to cut expenses as budgets were reduced based on changes in finance at the state level. However, if the limits did not exist, then local school districts could ask voters to pass an override to offset lost revenues resulting from a statewide tax revolt.

Construction is typically a local responsibility. Catherine Sielke (2001) stated that local communities have historically been responsible for all of the expenses associated with building construction (p. 653). There is no indication that the trend of requiring local communities to pay for new construction, as well as renovation of existing buildings, is going to change in the immediate future. State budgets are overextended and, as a result, cannot offer local communities much relief related to construction. The federal government is constitutionally limited in its involvement with public education. Glen I. Earthman (2009) stated that the costs associated with new construction have increased in recent years (p. 28). As a result of these increases in costs, local communities are being asked to assume more debt, but the state limits could impede the amount of construction that actually takes place. The state imposed limits could condemn a student to an outdated or dilapidated facility because the school district cannot even ask the local community to consider approving an additional bond.

Limits deny growth. State imposed limits on indebtedness ultimately restrict those who desire a superior system of education access to such a system (Zimmer & Jones, 2005, p. 534). Some communities value education and are willing to pay more taxes to ensure the local school district provides its students with the highest quality educational experience but cannot do so because of limits on indebtedness. If all students have access to an adequate education, then limits are not necessary, and those communities that want to pay additional taxes to augment the state offering should be allowed to do so.

Control is local. Local control is a concept that is highly valued by most Americans (Alexander & Alexander, 2008, p. 125). Local control, by definition, provides the school district's elected board members with a degree of plenary power delegated from the state legislature. Ron Zimmer and John T. Jones (2005) argued that school districts should have the discretion to manage these additional funds raised locally to support public education (p. 543). At the heart of local control is the idea of empowering each community to identify the most pressing issues and then develop solutions for those issues. State imposed limits on indebtedness infringe on local control by restricting the amount of money that can be raised to fund solutions to problems, and evidence indicates that a more state-centralized funding formula results in a lower per pupil expenditure (Zimmer & Jones, 2005, p. 534).

Eight arguments against the use of limits on indebtedness have been presented in this section. These arguments illustrate the dangers associated with the use of limits. Specifically, state imposed limits significantly hinder the development of education, restrict local control, and are ineffective.

CONCLUSION

Should states limit the indebtedness of local school districts? Assuming that the state is funding public education at an adequate level, then the answer to this question is a resounding no. These state limits only suppress free market concepts such as motivation, invention, and innovation. Advocates for public education should call for the elimination of limits on indebtedness because these limits deprive all children from receiving the highest quality system of education.

FURTHER READINGS AND RESOURCES

Alexander, K., & Alexander, M. D. (2008). *American public school law* (7th ed.). Belmont, CA: Wadsworth.

Alexander, K., & Salmon, R. G. (1995). *Public school finance.* Boston: Allyn & Bacon.

Brimley, V., Jr., & Garfield, R. R. (2001). *Financing education in a climate of change* (8th ed.). Boston: Pearson.

Buchholz, T. G. (1989). *New ideas of dead economists: An introduction to modern economic thought.* New York: Plume.

Colorado Department of Education. (2010). *Understanding Colorado school finance and categorical program funding.* Retrieved from http://www.cde.state.co.us/cdefinance/download/pdf/FY2010-11BrochureWeb.pdf

Crampton, F., & Thompson, D. C. (2004). When the legislative process fails: The politics of litigation in school infrastructure funding equity. In K. DeMoss & K. K. Wong (Eds.), *Money, politics, and law: Intersections and conflicts in the provision of educational opportunity* (2004 Yearbook of the American Education Finance Association, pp. 65–88). Larchmont, NY: Eye on Education.

Dothan, M., & Thompson, F. (2009). A better budget rule. *Journal of Policy Analysis and Management, 28*(3), 463–478. doi: 10.1002/pam.20441

Earthman, G. I. (2009). *Planning education facilities* (3rd ed.). New York: Rowman & Littlefield.

Figlio, D. N. (1998). Short-term effects of a 1990s-era property tax limit: Panel evidence on Oregon's measure 5. *National Tax Journal, 51*(1), 55–70.

Guthrie, J. W., Springer, M. G., Rolle, R. A., & Houck, E. A. (2007). *Modern education finance and policy.* Boston: Pearson.

House, E. R. (1998). *Schools for sale: Why free market policies won't improve America's schools, and what will.* New York: Teachers College Press.

King, R. A., Swanson, A. D., & Sweetland, S. R. (2003). *School finance: Achieving high standards with equity and efficiency* (3rd ed.). Boston: Allyn & Bacon.

Lipka, S. (2005). Debt: Credit ratings head for an even keel. *The Chronicle of Higher Education, 51*(18), A9.

Odden, A. R., & Picus, L. O. (2008). *School finance: A policy perspective* (4th ed.). New York: McGraw-Hill.

Rebell, M. A. (2004). *Adequacy litigation: A new path to equity?* (New York Practice Skills Course Handbook Series). New York: Practicing Law Institute.

Schrag, Peter (2005). *Final test: The battle for adequacy in America's schools.* New York: The New Press.

Sielke, C. C. (2001, Fall). Funding school infrastructure needs across the states. *Journal of Education Finance, 21*, 653–662.

Smith, A. (1976). *An inquiry into the nature and causes of the wealth of nations* (R. H. Campbell, A. S. Skinner, & W. B. Todd, Eds.). Oxford, UK: Clarendon Press. (Original work published in 1776)

Spring, J. A. (2004). *American education* (11th ed.). New York: McGraw-Hill.

Thompson, D. C., Wood, R. C., & Honeyman, D. S. (1994). *Fiscal leadership for schools: Concepts and practices.* White Plains, NY: Longman.

Verstegen, D. A., & Knoeppel, R. C. (1998). Equal education under the law: School finance reform and the courts. *Journal of Law and Politics, 14*, 555–589.

Wood, R. C., & Baker, B. D. (2004). An examination and analysis of the equity and adequacy concepts of constitutional challenges to state education finance distribution formulas. *University of Arkansas at Little Rock Law Review, 27*, 125–167.

Zimmer, R., & Jones, J. T. (2005). Unintended consequences of centralized public school funding in Michigan education. *Southern Economic Journal, 71*(3), 534–544.

Court Cases and Statutes

DeRolph v. State, 78 Ohio St.3d 193 (1997), 677 N.E.2d 733 (Ohio 1997) [DeRolph I].

DeRolph v. State, 89 Ohio St.3d 1 (2000), 728 N.E.2d 993 [DeRolph II].

DeRolph v. State, 93 Ohio St.3d 309 (2001), 754 N.E.2d 1184 (Ohio 2001) [DeRolph III].

DeRolph v. State, 97 Ohio St.3d 434 (2002), 780 N.E.2d 529 (Ohio 2002) [DeRolph IV].

Rose v. Council for Better Education, 790 S.W.2d 186 (Ky. 1989).

Serrano v. Priest, 5 Cal. 3d 584 (1971), 96 Cal. Rptr. 601 (Cal. 1971) [Serrano I].

Serrano v. Priest, 18 Cal. 3d 728 (1976), 135 Cal. Rptr. 345 (Cal. 1976) [Serrano II].

Should the leadership of each individual school have the authority to determine how money is spent at that school?

POINT: Carlee Poston Escue, *University of Cincinnati*

COUNTERPOINT: Luke M. Cornelius, *University of North Florida*

OVERVIEW

This debate asks whether individual schools should have substantial autonomy over funding. As with other debates in this volume, the issue is one of local autonomy. Those who favor the constitutional value of local control argue that just as local boards should be empowered, individual schools should have autonomy. Principals, parents, and teachers should have the authority to do what they think is best for their students. The advocates of local control believe that school leaders, in conjunction with the school community, are in the best position to make decisions based on the individual school and community needs. In opposition, those who favor the constitutional value of equality contend that current disparities between school districts should not be exacerbated by allowing additional disparities between schools.

Autonomy at the School Level Can Lead to Inequality

As noted in other chapters in this volume, there is often tension between the state constitutional values of equality and local control. On the one hand is the argument that all public schools should be equal. Education is a function of the states, and all states provide for the establishment, maintenance, and support of public schools. The education clauses of many state constitutions, in addition to stipulating that school systems should be thorough and efficient, specify a level of quality. Such constitutional mandates can, and frequently are, interpreted to mean that the public schools throughout the state will be of similar quality. State financing systems often authorize local school districts to impose property taxes for the support of public schools, supplemented by additional revenues for districts having low property values. Under such a system, all school districts receive a minimum level of funding that, in theory, should be sufficient for meeting the state's standards of quality. Further, such systems are designed to ensure educational equality by supplementing property tax revenues in less affluent districts.

On the other hand, and central to this debate, is the question of local control. Except for Hawaii, all states are subdivided into local school districts that have responsibility for the public schools within their boundaries. School districts are usually overseen by school boards that have broad discretion regarding the operation of the district, particularly its financial affairs. Thus, boards generally have the autonomy to spend the available money as they see fit, subject to state laws and regulations. The quality of the local public schools is the result of decisions made by the local school board regarding hiring of personnel, establishment of the curricula, and the allocation of funds.

In some instances, the idea of local control is taken a step further—individual schools are empowered to make financial and hiring decisions. Decisions are made not by a board, but by principals, parents, and teachers. The debate in this chapter centers on the propriety of taking local control to the individual school level. The great discretion given to local school boards almost inevitably leads to some inequality among school districts. Because some local school districts are better at making decisions than others are, some local districts become better than others even where the school districts have approximately the same level of funding. As can be expected, all resources between schools are not equal: Some teachers are better than others, some principals are superior administrators, some curriculum approaches are more effective, and some textbooks are of a higher quality. Although these differences are of concern, local boards may lessen and even eliminate these disparities simply by altering their hiring and curriculum approaches. In other words, local boards need to make better use of the resources available to them.

If the principles of local control are extended to the individual school, it seems inevitable that there will be disparities within a single school district, as well as between school districts. Quite simply, some groups of principals, parents, and teachers will be better at using the resources and autonomy than other groups will be. Some will succeed and others will fail.

Of course, although greater autonomy at the school level may lead to inequality, it will also lead to pockets of excellence. Children and the community in general will benefit if an individual school rises above the other schools. Moreover, if some schools succeed, other schools presumably will seek to emulate those practices and policies that have led to success. By allowing inequality in the short run, the overall quality of all schools may improve in the long run.

Summary of the Debate

Carlee Poston Escue, a professor of education at the University of Cincinnati, takes the affirmative view. As she notes, the funds necessary to achieve an adequate education will vary from school district to school district. Schools having numerous students with special needs or facing unique problems will need more money than other districts need. The same principle applies with comparisons between schools. Just as local school districts should have a degree of financial autonomy, individual schools within districts should have a degree of financial autonomy.

Luke M. Cornelius, a professor of education at the University of North Florida, takes the negative view. One of the basic premises of economics is that the price of producing a good or service is lowered when the producer is able to buy materials in quantity. A district that purchases 1,000 textbooks will pay less per book than will an individual school that purchases 100 textbooks. Moreover, the costs of maintaining and operating schools vary greatly depending on the age of the building and the experience level of the faculty. A school with a new building and a young faculty will have far more flexibility than a school with an older facility and an experienced staff will have. Furthermore, not all educators are capable of making the complex managerial decisions that come with financial autonomy. Finally, greater autonomy may make accountability more difficult.

William E. Thro
Christopher Newport University

POINT: Carlee Poston Escue
University of Cincinnati

Adequacy in education has become one of the most discussed and sought-after funding priorities for 21st-century education in the United States. The basic principle of adequacy is that the allocation of educational resources must consider the differences between children; because the needs of children differ, spending on each child should differ as well. This same principle also can be applied to schools. The funding received by individual schools should reflect the differences in the needs of those schools and their students. Most states around the country provide funds to school districts, and the school district determines how schools will be funded. To simplify the management of funds, most school districts follow a standardized budget that treats all schools in a similar manner. Equality in the distribution of resources does not recognize the differing needs of students and schools. Thus, school leaders are often plagued with the burden of meeting their individual school needs because this bureaucratic system of allocating funds essentially ties the hands of principals. School-level authority over funding decisions would allow school leaders to make decisions within their school allocations on the basis of individual school and community needs, thus meeting the students and the families where they are, not where the district averages them out to be. Stated another way, individual school leaders could prioritize their schools' needs and spend allotted funds based on those priorities rather than as assigned in a line-item district budget.

In many ways, school-level autonomy is a value system. Is the financial interest of a school protected best by the individual school leadership or by the encompassing school district? This question can be answered with certain caveats. If specific financial and legal training is provided for the school leadership, district auditing and accountability measures are in place and practiced, and there is a passionate focus on avoiding high principal mobility, it is fair to argue that an individual school leader would have more insight regarding the school needs in comparison with district personnel. This argument is even stronger with respect to large school districts where a school district may be composed of hundreds of schools. For example, the state of Florida is made up of 67 school districts. Some of these school districts are among the largest in the United States, and the schools within a district are drawn from diverse communities whose members have differing socioeconomic backgrounds.

WHAT IS SCHOOL-LEVEL FINANCIAL AUTONOMY?

Before the argument supporting school-level authority is discussed, a brief description of financial autonomy needs to be provided. Financial autonomy as described in this chapter incorporates financial decisions including teacher and staff hiring, curriculum material, professional development, building needs, and other financial components that could be made at the school level. This does not include bonds, tax rates, and other components that demand the general public to vote on or approve.

CENTRAL-OFFICE-BASED MANAGEMENT VERSUS SCHOOL-LEVEL MANAGEMENT

Education systems are managed in one of two ways or in a hybrid form. In central-office-based management, a district office makes most of the decisions. When decisions are made, the information is then handed down to the schools for full implementation. Many supporters of central-based management consider the model more efficient and consistent within the school district because having one person responsible for many schools allows that person to know the needs of the entire district and decide what each school is to do.

School-based management allows schools to have the final decision-making power. Schools determine their individual needs, whether it is for purchasing office supplies or hiring teachers. The school can assess the needs and manage the decisions without the need for approval from the central office.

Many school districts throughout the nation follow a hybrid model of the two. This gives certain powers to school principals but also controls larger situations at the central office. The Cincinnati Public School (CPS) district follows a hybrid model for allocating funding. CPS principals have the power to hire teachers and make many business decisions. However, CPS principals cannot hire certain staff that may need to be moved throughout the district. For example, paraprofessionals are usually assigned to a special needs student. The CPS central office manages the paraprofessionals because if the student were to move, the paraprofessional would need to move with the student. This saves principals money in the long run because they do not need to hire someone whose services may no longer be needed if the student withdraws.

BURDEN OF CHIEF FISCAL OFFICERS

Although the counterargument presents some serious and valid concerns regarding autonomy, it is important to note that most of the negative outcomes can occur in central-office-based school systems as well. To imply that central-based finance management somehow protects taxpayer money without any occurrence of inequity, fiscal mismanagement, or ineptitude would be inaccurate and more likely misleading. There are school districts throughout the nation that are mismanaged by chief fiscal officers to the point of emptying the coffers. Throughout the nation, there are school districts where gross inequities exist within the district, and there are inequities among neighboring districts, even when a central office is responsible for managing the distribution and equity of funds.

California's Department of Education listed 174 California school districts at high risk of being unable to meet their financial obligations for fiscal years 2009–2010, 2010–2011, and 2011–2012. Many of the school districts have financial officers with MBA degrees and backgrounds with many years of fiscal experience, yet there is a disconnect between the formal training of the fiscal school district executors and the fiscal soundness of the corresponding districts. With all of this said, school autonomy generally is advantageous and effective only when principals are given training and support regarding fiscal aspects involved with the entrepreneurial landscape concerned with autonomy.

INEQUITIES IN FUNDING

In a report by the Education Trust–West (2005), enormous disparities within districts were discovered between teacher salaries at high wealth schools and low wealth schools. Wealthier schools with less teacher turnover received more funding dollar for dollar compared with low wealth schools within the district because of differences in the salaries of senior faculty compared with those of newer faculty. Such disparity exists across the nation even with the involvement of a central office. One could even argue that the central office perpetuates this type of disparity by actively ignoring the disparity in teacher salaries. High-performing schools tend to have faculty who have been teaching for many years. These faculty members will have higher salaries because of their length of service in the school system, but newer faculty will have salaries that are much less. Thus, more money to pay for salaries will be allocated by school districts to schools with more senior faculty than to those with large numbers of teachers who are at the beginning level.

As the economy has struggled over the past few years, this disparity is also being exacerbated as many school districts are attempting to cap salaries by requiring that new teachers have less than three years of experience. This practice requires schools to replace faculty who resign or retire with new faculty who earn smaller salaries and thus prevents principals from hiring faculty with many years of experience because those salaries would be too expensive. This is another dilemma associated with central office control, student achievement, and autonomy. If a principal were to have many teachers retire within a few years of each other, the principal would not have the flexibility to hire new and experienced faculty to maintain a successful school. If the principal were to have autonomy, he or she could assess the school needs and hire faculty based on that assessment. This example demonstrates that sometimes efficiency is not always the most practical approach.

In an autonomous situation, a principal has more control over the salary disparity. When principals have control of teacher salaries, they can decide how to allocate these funds as they make hiring decisions. For example, a principal with $150,000 allocated for hiring faculty could determine whether to hire fewer higher paid teachers with multiple years of experience or more inexperienced faculty who may be coming straight from college.

Currently, principals have permission to hire teachers, but it is not common for districts to tell principals that they can hire a teacher in a specific salary range. However, this is common practice in higher education. Deans determine whether they want to hire at the assistant, associate, or full professor rank. These levels are usually associated with a salary level. Hiring one full professor may cost as much as hiring two assistant professors, and institutional needs will determine which choice is most likely to be advantageous. Such flexibility at the K–12 level would allow principals to determine their school needs and thus to staff schools with more specificity. For example, a principal could hire two beginning teachers earning $32,000 each, or the principal could hire one teacher with 15 years' experience earning $60,000. Depending on the school needs, one may make more sense than the other. A principal who has many experienced teachers retiring in the next year may want an experienced teacher to help with leadership needs. A principal who has a strong group of experienced teachers who will be retiring in 5 to 10 years may feel that training new teachers to be ready to take on leadership roles in 5 to 10 years would be more advantageous to the school in the long term. When the principal has the autonomy to make such decisions, there will be more individual school assessment and decision making. When a central office controls this decision making, it is difficult to ascertain the individual needs of each school. Central office decisions can often generalize solutions when perhaps there is more need for individual customization for schools.

THE PRINCIPAL'S ROLE IN AUTONOMY

School-level autonomy results in multiple positive outcomes associated with principal training and reduced principal mobility. In 2010, the Wallace

Foundation published results from the largest study of its kind examining principal influence on student performance. This study incorporated 9 states, 43 school districts, and 180 schools using surveys, interviews, and various forms of school demographics. The *Learning From Leadership Project: Investigating the Links to Improved Student Learning* (Wahlstrom, Louis, Leithwood, & Anderson, 2010) found that rapid principal turnover consisting of one new principal every 3 or 4 years has significant negative effects on student achievement. Allowing principals to manage school funds with autonomy may encourage principals and school boards to reduce principal mobility, benefiting the school and the students within it. This would address the student achievement concerns and increase autonomy and entrepreneurial decision making.

FACETS OF AUTONOMY: TRADITIONAL PUBLIC AND CHARTER SCHOOLS

Two examples can further illustrate the advantages of school-level authority.

Empowerment Schools Program in New York State

First, New York State's Empowerment Schools Program in 2010 gave more than 500 New York City public schools the ability to manage financial decisions at the school level. Empowerment Schools evolved out of a pilot program called the Autonomy Zone, which began in 2004 with 29 participating schools. Since 2004, Empowerment has grown from its roots as the Autonomy Zone (4 networks, 29 schools), to the first year of Empowerment (14 networks, 332 schools), to its current size (22 networks, 535 schools). The number of participating schools nearly doubled. Empowerment schools in the program are organized into networks that allow schools to group based on similar interests and student bodies. Principals of empowerment schools have more discretion regarding professional development, curricula, and budgeting decisions. Included with the ability to spend moneys with more flexibility is the option to apply for waivers and exemptions from many administrative obligations expected of traditional principals. All these components of the Empowerment Schools Program have allowed school leaders to manage their individual school needs without feeling that they are standardized within the education system.

School-Level Autonomy in New Orleans Charter Schools

Following the devastation resulting from Hurricane Katrina, New Orleans was offered the opportunity to test the charter school movement on a large scale.

The expansion of the charter school movement in New Orleans post-Katrina was adopted partly as a fairly quick way to establish schools in a community that was destroyed so rapidly and on such a large scale. New Orleans lost many teachers, students, and district personnel following Katrina. The city needed schools, and it needed flexibility. Charter schools provided that opportunity for New Orleans. More than 70% of New Orleans K–12 students were educated in a charter school in 2010. New Orleans provides a unique example of what might be possible if schools were allowed more autonomy.

In recent years since the inception of charter schools, school-level autonomy has been in full effect. Charter schools have served as the pioneering public school entity testing the possibilities for increased school-level autonomy. As with any inaugural expedition, there are struggles, failures, and successes. One component of charter schools needing more examination is the financial autonomy provided to charter schools. Does this allow opportunities for traditional public schools? Are there benefits to individual school-level authority? Does a one-size-fits-all approach to financing education work? Although this chapter is not intended to evaluate charter schools, the discussion does note similarities between autonomous traditional schools and the charter school movement. Many of the school-level authority decisions would relate to the management responsibilities of a charter school.

The counterpoint essay argues that the charter school comparison is moot because of the size of school districts compared with charter schools. The example presented in this point section of the chapter did not discuss an individual charter school as a comparison; the argument is focused on the charter school system in New Orleans. This example demonstrates the large-scale comparison of a charter system compared with school districts. The size is comparable to that of many school districts throughout the nation. In fact, the size of the New Orleans charter school system is larger than many school districts throughout the nation. For example, the state of Ohio has school districts with as few as 460 students. There are many charter schools in New Orleans with populations significantly larger than the small districts in Ohio.

ECONOMIES OF SCALE

Finally, the counterpoint essay makes a simplistic observation associated with supply and demand. The rationale is that a larger school district will have more buying power because of its ability to buy wholesale or in mass. Buying in bulk should not be a solid reason for central office management. There are many ways to make cost-effective purchases of material for office use without relinquishing autonomy and independence. For example, orders for all schools can be combined and placed through the central office to take advantage of bulk order discounts. Small business entrepreneurs wrestle with this dilemma continually; it is not a valid argument to eliminate small business and support only large corporate enterprises.

CONCLUSION

Although standardization at times can be considered more convenient, the marginalization of individual identity and needs can be detrimental to the success of our students, schools, and communities. School-level autonomy allows for more differentiated management recognizing the unique needs of communities, cultures, and values incorporated within the individual school.

Many problems with a school-level system that a counterargument could identify also exist in central-based funding systems. Fiduciary responsibility and ethical decision making are needed if school-level autonomy is to be successful. School-level autonomy allows schools to remove the obstacles preventing principals from making sound financial decisions that meet their individual school needs. The No Child Left Behind Act aims to individualize education as much as possible by meeting the needs of all of the nation's children; it only makes sense to allow schools to have the financial will to address those needs at the school level without the bureaucracy of central governing clogging the system.

COUNTERPOINT: Luke M. Cornelius
University of North Florida

It is not hard to appreciate the periodic and transitory appeal of school-based management (SBM) and budgeting. One need only read the newspapers to see that many taxpayers and citizens view centralized school administration with its built-in bureaucracy, particularly in large districts, as draining large amounts of money that could be better spent directly on students. Even in smaller and less bureaucratized systems, there is a certain libertarian and democratic appeal in ensuring that moneys collected to educate children be spent as directly as possible for that purpose, without the corrosive attrition imposed by additional layers of hierarchy and administration. It even appeals at a certain political level, as school-based solutions relate well to concepts of government that is smaller, more local, and more direct. Given such attractive and persuasive rationales, it seems hard to defend the entrenched status quo of state- and district-level controls over school funding. Viewed through the eyes of school decentralization advocates, resistance to school-based management must reflect nothing but the counterrevolutionary efforts of entrenched bureaucracies that place their own power and self-interest above that of the children they are supposed to serve. No doubt there is more than a little truth in this characterization. Yet, this is far from the extent of the argument against greater school-site budget autonomy.

ECONOMIES OF SCALE

One economic argument that advocates of SBM and similar reforms conveniently overlook is the classical theory of economies of scale. From textbooks to toilet paper, from school busses to sloppy joes, there remains a simple truth that those who purchase in greater quantities and at wholesale receive a lower relative unit cost. Does the value of allowing principals to select their own texts and materials truly outweigh the additional surcharge of higher unit prices inherent in such an arrangement? Even in the literature of charter schools, there is no evidence that localizing spending authority produces better purchase choices or cost-effectiveness. Indeed, one need only look to the inimical "purchase card" or P-card, to see that the real efficiency of localized spending is one of speed and convenience, not economy. A case of copy paper purchased at retail may be quicker and more responsive, but it cannot compete on a cost basis with purchases of hundreds or thousands of cases at wholesale.

RESPONSIBILITY FOR FISCAL MANAGEMENT

The transfer of higher-level budgetary functions is even more problematic. What happens at the schools where innovative and empowered leaders inherit disproportionately senior faculties, aged and maintenance-intensive facilities, or unduly high concentrations of high need and at-risk students? Does allowing, or requiring, principals to negotiate their own staff salaries and employee benefits truly justify the time-consuming nature of these activities? And, because among tens of thousands of school leaders, some must, a priori, be better than others at budget and fiscal management, how will the inevitable inequities that arise, some no doubt acute, be managed? For that matter, does not the allocation of greater fiscal authority to the school site simply invite even greater conflict on issues of equity and adequacy at a more microeconomic level? And are we inviting beneficial innovation or dangerous experimentation? What will be the response when some principal decides that using out-of-date texts is a fair trade-off for higher-paid staff? Or when some incapable or irresponsible school leader redlines the school's budget by early October? When it directly affects the quality of education for actual students, how do we rationalize the inevitable disasters, whether they are legion or merely outliers?

A further issue concerns leadership and business acumen. In a day and age when the focus of leadership preparation is increasingly driven by accountability and student achievement, where do we expect building-level leaders to acquire such expertise? Advocates of SBM and similar schemes often cite parallels to the private sector and industry, while conveniently overlooking that these managers are trained almost exclusively in specialized business skills such as human resources, purchasing, and risk management. There is, of course, no reason why educational leadership training cannot expand to incorporate such skills, but doing so means either the sacrifice of currently emphasized skills in curricular leadership or a vast increase in the required course load for certification. Although many principals may doubtlessly yearn for the freedom and control school-based finance gives them, many others will likewise resent the considerable diversion of time and effort from more pedagogical concerns. For although greater fiscal authority may facilitate greater school improvement, it also implies the addition of other fiscal tasks that may be more time-consuming than innovative.

The statement is made in the point essay that mismanagement exists among some segment of school district chief fiscal officers, and this statement is likely accurate. However, the argument is then made that the solution to this problem is to again train a much larger number of school-site administrators in budget and finance. Overlooked in this suggestion is that logic and efficiency indicate that it is far simpler and easier to train, retrain, or replace even a few hundred low-performing school business officers, rather than to provide comparable training to thousands of school building leaders. Here the point can be made that professional school business officers serve one main function. Those who cannot perform adequately in this role should have their skills upgraded, if possible, or be replaced by more capable practitioners. Certainly, there is a need for better and more specific training of school business professionals. Colleges of education should consider creating dedicated programs to train high quality school finance officers. In the meantime, school districts may want to consider broadening their recruitment of business officers by considering candidates with degrees and experience in budget and finance in public administration or even private business. By contrast, providing comparable training to all school-site leaders requires them to master yet another function, on top of the multiple roles they already have, and raises the questionable theory that somehow it is more feasible to train all principals adequately in finance and budget than it is to train central office business personnel. This suggestion also implies that building principals, who may be highly competent as curriculum and organizational leaders, will nonetheless be discarded if they demonstrate an inability for fiscal management similar to the criticisms of those currently inadequate central office business officials. Once again, the point essay suggests that it is far easier and more desirable to burden dozens or hundreds of school-level leaders with an additional training credential requirement, than to hire or adequately train a mere handful of dedicated district-level school business professionals.

CHARTER AND OTHER DECENTRALIZED SCHOOLS

In this debate, there is always a temptation to reason by analogies, false or otherwise. The example of charter schools always tops this list. This is of course an inaccurate comparison. Not only do charter schools often result in an *increase* in per student expenditures on administration, but comparing typically small and homogenous charter schools with larger and more diverse traditional district schools is invalid. Asking the leader of a school of maybe a few hundred students, to say nothing of high parent and community support, to assume the greater budgetary duties implied by the creation of a specialized curriculum and student focus is a far cry from imposing similar duties on the principal of a metropolitan high school with 6,000 or more students. Of course, this distinction of scale invites consideration of all-charter systems, such as those currently attempted in New Orleans, or of restructuring the size and purpose of traditional schools. Unfortunately, such discussions are contingent on much larger and more problematic political and fiscal policy-making issues. Likewise, although the Empowerment Schools Program in New York City may raise the enthusiasm of school-based budget and management proponents, all too many, even supporters of greater school autonomy conclude that the result was to replace centralized inefficiency and waste with localized incompetence and corruption. Even more sobering are recent revelations by researchers that charter and other decentralized schools, on average and during 2 decades of operation, do no harm. This is rather faint praise for such experiments, given the enthusiasm with which they were launched. And for those who endorse an analogical approach, perhaps it is also appropriate to consider the example of larger and better-established private and charter schools, where fiscal independence is often accompanied by the necessity of increased school office staff, often including dedicated professional school-site business officers or the bifurcation of the school leadership role into separate positions for the chief executive and chief academic officers.

CHANGING ROLES FOR SCHOOL LEADERS

There is also the context of history to consider. Many older school administrators can recall a day and age when building principals actually held greater fiscal autonomy as a matter of tradition and structure. The gradual removal of responsibility for auxiliary services such as transportation, food service, and building maintenance was seen then as empowering principals to focus on their role as pedagogical and curricular leaders. Thus, although building-based management initially seems attractive in the sense of fiscally empowering school improvement, given the time constraints of school principals, it remains to be seen whether building-level textbook selection processes and independent salary and benefit negotiations truly empower or encumber school leaders in carrying out their main task of being instructional leaders. Additionally, proponents of greater school autonomy, in areas beyond finance, must acknowledge that the noble goal of school-level empowerment comes with the cost of placing considerable added burdens on building-level leaders. Each new added authority must be considered in the context of the existing tasks and responsibilities of serving as a principal, such as academic leader, building manager, staff supervisor, disciplinarian, community resource, and even senior athletic director. Given the limited amount of time in a day, it must be recognized that each new task added will take time away from a principal's other tasks. With workdays that can extend to 12 hours or more at times, extreme care must be used when assigning greater fiscal autonomy, and the concurrent greater responsibility, to school leaders who are already all too often overburdened with other demands. Will transferring these duties from dedicated central office professionals to already busy school-site leaders truly result in improved decision-making processes and significant school improvement, or will they take a principal's attention away from other tasks directly related to student learning?

PRINCIPAL MOBILITY

Furthermore, there is the issue of how school-based initiatives correspond with other theories of effective school leadership. Advocates of decentralization argue that an essential condition for successful school-based solutions is the establishment of greater stability in the principal's position in particular. There are two basic problems with this assertion. The first is reconciling this requirement with competing theories of principal mobility. The regular rotation of principals is well supported in much of the leadership literature for reasons such as assigning the most effective leaders to the most at-risk schools and to avoid the establishment of local school "fiefdoms" in which long-term leaders can establish local power bases that may rely more on community relationships than objective measures of actual school effectiveness. Furthermore, the very market-based philosophies that underlie school-based models would tend to indicate the potential for greater, not lesser, principal mobility. It is not difficult to postulate a school leadership free market in which particularly successful school leaders, much like star athletes or coaches, are constantly relocating to new schools for ever increasing salaries while less successful principals are continually replaced in the quest for greater effectiveness.

ACCOUNTABILITY FOR EDUCATIONAL OUTCOMES

Finally, there are larger policy concerns. Much of the focus of recent political efforts at school improvement, such as the No Child Left Behind Act and the Race to the Top program, focus on district- and state-level accountability for educational outcomes. There is a logical inconsistency with devolving greater authority and autonomy to the individual school while increasing the responsibility and accountability of district and state systems. And even without such legislative acts, valid arguments remain for retaining, or increasing, centralized fiscal decision making. In an era of increasing family and student mobility, critical issues of establishing and maintaining consistent curricula are becoming apparent. What good does local innovation in text selections, teaching materials, and pedagogical approaches do for the student who moves from one attendance zone to another once or more in a given school year? Again there exists a vast divide between charter schools' students, often the children of families that are both highly motivated and deeply rooted in a given community, and the increasingly transient and diverse learners who populate more attendance zone–oriented schools. At a time when high-stakes testing causes many to argue, for example, for regional or statewide uniformity in curricula and text selection, does devolving these decisions to the building level truly serve either higher policy concerns or the needs of many learners and their families?

POLICY ALTERNATIVES

It would be all too easy to completely dismiss the concept of school-level fiscal autonomy altogether for the reasons already enumerated and many others too numerous to discuss. But this would be inappropriate for a number of reasons. First, it must be acknowledged that school-based management is itself an artifact of policy debates that often produce internally inconsistent and illogical directions. Within the debate about No Child Left Behind, for example, President George W. Bush's administration and its allies in Congress called for both greater state and district accountability while promoting an agenda of decentralization of school control and decision making, goals often echoed by members of the then opposition party as well. Second, in examining the underlying motivations and methods surrounding school-based approaches, it is possible to identify both legitimate concerns and effective alternative responses to these concerns.

Writing about school-based management a decade ago, Lawrence O. Picus (1999) suggested several attributes necessary for effective SBM. One of these was the need for greater professionalism within the school district business office. In the literature favoring school-based approaches, it is not hard to discern a strong undercurrent of resentment and criticism of centralized district business officers and their bureaucracies. But it may be possible to find alternatives to the current system less radical than burdening school leaders with dramatically increased fiscal responsibilities and the reduced purchasing power entailed in such a transition. Among the school district chief business officers of most states, there is great variety, from university-trained school finance experts to former business teachers, ex-principals, failed business owners, church managers, and many others. Before radically deconstructing the central school district, it may be time to consider placing a greater emphasis on the professionalization of the district business function to a level equivalent to that of the academic leaders of a system. There is a reason why calls for decentralization of fiscal authority are rarely heard with other municipal services such as police, fire departments, and public works. In most organizations, public and private, business and finance issues are controlled by experienced and well-trained professionals holding qualifications such as master's degrees in business or public administration. In most organizations, finance professionals work both through formal budget committee and appropriation processes and informally with agency and site managers to assess and meet their needs. Perhaps the time is long overdue when school districts, and state education departments, adopt similar structures and qualifications, most likely through means such as licensure and certification, so that highly qualified school business professionals, trained in the needs and functions of schools, become the norm. Consideration should at least be made to the concept that the district business and finance function can be improved, including its communication and cooperation with building leaders, before moving to the rather more problematic position of assuming that all, or at least most, principals can and must become fiscal experts themselves.

Another alternative proposition can be found already in a more *silent* revolution sweeping states in the form of school-based accounting. Another concept cited by Picus and others is the utility in mandating that specified percentages, such as 85%, of certain categorical funding lines be accounted for as having been spent directly for goods and services at the school site rather than for general district purposes and fiscal overhead. This concept, which has been quietly implemented in many states such as Georgia, may offer the best way to address the concerns of both sides in this debate. For example, school districts would be required to show that state appropriations for textbooks designated for a specific school, and even grade level, be accounted for by ensuring that new texts delivered to that site represented a value of at least 85% of the amount appropriated. Overages, if any, would revert to the building administrator to be spent on supplemental texts and other materials. In this way, districts could still employ the enhanced economy of central purchasing of texts and other staples while ensuring that the overwhelming majority of funds allocated to a specific school are actually spent on that site and not on bureaucratic overhead. (Such mandates, limiting administrative costs to 15% or even 10%, would also bring about the necessity of better managed and more efficient central operations.)

Although somewhat more complex, similar policies could even be applied to issues of staffing and salary, ensuring that all schools have a mix of teachers at different experience and seniority levels. It might even be possible to create a hybrid system of school-based accountability and budgeting whereby basic and standardized needs are met by the district, with site-based accountability, while mandating that some significant but manageable percentage is retained for the discretion of the school leadership itself.

FURTHER READINGS AND RESOURCES

Bull, B. (2000). Political philosophy and the balance between central and local control of schools. In N. Theobald & B. Malen (Eds.), *Balancing local control and state responsibility for K-12 education* (2000 Yearbook of the American Educational Finance Association, pp. 21–46). Larchmont, NY: Eye on Education.

Dragona, A. N. (2011). Tuning the tin ear: In search of fiscal congruency. *School Business Affairs, 77*(1), 23–26.

Education Trust–West. (2005). *California's hidden teacher spending gap: How state and district budgeting practices shortchange poor and minority students and their schools.* Oakland, CA: Author.

Guthrie, J. W., Rolle, A. M., Springer, M. G., & Houck, E. A. (2007). *Modern education finance and policy.* Boston: Pearson.

Howley, C., Johnson, J., & Petrie, J. (2011). *Consolidation of schools and districts: What the research says and what it means.* Boulder, CO: National Education Policy Center.

King, R. A., Swanson, A. D., & Sweetland, S. R. (2003). *School finance: Achieving high standards with equity and efficiency* (3rd ed.). Boston: Allyn & Bacon.

Picus, L. O. (1999). Site-based management: A nuts and bolts approach for school administrators. In M. E. Goertz & A. Odden (Eds.), *School-based financing* (pp. 22–39). Thousand Oaks, CA: Corwin.

Robelen, E. W. (2010). New Orleans schools seize post-Katrina momentum. *Education Week, 30*(1), 1, 13, 16–17.

Wahlstrom, K., Louis, K. S., Leithwood, K., & Anderson, S. E. (2010). *The Learning from Leadership Project: Investigating the links to improved student learning executive summary of research findings.* Retrieved from http://www.wallacefoundation.org/KnowledgeCenter/KnowledgeTopics/CurrentAreasofFocus/EducationLeadership/Documents/Learning-from-Leadership-Investigating-Links-Ex-Summary.pdf

Court Cases and Statutes

No Child Left Behind Act of 2001, 20 U.S.C. §§ 6301 *et seq.*

Should states rely on local property taxes as a primary method of financing public schools?

POINT: Steven A. Hinshaw, *Director of Finance, Centerville, Ohio*
COUNTERPOINT: C. Daniel Raisch, *University of Dayton*

OVERVIEW

A critical issue in school finance concerns exactly how the public schools are financed. Although local school districts receive funds from both federal and state sources, all local school districts, except those in Hawaii, raise much of the money necessary for operations through a percentage tax, with the rate set by the local residents, on the value of the real property in the district. This system, known as a property tax or millage tax, results in vast disparities because of differences in rates and in the value of real property within a school district's boundaries. As a consequence, some districts struggle to provide even the basics, but others, in more affluent areas, are able to offer educational luxuries. Given the probable relationship between level of expenditures and the quality of the education received by the students, disparities in funding will often lead to disparities in educational achievement. Although state legislatures and executives have adopted various mechanisms to correct this financial inequality, the disparities remain.

Property taxes are levied on the value of land and of improvements to the land. In some jurisdictions, personal property, such as automobiles, is also taxed. The property tax is the main means of supporting the public schools, but it is also used to finance other municipal services, such as police and fire departments. Thus, the schools often must compete with other local govern-mental agencies for scarce tax dollars. The debate in this chapter centers on whether states should abandon the historical practice of relying on local prop-erty taxes. Those who believe the constitutional value of equality is paramount generally favor such an approach. Those who favor local control and fear the consequences of centralization, however, generally oppose such an approach.

Because reliance on local property taxes results in significant disparities in the amount of funding available, school finance systems that rely on local prop-erty taxes are constitutionally problematic. The education clauses of the 50 state constitutions mandate the establishment of a system of free public schools and, in many states, these clauses actually specify a level of quality. Implicit, if not explicit, in this constitutional command is the concept that the public schools throughout the state will be of similar, if not virtually identical, quality. When states rely on the property tax to fund education, disparities exist because all school districts are not able to generate the same amount of rev-enue. When significant disparities in the amount of money available exist, then arguably there is a constitutional violation.

Given the obvious conflict between the constitutional value of free public education for all and the funding disparities created by the states' reliance on property taxes, it is not surprising that there has been litigation. Indeed, during the last 4 decades, the highest court in virtually every state has wrestled with the question of whether the state's school financing system is constitutional. The plaintiffs typically argue that the state constitution requires nearly equal funding (equity suit) or that the state constitution requires some specific level of funding for each district (adequacy suit). In some instances, the state has experienced multiple lawsuits. As discussed in other chapters in this volume, the issues in school finance litigation have been particularly contentious.

Given this constant litigation, it is easy to suggest that the states should abandon reliance on property taxes as the primary means of financing the public schools. However, abandoning local property taxes as the primary means of financing the schools seems to conflict with another state constitu-tional value—local control of the schools. As the U.S. Supreme Court observed in *Milliken v. Bradley* (1974), "No single tradition in public education is more deeply rooted than local control over the operation of schools . . ." (p. 741). Moreover, in some states, the state constitution actually would prohibit such a measure.

All states, with the notable exception of Hawaii, provide for the delivery of educational services through smaller political units—typically called school districts—that are responsible for the public schools in a given geographic area. Each school district is controlled by a school board, which generally is elected by the voters of the school district, but in some cases may be appointed by an executive, such as a mayor. The local board normally has broad discretion for hiring, financial, and curriculum decisions. If the board is to exercise such autonomy, it must have control of its finances. If the board depends on the state, then the state will wish to dictate how money is spent. Thus, as a historical norm, schools are financed from local sources and property taxes are the primary local source. Indeed, before the 20th century, local property taxes were the exclusive source of funding for the local schools.

Summary of the Debate

Steven A. Hinshaw, the director of finance for the City of Centerville, Ohio, takes the affirmative view. As Hinshaw notes, it is imperative that schools have a stable revenue source. Unlike revenue from income taxes or sales taxes, which frequently vary as economic conditions change, revenue from property taxes is relatively constant and stable. Moreover, although income taxes and sales taxes depend on highly complex methods of collection and, in the case of income taxes, a large degree of voluntary compliance, property taxes are relatively simple to implement. Furthermore, because wealthy individuals tend to own more valuable property, wealthy individuals end up paying a greater share of taxes in a property tax system.

C. Daniel Raisch, a professor of education at the University of Dayton, takes the negative view. Raisch focuses on the vast disparities that result between school districts. Even if two districts tax property at the same rate, one district may have substantially more revenue because the assessed value of real property in that district is greater. As an alternative, he suggests that states should rely more on income taxes. He further suggests that changes in the property tax structure could reduce the effects it has on communities.

William E. Thro
Christopher Newport University

POINT: Steven A. Hinshaw
Director of Finance, Centerville, Ohio

The principal use for property taxes in the United States is to support primary and secondary education. The Old Deluder Satan Act of 1647 was passed by the General Court of Massachusetts to require all towns of 50 or more families to provide an elementary school. Towns that had 100 or more families were required to have grammar schools teaching Latin and Greek. In 1648, Dedham, Massachusetts, became the first town in the United States to authorize a property tax to fund a public school.

From 1648 to 1920, local property taxes were almost exclusively the source of funding for local schools. Then in the 1920s, most states began to give flat grants to local school districts based on the number of students enrolled in the district. As state support of public education became an increasingly larger share of funding, lawsuits challenging the way state support was calculated began to increase. Throughout the decades of litigation, states continued to determine that property tax was the best measure of a local community's wealth.

According to the National Center for Education Statistics (2011), the revenue sources for public schools in 1989 to 1990 were 6.1% from federal sources, 47.1% from state sources, 35.9% from local property taxes, and 10.9% from other local sources. Property taxes accounted for 77% of the total local portion with the remainder coming from student fees and other local taxes. In 2006 to 2007, 8.5% of the revenue sources for public schools were from federal sources, 47.6% from state sources, 33.7% from local property taxes, and 10.2% from other local sources. Property taxes accounted for 77% of the total local portion, with the remainder coming from student fees and other local taxes. Yet, the reliance on property taxes varies greatly, with the most reliance in the Northeast at 45.8% and the least reliance in the West at 23.4%. But even in the West, property taxes accounted for 73% of the total local portion of school revenues, with the remaining 27% of local support coming from student fees and other local taxes.

As the data from 1990 to 2007 show, public schools have depended on the property tax as a large percentage of the local revenue. This long-term and high degree of dependence is possible and sustainable only to the degree that the tax is a reliable, stable source of revenue.

PROPERTY TAXES IN STATE FUNDING FORMULAS

Despite its unpopularity, the property valuation within a public school district has been imbedded in many state formulas when providing financial support to local school districts. The flat grant programs in the 1920s that were the first form of state support to local public schools evolved into foundation programs that used the property valuation as a basis to determine the level of state support to local public schools. From the foundation programs, the guaranteed tax base programs evolved to guarantee a fixed level of funding regardless of property valuation.

The flat grant programs started as a way to provide funding to the poorest locations in a state that could not support local public schools. These programs started as funding on a per school basis then evolved to funding on a per student basis. The primary problem with flat grant programs was that the state provided equal funding on a per student basis (hence, flat grant) regardless of the local public school district's ability to pay for public schooling, thus creating a great inequity in funding. Today, states do not use flat grants as the formula to distribute state aid to local public schools. The use of the property tax base was seen as a missing component in this state aid public school funding program.

The foundation program has become the standard formula states use to distribute money to local public schools. The basic formula for foundation programs is that state aid equals the difference between the base amount of required funding per pupil determined by the state and the local capacity required by the state. The local capacity is defined as the minimum tax rate times the taxable property valuation. Property valuation per pupil then simply taxes the taxable property valuation divided by the number of students in the public school district. The lower the property valuation per pupil, the higher the amount of state aid received in the local public school district. The use of the property tax base is seen as a valuable component in the state aid public school foundation program.

A newer state formula program is the guaranteed tax base (GTB) program. Instead of guaranteeing a fixed level of funding found in foundation programs, the GTB provides the same amount of revenue per pupil from a specified property tax base determined by the individual state. The public school district receives state aid through the equalization process when a public school district's assessed values do not equal the minimum property tax base. Again, the use of the property tax base is seen as a valuable component in the state aid public school GTB funding program.

In every state program (flat grant, foundation, GTB), the property tax base is essential. Removing the property tax base would undermine most states' distribution formulas, thus causing instability to public school funding.

PROPERTY TAXES IN SCHOOL FUNDING LAWSUITS

The reliance on property valuation and property taxes in the state formula to distribute state aid to public school districts was a primary argument in early school finance litigation. The first wave of litigation challenged the states' school funding systems on the basis that they violated the Equal Protection Clause of the U.S. Constitution. These early cases included the *Serrano v. Priest* (1971, 1976) lawsuit in which the California courts did not find that the use of property taxes to fund schools was unconstitutional but did find that finance systems that used property taxes in their state aid formulas were more at risk of future lawsuits.

The second wave of litigation included many lawsuits that challenged states' "thorough and efficient" clauses related to the public education system. The quintessential case in this wave was the *Robinson v. Cahill* (1973) lawsuit in New Jersey, which successfully argued that spending per pupil cannot be strongly linked to local property wealth per pupil. Foundation programs and GTB programs in other states were reinforced during the years following this litigation to avoid similar claims.

The third wave of litigation shifted from an equity argument with regard to property taxes to an adequacy argument. The first lawsuit to reach a state supreme court was in Kentucky with *Rose v. Council for Better Education* in 1989. Although the initial argument was that the finance system placed too much emphasis on property taxes, thus causing public schools to be both unequal in opportunity and inadequate in quality, the courts focused on the adequacy. Kentucky introduced a GTB-type program to address the inequity based on the property tax system.

The one constant in each wave of school finance litigation is that more funding for public schools has been required—regardless of where the money comes from, whether property taxes, state aid, or some other source of funding.

ANALYSIS OF REVENUE SOURCES

Traditionally, there have been three major forms of taxation to support governmental activities, including public schools: individual income tax, sales tax, and property tax. The individual income tax is the largest revenue source for the federal government. For state government, the individual income tax is considered a major revenue source—along with sales tax. Forty-one states collect an individual income tax, and another three states impose the income tax on interest, dividend, or capital gains. The sales tax was introduced in 1932 when Mississippi was looking for a tax to help the state fund essential services (most commonly police and fire services, rather than public schooling services) during the Great Depression. Today, 45 states have enacted a sales tax. The property tax has been used to support public schools in the United States since 1648. Today, all 50 states use property taxes to support public schools.

Seeking a stable revenue source is most important to fund public schools. Among the major sources of tax revenue that fund governmental activities, the property tax has historically been the most stable compared with general sales taxes or even individual income taxes. A closer look at the major sources of tax revenue with respect to the tax base, tax administration and compliance, tax equity, and tax yield will confirm the belief that property taxes are the most stable source, and consequently best form, of revenue for public schools.

Tax Base

Simply put, the tax base is the entity to which a tax rate is applied to generate a tax yield. However, determining the tax base can be complex. This complexity is evident with the individual income tax. Federal, state, and even local income tax ordinances frequently modify the definition of "income." With the myriad of income adjustments, itemized and standard deductions, and exemptions, the individual income tax base can become almost unrecognizable.

The sales tax base is rather straightforward. It is a tax on retail sales. Many states do exempt the sales tax on certain purchases, such as prescription drugs and food, for reasons discussed later with respect to tax equity.

The property tax base is rather straightforward, too. Generally, it is the land and improvements on the land. Property owned by governments and charitable organizations are exempt from the property tax. The complexity of determining the property tax base comes from the assessment process. When analyzing the tax base, the property tax is a straightforward tax.

Tax Administration and Compliance

Several factors encompass the cost of tax administration and compliance such as maintaining and gathering of records, computation of the tax liability, remittance of the tax liability, collection, audits, appeals, and enforcement. Generally speaking, though, the more complex the tax, the higher the costs of both administration and compliance.

As discussed with the tax base, the individual income tax is a complex tax. Individuals and accountants spend much time preparing and filing tax returns. Federal, state, and local income tax agencies spend much time collecting and auditing the tax returns. The same governmental agencies spend even more time and money collecting delinquent taxes and chasing income tax avoiders. Typical public school districts would need to create new income tax revenue departments to collect and monitor the income taxes or would need to contract this service to another governmental agency but would lose the local control to effectively and efficiently monitor the tax collections.

The sales tax is a lower cost tax with regard to administration and compliance. The collection costs of a sales tax are maintained by the retailers. Total sales are generally easy to measure and audit. Several studies have stated that because of the low cost of collecting the sales tax, the compliance with the state sales tax laws increase. If a sales tax were to be enacted for public schooling purposes, the cost of distributing the tax would increase.

The property tax is a low cost tax for individual compliance. Property tax payments are submitted annually and semiannually. Today, financial institutions have made it even easier for individuals to pay their property tax monthly with their mortgage payments. The administration of the property tax is higher for the governments to assess the property values and conduct the tax appeals process. When analyzing the cost of tax administration and compliance, the property tax remains a cost-effective tax for the individual.

Tax Equity

Tax equity studies the issue of whether a tax treats individuals equitably. Horizontal equity is the equal tax treatment of individuals in the same or equal circumstance and is easier to estimate than vertical equity. Because most individuals are not in the same or equal circumstances, vertical equity would be the appropriate equity principle to use and is defined as the different tax treatment of individuals at different circumstances, such as ability to pay. Vertical equity has three broad terms to distinguish itself: progressive, regressive, proportional. *Progressive* taxes state that as the ability to pay increases, the proportion of income taxed increases. *Regressive* taxes state that as the ability to pay increases, the proportion of income taxed decreases. *Proportional* taxes state that as the ability to pay changes, the proportion of income taxed remains the same. Other equity issues are with the tax incidence, or who actually pays the tax.

The individual income tax is the most progressive tax among the major forms of taxation, especially at the federal level. At the state level, the individual income tax is still considered progressive, although with state-targeted income tax relief programs, some of the progressivity decreases. Some states allow local governments (including local school districts) to collect an individual income tax. In those cases, the tax becomes more proportional in nature.

The sales tax meets the horizontal equity standard quite well: the equal treatment of individuals in the same situation. Several studies have proven that the sales tax is a regressive tax by placing a greater burden on those in low income brackets. This is the primary reason prescription drug and food purchases are excluded from many states' sales taxes. Other potential solutions to lessen the regressive nature of the sales tax include reducing the tax rate, changing the tax base, taxing services, and issuing refunds based on income.

Many view the property tax as a progressive tax at household income levels above $20,000 annually. In efforts to lessen regressive tendencies of the property tax and provide property tax relief, many states have enacted different types of property tax relief programs. Homestead exemption and credits programs are used by 48 states. These programs reduce the property tax for an individual who owns the home, and some states offer homestead exemptions to elderly, the disabled, the poor, and veterans. Circuit breaker programs are used by 36 states. These programs correlate property tax bills to a taxpayer's income so a portion of the property tax bill that exceeds a given percentage of income is returned to the taxpayer. Property tax limitation programs are used by 34 states. These programs generally limit the overall property tax rate, limit the overall property tax rate without a popular vote, or constrain the total revenue raised. When analyzing the tax equity, the property tax has been a progressive tax with property tax relief programs to complement the tax.

Tax Yield

The tax yield is the amount of revenue a tax will produce. The goal is for a broad-based tax with low rates. Two key considerations when analyzing the tax yield are the stability and the elasticity. The *stability* is the degree to which the yield rises or falls with national or state economic cycles. The *elasticity* measures the degree to which tax revenues keep pace with changes in either their base or in personal income.

Individual income tax revenues are typically the fastest growing revenue source. Studies have demonstrated that the long-run elasticity estimates show that growth in personal income tax revenues more than doubled personal income growth during the past 40 years. Because most states have a progressive income tax structure with tax brackets, the growth in the individual income tax revenue may be slightly exaggerated as taxpayers are bumped into higher tax brackets, thus paying a higher percentage of additional income in taxes. Tax revenue from individual income is historically stable, although it has high elasticity, greatly subjecting itself to economic cycles.

During the past 40 years, general sales tax revenues have grown at about the same rate as personal income but are much less elastic than are individual income taxes. As the economy of a state grows and the more dependent the state is on income taxes compared with sales taxes, the faster state revenue will grow. Despite its relatively low elasticity (compared with the individual income tax), the sales tax is an unstable source of revenue. During recession periods, consumers spend less thus lowering sales tax revenue. Although sales tax revenues are affected less than are changes in personal income that affect income taxes, sales tax revenues are not as stable as property tax revenues.

Property tax revenue is the most stable form of taxation. Except in deep recessions, property values maintain their levels, which produces a steady revenue stream. In times of economic growth, as property values rise so, too, do property tax revenues. Although the elasticity of property taxes is relatively low, meaning as income increases, revenue from property taxes rises more slowly, property taxes provide stability during economically distressed times. When analyzing the tax yield, the property tax will generate the most stable revenue over time.

SUMMARY

Although the individual income tax can appear to be a viable, long-term solution to public school funding, the overall elasticity and instability of this tax is large. As economic cycles fluctuate, so, too, will this revenue source. The cost of administration and compliance with an income tax is large. Additionally, the federal government, the majority of state governments, and many local municipalities across the nation already collect an individual income tax. Layering an additional individual income tax on a heavily income-taxed population could be problematic politically.

Sales taxes are typically viewed as politically acceptable. If public schools were to lessen the burden from property taxes, then the sales tax is seen as the most politically viable option. In 1994 when Michigan reduced the property tax rates to fund public education, voters elected to increase the sales tax rate rather than to increase the income tax rate—despite the regressive nature of this election. In 1998, however, when Ohio had the option to increase the sales tax rate for public school and property tax relief, voters defeated the issue. Although the sales tax can appear to be a politically acceptable panacea to public school funding, the overall elasticity of this tax is great. As economic cycles fluctuate, so, too, will this revenue source.

Property taxes represent a lower portion of personal income today than they did 30 years ago—most likely because of property tax relief programs. Although the unpopularity of property taxes is undeniable, property taxes have been and continue to be the bedrock for funding public schools. Property taxes can generate large amounts of annual revenue and then sustain those levels of revenue in economic downturns. In economic upturns, then property taxes can generate revenue increases.

CONCLUSION

Historically, the property tax has been a more stable and less volatile form of taxation. Throughout the equity lawsuits, adequacy lawsuits, increased state funding, decreased state funding, recessions, great recessions, and the Great Depression, the property tax has been the mainstay in financing public schools—and should continue in the future.

COUNTERPOINT: C. Daniel Raisch
University of Dayton

S tates should not rely on local property taxes as a primary method of financing public schools; yet, property taxes in this country are linked closely to school funding. The two are so tightly connected that studies of property taxes must also examine school funding. Advocates of the property tax as the major means of local funding for public schools maintain that the states should not encroach on this funding source. Daphne A. Kenyon (2007a), in a study published by the Lincoln Institute of Land Policy, estimates that local school districts derive more than 95% of their tax revenues from property taxes. This clearly indicates that schools, more than any other type of governmental agency, rely heavily on property taxes to provide income for operations. Additionally, approximately half of the total property taxes collected in the United States are used to support public schools. States should not expect the local taxpayer to add to the property tax revenue to support additional growth in income for public schools at the state level. At most, property tax revenues should be reserved for and controlled by the local community, and states must find other sources of income to support the states' contribution to financing education.

Even though property taxes continue to be the primary income source for local government agencies, primary of which is schools, these taxes also continue to be remarkably contentious. The universal objection to property taxes is that they are "unfair, inequitable, unwarranted, unjust, unreasonable"—for example, they are inequitable in their distribution across earnings groups for financial support of education and because of broad disparities in property values, unfair to specific groups of taxpayers such as the poor and those on fixed incomes, and unreasonable because increases in property value are taxed without a gain to offset the increase in taxes.

CONCERNS WITH PROPERTY TAX IMPLEMENTATION

Local school systems vary noticeably in the way they are backed through state financial support. The rate of support varies from approximately 8% in New

Hampshire to nearly 75% in New Mexico. However, on average, states fund approximately 50% of the total dollars needed to maintain the general education budgets of local districts. Local boards and, in some states, local governments fund approximately 44% of the income needed. The majority of the local income is generated from property taxes. The remaining percentage (generally less than 10%) comes from the federal government, primarily through special or restricted funding. Nominally, half of all those fiscal resources come from property taxes.

Most local school tax funds result from property; however, the use of income taxes to support schools is on the increase in many states. Since the 1950s, the dependence of local governments on property taxes has declined, whether measured as a percentage of local tax revenue, general revenue, or total general revenue. During a 30-year period from 1952 to 1982, the decline was remarkable. Local governments, especially schools, received more state aid that relied on income or sales taxes.

Property taxes, as a percentage of private earnings, are the best measures of a property tax burden. Property tax burdens are similar to those of a half century ago, approximating more than 3% of personal income. Regardless of whether this is a reasonable percentage, ongoing legislative changes and judicial actions, coupled with the growing backlash against public sector bargaining that increases the cost of educating children, indicate that the general property taxpaying public is saying "enough."

Public school funds are generally distributed to local districts in two ways: as general operating funds typically circulated on a per pupil basis and as categorical money to maintain special programs or operations. School funding varies from state to state and among districts in each state. In some states, the expenditure per pupil may range from $5,000 to $15,000. The range is based primarily on the local district's ability to fund or supplement the state minimum guaranteed expenditure. As an example, two districts with approximately the same number of students could raise significantly different amounts of local funds based solely on the value of property, including residential, commercial, and corporate property.

CRITICISMS OF PROPERTY TAXES FOR SCHOOL FUNDING

As a result of claims that property taxes are unfair, the property tax seems to be constantly under attack, often with the goal to reform, reduce, or eliminate it. Examples include the adoption of Proposition 13 in California and H.B. 920 in Ohio, both implemented in the late 1970s. Since then, state legislatures, by court order or other pressures, have attempted to reform the funding of public education, which generally has changed the configuration of property taxes and often replaced funds derived from property taxes with other sources, including sales, income, and use taxes, although the overall largest percentage of local funding of schools remains reliant on property taxes.

Among the strongest criticisms of using property taxes to fund local governments, especially schools, are the claims that they create inequities in revenue for education and, thus, inequities for students; that they produce significant tax burdens on retired persons; and that they generally do not adjust equitably with inflation because they do not keep pace with economic growth. States all over this country have or are attempting to resolve the high reliance on property taxes to fund schools. However, there clearly is a fine line between keeping the local community involved in the support of the local governments, including schools, and the overreliance on one primary source of revenue to do so.

The link between the property tax and school funding starts with a focus on education needs and incorporates the preference for local autonomy and local involvement. Property, sales, or income taxes are often seen as the big three tax bases for supporting local governments, with the property tax often seen as the most appropriate. City governments often assume that the income tax is "their" tax and the property tax is the "school" tax. But those lines are becoming more and more blurred as local governments vie for ways to produce additional revenue streams.

In some states, such as Ohio, this is an issue because income tax revenue for schools increases as income increases, but property taxes are essentially capped, thus requiring schools to request additional property taxes to produce additional revenue. However, in recent years, an average of about 70% of attempts to pass additional operating levies in Ohio have failed. This clearly indicates that local taxpayers are making statements about their opposition to more and higher taxes, especially property taxes.

The vast majority of new levies requested in Ohio are based on property taxes; only a small number are income based. In fact, only about 28% of Ohio's 613 school districts have an income tax to support public education. The number is relatively small but growing in contrast to the nearly 550 municipalities in Ohio that have an income tax.

An added concern regarding the property tax is the notion that it discourages maintenance and modernization primarily because of frequent assessments. Therefore, as improvements are made, values increase, and taxes owed increase. Owners may then be deterred from improving property assuming the observable results will more likely draw the awareness of the assessor.

LEGAL IMPLICATIONS

Plaintiffs have succeeded in challenging the equity of their state systems of funding public education in about half of the cases that have been filed since litigation began in the early 1970s. Yet, despite the tinkering with state systems of paying for public education, local property taxes remain the primary means of funding local schools. Logic might equate property-wealthy districts with high income districts and property-poor districts with low income districts, but that is not necessarily the case. A community's per pupil wealth depends on the magnitude of industrial or commercial property that shares the property tax burden with homeowners. It is reasonable to assume that a low income community may have a large quantity of industrial and commercial property compared with a high income community, and high income communities may have little or no industrial or commercial property. Thus, because per pupil property value is not necessarily the best indicator of a school district's financial condition, many states now use a formula that considers the income level associated with parcels of real property in relation to per pupil need to measure a community's fiscal need in their school funding formulas.

Most school finance cases have centered on the concept of equity or adequacy with varying degrees of success. The typical claim, at the state level, is that the differing levels of support for students between and among school systems is unconstitutional. Since the 1970s, most of the cases have been processed in the local and state court systems, with about half of them resulting in having state systems struck down, primarily on the basis of adequacy and equity provisions in state constitutions.

At the heart of the claims filed by the plaintiffs is that if all children are to be treated fairly, then schools must be funded equitably. Proponents of school finance reform have argued that states will have to levy statewide income, sales, or property taxes to ensure greater equity. States are being pressured to provide adequate funds for all school children, while local taxpayers are insisting on reducing the local property tax burden. The political dilemma then revolves around the need to serve the students of a state and community adequately and fairly while fairly addressing the concerns of the taxpaying public.

It is vital to differentiate between property taxes put into operation by local governments and those put into operation by state governments. Some states have substituted a portion of their local property taxes with a state property tax whose rate will not fluctuate by district. In this case, neither the issue of monetary differences nor that of fiscalization of land (meaning its value in terms of per pupil expenses) arises, but the argument that the property tax is a benefit tax, in the sense that it is used to fund schools for the common good, will be undermined. However, other drawbacks of centralizing educational funding at the state level may exist, including political changes in government.

ADVANTAGES OF PROPERTY TAXES

One significant benefit of property taxation is its constancy as an income stream. It is clear that the income and sales taxes are far less stable as sources of revenue. If the alternative to a local tax is state aid to schools, local governments have less authority over the amount of income they obtain. In good economic times, state governments may be generous in their payouts including state aid to schools, but in down economic times, they may reduce state aid. Thus, moving from local property taxes to state revenue for education may make education more vulnerable to swings in the political and economic cycles of state budgets.

The property tax has other advantages in addition to the consistency of revenue. One is the fact that local community members have a say in whether to support local government agencies. This type of local control has been a benchmark since the early beginnings of our country. William A. Fischel (2001) concluded that the use of property taxes by local schools and communities motivates homeowners who are voters to pay close attention to local governments. This is true mostly because for most homeowners, their home is generally their most important asset.

Even with the advantages mentioned, however, local taxpayers are reluctant to support additional funding for governmental agencies through increased property taxes. Leaders must continue to seek alternatives to the property tax to support government functions.

REPLACING PROPERTY TAXES

Replacing all of a state's property taxes with a state sales tax would require more than double the current state sales taxes. To stabilize or even reduce property taxes, legislators will have to figure out solutions that allow some reasonable growth in revenue for schools. Although it is unreasonable to assume that property taxes will be eliminated, it is important to implement school funding formulas that provide for inflation. In other words, it is important for decision makers to protect the property tax for the local communities' use, provide a state tax base that allows for inflation, and develop a funding formula that provides equity and adequacy among school districts.

Barbara M. De Luca and Steven A. Hinshaw (2009) conducted a study that examined the impact of shifting from a property tax base to an income tax base to support local schools. The importance of their study is that it covered a range of districts from high poverty to high wealth and included urban, suburban, and rural systems. This study examined three scenarios: first, a universal, statewide income tax where some districts gained revenue and some lost; second, an increase in income tax rates, in 0.25% increments, in each district to produce local revenue as close to the current level as possible; and third, an income tax rate that varied with each individual school district. The results of their study suggest that many districts classified as urban would lose local revenue under the identical statewide rate. However, if the rates vary by district, the urban districts would have elevated income tax rates to balance the loss of property tax income. Additionally, suburban districts in their study gained local revenue under the first scenario. Using scenario 2 with individual school district income tax rates set to increase at 0.25% increments and no district losing local revenue, the tax rate ranged from 1.25% in one district to 13.5% in another. Almost all districts gained revenue in this scenario; however, the tax range was significantly different. In scenario 3 where each school district's income tax rate was set so that no district gained or lost revenue, the rates ranged from 1.19% to 13.47%.

Scenarios 2 and 3 would satisfy the criterion of Pareto optimality (i.e., they would ensure that at least one person benefits without making anyone worse off financially). However, both scenario 2 and 3 were constructed so that no district lost resources. Therefore, it is reasonable to assume that it is possible to shift some if not all of the local property tax to a local or statewide income tax. However, the study points out that shifting the tax would not address the wide disparities caused by the current funding system in Ohio, and this is generally true in most other states. In addition, the researchers noted that the corporate and business property taxes would have to be accounted for in the scenarios. In many communities, this would dramatically change the look of the income tax rates if the property taxes for commercial and business real estate were eliminated.

This said, levying additional taxes on business and industry affects how corporate decisions are made—in particular, how much and in what forms to invest in productive operations. For business and industry, in general, taxes are operating costs without direct benefits to the bottom line. Although some companies are, for various reasons, attached to specific locations, it is unclear whether this is a universal condition. Consequently, increasing tax burdens on some businesses could result in their changing their location.

PROPERTY TAX REDUCTIONS

A nationwide reduction in property taxes would benefit all owners of capital, proportional to the amount of capital owned. Such a change clearly would favor the rich, who own relatively more capital. Perhaps property taxes for commercial and business properties would not be included in the process and only include residential properties.

Some changes could be made in the property tax structure to help reduce the effects it has on local communities. Land could become the primary base for the property tax and less of a burden could be placed on buildings, equipment, and inventories. Lowering the tax on improvements could increase the attractiveness of investments in certain sections of a community. Conversely, investment in land deserves, in certain sections of a community, some of the same considerations as investing in buildings and equipment. If a community cares about controlled growth, it will become creative in how it structures its tax base.

FURTHER READINGS AND RESOURCES

De Luca, B. M., & Hinshaw, S. A. (2009, March 19–21). *Reducing the reliance on property taxes: An effort and analysis for state funding in Ohio.* Paper presented at the annual conference of the American Education Finance Association, Nashville, TN.

Fischel, W. A. (2001). Municipal corporations, homeowners, and the benefit view of the property tax. In W. E. Oates (Ed.), *Property taxation and local government finance* (pp. 33–78). Cambridge, MA: Lincoln Institute of Land Policy.

Harriss, C. L. (1974, January). Property taxation: What's good and what's bad, how to use property taxes more rationally and effectively. *American Journal of Economics and Sociology, 33*(1), 89–102.

Kenyon, D. A. (2007a). *The property tax–school funding dilemma.* Cambridge, MA: Lincoln Institute of Land Policy.

Kenyon, D. A. (2007b, March 23). *Reexamining the role of the property tax in school funding.* Paper presented at the American Education Finance Association meetings, Baltimore, MD.

National Center for Education Statistics. (2011). Contexts of elementary and secondary education—Finance. In *The condition of education 2011.* Retrieved July 14, 2011, from http://nces.ed.gov/programs/coe/indicator_sft.asp

COURT CASES AND STATUTES

Milliken v. Bradley, 418 U.S. 717 (1974).

Robinson v. Cahill, 62 N.J. 473 (1973), 303 A.2d 273 (N.J. 1973).

Rose v. Council for Better Education, 790 S.W.2d 186 (Ky. 1989).

Serrano v. Priest, 5 Cal. 3d 584 (1971), 96 Cal. Rptr. 601 (Cal. 1971) [Serrano I].

Serrano v. Priest, 18 Cal. 3d 728 (1976), 135 Cal. Rptr. 345 (Cal. 1976) [Serrano II].

5

Should the federal government condition federal funds for school districts on the implementation of federally mandated curricula?

POINT: Shana Goldwyn, *University of Cincinnati*
COUNTERPOINT: Scott R. Bauries, *University of Kentucky*

OVERVIEW

The U.S. constitutional system is unique, even in comparison with other federations, in that it "protects us from our own best intentions: It divides power among sovereigns . . . precisely so that we may resist the temptation to concentrate power in one location as an expedient solution to the crisis of the day" (*New York v. United States,* 1992, p. 187). Although the states surrendered many of their sovereign powers to the new national government, they retained "a residuary and inviolable sovereignty" (*Printz v. United States,* 1997, pp. 918–919). That the Constitution divides power between *dual sovereigns,* the states and the national government, is reflected throughout the Constitution's text, particularly in its conferring on Congress only discrete, enumerated governmental powers, not all powers. The states retain extensive sovereign powers under the federal constitution, and Congress does not readily interfere with those powers (*Gregory v. Ashcroft,* 1991). Thus, "the States may perform their role as laboratories for experimentation to devise various solutions where the best solution is far from clear" (*United States v. Lopez,* 1995, p. 581, Justice Kennedy, concurring). In sum, the U.S. constitutional system values decentralization (*Alden v. Maine,* 1999).

This federal constitutional value of decentralization is best illustrated in the context of public education. Although the national government has long been involved in the promotion of public education and although that involvement has increased dramatically in recent years, education generally remains the prerogative of the states (*Honig v. Doe,* 1988, p. 309). Thus, the individual states, not the national government, make the fundamental decisions about school governance, finance, curricula, textbooks, academic calendar, and eligibility to attend school, as well as the certification and compensation of teachers. Moreover, with the exception of Hawaii, all the states engage in further decentralization by delegating some of these fundamental decisions, including the ability to raise and spend additional monies, to local school districts. Because each state and each school district within a given state make different choices when making these fundamental decisions, there is a wide variance in public schools even within the same state. Furthermore, many states and school districts within a state do not make wise choices when making these fundamental decisions. Thus, some children receive superior educations simply because their local and state policymakers made better choices.

To alleviate these disparities, some have suggested that the federal government should demand that the states and, by extension, local school districts conform to certain standards as a condition of receiving federal funds, often in the form of reimbursements. Such a suggestion raises both constitutional and policy concerns.

From a constitutional standpoint, it is not clear that Congress could interfere in a function that clearly is a sovereign prerogative of the states. However, Congress may be able to use the Spending Clause to circumvent that limitation. As the U.S. Supreme Court observed during the 1930s, the direct grants of legislative power that are found in the Constitution do not limit the power of Congress to authorize expenditure of public funds for public purposes (*United States v. Butler,* 1936). In other words, objectives not thought to be within the Constitution's enumerated legislative fields may still be attained through the use of the spending power and the conditional grant of federal funds (*South Dakota v. Dole,* 1987). Thus, the Spending Clause is limited only by Congress's view of the general welfare. Given the vast financial resources of the federal government, the reality is that the Spending Clause gives Congress the authority to remove the barriers and trespass on the states' jurisdiction (*United States v. Butler,* 1936, Justice O'Connor, dissenting). Indeed, it appears that Congress has an easy means to circumvent any restrictions the Constitution might impose on its ability to regulate the states. Congress need only attach its otherwise unconstitutional regulations to the large sums of money that it offers the states (Baker, 1998). Nevertheless, it is unclear that the Court would uphold direct federal involvement.

With respect to policy concerns, federal involvement may not be prudent. Our nation is large and diverse. A national curriculum, like many one-size-fits-all solutions, may be inappropriate.

Summary of the Debate

This debate explores the constitutional and policy considerations surrounding whether the national government should use its spending power to dictate curriculum choices.

Shana Goldwyn, a professor of education at the University of Cincinnati, takes the affirmative view. She notes that the Supreme Court's current Spending Clause jurisprudence seems to permit such a measure. Moreover, in her view, there are sound reasons for having a national curriculum. If the United States is going to compete globally, it cannot have inadequate curricula or educational systems in any part of the nation.

In contrast, Scott Bauries, a law professor at the University of Kentucky, takes the negative view. He acknowledges that the Court's current Spending Clause jurisprudence gives vast discretion to Congress, but argues that the Court should draw the line at dictating curriculum decisions. Drawing on the work of Lynn Baker as well as Justice Sandra Day O'Connor's dissent in *Dole*, Bauries contends that there is a distinction between reimbursement spending and conditional or regulatory spending. In reimbursement spending, Congress provides money and tells the state exactly how to spend the money. Conversely, in regulatory spending, Congress provides money for some general purpose but then imposes other conditions that effectively limit sovereign choice. Bauries believes the former should be constitutional, but the latter should be unconstitutional. Although he acknowledges the policy questions, he contends that the issue essentially is a constitutional one.

William E. Thro
Christopher Newport University

POINT: Shana Goldwyn
University of Cincinnati

Federal funding has been a significant aspect of school leaders' budgeting and long-term planning for many years. However, in this era of accountability and with the growing economic challenges schools are dealing with, maintaining federal funding has become a critical aspect of school success. And yet, the distribution of federal funds often comes with specific requirements that need to be met to maintain this funding. With the reauthorization of the No Child Left Behind Act, as well as the discontinuation of federal Reading First monies, the imposition of federally mandated curriculum and standards, particularly in the area of reading, as a condition of receiving federal funding has become a highly contentious issue in the field of curriculum. Nevertheless, despite the contentiousness, there is a fair bit of support from curriculum experts for the idea of a federally mandated curriculum in return for federal money. There are several reasons for this. First, despite the challenges associated with Reading First, several extremely positive aspects emerged from the implementation of the curricula associated with this program. Second, the link between curriculum and funding also allows for training and an implementation of best practices that can be consistent among some of our poorest schools. Finally, linking federal curriculum and federal funding allows state education agencies to work simultaneously with the federal education agency to merge accountability structures and funding formulas to emphasize the need to invest in curricula to yield student achievement results.

LESSONS FROM THE READING FIRST PROGRAM

One of the primary arguments against the linkage between curricula and federal funding concerns the difficulties that emerged during the implementation of Reading First. One of the controversies that emerged surrounding Reading First was that recipients were under the false impression that those involved in the development of the legislation were impartial with respect to the specific curricula from which recipients of the monies could choose. Because of this, many opponents of a federally mandated curriculum use this as an argument, again linking funding and curriculum. Opponents contend that schools receiving funds should have more choices in curricula rather than being restricted to reading programs from an approved list, many of which were developed by researchers who had ties to the Department of Education.

However, we must be cognizant of the positive conclusions that have come from the implementation of Reading First. To begin with, and perhaps most importantly, Reading First was part of Title I funding, which targets our neediest schools. Our neediest schools are less likely to have large percentages of students who are performing at or above proficient levels. There are several reasons for this, but one of the main reasons is access to high quality, research-based curricula. Reading First provided high poverty schools with selections of specific high quality research-based curricula and with funding to invest in these programs. Although indeed this aspect of Reading First may seem convoluted because of the aforementioned conflict of interest, we cannot discount the importance of providing curriculum options that have been proven to yield results in student achievement. Further, although achievement results for Reading First were not as great as were expected, we cannot discount the impact of Reading First on student achievement. Impact studies continue to emerge surrounding Reading First, exploring the relationship between best curricular practices and increased student performance.

Mandating specific curricula or aspects of curricula offers the same potential. Schools will be able to advocate for curricula that are high quality and research based and have been proven to be linked to increased student performance. In some ways, this dissipates the ambiguity surrounding the selection of specific curricula. Often schools that fluctuate within the accountability structures are able to examine data trends through changes in curricula or an implementation dip that is caused by gaps in student knowledge arising from instructional variability. Curricula linked to funding presents districts with a list of targets, with monies specifically dedicated to curriculum selection and adoption, and can eliminate these same performance issues. Students will avoid gaps in knowledge as a result of curriculum reform because of the consistency involved with using a mandated curriculum. These gaps can be predicted and rectified before this becomes problematic for school and district assessments of performance.

ASSESSMENT

Perhaps one of the most challenging tasks for a school district, and one of the hallmarks of the Reading First program, is the ability to develop a seamless assessment system that is both vertically and horizontally aligned. Understanding how to do this requires knowledge of how specific curriculum programs are linked to standards, how each of these standards is assessed, and the specific elements of the curricula that address the mastery of each of these standards. Though the development of this assessment program is a key component in understanding a student's "snapshot" performance on standardized tests, beyond that the value-added scores for each student are often computed through these assessment systems. These ongoing assessments are associated with additional long-term explorations of student performance such as graduation rates and comparisons between schools, districts, states, and international competitiveness.

The development of such an assessment system—one that reaches beyond school- and district-level assessment and integrates it into state and national performance measures—is not feasible without consistencies in both standards and specific curricula that address these standards. With such consistency in curricula, standards, and assessments intended to measure these standards in such a way that they are able to be linked back to the curriculum, there can be a wealth of information, similar to that of the Progress Monitoring and Reporting Network, available surrounding student performance and the discrepancies that are caused specifically by curricula and teacher implementation of curricula.

NATIONAL STANDARDS

Perhaps at this point, there should be a clear distinction between curricula and activities associated with curricula, such as instruction, best practices, assessment, and standards. This is an important distinction to make as advocates of national mandates of curricula often embrace a broader concept definition of *curriculum*. The concept of curriculum has evolved to be a specific layout of what is taught, including details on teaching methods, timelines, assessments, and connections to standards. This concept is often interpreted as the systematic, step-by-step programs that go beyond a layout of concept, with detailed instructions on implementation and follow-up. Yet, the implementation of curricula extends beyond these individual programs to include all materials and instructional practices associated with meeting specific standards. It is important to note this distinction because advocates for nationally mandated curriculum often are referring to standards, best practices, or common assessments rather than programs.

The discussion of a common set of national standards has been an ongoing debate since the standards-based movement. During the standards-based movement, states were charged with developing learning standards that were aligned with the state assessment system each state uses to adhere to the mandates set in the No Child Left Behind Act. This resulted in different sets of standards for each state. The vast variability in states' standards has made it difficult, if not impossible, to compare student performance between states. One of the additional, and perhaps greater, problems with different standards for each state deals with rigor. No Child Left Behind mandates accountability for all states and all students. This incentivizes states to develop and maintain low standards of learning. This means that students in one state can fail to meet state standards even though they are performing significantly higher than students in a different state with much lower standards. The magnitude of this discrepancy between standards is vast. As we look beyond K–12 or K–20 education, it is easy to see why, as a nation, we are decreasing in international competitiveness. The focus has shifted from implementing curricula in such a way that all students are provided the opportunity to meet rigorous content standards, to implementing curricula as a catalyst for "teaching to the test" so that districts and states are able to meet current accountability structures.

The acceptance of national curriculum standards is already present in the field. The Common Core State Standards is an initiative that emerged separately from the federal Department of Education, which is, in part, why it has gained a large amount of support. The National Governors Association Center for Best Practices and the Council of Chief State School Officers have used the states that have the best and most rigorous standards as models to develop a set of common standards in English language arts and mathematics that are to be adopted by states. Accepting the Common Core as state standards is not mandatory; however, the majority of states have adopted and begun implementing these standards. In exploring the proposed reforms, adopting these standards is one of the elements that is proposed to be tied to school funding. If states do not wish to adopt this common core of standards, they must each propose an alternate set of standards that is comparable.

This is the first step in truly understanding the vast importance of both rigor and consistency between states. To regain previously high levels of international competitiveness, students from all states need to be provided the opportunity to engage in high quality rigorous instruction. The adoption of these state standards is likely the beginning step for ongoing national changes in curricula. A set of common standards allows consistency, which consequently leads to assessment systems, such as those mentioned earlier, that allow for better comparisons and assessments of student performance. Certainly, this level of consistency will also lead to better assessments of scientifically researched curricula, and consequently better adoption and implementation of curricula programs.

TEACHER QUALITY AND PROFESSIONAL DEVELOPMENT

Though there is a great deal of merit in using sound research-based curricula, curriculum is not absent from issues of teacher quality. The quality of curriculum largely depends on the teacher's ability to implement it successfully. Understanding best practices as they relate to specific standards is critical to the successful implementation of any curriculum. Teachers need to know how to implement curricula that meet the standards, but also how to implement curricula in such a way that all students are able to access and be successful at the standards. Yet, currently, professional development in the area of best practices is often left to the discretion of the building principal or the district level. Again, this raises the variability of both the ongoing training that teachers have in the field, as well as the determination of what constitutes best practices and how it is decided.

Principles such as Universal Design for Learning (UDL) are some of the best practices that are emerging at a national level. The concept behind UDL is designing curricula and lessons in such a way that they are accessible by all students. The very nature of UDL speaks to the prospect of understanding curricula at a national level. One of the arguments against nationally mandated curricula is that the needs of each student vary, and a national curriculum takes away a teacher's ability to determine the needs of each of the students and design lessons that meet each student's needs. UDL provides a framework that allows us to conceptualize a national curriculum with the understanding that we use a core program as the foundation, designing it in such a way that it can be adapted and modified for all students. A number of states are adopting UDL principles to be used in teacher training programs and lesson planning. This is another step in moving toward national curricular mandates.

Beyond the design of a national curriculum through UDL, professional development in this type of design is also critical to the success of all students. As mentioned earlier, professional development is often left to the building principal or the district level. Research shows us that teacher quality is greatly enhanced by professional development opportunities: specifically, professional development opportunities that allow teachers to implement their knowledge in practical applications. Research also shows us that the impact of a poor teacher on student performance is far-reaching. The more years a student spends with a poor teacher, the more likely the student is to perform below proficient levels. Therefore, understanding professional development as it relates to curriculum is critical. A nationally mandated curriculum is a wealth of opportunity to provide high quality professional development for all teachers. With a common set of frameworks to center curriculum around, greater numbers of opportunities are available for coaching, fidelity of implementation of programs, and using assessment results to inform teaching practices.

PURPOSES OF LINKING FEDERAL MANDATES AND FUNDING

Although there is a strong case for the need for a nationally mandated curriculum, it is important to understand the benefits of linking this curriculum to funding structures. There are three main reasons for the use of federal funding dollars as a directive for curriculum:

1. The growing number of federal funding initiatives that are intended to yield higher student achievement levels.

2. The continued need for increased funding in all areas of curriculum.

3. The thrust for states to participate in both state reform initiatives and federal reform initiatives.

Currently, the challenges schools, districts, and states are facing in meeting accountability structures do not go unnoticed by the federal government. As incentives for schools, districts, and states to engage in the challenging reform work surrounding curricula, a necessary and ongoing component of increased student achievement, a number of grants and federal incentive dollars are being offered to districts and states that are willing to engage in that kind of work. The most notorious type of this incentive is Race to the Top. Like Race to the Top, tied to these incentive grants is a component that requires changes in curricula. The federal government is also restructuring the Elementary and Secondary Education Act (to replace the current No Child Left Behind). Built into this reform are changes in the education accountability structures to include ongoing measures of value-added and continued commitment to the implementation of research-based curricula. Simultaneously, schools are cutting budgets, resulting in a loss of key personnel related to curriculum and instruction, as well as loss of monies for new materials and professional development. Participating in these incentives will help schools embrace national mandates on funding and use the money in a way that is productive in increasing student achievement and meeting accountability structures.

Coupling federal funding with a mandated curriculum greatly increases a district's or state's financial capacity. This allows the level of funding spent at the district and state levels to decrease, while being grounded in research-based standards, programs, and best practices. Those who argue against the link between federal aid and curricular need will explore this idea of financial capacity as it is clouded by teacher and administrator autonomy. It allows us to focus our funding more clearly on rigorous high standards, which is critical to the success of all students, rather than on management and organization.

Although the author of the accompanying counterpoint essay makes a strong legal case for the absence of politics in curricular legislation, he provides an argument void of the critical link between curriculum and student achievement. A federally mandated curriculum is not an attempt to provide a personal frame of reference but, rather, to provide materials and resources in such a way that all schools and districts have access to high quality curricula that enable all schools to succeed within an increasingly difficult accountability structure. Though there is a possibility of personal and political "agendas" to manipulate power within the curriculum, it is important not to overlook the most important quality of federally mandated standards and curriculum: the notion of *research based*. A true research-based curriculum would be tested against the standards that are intended to be covered by that program. If indeed a personal or a political frame of reference were to be evidenced within a specific curriculum, rather than a direct connection to specific state standards, it would not withstand the research trials because it would not yield significant results in student assessment gains.

COUNTERPOINT: Scott R. Bauries
University of Kentucky

This counterpoint essay takes the position that the best answer to the question posed in this chapter is "No." This issue has generated debate since at least the establishment of the Department of Education as a federal agency during President Lyndon Johnson's administration, but it has reached a crescendo lately as a result of the No Child Left Behind Act (NCLB), enacted during President George W. Bush's administration. Good policy arguments exist on both sides of the question, but the central inquiry is a legal one—whether the federal government should have the *power* to dictate local curricular choices as the result of allocating money to local school districts through state legislatures.

LEGAL BACKGROUND

To answer this question on Congress's legislative power, one must begin with the U.S. Constitution. The Constitution, it is often repeated, sets forth a federal government of limited and specifically enumerated powers. Among these powers are the regulation of interstate commerce, the enforcement of the rights to equal protection and due process against the states, and the raising of a national army. Notably, the U.S. Constitution contains no reference to public schooling, or even to education in general. This absence of mention has been interpreted to mean that public education is purely the realm of state government. The Tenth Amendment supports this interpretation through its guarantee that all powers not specifically delegated to the federal government through the Constitution, or prohibited by the same document, reside with the states or the people.

However, it is clear that Congress does indeed legislate substantially in the area of education. To pick a recent example, the federal NCLB imposed comprehensive testing and reporting requirements, along with strict standards for teacher preparation, among other requirements, on the states. Debates continue to swirl in educational and political circles about the wisdom of this legislation, but it imposes no curricular changes on local school districts, so these debates will not be of much help in addressing the question that frames this essay. In addressing the question, then, it will be helpful to refer to a hypothetical piece of legislation. Imagine that Congress enacts a statute containing the following text:

> Beginning in the 2011–2012 academic year, no local educational agency (i.e., school district) accepting any federal funds for that school year or any other thereafter shall offer any instruction to students in any grade on the subject of Darwinian evolution or the origin of species through processes of natural selection. All federal educational funding shall be revoked from any local education agency that fails to comply with this condition.

From a political or policy perspective, some may find this hypothetical statute laudable, but others (perhaps most) may find it quite disappointing. Notwithstanding the conclusions presented in this essay, the policymakers will have to work that debate out among themselves. The proper question for the purposes of this essay is whether such a conditional grant of federal funds to the states should be constitutionally permitted.

To begin with, considering the enumerated and limited nature of Congress's legislative power, one is forced to wonder what basis Congress might cite in support of its enactment of this hypothetical legislation. The answer is Congress's enumerated "spending power." Referred to generally as the Spending Clause, Article I, Section 8, Clause 1 of the Constitution specifically empowers Congress to "pay the Debts and provide for the common Defence and general Welfare of the United States." At the time of the founding, a contentious debate existed regarding the scope of this power. The narrow or strict view in the debate, represented by James Madison, held that Congress's power to spend allowed it to expend funds from the public treasury only to fulfill the other legislative powers enumerated in the Constitution—for example, to fund a national army or to regulate interstate commerce. The broader view, articulated by Alexander

Hamilton, held that Congress's power allowed it to expend funds for any purpose, as long as such spending was in pursuit of the general welfare of the citizens of the United States.

Nearly two hundred years passed before this initial debate was resolved. In deciding the case of *United States v. Butler* (1936), the U.S. Supreme Court explicitly adopted the Hamiltonian view, holding that Congress's power to appropriate funds is not limited by the other powers enumerated in the Constitution. However, in the same case, the Court ultimately struck down an exercise of the spending power to appropriate funds to farmers in exchange for their agreeing to reduce their crop yields, holding that this particular exercise of the spending power was merely a subterfuge to accomplish a legislative end that could not be accomplished directly—the regulation of local agricultural production. The contradictory nature of this opinion created a good deal of confusion.

THE FIVE-PART TEST FOR CONSTITUTIONALITY OF SPENDING LEGISLATION

One of the points of contention created by *Butler* and subsequent cases reaching divergent results was whether Congress could use its spending power to impose conditions on the receipt of federal funds, where the conditions would have been outside the enumerated powers of Congress to impose directly—what is now referred to as *conditional spending*. Over the years, the courts developed a conception of the spending power as Congress's power to form "contracts" with the states, whereby Congress exchanges funding for state-level behavior that Congress lacks the power to compel on its own. Underlying this contract-based theory of conditional federal spending lies the assumption that states are free to accept or reject federal funding depending on whether the states are willing to comply with the conditions accompanying such funding. However, underlying contract doctrine itself is the notion that not all contracts are completely volitional for both parties. For example, less powerful parties at times may be coerced, tricked, and even forced to enter contractual arrangements that they would prefer not to enter. Thus, the courts over the years were asked to evaluate the "contracts" between Congress and the states and to develop standards for doing so.

This activity ultimately culminated with the landmark case of *South Dakota v. Dole* (1987). In *Dole,* the Supreme Court considered whether Congress exceeded its spending power by threatening to withhold 5% of federal highway funding from any state that failed to raise its drinking age to 21. To resolve the case, the Court promulgated a five-part test for evaluating Congress's use of its spending power. To be a valid use of Congress's power, Spending Clause legislation must

1. be in pursuit of the "general welfare of the United States,"

2. contain a clear and unambiguous statement of the conditions imposed on the receipt of federal funds,

3. impose only conditions that are related to the federal interest in funding,

4. avoid imposing conditions that would require the states to violate other sections of the Constitution, and

5. avoid impermissibly "coercing" the states' acceptance of undesirable conditions in exchange for funding.

Each of these factors has been further defined, but the result of these later cases has called the workability of the *Dole* factors into question. The courts have treated the "general welfare" requirement deferentially, essentially accepting Congress's judgment in each case that a particular program is directed at the "general welfare." Legislation has been struck down for Congress's failure to state its conditions clearly enough, but as a result, Congress soon became wise to this requirement, which is now fairly easy to meet. Courts have had little occasion to apply the fourth criterion that conditional spending legislation not violate an independent constitutional provision. However, this requirement is more a limitation on all congressional legislation than a limitation on the spending power. Also, Congress is unlikely to violate this factor because the public nature of the political process would tend to correct independently unconstitutional conditions before a statute's passage. This leaves the third requirement—relatedness—and the fifth—noncoercion—as the only two of the five with much potential limiting force on the conditional spending power.

However, under current jurisprudence, even these two factors would not stand in the way of congressional action to condition the receipt of federal education funds on the elimination of the scientific process of natural selection from the curriculum. Forbidding the teaching of evolution by natural selection— although inadvisable from a biologist's perspective—would certainly be "related" to Congress's interest in spending money on education. Congress could easily defend the condition on the basis of a professed desire to eliminate controversy from the classroom and to foster harmony between those of differing belief systems. Most would doubt the veracity of such a justification, but the courts would grant substantial deference to Congress, and the measure would likely survive a challenge. Further, it is unlikely that the courts would require any sort of direct relationship between the funding at issue and the condition imposed. The courts have never imposed any strict requirement that the compliance with a condition on which funding depends actually be paid for directly by the funds. Thus, as long as Congress is willing to justify a ban on the teaching of evolution on the basis of Congress's own educational goals, the condition will likely survive the relatedness inquiry.

As to coercion, the Supreme Court has never made clear the point at which, as the Court stated in *Dole,* "pressure turns to compulsion," and the states become "coerced" by the spending accompanying federal conditions. The dominant view is that the pressure that federal conditional spending legislation imposes depends on the magnitude of the funding put at risk. In *Dole* itself, states that chose not to comply with the condition of raising the drinking age would risk losing only 5% of federal highway funds, and the Court found that this minimal loss of funds was not enough to constitute coercion.

The hypothetical law described earlier makes this question more difficult because it ostensibly puts all federal educational funding at risk for school districts that refuse to eliminate evolution from the curriculum. Nevertheless, federal funding makes up less than 10% of overall public elementary and secondary education funding, whereas federal highway funding constitutes the bulk of overall highway funding nationwide. Comparing this budgetary impact of the condition imposed in *Dole* and the condition imposed in the hypothetical evolution legislation therefore shows that the impacts are of similar magnitude. Each presents the risk of losing less than 10% of the total funding for any state that chooses not to accept the condition.

Based on the law as its stands, therefore, it appears that even the hypothetical law set forth would be upheld as a constitutionally permissible exercise of Congress's conditional spending power. Nevertheless, the question is not whether Congress *is* permitted to condition its funding in such a way, but whether it *should be* permitted to do so. The remainder of this essay draws on the scholarship of Lynn Baker, a leading academic writing in this area, as well as the dissent of Justice Sandra Day O'Connor in *Dole,* to argue that Congress should not be so permitted.

THE ARGUMENT AGAINST CONDITIONAL SPENDING FOR EDUCATION

The argument must begin from the premise that *United States v. Butler* resolved a long-standing and contentious dispute regarding the extent of the spending power. Under James Madison's strict view, the power would have allowed only expenditures on other proper legislative objects. In Alexander Hamilton's view, the power would have allowed expenditures on any legislative object, whether permitted under the other enumerated powers or not. Importantly, neither of these views explicitly embraced the idea that spending could be used to impose conditions on the states or the people, other than conditions as to how the federal money itself was to be spent.

In *Butler,* the United States argued that the phrase *general welfare* in the Spending Clause constituted a separate and distinct enumerated power, allowing Congress to use its power to appropriate funds to exact contract-like concessions from individuals or the states going beyond the intended uses of the money itself. The *Butler* Court rejected this interpretation, holding that federal spending could not be used to compel those accepting federal funds to accept federal regulation in areas outside the enumerated powers of Congress. Accepting this account of *Butler,* one may reasonably wonder why the *Dole* Court found it so easy to hold that Congress could compel the states to cede their power over regulating the drinking age to Congress based on funding for highways.

The explanation is twofold. First, in between *Butler* and *Dole* lay the development of the 20th-century U.S. welfare state. Striking down the legislation at issue in *Dole* arguably would have required striking down massive federal programs in health care, unemployment, and of course, education. It may be that the Supreme Court recognized this possibility and chose to avoid it by finding a way to decide *Dole* in favor of the federal legislation.

Second, the cases following *Butler* have improperly focused on its holding resolving the Hamilton–Madison debate in favor of Hamilton's broad view, although seemingly ignoring the Court's actual decision in the case, which struck down a piece of legislation for attempting to impose conditions on the receipt of federal funds other than how those funds were to be spent. The *Butler* Court's justification for striking down the federal program was that Congress could not use federal funds to force actions that it could not otherwise compel. Somehow, since *Butler,* this aspect of the Court's decision has dropped away, and it has been replaced with the general notion that Hamilton's side won the debate, and that Congress is therefore not limited in the subjects on which it may impose conditions, as long as its legislation does not run afoul of the *Dole* factors.

As Justice O'Connor pointed out in her well-reasoned dissent to the *Dole* decision, the *Dole* approach to conditional spending constitutes an improper and mistaken reading of *Butler.* It should be rejected in favor of a *Butler*-based approach that distinguishes between what Professor Baker has referred to as reimbursement-based spending (funding accompanied by conditions about how the precise funds allocated are to be spent) and regulatory spending (funding accompanied by conditions other than how the precise funds are to be spent, and also outside Congress's enumerated legislative powers). Under this approach, reimbursement spending would remain constitutional because such spending is clearly what both Hamilton and the *Butler* Court had in mind. In contrast, regulatory spending of the kind at issue in *Dole* would not be constitutional. This form of contractual expansion of Congress's powers was never an explicit part of Hamilton's conception of the spending power, and it was the precise form of spending struck down as unconstitutional in *Butler.*

Applying this view to the hypothetical evolution legislation set forth earlier, the result becomes clear. The legislation does not direct how any particular federal funds are to be spent. Rather, it threatens local school districts with the loss of all of their federal education funding unless the districts comply with federal curricular regulations that Congress would otherwise have no power to impose. Thus, it regulates through a spending "contract" that which Congress would otherwise have no power to regulate. Accordingly, it ought to be unconstitutional.

Contrary to the reading of the point essay, this essay's main point is not that the possibility of politically or personally motivated conditional spending should alone justify skepticism of the current approach. Rather, the admittedly extreme political example used herein is employed to illustrate the lengths that current jurisprudence would allow conditional spending to reach. Applying this essay's conclusion to other legislation exchanging federal funding for curricular reforms should yield similar results unless (1) the cost of such reforms is *fully covered* by the federal funding at issue, and (2) *only* the federal funding used to pay for the specific curricular reforms imposed is placed in jeopardy if a state chooses not to accept the reforms. Under this approach, the Reading First example capably employed by the opposing essay would fail a constitutional challenge simply because, under NCLB, a state failing to adopt the program places itself in jeopardy of losing *all* federal education funding. If the Reading First program were modified to place in jeopardy *only federal Reading First funding* for states choosing not to adopt the program, then it would likely survive a constitutional challenge under the approach promoted herein. Nevertheless, the current *Dole* approach, which does not contain either of the requirements outlined previously, would uphold the program and its greatly outsized sanction for noncompliance, just as it would uphold the hypothetical antievolution condition presented as an example in this essay. Given these likely results, one must conclude that the current approach to federal spending as set forth in *Dole* places the other enumerated powers in the Constitution in danger of being swallowed by the essentially unlimited power to conditionally spend. This result would be a regrettable departure from the genius of our

Constitution in balancing enumerated federal powers with residual state powers. As Congress moves forward with its redesign of the Elementary and Secondary Education Act, the courts should similarly reconsider *Dole* with an eye to restoring this balance.

FURTHER READINGS AND RESOURCES

Baker, L. A. (1995). Conditional federal spending after *Lopez*. *Columbia Law Review, 95,* 1911–1989.

Baker, L. A. (1998). The revival of states' rights: A progress report and a proposal. *Harvard Journal of Law & Public Policy, 22,* 95–101.

Baker, L. A., & Berman, M. N. (2003). Getting off the *Dole*: Why the Court should abandon its spending doctrine, and how a too-clever Congress could provoke it to do so. *Indiana Law Journal, 78,* 459–543.

Common Core State Standards Initiative: http://www.corestandards.org

Drake, S. M. (2007). *Creating standards-based integrated curriculum: Aligning curriculum, content, assessment, and instruction.* Thousand Oaks, CA: Corwin.

Engdahl, D. E. (1994). The spending power. *Duke Law Journal, 44,* 1–109.

Foorman, B. R., Petscher, Y., Lefsky, E. B., & Toste, J. R. (2010). Reading First in Florida: Five years of improvement. *Journal of Literacy Research, 42,* 71–93.

Gordon, D. T., Gravel, J. W., & Schifter, L. A. (Eds.). (2009). *A policy reader in Universal Design for Learning.* Cambridge, MA: Harvard Education Press.

Heise, M. (2006). The political economy of education federalism. *Emory Law Journal, 56,* 125–158.

Jennings, J. (2010/2011). The policy and politics of rewriting the nation's main education law. *Phi Delta Kappan, 92*(4), 44–49.

McKenna, M. C., & Walpole, S. (2010). Planning and evaluating change at scale: Lessons from Reading First. *Educational Researcher, 39*(6), 478–483.

COURT CASES AND STATUTES

Alden v. Maine, 527 U.S. 706 (1999).

Elementary and Secondary Education Act of 1965, 20 U.S.C. §§ 6301 *et seq.*

Gregory v. Ashcroft, 501 U.S. 452 (1991).

Honig v. Doe, 484 U.S. 305 (1988).

New York v. United States, 505 U.S. 144 (1992).

No Child Left Behind Act of 2001, 20 U.S.C. §§ 6301 *et seq.*

Printz v. United States, 521 U.S. 898 (1997).

South Dakota v. Dole, 483 U.S. 203 (1987).

United States v. Butler, 297 U.S. 1 (1936).

United States v. Lopez, 514 U.S. 549 (1995).

Should the federal government pay all the costs of special education services?

POINT: Michael Hazelkorn, *University of West Georgia*

COUNTERPOINT: Dana K. Bagwell, *D'Youville College*

OVERVIEW

The Individuals with Disabilities Education Act (IDEA), originally enacted in 1975 as the Education for All Handicapped Children Act, is a comprehensive, extensive, and expensive federal mandate that requires all states to provide a free appropriate public education (FAPE) for all children with special needs. Children who have been identified under IDEA as having special needs are those who require specialized instruction, support, and services to access the general school curriculum. IDEA is comprehensive because it covers all children with disabilities, from birth to age 22. It is extensive because it requires that schools provide appropriate and individualized programs and services that address the underlying physical, emotional, educational, and social impediments that hamper these students from having the benefit of educational opportunities that their nondisabled peers enjoy. It is expensive because the additional internal and external expenses that are incurred are not readily applicable to the general student population. These costs include but are not limited to additional teachers, paraprofessionals, therapists, equipment, technology, transportation, diagnostic testing and evaluation, environmental and instructional modifications, instructional materials, and, unfortunately, legal fees.

This latter point, the expense of special education, is the focus of the debate depicted in these essays. Everyone agrees that special education is a "budget buster" for both state and local education budgets. The question is, however, who is responsible for covering these costs—the federal government (since the

U.S. Congress was the author of IDEA), or the state, which is the constitutionally required provider of public education for *all* children.

The Massachusetts Department of Elementary and Secondary Education reported that more than $2 billion was expended by school districts on special education students for fiscal year (FY) 2010. That figure represented 20% of combined school district operating budgets. The state also published each district's fiscal report, which totaled special education expenditures, both as total dollars and as percentage of the operating budget, over a 10-year period, FY 2001 to 2010. These spreadsheets provided a trend analysis of expenditures that were directly attributable to special education. The costs that were identified for this analysis were those related wholly to special education students, but they did not include transportation or capital expenditures.

For example, the Abington Public School District expended more than $2.5 million, or 17.4% of the school operating budget, to meet the needs of students with disabilities in FY 2001. For FY 2010, the amount grew to almost $5 million, or slightly more than 23% of the budget. More importantly, these increases in the amount spent toward special education grew at a faster rate than the operational budget did. In those 10 years, special education costs in Abington swelled by more than 90%, almost double. However, the overall operating budget grew by only 43%. In other words, costs for special education are consuming more of the fiscal pie.

Summary of the Debate

Michael Hazelkorn, professor of special education and speech-language pathology at the University of West Georgia, who supports the position that the federal government should be picking up the full tab for special education costs, worries that the supersized costs of educating children with disabilities is being underwritten at the expense of general education children. He reports that it costs an average of $6,000 per pupil per year more to educate and meet the needs of students with disabilities than it does for a general education student.

Moreover, when budgets are tight, the general education program feels the knife. Education funding is already being strangled by a dysfunctional economy, which has resulted in states slashing their education contributions to local school districts. Likewise, local taxing authorities, eager to reduce burdensome tax levies for their constituents suffering from high unemployment rates and upside down mortgages, are drastically diminishing educational budgets.

However, special education services and programs are spared most of the downsizing. As Professor Hazelkorn warns, the federal government forbids states from decreasing funding for special education, except when there is exceptional economic distress. A few states have requested waivers, but this does not address the underlying problem of the high cost of funding special education and the fiscal burden it places on educational providers.

Hazelkorn also notes that no child's educational opportunity should be a function of where he or she lives or who he or she is. This refers to horizontal and vertical equity, a perennial problem embedded in state and local funding of public education. He reasons that the federal government is in a much better position to ensure that adequate special education funding is afforded to schools that educate students with special needs, irrespective of the disability or of the state or town in which the child resides.

The author of the counterpoint essay, Dana K. Bagwell, disagrees with the premise that a mandate such as IDEA should be funded entirely by the federal government. As a private researcher in the field of mental health, Bagwell argues that the federal government has already excessively intruded into the states' constitutional domain, public education, and to take more money from the federal government would result in more federal control.

He also worries that more federal money would result in fiscal incentives that might result in the overidentification of children for special education services. States and localities eager to fatten their education budgets with federal money and to alleviate them of responsibility for funding special education, might liberalize the identification of students with special needs, especially in categories that are more subjectively diagnosed, such as *learning disabled*. This notion is not far-fetched inasmuch as students diagnosed as learning disabled are most often placed in fully inclusive classrooms, which means there could be additional resources to fund paraprofessionals, collaborating special education teachers, and technology. These are all resources that could benefit all children in the classroom.

Finally, Bagwell argues that money does not matter. It is not the answer to the myriad problems associated with special education, such as late identification, misdiagnosing, or unhelpful categorization of children with special needs and the inability of school districts to narrow the achievement gap that exists between special education and general education students. As he puts it, it makes no sense "to throw good money after bad."

Regardless of the reader's own position in the debate, he or she will find something to ponder on both sides. One hopes this will result in reflective policy development and ethical implementation of IDEA.

Jennifer A. Sughrue
Old Dominion University

POINT: Michael Hazelkorn
University of West Georgia

Special education refers to "specially designed instruction, at no cost to parents or guardians, to meet the unique needs of a child with a disability" (IDEA, 20 U.S.C. §1401(a)(16)). Since the passage of the Education for All Handicapped Children Act of 1975 (EHCA), the federal special education legislation, the number of students with disabilities being educated in the public schools has increased considerably to approximately 7 million children.

The debate surrounding special education and how it is funded requires maintaining a delicate balance. With limited budgets, every dollar school districts spend on the education of students with disabilities may come at the expense of children without disabilities. Many of the services that districts must provide for students with disabilities are mandated by federal law, so districts must often take funds from the education of students without disabilities to provide the mandated services. Thus, the source of special education funding becomes critical in balancing the needs of both groups of students.

BACKGROUND

Before the enactment of EHCA, the majority of children with disabilities were either entirely excluded from schools or were sitting idly in regular classrooms waiting until they were old enough to drop out. Children with disabilities were unserved and underserved. EHCA, later renamed the Individuals with Disabilities Education Act (IDEA) in 1990, brought about the promise that with special education services, children with disabilities would achieve educational equity with their peers without disabilities. Children with disabilities are to receive a free appropriate public education (FAPE), that is, special education and related services are to be provided at no cost to parents or guardians and must be delivered in conformity with the Individualized Education Program (IEP) to meet the unique needs of a child with a disability.

IDEA is a Spending Clause statute that seeks to ensure that all children with disabilities have a FAPE available to them. It is a commitment by the federal government to provide states with supplemental federal dollars so that they will be able to offer students with disabilities equal educational opportunities. Although the IDEA

> leaves to the States the primary responsibility for developing and executing educational programs for handicapped children, it imposes significant

requirements to be followed in discharge of that responsibility. Compliance is assured by provisions permitting the withholding of federal funds upon determination that a participating state or local agency has failed to satisfy the requirements of the Act. (*Board of Education of Hendrick Hudson Central School District v. Rowley,* 1982, p. 183)

Participating states must certify to the secretary of education that they have policies and procedures that will effectively meet the act's conditions. State educational agencies in turn must ensure that local schools and teachers are meeting the state's educational standards (IDEA, 20 U.S.C. §1412(a)). Local educational agencies (school boards or other administrative bodies) can receive IDEA funds only if they certify to a state educational agency that they are acting in accordance with the state's policies and procedures (IDEA, 20 U.S.C. §1413(a)). Regardless of how much or how little the supplemental dollars are, states and local school districts must comply.

THE EXTENT OF SPENDING ON SPECIAL EDUCATION

EHCA originally authorized Congress to appropriate 40% of the national average per pupil expenditure (APPE) for public elementary and secondary schools. This percentage was to increase from 5% of the APPE in 1978 to becoming "fully funded," that is at 40% of the APPE in 1982. Unfortunately, "full funding" has never become a reality. States have failed to make up the difference, and many children with disabilities continue to be unserved or underserved. In 1999 to 2000, federal IDEA funding amounted to approximately 10.2% of the additional total expenditure on special education students, or approximately $605 per student with disabilities. Federal funds supported 7.5% of the total special education expenditures at the local level.

According to Jay G. Chambers, Thomas B. Parrish, and Jenifer J. Harr (2004), $50 billion, or approximately $8,080 per student, was spent on special education services during the 1999–2000 school year. The difference between what school districts pay to educate children with disabilities and what they recoup from the IDEA is considerable. Who makes up the difference? Where do the funds come from? The difference between what is spent to educate a child with disabilities and a child without disabilities is approximately $6,000. The dollars at the local level that are supporting special education come from the district general funds. These dollars must be spent on special education and cannot be directed elsewhere. Considerable dollars are spent at the local level and are contributed at the local level to educate children with disabilities. Combined with the fact that the dollars cannot be spent elsewhere, the limited amount of available funds contributes to a tension between general education and special education; some educators and policymakers believe that the "excessive" cost to educate children with disabilities is at the expense of students without disabilities. Yet, the federal government with its minimal contribution still imposes requirements and ensures compliance by threatening to withhold funds.

With the reauthorization of IDEA in 2004, Congress pledged to achieve full funding (i.e., 40% of the APPE) within a 7-year time frame. Some may argue that federal government funding of 40% of the APPE is sufficient and that states and school districts should be grateful if the federal government ever upholds its promise of 1975. As of this writing, that promise has not been ful-filled. The promised funding would relieve states and school districts of some of their fiscal responsibility. However, the federal government has been derelict in paying its share since 1975. Promises were made, programs were built on those promises, considerable dollars were spent, and compliance was enforced. The federal government owes states and school districts money and should pay them back for their costs. As long as the federal government is going to attach strings to funding—no matter how much money it gives—it might as well fund special education and take away the pretext that local school districts have local control. Rather than imposing regulations and sanctions for a minimal contribution, the federal government should fully fund special education at 100%. Full funding at 100% would allow children with disabilities to reach for that unfulfilled promise from 1975.

INEQUITIES IN ACCESS TO SPECIAL EDUCATION

Special education has long been underfunded. This underfunding has led to a disparate education based on the place of residence. Children who live in wealthy school districts receive a better education than do those children who live in school districts with fewer resources. The special education and related services a child receives should not depend on where the child lives. Progress and innovation are possible when children are appropriately educated. Children with disabilities can contribute to that progress if they have received an appropriate education. It is less likely that they can contribute to their potential if they haven't received an adequate education that will teach them the knowledge and skills they need. By fully funding special education at 100%, the government can provide the monetary incentive to ensure an appropriate education for all children with disabilities regardless of where they live or go to school.

States and school districts have been unwilling or have been unable to fund special education with the dollars needed to provide every child with a dis-ability with an appropriate education. Many states and local school districts resent federal interference. On average, states provide approximately 45% of the costs of special education programs, districts provide approximately 46%, and the federal government picks up the rest. As long as state and local taxes support a considerable percentage of the costs of K–12 education, proponents of less government interference and involvement are able to make the case for local control and resist federal regulations. New Mexico initially refused its IDEA funds and hoped to not be required to comply with the act's mandates. State and local school districts have considered refusing their No Child Left Behind Act (NCLB) of 2001 funds and have even gone to court to stop the federal government from enforcing its "unfunded" mandates. All of this has been for naught. Even if states and school districts don't accept funds, the federal government has other ways to ensure compliance.

SOCIAL IMPACT OF FEDERAL FUNDING

We have integrated schools, special education in inclusive environments, and increased standards because of federal interference. History has shown that without the full backing of the courts or the federal government, local authorities often have chosen segregation over integration. It took the Supreme Court's ruling in *Brown v. Board of Education* (1954) and the subsequent passage of the Elementary and Secondary Education Act of 1965 and the Civil Rights Act of 1964 to end racially segregated public schools (McDermott & Jensen, 2005). It took the IDEA to give students with disabilities their rights. Advances in special education have taken place through federal initiatives and funding. Because of federal funding, best practices in special education are promoted and disseminated. Because of federal funding, the Education Resources Information Center (ERIC) and the IRIS Center for Training Enhancements exist. Because of federal funding after the passage of the EHCA, universities received many grants to train personnel to teach children with disabilities and become the next generation of leaders. Think about how much farther we would be if the government had fully funded special education at 100%.

Unfortunately, rather than moving forward to provide all children with disabilities a FAPE, the state of the current economy may instead be moving special education backward. Almost every state has a deficit. In California, state funding for general education is being cut and teaching positions across the state are being eliminated. Yet, special education has not been cut as deeply because it is against the law to reduce special education funding. Local school officials have to look to find the necessary funds. Special education detractors complain that special education dollars are draining valuable resources from other children on whom the money would be better spent. Many states, while trying to maintain educational standards and meet the accountability requirements of NCLB and the IDEA, are revising their rules and regulations (e.g., length of the school year, minutes in class, class size) to allow districts greater flexibility. Although some are arguing that this is good practice, it appears at face value more like cost cutting initiatives that have nothing to do with best practice.

According to data from the U.S. Department of Education's National Center for Education Statistics (NCES), the national percentage of all students covered under the IDEA fell from a high of 13.8% in the 2004–2005 school year to 13.4% in the 2007–2008 school year (NCES, 2010). Yet, some states and districts report that their numbers are rising. New York City, for example, reported that the number of special education students increased by 18,000 students this year and that special education costs will increase by $140 million. Although claiming that it still should be held accountable, the city wants flexibility from the state's IDEA mandates. Not requiring that all teachers get copies of students' IEPs and increasing the number of students with disabilities in general education classrooms moves away from best practices and the interests of students. It is hard to imagine that the present budget crisis did not precipitate these proposals being made.

Nationally, the percentage of children identified as children with disabilities is down from previous years. Is this because school districts are doing a better job of remediating children's educational deficits so that referrals are not being made to special education? Or, are school districts using the current economic situation to not identify students in need of special education services and thereby save dollars that could otherwise be used to fund general education services? In *Jamie S. v. Milwaukee Public Schools* (2007), the court ruled that the school district had failed to meet its obligations under the IDEA, specifically in regard to its child find obligations and its failure to refer children in a timely manner. The school district recently appealed a federal judge's orders requiring that it search for current and former students that it had failed to serve under the IDEA from 2000 to 2005 because it claims it is too costly to implement. If the federal government paid 100% of the costs, would the Milwaukee school district still be making the same argument?

Are school districts using the current economic situation to cut back on services and thereby save dollars that could otherwise be used to fund general education services? Is this affecting the quality of education that students with disabilities receive? Some states (e.g., Iowa, South Carolina, West Virginia, and Kansas) have requested waivers because of unforeseen financial problems to temporarily reduce the amount of money they give to districts for special education programs. Many states and school districts across the country are now educating more students who have disabilities in district schools rather than sending them to out-of-district schools. Is this because they have become more mindful of educating students in their neighborhood schools and in more inclusive environments? Or, is it because they no longer have the dollars to provide the education that the IEP team once thought was so necessary? Washington, D.C., hopes to cut its annual $280 million expense of educating students with disabilities in private schools by educating those students in the city's public schools. New Jersey has cut state aid and imposed budget caps, while cutting the percentage of students with disabilities who were educated in out-of-district programs. Is this a best practice, or is this trend driven by the need to reduce costs? Would the situation be the same if the federal government provided 100% of the cost of the special education?

Is the decline in the percentage of children with disabilities at the national level caused by changes in the IDEA? The reauthorizations of IDEA in 1997 and 2004 added specific requirements regarding the distribution of state special education funds establishing placement-neutral funding formulas so that districts were not rewarded for segregating children with disabilities. Whether school districts sought to overidentify children and then believed that segregated classrooms were better than more inclusive classrooms is doubtful. The costs to a school system of educating children with disabilities are just too high. A more likely scenario is that school districts actively try to under-identify children with disabilities. Regardless, if the federal government funded 100% of the costs of special education, school districts could devote less of their time worrying about overidentifying or under-identifying children for special education, and instead devote their time to providing the best education possible to children with disabilities.

The recent stimulus bill in part was to shore up education dollars and in particular dollars for special education. However, this is at best a stopgap measure. Full funding of special education at 100% on a permanent basis would relieve the current economic pressures faced by states and local school districts. The federal government already has the authority to get states and local school districts to comply with its rules and regulations. As long as the federal government is using that authority, it should pay 100% of the costs to support that authority. Although full 100% funding from the federal government may shift control of education away from states and school boards, this may not be a bad thing. As the entity paying 100% of the costs, the government would have the ability to demand 100% compliance with the IDEA. As a result, there may be fewer inconsistencies about the way rules and regulations are interpreted between and among states. This would help equalize the education students with disabilities receive with their peers without disabilities and across districts in the state and across states. Although some states are progressive and push their districts to "best" practices, not all states have the resources to provide the technical assistance and professional development to make it happen. Federal funding of 100% of the costs of special education would help equalize technical assistance and professional development across states. Essentially, special education is an unfunded mandate. The federal government has the opportunity to make it right and can do that by funding 100% of the costs of special education. With 100% funding, the goals guaranteed by the IDEA may finally be realized. Ultimately, everyone would benefit when students with disabilities receive a free appropriate public education.

COUNTERPOINT: Dana K. Bagwell
D'Youville College

The U.S. Constitution does not mention nor provide for public education. Historically, public education is considered to be the purview of each individual state inasmuch as the Tenth Amendment reserves powers not specifically enumerated in the Constitution to the states. Most often, the federal government's involvement in education has been on an as-needed basis—it steps in only when national or international events dictate swift and comprehensive change. Some notable examples include the Servicemen's Readjustment Act (GI Bill) in 1944, the National Defense of Education Act in 1958 (responding to the Soviet launch of Sputnik), and Section 504 of the Rehabilitation Act of 1973, which guaranteed basic civil rights in education to all Americans. This essay is not about the utility of special education in general; certainly no one denies the humanity of providing extra assistance for children struggling to learn. Rather, this essay examines the role of the federal government in education, states' rights in education, and the data regarding special education outcomes and current funding. In 2008 alone, the total spent on special education programs across the nation was a mind-numbing $96.6 billion. It is important to remember that the federal government has never fully funded any public educational program because it is not its role to do so. In this accountability-focused era, is special education in such a crisis that a federal bailout is necessary?

BRIEF HISTORY OF SPECIAL EDUCATION IN THE UNITED STATES

The U.S. Office of Education adopted and implemented an age-to-grade system of school categorization in the 1880s. In 1965, the Elementary and Secondary Education Act, and its subsequent amendments, laid the groundwork for future special education legislation by authorizing aid for disadvantaged (poor) and disabled (physically handicapped) students. The first civil rights law protecting handicapped children was enacted in 1973 under Section 504 of the Rehabilitation Act. Although the 1975 Education for All Handicapped Children Act (EHCA) mandated four overarching guidelines for special education (a broad "zero reject" policy stating that no child can be denied an education on the grounds that he or she is uneducable), no plan for funding or designation of financial responsibility was included—an oversight that continues to plague the relationship between states and the federal government. The Individuals with Disabilities Education Act (IDEA), a reauthorization and renaming of the EHCA, and the Americans with Disabilities Act (ADA), both passed in 1990, solidified the federal government's commitment to mandating equal educational access across the nation; individuals with autism and traumatic brain injury are now eligible for special education services. With the IDEA Amendments of 1997, the federal government required special education programs to provide severely impaired children with health care, including parental training, psychological management plans, and training in basic movement and awareness skills. In an attempt to reform public education, the 2001 No Child Left Behind Act (NCLB) mandated that all states report adequate yearly progress (AYP) goals in reading, mathematics, and science without providing a standardized assessment platform and left the majority of the expenses to individual states. The American Recovery and Reinvestment Act (ARRA) of 2009 expanded special education eligibility to include children from birth to age 2 and their parents. Whether right or wrong, the federal government's intervention in education is a relatively new phenomenon associated with the expansion of the welfare state. Nowhere in the history of education in this country has the federal government stepped in to provide such extensive financial funding in education for any subcategory, not even during the court-mandated integration of public schools after *Brown v. Board of Education* (1954).

FEDERAL GOVERNMENT SPECIAL EDUCATION LEGISLATION

The IDEA provides a detailed framework explaining the funding relationship between the federal government and states regarding special education. This relationship is not new, unusual, or without precedent. Although federal funding for all educational programs has increased throughout history, it has been and currently remains the responsibility of the states and local school districts to fund the majority of their public education programs. To prevent state governments from charging poor individuals for the extra services, the IDEA required states to provide a free appropriate public education for all students with disabilities qualifying for special education. State opposition to the federally imposed NCLB continues almost a decade after its passing. In 2005, Michigan, Vermont, and Texas, home state of former President George W. Bush (who signed the NCLB into law), along with the National Education Association (NEA), filed a lawsuit, which was eventually suspended and then reintroduced in January 2008, claiming that NCLB was unconstitutional and created an undue burden on the states. One of the major critiques of the NCLB is the state-to-state variability in the type, validity, reliability, and academic rigor of the assessments used. Statewide variability in testing outcomes during the 2005–2006 school year ranged from 30% to 90% passing rates, but determining what these numbers really mean is impossible. The federal government states NCLB permits flexibility in accountability systems, thus leaving the states in control of education, but the states complain that standardized testing fails to measure what is being taught.

Since its inception, special education has received an inappropriate share of blame for schools failing to reach AYP goals in NCLB. Special education programs often account for 80% or more of schools that do not achieve AYP. Baseline scores on standardized tests are typically much lower than those of regular students; therefore, closing the test gap is more difficult especially when learning new material is already a challenge. It is insidious to require progress of special education students parallel to that required for their classmates who do not have disabilities, and even more unfathomable to fail the entire school because of lack of progress in a subcategory of students. However, is throwing more federal taxpayer money at the problem really the answer, given the inability to measure what is wrong or how much progress is even possible? Is it too much to ask for a modified measure of progress for special education students?

The question posed in this chapter is whether the federal government should pay all of the costs of special education services. This essay argues that the financial responsibility for funding special education should be shared by the federal government, states, and local school districts. Even though the federal government has mandated a minimum level of educational quality for students with disabilities, it should not be fully responsible for the costs of special education, any more than it is responsible for the costs of educating students who do not have disabilities.

PROBLEMS IN THE IDENTIFICATION AND CLASSIFICATION OF STUDENTS WITH DISABILITIES

Since the enactment of special education legislation in 1975, the number of children receiving special education services has increased more than 150%. In the last decade alone, special education numbers have risen more than 30%.

More than 75% of these students spend some, part, or all of their days in traditional classrooms. Accordingly, are such diagnoses accurate and are all currently provided services necessary? Nonetheless, this large increase in special education labeling results from myriad factors, including increasingly accurate diagnostic procedures and medical advances that increase survival odds of premature babies. However, the largest increases have occurred in categories where subjectivity in diagnosis is more the rule than the exception. For example, the broadly inclusive category of *learning disabled* has experienced a 300% increase since the late 1970s, and often a medical doctor is never consulted before a student receives such a label. More recently, *specific learning disabled* (SLD) has become the preferred nomenclature; oddly enough, however, there is an utter lack of diagnostic specificity and broad inclusion of quite disparate conditions. The SLD condition accounts for 40% of special education and represents an unfathomable 1-in-20 public school students. Accordingly, with such broad inclusion criteria, many of the behavioral symptoms associated with these new definitions of special education seem like the very definition of childhood itself: disorganization, difficulty with authority, difficulty sitting still, or difficulty concentrating.

The special education subcategory of emotional disturbances is a grab bag of symptoms that can include an inability to maintain interpersonal relationships on one end and the severe disorder of schizophrenia on the other end. Using such inconsistent categorization and lumping all childhood disorders under the special education label inevitably leaves schools to sort out the mess. Gifted and talented students are categorized by their performance on standardized tests and receive instruction according to their strengths and weaknesses. For example, a student might score in the upper percentile on math but score in the average range on social studies; accordingly, that student would receive advanced math classes but regular social studies classes. Is it so inconceivable that special education students receive similar treatment? A director of special education services in Framingham, Massachusetts, laments the increase in severity of special education children during the last 10 years and feels powerless to provide sufficient services. It is no wonder school districts and parents alike exploit loopholes in educational policy. The special education designation becomes the particular purview of parents and school administrators who move children in and out of special education to fit the current economic needs. Such flip-flopping might produce financial stability in the short run, but children are ultimately the ones who suffer. And yet, here we are arguing about whether to pump more federal money into a system that encourages such abuses.

Further, there is an inherent, yet familiar, problem with the special education classification system currently in use—its inconsistency. Some school districts count gifted and talented students in the special education category. Other districts lump children with noncognitive and nonemotional disabilities, and other disabilities that do not impair the child's academic achievement into the special education pool—for example, arthritis complications that hinder writing for extended periods. Some schools count students with multiple classifications, such as the high-performing student with arthritis, twice (i.e., once as gifted and talented and once as physically impaired), effectively increasing their special education needs without expending additional resources. Although it might be tempting to blame the schools, the federal government's classification of special needs is equally as murky. Serious organic brain disorders—for example, schizophrenia, traumatic brain injury, and similar lifelong disorders—are classified under "student disabilities" along with dyslexia. A 2007 amendment to NCLB permitted states to "modify academic achievement standards" for students with disabilities—as originally classified under the IDEA. This legislation modifies AYP scores, a mandatory condition for funding under NCLB, for this group of state-created special education students, although this loophole is used inconsistently, further complicating this discussion. Whether the modification of learning difficulty categorization, testing procedures, and AYP is good or bad is irrelevant in this argument. However, highly relevant is whether this loophole provides a slippery slope toward the overcategorization of students as learning disabled, as in the autism epidemic discussed earlier, to avoid federally mandated AYP scores and increase the 100% free funding for special education, as proposed in the point essay of this chapter. After examining these facts, how could one conceive that complete and unconditional funding would not further distort the actual number of special education students?

Numerous research studies have demonstrated the current growth in special education is inextricably tied to funding: When schools receive resources based on the total number enrolled in special education programs, the number of special education students magically increases. Julie Cullen (2003), a University of California economist, discovered that 40% of special education enrollment in Texas during the 1990s was directly linked to financial incentives. Unfortunately, some attempts to rein in such errant fiscal irresponsibility have backfired. Resource-based funding allocated specific education resources based on specific needs of the special education students and school accommodations, such as student-to-teacher ratios. Ultimately, schools began over-referring students into separate classrooms to drive up the number and therefore funding for special education. However, the inconsistent labeling is not a one-way street. Sometimes funding incentives inhibit special education labeling. In 2009, the Manhattan Institute examined Florida's voucher program, which permitted student transfer to a private school with full or partial tuition funding (Winters & Greene, 2009). Such vouchers redirect money that was allocated for public schools and have been legally challenged as unconstitutional. However, the authors of the report, Marcus Winters and Jay Greene, hypothesized that if parent preferences were driving the increase in SLD designations, Florida private schools that were both proximally near and accepted the vouchers would see an increase in special education students. Still, Winters and Greene's research showed that voucher-eligible fourth through sixth grade students were about 15% less likely to receive an SLD diagnosis in these areas. In this case study, public schools inhibited the SLD diagnosis to retain funding; when a student leaves the public school with a private school voucher, the school loses that money—the taxpayer still foots the bill. Whether parents or schools are driving the inflated special education numbers is unimportant. What is important is ceasing the manipulation of children to secure funding. What is equally important is that labeling of children should not be manipulated for self-interest. How are we serving the best interests of students when we falsify a medical record for money? What are the long-term consequences, psychologically, financially, and educationally of these unethical behaviors? How would most Americans feel about these behaviors if they knew? Unquestionably, increased federal funding for special education, particularly when tied directly to the number of students served, will most certainly escalate this trend and likely do nothing to improve educational outcomes in the process.

SPECIAL EDUCATION FUNDING

In 2008, the United States spent more than $584 billion for K–12 public education, state and local governments provided 92% of these funds—the federal government provided 8%. Presently, 2011 federal appropriations are $50.7 billion for the Department of Education—a $4.5 billion increase over 2010 funding. Special education state grants from the federal government are proposed at $250 million over the 2010 funding level. However, there is still no evidence that more federal money will result in better services for students with disabilities or better outcomes. In fact, a 2010 policy report from Vanderbilt University revealed that offering performance-pay bonuses of as much as $15,000 directly to teachers did not raise student's test scores (Springer et al., 2010). Therefore, money is most certainly not the driving force behind educational reform. In 2009, Massachusetts spent almost $2 billion on special education alone, with almost $436 million subsidizing private tuition; their private school spending on special education ranks third in the nation despite the state ranking 32nd in overall population size. Again, money did not fix special education there either, as Massachusetts ranked 32nd in the percentage of special education students who graduate from high school (Sullivan & Mohl, 2009).

Full funding of special education has actually been implemented before—with no real success. In the 1980s, Pennsylvania provided 100% funding for special education programs. The point side of this argument wants the taxpayer to believe this is the best way to fix special education. But did full funding, by the state in this case, increase the quality of special education? No. Full funding increased the quantity of students destined for special education. This increase occurred despite an overall declining population of school-aged children during this period. It took a decade of accountability and specially designed instructional packages to rein in costs and to reduce the number of misidentified students.

The best solution is for each entity—the federal government, state, and local school district—to pay a share of special education costs, as they are now doing, with federal and state reimbursements tied to outcomes, not numbers of students served. The education gap continues to widen between special education and traditional students, not decrease, even as more money is dumped into the special education system. This is not the time to throw good money after bad; this is the time for accountability in education. Regardless of the source of funding, empirical, accurate, and appropriate outcome measures are needed to ensure that the funds are well spent. We owe it to our children.

FURTHER READINGS AND RESOURCES

Chambers, J. G., Parrish, T. B., & Harr, J. J. (2004, June). *What are we spending on special education services in the United States, 1999–2000.* Washington, DC: American Institutes for Research, Center for Special Education Finance, Special Education Expenditure Project. Retrieved from http://csef.air.org/publications/seep/national/AdvRpt1.pdf

Cullen, J. B. (2003). The impact of fiscal incentives on student disability rates. *Journal of Public Economics, 87,* 1557–1589.

Eckes, S. E., & Swando, J. (2009). Special education subgroups under NCLB: Issues to consider. *Teachers College Record, 111,* 2479–2504.

McDermott, K. A., & Jensen, L. S. (2005). Dubious sovereignty: Federal conditions of aid and the No Child Left Behind Act. *Peabody Journal of Education, 80*(2), 39–56.

National Center for Education Statistics. (2010). *Digest of education statistics, 2009* (NCES 2010-013), Chapter 2. Washington, DC: U.S. Department of Education, Institute for Education Sciences, National Center for Education Statistics. Retrieved from http://nces.ed.gov/programs/digest/d09/ch_2.asp

President's Commission on Excellence in Special Education. (2002, July). *A new era: Revitalizing special education for children and their families.* Washington, DC: U.S. Department of Education. Retrieved from http://www2.ed.gov/inits/commissions-boards/whspecialeducation/reports/index.html

Springer, M. G., Ballou, D., Hamilton, L., Le, V., Lockwood, J. R., McCaffrey, D., et al. (2010). *Teacher pay for performance: Experimental evidence from the project on incentives in teaching.* Nashville, TN: National Center on Performance Incentives at Vanderbilt University.

Sullivan, J., & Mohl, B. (2009, April). Spending spiral. *CommonWealth,* Spring, 34–47.

Winters, M. A., & Greene, J. P. (2009). How special ed vouchers keep kids from being mislabeled as disabled. *Civic Report, 58,* 1–12.

Court Cases and Statutes

American Recovery and Reinvestment Act (ARRA) of 2009, Pub. L. 111-5, 123 Stat. 115.

Americans with Disabilities Act (ADA) of 1990, 42 U.S.C. §§ 12101 *et seq.*

Board of Education of Hendrick Hudson Central School District v. Rowley, 458 U.S. 176 (1982).

Brown v. Board of Education, 347 U.S. 483 (1954).

Civil Rights Act of 1964, 42 U.S.C. §§ 2000d *et seq.*

Education for All Handicapped Children Act of 1975, 20 U.S.C. § 1401 *et seq.*

Elementary and Secondary Education Act of 1965, 20 U.S.C. §§ 6301 *et seq.*

Individuals with Disabilities Education Act (IDEA) of 1990, 20 U.S.C. §§ 1400 *et seq.*

Individuals with Disabilities Education Act Amendments of 1997, 105-17, 111 Stat. 37.

Individuals with Disabilities Education Act Regulations, 34 C.F.R. §§ 300 *et seq.*

Jamie S. v. Milwaukee Public Schools, 519 F. Supp. 2d. 870 (E.D. Wis. 2007).

National Defense of Education Act of 1958, 20 U.S.C. §§ 401 *et seq.*

No Child Left Behind Act of 2001, 20 U.S.C. §§ 6301 *et seq.*

Rehabilitation Act of 1973, Section 504, 29 U.S.C. § 794.

Servicemen's Readjustment Act (GI Bill) of 1944, 38 U.S. C. §§ 3701 *et seq.*

When individual states require local school districts to provide gifted education, should the state pay all the costs?

POINT: Nicola A. Alexander, *University of Minnesota*

COUNTERPOINT: Victoria Carr, *University of Cincinnati*

OVERVIEW

As a matter of state constitutional law, each state is required to establish a system of free public schools and, in many states, to ensure that those schools meet a level of specific quality. Implicit, if not explicit, in this constitutional command is the notion that the public schools throughout the state will be of similar, if not virtually identical, quality. One way to ensure substantial equality is for the state to mandate the provision of certain services.

Gifted education is a classic example of such a mandate. Children who are gifted have special needs and, arguably, require special services. They may need special classes where the pupil–teacher ratio is smaller or where there is greater use of technology. At the high school level, it may be necessary to have a special curriculum or advanced placement classes, which closely resemble a college curriculum. It may also be necessary for gifted students to participate in labor-intensive extracurricular activities such as Odyssey of the Mind, Future Problem Solving, debates, or the science fair. Of course, coordinating all of these activities may require additional administrators.

Yet, such mandates seemingly conflict with another state constitutional value—the value of local control. All states, except Hawaii, provide for the delivery of educational services through smaller political units—typically called school districts—that are responsible for the public schools in a given geographic area. Each school district is controlled by a school board, which generally is elected by the voters of the school district. The local board typically has broad discretion over hiring, financial, and curriculum decisions.

When the state mandates that a local district provide certain services, the state necessarily diminishes local control. Instead of spending money as the local board sees fit, the district must now spend money on particular services. In some instances, the district may be forced to fund policy choices that are substantially different from its own policy choices.

The tension between the state's promotion of the state constitutional value of equality and the local district's preservation of the state constitutional value of local control is exacerbated when the state mandates the provision of services but does not provide the money to perform the services. State mandates to provide gifted education, which are motivated by a desire to see that children receive the services necessary for them to fully develop as human beings, are a classic example of the unfunded mandate.

Summary of the Debate

This debate asks whether the states should have to pay 100% of the costs of gifted education when the provision of gifted education programs is mandated by state law.

Nicola Alexander, a professor of education at the University of Minnesota, takes the affirmative view. She contends that when a state mandates gifted education, the state is making a policy judgment that gifted students require additional services, and of course, additional services cost money. Having made that policy choice, the state has an obligation to provide the funds to implement the program. Her argument has four key points. First, in our constitutional system of federalism, the states, not the local school districts, have responsibility for educating the population. If the state imposes a mandate but does not provide the necessary funds, the state ignores its responsibilities and undermines the values of local control. Second, principles of equity require that the state ensure that local districts have the funds to meet their obligations. Third, principles of adequacy dictate that every school district have sufficient funds for gifted education. Finally, to the extent that state constitutional provisions require equal education or education that meets a particular quality level, the failure to provide sufficient funds for gifted education may constitute a constitutional violation.

Victoria Carr, a professor of education at the University of Cincinnati, takes the negative view. While calling for the continuation of state mandates for gifted education, she argues that mandatory state subsidies are unnecessary. Instead, she believes that focusing on the source of the money ignores the more significant question—how to best structure the educational environment so that gifted students may reach their full potential. Specifically, she suggests that gifted students be allowed to start school early, be allowed to skip grades, and, at the high school level, pursue advanced studies. Additionally, she advocates significant reforms in how the teachers of gifted students are trained and interact with students. In sum, her view is that local school districts must spend existing money more effectively but should be allowed to make their own choices. The problem, in her view, is not a lack of money for gifted education; it is the inefficiencies in how the money is spent.

William E. Thro
Christopher Newport University

POINT: Nicola A. Alexander
University of Minnesota

"Whoever pays the piper calls the tune" is a well-known adage that should be turned on its head with respect to funding for gifted education. Instead, we should demand that whoever calls the tune should pay the piper. If individual states mandate that local school districts provide gifted education, then those states should pay all the costs of gifted education.

By mandating gifted programs, state policymakers are reflecting the viewpoint that gifted and talented students *require* additional services in order for the students to receive an appropriate education. In other words, these states are adopting a resource–cost approach to the education of gifted and talented children. The resource–cost approach "involves costing out the physical ingredients of the generally accepted set of required resources for providing an appropriate education to a child with a given set of educational needs" (Baker, 2001, p. 230). This strategy contrasts with the standards-based view where children are funded based on the level of funding needed for them to meet basic performance standards.

By requiring districts to provide gifted and talented programs, state policymakers explicitly recognize that gifted and talented children have needs different from those of typical students. There is an explicit recognition that gifted and talented students require a specialized program, and there is an implicit commitment that public dollars will pay for it. In other words, state policymakers are signaling to schools that they should offer to the gifted child an individualized program that adapts to his or her needs. However, according to the National Association for Gifted Children, of the 32 states that mandated gifted and talented programs in 2008, only 6 fully funded these programs. Five states with mandates required these programs but offered no additional funding.

Despite the nod given to excellence and expressive individualism that a mandate for gifted education implies, policymakers have accorded low priority to funding the intellectual needs of gifted youth. According to data from the U.S. Department of Education, National Center for Education Statistics (2010), the federal, state, and local governments combined to raise more than $584 billion for elementary and secondary programs in 2007 to 2008. Of this amount, less than one tenth of 1% (i.e., $577 million) was allocated to gifted and talented programs. This represents about one fifth of 1% (.21%) of total state moneys raised for K–12 programs. Conventional wisdom indicates that gifted and talented children account for 3% to 5% of the student population and number at least 2.5 million children. Thus, in 2008, public expenditures for gifted programs typically accounted for less than $231 per student eligible to participate. Indeed, more than a quarter of the states provided no funding at all to gifted programs.

Notwithstanding, the mandating of gifted services sine qua non suggests that state policymakers accept that gifted children need supplemental services. This places the obligation to fund gifted services in a similar context as the funding of children with disabilities. However, research during the last 2 decades indicates that states on average spend more than 100 times more on children with disabilities than they do on children performing at exceptionally high levels. Although some difference in funding is certainly warranted, 10,000% higher seems a bit extreme. The substantial gap in funding between students at either end of the performance spectrum suggests that much of the additional cost for gifted children is left uncovered by the government. When public funding does not cover the full costs of additional services required by gifted students, these children have to fend for themselves. For example, Bruce D. Baker and Craig E. Richards (1998) find that reducing the number of public-supported elitist programs simply resulted in the growth of fee-based private programs for gifted children (as cited in Baker 2001, p. 233). Consequently, gifted children from families with means have access to supplemental services while less privileged children have to do without those very services that state policymakers deem essential.

State policymakers need to fund fully their mandate that districts provide gifted programs for several reasons. First, principles of federalism cede to states the responsibility of educating their citizens. Second, ideals of equity require states to play a key role in the distribution of educational resources. Third, considerations of adequacy make it necessary for states to fund their education system appropriately. Fourth, legal implications are tied to states not providing an equitable and adequate system of education. The rest of this essay will elaborate on these key points.

ARGUMENTS FOR REQUIRING STATES TO FULLY FUND GIFTED EDUCATION

Federalism

The balance of power between states and federal government puts the responsibility of educating citizens squarely on the states. The residual power authorized in the Tenth Amendment to the U.S. Constitution is emphasized in the education clauses present in the constitutions of all 50 states. The state is responsible for providing a "thorough and efficient" or "adequate" system of education. When states mandate gifted and talented programs, they are essentially indicating that those programs are a key element in their system of education. States should be responsible for covering all the costs that they deem to be essential.

By not fully funding state-mandated programs, states infringe on local choice. When state policymakers mandate programs without fully covering the costs, they are really requiring localities to foot the bill of that mandated service. However, districts may not always choose or be able to cover these costs. Indeed, research suggests that most schools located in states with mandates not accompanied by state funding are less likely than average to offer gifted programs. Thus, mandating gifted programs and essentially requiring local districts to pay their costs is not an appropriate stance if localities are not equally advantaged. Districts have different needs and face different costs. There are large variations in their fiscal ability to meet the mandate of providing gifted and talented programs. This variation at the district level has a big impact on the ability of students to participate in gifted programs. Without full state funding, a child's participation in a gifted program may be more associated with the size of the district and the typical income of its residents, than it is to his or her exceptional talents.

Some policymakers would argue that the states can help localities but do not need to fully fund the mandate. However, the answer is not simply to allocate some funds to districts based on pupil count or other criteria. Partial funding through flat grants, weighted student formulas, and incomplete reimbursements often does not cover the additional costs of gifted supplemental services. Consequently, these funding approaches leave district policymakers holding the bag, without the necessary ability or will to keep gifted programs going. Moreover, research has long demonstrated that flat grants have exacerbated inequities in service for gifted children, where children in wealthy communities received more money from the state than their peers in less wealthy districts received. Further, when states only partially reimburse costs, state dollars are often not sufficient to support needy local communities in their provision of gifted and talented programs. For these programs to work, localities end up having to use substantial amounts of their own limited funds. In sum, research shows that without full state funding, rural districts, smaller communities, and districts with less-wealthy students seldom receive enough state dollars for gifted education to make running these programs meaningful.

Anything less than full state coverage of the supplemental costs of gifted programs falls short of the state fulfilling its obligation to districts and to the children they serve. By not covering the full costs of the mandated gifted programs, states leave children who are in the less advantaged districts facing lower prospects of participating in gifted education than their peers who live in more wealthy communities. Although it is understandable that different localities have different capacities, it is not acceptable for those differences to impede local effort to meet the needs of a state mandate. Even less tolerable is the impact that this differential capacity has on the opportunities of gifted children.

Equity

Notions of fairness are grounded in perceptions regarding the distribution of rights and resources. In the field of education finance, policies are called on to distribute educational resources so that there is horizontal equity, vertical equity, and fiscal neutrality. Once states have mandated gifted services, it is the responsibility of each state to ensure that its jurisdiction can provide these programs in an equitable manner.

Horizontal equity requires the equal treatment of equally situated entities. For gifted and talented programs, districts should be given the same capacity to pay for the costs of gifted programs, and gifted children should have the same opportunity to receive the required supplemental services. However, without equal capacity, districts will not have the same opportunity to provide each gifted child with the supplemental services needed. States, on the other hand, have the broad revenue base, the fiscal capacity, and the authority to equalize funds among districts.

Vertical equity calls for the unequal treatment of unequally situated entities. To the extent that districts have different capacities and tastes for gifted education, state policymakers must assure children that their opportunities will not be conscribed by the district in which they live. Those children who live in districts that are less able to fulfill their obligations under the mandate must not be penalized. If districts are unequally willing or able to pay the full costs of gifted and talented programs, states must step in.

Fiscal neutrality calls for there to be no significant relationship between the distribution of resources and "illegitimate" characteristics, such as district property wealth, district size, and the income levels of the community. Notwithstanding, the capacity of schools to meet state and district requirements typically depends on school size, composition, and institutional setting. For example, Bruce D. Baker and Reva Friedman-Nimz (2004) find that larger schools were significantly more likely to offer gifted programs than were smaller schools. Larger schools were also more likely to have higher participation rates among students. If the size of school matters in the way described, students attending smaller schools are at a disadvantage if states do not fully fund the additional costs of gifted and talented programs. Further, because research indicates that suburban and rural schools were more likely to offer gifted programs, students attending schools in urban districts would be at a disadvantage relative to their nonurban peers. Similarly, because of the additional costs, schools with higher portions of low income students also tended to have fewer gifted and talented programs. Even when poorer districts could afford to offer a few programs, the number of gifted students that they could serve was limited. This disadvantage would be mitigated if states took on the full responsibility of funding the full costs of the supplemental services for gifted children.

Although equity and fiscal neutrality are important markers of fairness, they are not sufficient. For example, state policymakers may design systems where equity among districts is high but state funding is not provided, resulting in districts that invest equally little in gifted programs. That is, equity and fiscal neutrality exist not because governments adequately fund these programs, but because districts, and the children they serve, are in equally bad shape. To ensure adequate (and not just equitable) funding of gifted programs requires the full state funding of these mandated services.

Adequacy

To determine adequacy, it is important for policymakers to distinguish between the "wants" and "must haves" of a schooling system. With a mandate, state policymakers indicate that gifted and talented programs are "must haves" and are thus an essential component of the state's education system. When state policymakers prescribe what programs districts are required to offer, they also provide a working definition of what educational components are included in that state's definition of what an "adequate" educational system looks like. That definition may be used as a benchmark to evaluate the capacity of districts to meet adequacy requirements. Given the large variation in the existing capacities of districts to meet the mandate to provide gifted education, the proper role of the state is to fill in those gaps.

The imposition of mandates that do not account for fiscal and other structural differentials among districts exacerbates negative consequences that prevail in the most troubled schools. Ensuring that contextual differences are appropriately captured is crucial in formulating policies for funding an adequate system. For example, Andrew Reschovsky and Jennifer Imazeki's (2001) observations regarding the state role in funding general education apply here. As they note, "These schools [with above-average costs] will fail, not necessarily because of their own inability to effectively educate children, but because they were provided with insufficient fiscal resources to do the job" (p. 375).

If state policymakers have high expectations that they do not support, the educational actors needed to implement state aims may simply give up. Ensuring that localities have sufficient capacity to fulfill the objectives of policy is thus important and has far-reaching implications for supporting adequate school systems. States are the entities that are best able to ensure that the greatest subsidies exist for those who receive the lowest levels of private rates of return from schooling. States can do this if they take on the responsibility of fully funding gifted and talented programs. For example, Baker and Friedman-Nimz (2004) find that schools in states providing funding for gifted and talented programs were more than two times more likely to offer gifted programs. Moreover, schools located in states providing funding for gifted education tended to serve more gifted students.

More needs to be done to focus on the contextual differences that exist between schools and among students in determining appropriate measures of adequacy. This essay argues that if states do not fully cover the costs of mandated programs, they are not providing an adequate educational system. Tying judgments on adequacy to the standards set by state policymakers is consistent with recent trends in the legislative and judicial arena, including lawsuits filed in New York State, Ohio, and Kentucky.

Legal Considerations

There is a lack of protection provided to gifted children under federal case law. However, the general trend in adequacy litigation at the state level illustrates the appropriateness of mandating full payment of these services for states that require that they be provided. Carolyn D. Herrington and Virginia Weider (2001) indicate, "Adequacy challenges have focused on whether the amount of money appropriated for public education in general is enough to meet the costs of providing the standard guaranteed in the state constitution" (p. 523). Similar arguments may be used for the funding of gifted and talented programs once states have established a mandate. The inability of some districts to meet their state mandate provides prima facie evidence that not all eligible children are given the appropriate educational support required by law.

In the end, when states do not fund programs that they mandate, fairness in educational investments and educational outcomes is often compromised. This is why individual states that require supplemental services for the gifted should pay for them. It is simply the right thing to do.

COUNTERPOINT: Victoria Carr
University of Cincinnati

U.S. education has a long history of providing children who are highly gifted with a "special" education on a shoestring budget. Shrinking budgets and stereotypes about giftedness make it highly unlikely that enough funding will be set aside in future state budgets to make significant impacts on specialized programs for gifted and talented students in public schools. One stereotype is the belief that children who are gifted or talented will do well in any setting because of their gifts. This view counters arguments for state funding for programming targeted to these bright and talented individuals, particularly because so many children struggle to meet minimum standards of achievement, an area in which supplemental aid is targeted. However, children who are gifted can do well in the general education setting when the setting addresses the diverse needs of the individuals in the classroom. Educating children with a focus on problem solving and critical, creative, and higher-level thinking processes should not just be part of a specialized gifted program. All children should have these opportunities. Therefore, a special subsidy should not be expected from states. Given the history of gifted education, waiting for funding to specially serve children who are gifted and talented is irrational.

State mandates, however, should be in place directing local school districts to provide gifted education. Without mandates, districts may adopt the perception that children with gifts and talents will do fine without any special attention, but history has shown this is not the case. There are many ways to provide "special" attention to children who are gifted and talented with minimal state funds. For example, grade acceleration, advanced placement coursework, differentiated instruction, and inquiry-based education should be the norm for meeting the needs of gifted and talented children. Professional development funding provided to schools should be used to support administrators and teachers to learn how to implement gifted education systemic reform that provides an appropriate education for all children within the general classroom.

EQUITY IN EDUCATION

There have been numerous policy directives from the legislative level to provide quality education to all students, but these attempts have not worked. As state school finance policies aim to provide local districts with moneys for equal funding per pupil across districts, this generally provides for what Bruce D. Baker and Reva Friedman-Nimz (2004) call an "adequate" education. Supplemental aid is usually provided to districts that have a higher need or lower fiscal capacity to ensure that students in those districts receive an adequate education. Yet, an adequate education is not necessarily an *appropriate* education, and in many schools across the nation, it does not even come close. Providing extra funding for gifted programs may provide enrichment for some children, but far too many will still not have an adequate, much less appropriate, education. Focusing funding on addressing systemic issues within schools would better ensure that all children receive an appropriate education. Leaders in education must support equity and quality for all children who are gifted within the general education classroom.

Beginning with the Marland report to Congress in 1972, the argument that children who are gifted and talented are not being served in the public schools has been debated. To best serve all students in the public schools, state policies will need to mandate learning for all students in ways that all students can become engaged with school learning and forego the systems that have failed. As Joseph Renzulli (Renzulli, Leppien, & Hays, 2000) and others have argued, the drill-and-practice, test-teaching, textbook-driven, worksheet-oriented, and boredom-producing curricula must evolve into a 21st-century curriculum where engagement, inquiry, and learning are the focus of classroom pedagogy. This, however, will be challenging, particularly given the drive toward common national standards and accountability for these standards based on high-stakes testing. The reauthorization of the Elementary and Secondary Education Act (ESEA) in 2011 has the potential to alleviate some of the issues that hinder quality appropriate education for all children and provide clear national directives for gifted and talented education, but with a divisive Congress and reform-oriented education groups competing for ESEA influence, changes will be difficult, but necessary.

The federal government's reluctance to fund gifted education has been made even more evident by the significant reduction in funding during the past 5 years for the ESEA Jacob Javits Gifted and Talented grants. Although this certainly sends a clear negative message to state education legislators, the solution to providing an appropriate education for children who are gifted and talented lies with state mandates and reforms that provide an appropriate education, not just an adequate education, within individual school districts. These mandates do matter. It has been shown that with belief in the policies and accountability for implementation of those policies, states yield higher academic results. Furthermore, state policies can eliminate misperceptions about gifted education and promote best practices in the schools through the development of guidelines and strategies to meet the needs of individuals who are gifted and talented. Although current mandates and policies vary by state, when state manuals are created, they reflect best practice initiatives in gifted education (Brown, Avery, VanTassel-Baska, Worley, & Stambaugh, 2006).

BEST PRACTICES IN GIFTED EDUCATION

The National Association for Gifted Children and the Association for the Gifted, a subdivision of the Council for Exceptional Children, have created position statements on the education of gifted and talented children, including information about how to identify those children who are at risk and children who have gifts and disabilities. In addition, gifted education standards for teacher education were created to promote foundational knowledge and skills in gifted education that are to be used by university teacher preparation programs and as a model for district-based professional development. These standards should not be limited to those individuals who are designated as teachers of children who are gifted and talented. Rather, these standards should be part of all teacher preparation programs and professional development for all teachers. More than funding, it is important that state legislators, administrators, and teachers understand how to meet the needs of children through systemic change that addresses the needs of all children in the classroom.

Education Leaders and Administrators

Those who are responsible for establishing funding allocations, assuming school management, providing instructional leadership, and facilitating reforms to raise student achievement, have the influence to make systemic changes to how the needs of children who are gifted and talented are educated. First, early entry into kindergarten must be allowed. Currently, most states base kindergarten entry solely on age. Second, in early and middle grades, children who demonstrate academic prowess across subject areas should be allowed to skip grades so that their academic needs are appropriately met. In addition, those children who are gifted in specific areas should receive subject-matter acceleration. Third, high school students should have opportunities to participate in advanced placement courses or dually enroll in high school and university coursework. Funding for these practices is minimal. Any additional funding should be spent on reduction in classroom teacher–student ratios.

These acceleration practices must be led and facilitated by state and district administrators. It should be common, not exceptional practice, for those children who would benefit from acceleration to have the opportunity to do so.

The research strongly squelches the misinformation about acceleration being detrimental to the social-emotional growth of gifted individuals, an old argument for not accelerating children. Therefore, education leaders and administrators need to support and facilitate acceleration. Ultimately, they need to provide teachers with the tools and time needed to implement best practices in classroom pedagogy to fully realize best practices in gifted education.

Classroom Teachers

School leaders should also support and assist classroom teachers as they implement practices that will benefit all children in the classroom while supporting the intellectual growth and development needs of children who are gifted. Teachers need time to collaborate with one another, access high and low tech resources, and obtain information about ways in which the curriculum can be enriched and studied in depth.

With regard to acceleration, early and middle grade teachers need opportunities to learn how to universally design curricula so that all children can access the curriculum content and engage with it in various ways. Pedagogical skills such as curriculum compacting (eliminating repetitious work that has been mastered to provide content acceleration and enrichment) and telescoping curricula (allowing students to complete curricula in less time, e.g., doing Grades 7, 8, 9, and 10 in 3 years instead of 4) should be part of on-site teacher professional development. At the minimum, teachers must be able to understand content knowledge themselves and differentiate curricula to provide multiple ways for children to access information and make sense of ideas. Many curricular models support the learning and cognitive needs of children who are gifted, but as Joyce VanTassel-Baska and Elissa F. Brown (2007) assert, the level of commitment by the administrators and teachers involved with the student determines effectiveness.

Teacher Education Programs

Commitment to teaching children who are gifted can be fostered in teacher education programs. If teachers do not believe that children who are gifted have varied learning needs, they will not make an effort to accommodate those students. Although most preservice teacher education programs present information about identifying and serving children with disabilities, little is typically taught about working with gifted learners in undergraduate coursework. Thus, given the job of teaching in a general classroom with learners who have special needs along a broad spectrum is overwhelming when preservice teachers practice in the field. Therefore, to become effective teachers in general education classrooms, university teacher education coursework should include content related to the needs of and practice in pedagogy for gifted learners. Minimum preservice learning should include a thorough understanding of child and adolescent development and its variations, knowledge of the nature of intellectual giftedness, the special social-emotional characteristics of highly gifted individuals, ideas for flexible grouping, and strategies for differentiating instruction and providing in-depth study in the general classroom.

This knowledge is particularly important in the realm of curriculum building. As Renzulli (2010) pointed out at the keynote address for the National Association for Gifted Children 2010 conference, there are curricula that are built to fit children into, and there are curricula that assess children's abilities, interests, and learning preferences to build the curricula around children. Consider how this second concept fits into the general education classroom and how recognizing, developing, and nurturing the abilities and talents of all children can establish a pattern of successful learning that can continue throughout children's lives.

CONCLUSION

It is the responsibility of school districts to provide, and pay for, an appropriate education for all children. States should mandate gifted education and provide training and professional development necessary for teachers to serve children within the district through acceleration and classroom pedagogy because this is how the needs of children who are gifted will be met on the school district's "shoestring" budget. It is important that all children participate in engaging experiences that set in motion a lifetime of learning where their abilities are nurtured and their diverse interests are respected. Acceleration should be standard practice and state funds should support the education of gifted learners by reducing classroom size and putting supports in place for the general education teacher to design curricula that meets the needs of all learners in the classroom.

Response to the Counterpoint Essay

Nicola A. Alexander makes a compelling argument for funding gifted education based on *implicit* commitments. Although mandates for gifted education do acknowledge that children who are gifted and talented require additional services for them to receive an appropriate education, the resource–cost approach to addressing this mandate is not one that is specific to gifted education nor does it consider the quality and value-added aspects of gifted programming when it is provided. Thus, even if programs are funded, are they effective? It is, however, as, Alexander states, a fairness issue directly related to a standards-based view of education. Academic rigor for *all* students is what is needed for children to be ready for college. An adequate system of education lacks the rigor necessary to meet the needs of *most* children, much less those who are gifted and talented. Fairness in educational funding, then, is a misdirected issue when only targeted to gifted education. Until states focus on supporting teachers as they build curricula around all the children they educate within academic environments that are universally designed to stretch the intellect, it is as Alexander points out, unfair, especially in the poorer school districts. Adequate systems are antiquated. States should require and fund excellence for all, a message inherent in providing public education and a decree that is inappropriately measured and rewarded. An unintended outcome from educational systems that actually *educate* children instead of training them up to standards might be more individuals performing at high levels and less need for specialized programming.

FURTHER READINGS AND RESOURCES

American Educational Research Association (AERA). (2004, Fall). Closing the gap: High achievement for students of color. *Research Points: Essential Information for Education Policy, 2*(3), 1–4.

Baker, B. D. (2001). Gifted children in the current policy and fiscal context of public education: A national snapshot and state-level equity analysis of Texas. *Educational Evaluation and Policy Analysis, 23*(3), 229–250.

Baker, B. D., & Friedman-Nimz, R. (2004). State policies and equal opportunity: The example of gifted education. *Educational Evaluation and Policy Analysis, 26,* 39–64.

Brown, E., Avery, L., VanTassel-Baska, J., Worley, B., & Stambaugh, T. (2006, September 22). A five-state analysis of gifted education policies (Legislation and policies: Effects on the gifted). *Roeper Review, 29*(1), 11–23.

Clinkenbeard, P. R., Kolloff, P. B., & Lord, E. W. (2007). *A guide to state policies in gifted education.* Washington, DC: National Association for Gifted Children.

Colangelo, N., Assouline, S. G., & Gross, M .U. M. (2004). *A nation deceived: How schools hold back America's brightest students.* Iowa City, IA: The Connie Belin & Jacqueline N. Blank International Center for Gifted Education and Talent Development.

Delcourt, M. A. B., Cornell, D. G., & Goldberg, M. D. (2007). Cognitive and affective learning outcomes of gifted elementary school students. *Gifted Child Quarterly, 51,* 359–381.

Feldhusen, J. F., & Moon, S. M. (1992). Grouping gifted students: Issues and concerns. *Gifted Child Quarterly, 36,* 63–67.

Herrington, C. D., & Weider, V. (2001). Equity, adequacy and vouchers: Past and present school finance litigation in Florida. *Journal of Education Finance, 21,* 517–534.

Jennings, J. (2010/2011). The policy and politics of rewriting the nation's main education law. *Kappan, 92*(4), 44–49.

Kulik, J. A., & Kulik, C. C. (1992). Meta-analytic findings on grouping programs. *Gifted Child Quarterly, 36*(2), 73–77.

Marland, S. P., Jr. (1972). *Education of the gifted and talented: Report to the Congress of the United States by the U.S. Commissioner of Education and background papers submitted to the U.S. Office of Education* (2 vols.) (Government Documents Y4.L 11/2: G36). Washington, DC: U.S. Government Printing Office.

Purcell, J. H. (1992). Programs for the gifted in a state without a mandate: An "endangered species." *Roeper Review, 15*(2), 93–99.

Renzulli, J. S. (2010). *The gifted empire strikes back: Reexamining the role gifted education can play in the twenty-first century.* Retrieved January 30, 2011, from http://www.gifted.uconn.edu/nagc/NAGC_2010_Keynote_The_Gifted_Empire_Strikes_Back.pdf

Renzulli, J. S., Leppien, J. H., & Hays, T. S. (2000). *The multiple menu model: A practical guide for developing differentiated curriculum.* Mansfield Center, CT: Creative Learning Press.

Reschovsky, A., & Imazeki, J. (2001). Achieving educational adequacy through school finance reform. *Journal of Education Finance, 26,* 373–396.

Robinson, A., Shore, B. M., & Enersen, D. L. (2006). *Best practices in gifted education: An evidence-based guide.* Waco, TX: Prufrock Press.

U.S. Department of Education, National Center for Education Statistics. (2010). *Revenues for public elementary and secondary schools, by source of funds: Selected years, 1919–20 through 2007–08.* Retrieved from http://nces.ed.gov/programs/digest/d10/tables/dt10_180.asp

VanTassel-Baska, J., & Brown, E. F. (2007). Toward best practice: An analysis of the efficacy of curriculum models in gifted education. *Gifted Child Quarterly, 51*(4), 342–358.

VanTassel-Baska, J., & Stambaugh, T. (2005). Challenges and possibilities for serving gifted learners in the regular classroom. *Theory Into Practice, 44*(3), 211–217.

COURT CASES AND STATUTES

Elementary and Secondary Education Act (ESEA) of 1965, 20 U.S.C. §§ 6301 *et seq.*

Should schools base teacher salaries on student performance?

POINT: Janet R. Decker, *University of Cincinnati*

COUNTERPOINT: Carlee Poston Escue, *University of Cincinnati*

OVERVIEW

Money has always been the blunt instrument of government to solve myriad problems. It is often considered an expeditious solution to overcoming economic and social deficits. It is the buckets of water on the proverbial fires that are always raging in society. The irony is that decisions to spend money on short-term healing are often at the expense of long-term health. Certainly, merit pay is a short-term strategy. Government has never been willing to continually, over the long term, increase pay, even in the presence of productivity.

State legislatures are considering how to use salaries as both a carrot and a stick to address the perennial problem of low student achievement. Many argue that, to stimulate better and more effective teaching, salaries must be tied to student outcomes. Proponents are confident that dangling a carrot in the form of merit pay is the way to reward productive teachers who are moving in the right direction. They are equally confident that using it as a stick will motivate others to start moving or otherwise starve.

As has been the practice for a number of decades now, government believes that if it acts more like private industry, it will increase efficiency and effectiveness in the delivery of its programs and services. Merit pay is one more example of importing a business practice into the public sector.

The challenges of creating a workable pay-for-performance scheme are many:

Creating valid and reliable measures by which to assess student outcomes

Allowing for variables that affect student achievement that are external to the classroom

Improving the teacher evaluation process so that it is less subjective and more consistent

Comparing and contrasting the conditions under which the private sector successfully employs a merit pay system to that of the public school context

Guaranteeing a consistent and sufficient source of funding for the pay-for-performance program

These elements are not easily addressed, particularly in a political venue. A rich history of legislative action mimics private industry with poor results because shortcuts are taken and accurate data are not considered. By way of example, consider two of the factors, valid and reliable measures of student outcomes and an ongoing source of funding to sustain a merit pay initiative.

The No Child Left Behind Act of 2001 (NCLB) relies heavily on only a few measures of student outcomes, such as standardized tests and graduation rates to determine if school districts are achieving adequate yearly progress (AYP). The federal government leaves it to the individual states to construct their own curricula and achievement tests and to define and calculate their graduation rates. Both of these measures are replete with flaws because neither can be adjusted to the consideration of external factors, such as poverty, special needs, English language proficiency, and family education and support. Neither the federal nor state governments are much interested in "excuses." They have set arbitrary limits to how long and how many students with extenuating circumstances may be exempted from testing.

State governments have a variety of methods of calculating graduation rates, but many have inadequate data systems to accurately track student cohorts. Likewise, there is little evidence that states will incorporate other measures of student performance, such as portfolios. Although research concludes that portfolios effectively demonstrate students' acquisition of knowledge, skills, and dispositions, studies have warned legislators and other policymakers that such intensive and comprehensive measures are time consuming and expensive.

It is also questionable whether any state has the political commitment to maintain a stable and well-allocated pool of funds to support the merit pay initiative. Abundant evidence indicates that state governments have failed to fulfill promises of better pay for teachers under other incentive programs. For instance, teachers who are contemplating obtaining their National Board Certification have learned that those incentives are diminishing. Likewise, many states enacted school-based incentive plans, such as Florida's A++ Plan, in which schools receive monetary rewards to distribute to faculty and staff or to reinvest in instruction when their students make gains on standardized tests. The amount of money being allocated for these initiatives has been steadily decreasing in the wake of reduced state revenues. It is projected that eventually they will disappear altogether. Another state promise broken.

Generally, the success or failure of merit pay systems relies on a stable and committed organization willing to make the investment to ensure teachers and students have what they need to be successful. Private industry understands the value of quality inputs to generate desired outputs. In other words, you get what you pay for. Are states up to the challenge?

Summary of the Debate

Janet R. Decker, from the University of Cincinnati, believes conditions could exist that would support a pay-for-performance mandate. First, she understands that a single measure, standardized tests, is insufficient for the task of linking student performance to teacher salaries. She trusts that school districts could individually determine additional measures and develop a reasonable plan for measuring teacher effectiveness. Second, she argues that there are organizations that have adopted successful pay-for-performance designs and that states and schools could learn from them. Likewise, by virtue of these programs, organizations have been able to recruit and retain high quality and productive employees. Third, she hears the cry from school reform advocates who declare that doing something is better than doing nothing. In other words, let's try merit pay and see if it generates the desired results.

Carlee Poston Escue, also from the University of Cincinnati, strongly disagrees with the premise that merit pay will bring about better teaching and, consequently, higher student achievement. She argues that the logistics alone will sink that political ship.

For example, not every school-based instructor teaches courses that are subject to standardized testing, so there is a question about how the district would address issues of equity both in terms of performance and pay for different subject matter teaching assignments. As noted previously, creating multiple measures of student performance, measures that could span the entire curriculum, are costly and time consuming.

Escue also wants to know if the annual teacher evaluation will have a role in determining performance. There is substantial evidence that teacher evaluations are inconsistently applied, personality dependent, and, as a result, suffer from gross reliability and validity flaws.

She further presses her point by noting the role collective bargaining may play in designing such programs, if there is support for them. Protecting the due process rights of teachers may stifle political attempts to reduce teacher evaluations or other measures of effectiveness to the lowest common denominator.

Meeting the needs of the most vulnerable children also challenges the efficacy of pay-for-performance. School districts, particularly those in urban centers, already face extreme challenges in convincing high-performing teachers to move into schools where students are struggling to acquire grade level skills, to survive external factors that affect their ability to come to school and to study, and to overcome extenuating circumstances, such as language acquisition and special needs, that impede their grade level progress and their performance on standardized tests. Once teachers understand that their salaries will be tied to student performance, the only schools attracting highly qualified teachers will be those that have highly qualified students.

It may be that given the current fiscal climate, states may be reluctant to introduce merit pay legislation for the time being. And, as political winds blow left to right and right to left, it is unclear that the political will to enact such legislation will show up at the same time as money becomes available. One thing is abundantly clear, educational researchers will have new ground to explore if and when such legislation does come to pass.

Jennifer A. Sughrue
Old Dominion University

POINT: Janet R. Decker
University of Cincinnati

When a portion of an employee's salary is based on job performance, it is called *merit pay* or *performance-based compensation.* In recent years, some researchers have hypothesized that certain types of performance pay for teachers are ineffective (Springer et al., 2010). Yet, other scholars report positive effects (Podgursky & Springer, 2007b) or conclude that the results of the merit pay studies are inconclusive (Belfield & Heywood, 2008). Thus, it appears that it is too early to make broad conclusions about whether we have enough empirical evidence to support or refute merit-based pay for teachers. Given this inability to make empirically based conclusions, this essay does not present the many conflicting findings from research studies. Instead, it presents three practical reasons why many policymakers, educators, and parents believe schools should base teacher salaries on student performance.

First, proponents of pay-for-performance systems in education argue that it is wrong to assume the only way to measure student performance is by standardized tests. They contend that many additional student performance measures exist and should be explored. For example, proponents have clarified that it may be best to allow school districts to design and define their merit pay policies and procedures.

Second, many other organizations reward their employees for their job performance and have reaped the benefits of adopting a merit-based pay system. Specifically, these organizations are better able to attract the best job applicants, as well as retain and motivate their current employees.

Third, instead of complaining that public education needs to be improved, supporters of performance-based pay believe we should implement this reform effort. This endorsement for performance-based pay for teachers has come from a variety of stakeholders including policymakers, educators, and parents. They argue that only when it is put into practice will we be truly able to evaluate its effectiveness. Eventually, when we have sufficient data and if they indicate applying merit-based pay to education yields negative results, then the reform effort can be abandoned. However, we will not know until we allow initiatives such as this to be explored, and it appears that the time is ripe for this initiative to be implemented and evaluated.

MULTIPLE WAYS TO MEASURE STUDENT ACHIEVEMENT

The first argument presented by proponents who believe teacher salaries should be based on student achievement is that standardized testing is not the only way to measure student performance. Alternatively, multiple measures exist that can be used to determine whether teachers have influenced their students' learning.

Proponents often agree with the opponents of performance-based pay that basing teacher salaries *only* on students' standardized test scores would be problematic. To begin, researchers have identified the cultural bias inherent in many of the tests and have many other criticisms of the standardized testing system in its current form. Thus, many supporters of merit pay for teachers do not attempt to refute the many valid criticisms with standardized testing. Moreover, proponents have recognized that identifying a single measure to determine student achievement is no easy task. A measure that may appear to be fair in one school district may be completely inappropriate in another.

Despite these obvious challenges, as proponents of merit pay often argue, there are multiple ways merit pay could and should be defined. First, student performance could be one of many factors used in determining teacher salaries. For instance, the Teacher Advancement Program (TAP) proposed by the Milken Family Foundation proposes that teachers' salaries are based upon teacher achievements, teacher performance, teacher tasks, and student performance (Solmon & Podgursky, 2000). Additionally, some suggest that teacher training could be one part of the measure. When teachers seek additional professional development, credits, and degrees that are likely to increase their future student achievement, then the school could reward these teachers for their initiative to become more highly skilled at their profession (Center for Teaching Quality, 2008).

Yet, some supporters of merit pay, who think teacher salaries should be based only on student achievement, have suggested that teachers should be paid based on the collective student achievement of the entire school, rather than individualizing each teacher's salary. Others suggest that merit pay should be based on student growth or student achievement over time (Center for Teaching Quality, 2008). In sum, many proponents of merit pay have emphasized that it is beneficial to allow individual school districts to determine the best way to measure student achievement for their particular needs. For instance, if a school must raise its reading scores to achieve adequate yearly progress (AYP) under the requirements of the No Child Left Behind Act

(NCLB), then that specific school could provide increased salaries to its language arts teachers who have students excelling in reading (Center for Teaching Quality, 2008).

Some supporters who believe student achievement should be measured in multiple ways are motivated by political reasons. Specifically, there are supporters who are critical of the increased involvement of the federal government in public education as evidenced by controversial federal legislation such as NCLB. They believe that allowing states and school districts to determine what works best for them is one way to promote localized control of public education. Therefore, they support the idea of allowing local districts to identify which student achievement measure works best for them because it is one way to increase the authority of states and local school boards. However, one criticism of performance-based pay is that it will only be available in well-funded districts and, thus, inequities amongst districts will be heightened (Solmon & Podgursky, 2000). Yet, in response to this concern, supporters have countered that the opposite may occur. Instead of fostering inequities, merit pay programs will allow schools that have high needs and are low performing to actually attract the best teachers through incentive programs (Center for Teaching Quality, 2008). A single measure, such as standardized tests, is not a sufficient means of assessing student performance for purposes of determining teacher salaries. Multiple measures are needed.

USE OF PERFORMANCE PAY BY OTHER ORGANIZATIONS

Many effective organizations outside the field of education employ some type of reward system for their employees based on their employees' performance. These organizations have shown that merit pay attracts the best candidates, retains current employees, and motivates their workforce.

Thus, a strong argument for including merit-based systems in education is to attract the best and the brightest into the teaching profession (Podgursky & Springer, 2007a). Proponents contend a shortage of effective teachers has caused Congress to legislate under NCLB that teachers teaching some subjects must be "highly qualified." Proponents complain that to recruit highly effective teachers, schools need to be paying higher salaries. Thus, the argument is made that in addition to legislating mandates we must also be providing incentives to ensure schools have a pool of skilled applicants for teaching positions.

Moreover, effective teachers can be retained through the use of performance-based pay. Those who support this notion explain that successful teachers face frustrations when their hard work and extra efforts are ignored. When these exceptional teachers observe other fields rewarding their employees through differentiated salaries, then these valued teachers may decide to leave the teaching profession for positions where they feel more appreciated and can receive much higher salaries.

The other side of the debate on applying performance pay in education may argue that we need to help all teachers improve their teaching abilities and not simply provide rewards to a small percentage of teachers (Solmon & Podgursky, 2000). However, supporters of incentive pay explain that when a merit pay system is implemented correctly, it will positively affect the entire workforce. Individual employees are motivated to improve and collectively, employee morale is boosted. Other organizations have concluded that performance-based pay worked to motivate their workforce and increase productivity. Through a reward system, an employer can essentially communicate to the employees who are meeting and exceeding expectations. It makes sense that employers should only want a workforce that is fulfilling its responsibilities. Many Americans receive this type of assurance from their employers and are rewarded for a job well done by receiving end-of-the-year bonuses.

By not applying merit pay in education, however, we are unfairly and ignorantly failing to reward our teachers. This is disconcerting considering that learning theory has documented for more than 70 years that we can increase desired behavior through the use of rewards or operant conditioning. In other words, we can increase positive behavior if we reward it. This is why we are able to teach dogs to sit and beg, to teach dolphins to jump through hoops, and to teach employees to increase their productivity or the quality of their work product. Thus, an argument can be made that if we reward teachers who increase student achievement, we will in turn, increase student achievement.

These long-standing principles of learning theory are already applied in education, but are being applied to increase desired behaviors of students, not teachers. For example, teachers often have reward systems for students who read a certain number of books each week or who behave appropriately in class. Similarly, we hold students accountable for their academic achievement by passing or retaining them from grade to grade. Therefore, some may argue that it defies logic that we are hesitant to apply these empirically supported practices, rewards, and consequences to teachers.

Conversely, opponents of merit pay argue that it could cause contention among employees and foster problematic competition that we do not want in our school environments (Solmon & Podgursky, 2000). However, if implemented correctly, applying performance-based pay in schools should not decrease employee morale. The private sector does not appear to be crumbling because of its use of performance-based compensation. Instead, social norms prevent most employees from bragging or complaining about their individualized salaries and bonuses.

Moreover, if performance pay is awarded to teachers who share best practices with other teachers and who mentor new teachers, then it would actually foster collaboration, not competition (Center for Teaching Quality, 2008).

Alternatively, if merit pay amounts are publicized, then it could even produce healthy competition among employees rather than cause discontent. Proponents state that whether we all agree the competition is good or bad, the reality is that the United States is an individualistic society where competitive sports and free market principles are the current landscape. If we continue to allow our educational system to ignore those who work hard and achieve results, then our best and brightest citizens are likely to choose career paths other than teaching because other careers are more lucrative and attentive in rewarding their employees.

STRONG SUPPORT FOR PERFORMANCE-BASED PAY

A final argument made by those who believe teacher salaries should be based on student performance is that policymakers, educators, and the general public agree that public education needs to be improved. These stakeholders are eager to implement drastic changes to the public education system rather than wasting time complaining that the system is broken.

Specifically, many policymakers, teachers, and parents are enthusiastic about this reform effort. One requirement of the Obama administration's Race to the Top federal grant program was for states to tie student performance to teachers. President Barack Obama and Secretary of Education Arne Duncan publicly advocated for the positives of basing teachers' salaries on student performance (Hunter, 2010). In 2006, Congress enacted the Teacher Incentive Fund (TIF) as part of the American Recovery and Reinvestment Act (ARRA) to foster the development and implementation of performance-based pay in high need schools (U.S. Department of Education, 2010). Additionally, Michael Podgursky and Matthew G. Springer (2007a) found that many states and districts are actively implementing pay-for-performance systems in education or are considering the option.

Teachers, too, have advocated for this reform. One complaint made by some teacher organizations is that the purpose of a unitary system in which all teachers receive the same compensation is outdated. For instance, the Center for Teaching Quality (2008) disseminated a report, *Performance Pay for Teachers: Designing a System That Students Deserve,* that was written from a teacher's perspective. The report stated that teachers are no longer concerned about past issues of gender and racial pay inequities that necessitated a single salary schedule during the early 20th century. Instead, today's teachers would like to be paid at different rates.

In addition to policymakers and teachers, it appears there is strong support for performance-based pay from parents too. The 2010 Phi Delta Kappa/Gallup survey on the U.S. educational system indicated that 75% of parents would like teacher pay to be closely tied to student achievement (Mendes, 2010).

Thus, those who are eager to implement change believe that our democratic society needs to allow for democratic experimentation. By doing so, we are likely to identify some effective ways to improve the educational system and, in turn, the academic achievement of our students. Merit pay is one of many reform efforts that these stakeholders actually agree should be put into practice. Only after we give it a try will we be able to evaluate its widespread effectiveness. Testing a variety of merit pay systems for teachers will enable us to identify the potential benefits of performance-based pay in schools and to identify best practices. Educators already experiment in many other areas of education such as with curricular offerings. Thus, it does not make sense why the other side is so fearful of this proposal. As the supporters of merit pay point out, if we discover through careful, objective analysis that this reform effort is bad policy, then we can and should consider that and alter our efforts. Similarly, if pay-for-performance is deemed to be ineffective, then it can be abandoned. Yet, we will not be able to evaluate the merits of performance pay if we simply do not allow it to occur.

In conclusion, there are three main arguments for paying teachers based on student performance: Multiple measures can and should be used for student achievement. Additionally, other organizations have been able to recruit, retain, and motivate their employees through pay-for-performance systems. Finally, the time is ripe to implement this reform effort.

COUNTERPOINT: Carlee Poston Escue
University of Cincinnati

E ducating U.S. children is more complicated than taking a magic pill or finding the silver bullet. Ironically, most critics of education in the United States always have the quick and easy solution. Currently, merit pay is at the zenith of such reform agendas. Merit pay is the perfect solution: Pay teachers for performance, and the best teachers will rise to the top while the poorly performing teachers will drop away. These critics then put the finishing touch on the merit pay proposal by suggesting that this same model works in the private sector. In a country priding itself on the benefits of capitalism, the free market, and supply and demand, how could merit pay possibly fail? That question is easy to answer:

Public education does not fit within the tenants or theories of a capitalistic model.

PAY-FOR-PERFORMANCE PLANS

There are three basic types of performance-pay plans. The first type is termed *merit pay.* This approach gives teachers individual funding incentives based solely on student performance. Student performance can be determined by a number of criteria, but there does seem to be a trend in the direction of using standardized assessments in core subject areas to determine student achievement. The second type of performance-based plans is known as *knowledge- and skill-based compensation.* This approach still provides individual monetary incentives for teachers; however, it is measured by the skills and knowledge possessed by the teacher measured through supervisor evaluations or teacher created portfolios. Last, *school-based compensation* is a performance-based plan that rewards schools or groups of teachers as a whole. Funds are then divided within the school itself. At times, faculty members vote on ways to use the money. Some reinvest back into the programs or distribute the funds on some sort of scale based on active roles and the workloads associated with the success of the student achievement. Monetary incentives are the most common reward for all plans; however, some plans do use alternative incentives such as prestige and improvement in working conditions.

For the remainder of this essay, the term *merit pay* will be used interchangeably to refer to any performance-pay plans. This is to continue the discussion in a broad sense without getting bogged down in the minutia that delineates between the three plans. Logistically, ideally, and practically, all plans propose to fund teachers based on merit within the education system.

LOGISTICS

For argument's sake, let's say that merit pay is the best way to improve student achievement. A number of logistical concerns need to be addressed. First and foremost, what are the metrics to determine teacher performance? Will the use of standardized tests be part or all of the determination? If so, what of the teachers who do not teach courses that are tested? Do these teachers get merit pay? If the use of standardized tests is only part of the assessment, then what else will be used? Do teacher evaluations get incorporated? Basing pay on evaluations could work; however, another layer of teacher evaluation would need to be addressed. Evaluation reliability and validity would need to be significantly improved before such accountability measures were applied to them. Along the line of evaluations, collective bargaining contracts would need to be significantly altered. Teacher rights are protected in collective bargaining agreements. These agreements would need to protect the teacher as well as appropriately evaluate the teacher. State policymakers would need to amend policy to reflect the inclusion of such new measures and evaluations. This would take an enormous amount of negotiation, time, and money.

Money is the elephant in the room. Funding will be needed to implement any merit pay program—from the planning process to the implementation process to the final pay-for-performance portion. It is unclear how supporters of merit pay propose to pay for the bonuses incorporated into merit pay. In a time when education budgets are being cut and teachers are being laid off, where is the money to pay for bonuses coming from? If all teachers qualify for merit pay, does everyone get merit pay? Once again, where is this money coming from?

The final money component involves grievances. How do states plan to address the increase in litigation that will occur when teachers are dismissed from employment or not awarded merit funds? This nation is based on capitalism, but it is also strongly litigious. Lawsuits will be filed, and states will lose some of the suits. Are states prepared to legally stand behind their merit pay schema? In all likelihood, they are not.

ATTRACTING THE BEST AND BRIGHTEST

Merit pay supporters argue that merit pay is the way to attract the best and brightest educators. The problem with this approach is that the best and brightest educators will not always be willing to risk their own personal financial well-being. Educators will more likely choose student populations that are mostly like to demonstrate improvements in performance. The best and brightest will choose schools with higher wealth, more involved parents, and communities that support and value the school district. Research has indicated that students in more affluent schools may show growth even when the teachers are inadequate. This perpetuates the core problem with U.S. education. Less affluent children will once again be marginalized. Why would an individual choose to teach in a school where students are more likely to fail the standardized assessments, drop out of school, and have discipline concerns? A few altruistic educators may be willing to do this for a time, but it is not sustainable, and the merit pay system will fail the children that need help most—once again perpetuating the status quo and disenfranchising our poorest and most needy students.

Currently, many states that focus on student improvement, specifically value-added approaches, are already narrowing in on the students with the most possibility of improving, thus moving the school or district ranking within the state grading and ranking system. Including performance-based pay will make this approach even more vicious, creating an environment where teachers will vie for class loads comprising students with the greatest possibilities for improvement. Students who have the most need for improvement but are not the most likely to actually improve will have teachers who have not yet figured out the system or are less established within the education community. More often than not, these students with limited growth abilities come from impoverished backgrounds with weak or failed support systems at home.

As a society, while examining the greater good of the United States, it is important to recognize the enormous misstep involved in ignoring a growing impoverished percentage of our collective whole. By focusing only on education for the students who will give the most "bang for the buck," we are in essence inequitably and inadequately educating U.S. children. Disenfranchising these children does not benefit our society and our economic growth. This will fail the nation on a long-term perspective; it will also compromise state coffers in the short-term.

This brings to the conversation an enormous and expensive concern with our litigious society. Equity and adequacy cases are continually brought to state judicial systems, costing taxpayers incalculable dollars. Again, if districts and schools are actively focusing on students with the most possibility of improvement, it can be easily argued that students are not being educated equitably or adequately, thus violating multiple state constitutions' education clauses. If the purpose of performance-based programs is to improve the education of U.S. students, then this approach of schools and districts is failing the education system and all stakeholders involved.

COMPETITION

An additional concern with merit pay is competition within the field of education. Research suggests that culture, climate, and collaboration are essential components for successful schools. When money is added to the equation, competition will unfold. This again is a capitalistic theory that does not mesh well with the educational environment. Teachers will find themselves fighting over students, classrooms, materials, principals, and so forth. This level of competition is not helpful to the students, teachers, community, or the nation.

Another concern with competition is cheating. When stakes are high, desperate times can call for desperate measures. There are two major concerns with cheating for merit pay. One, teachers are put in a situation where cheating becomes something that they would entertain. The temptation may be powerful enough for them to consider and finally participate, thus cheating both the system and the children. The second concern is focused on cheating prevention. For schools to prevent cheating, a system of auditing or monitoring procedures will need to be developed, once again taking considerable time and money.

A by-product that would most likely occur with this added component of competition and monetary gain is the narrowing of the curriculum. Teachers will focus the lessons on improving test scores, rather than on building skill sets focused on innovation and 21st-century needs. The weaker teachers will, in all likelihood, teach to the test. If our nation is intent on improving our student quality and being notable factors in the international community, it is advantageous to train and educate our children to be able to adjust to the rapid growth of technology, innovation, and problem solving. Children who are educated to master a standardized assessment on core subject areas will be limited from the beginning, only growing the gap between the U.S. educated workforce and our international competitors. This will influence our nation's economy for the far distant future.

Finally, does money attract the best and brightest educators? It is simply a theory that does not have much traction in the real world. Studies suggest that money is not the sole reason top-performing employees remain in a position. Top performers want more than a dollar amount. Quality of work environment, appreciation, personal value, and other such quality concerns are imperative for top performers to find value in their place of employment. Once again, this falls along the lines of the magic pill theory. To assume that if we pay good teachers more money our education system will improve is primitive and not really worth the discussion when considering the complexity of educating more than 70 million U.S. children. If that was the solution, then education in the United States would be superior to all and the concern for education would not exist, because the solution was so simple.

EXTRINSIC MOTIVATION

In education, research says that students perform best when motivated intrinsically rather than extrinsically. Based on student performance data, why would one assume that extrinsic motivation is best for educators? Wouldn't the same follow that educators perform best with intrinsic motivation? However, merit pay defies that logic. Merit pay focuses on dangling a carrot in front of the teacher to ensure that the teacher performs better. If this approach does not work for children, why would it work for adults?

Vanderbilt University and the RAND Corporation recently completed a study of the influence of merit pay on student achievement. The research examined nearly 300 schools in Nashville from 2007 to 2009 (Moran, 2010). The study results indicated that merit pay does not improve student achievement. In addition to this research, Mathematica Policy Research performed a study on a merit pay pilot program in Chicago and again found no effect on student achievement (Glazerman & Seifullah, 2010). The study also indicated that teacher retention was not improved either. Interesting to note, this merit pay pilot program was funded by a $27.5 million federal grant. That is a large amount of taxpayer dollars used to have results indicating no effect. Perhaps there are better uses of taxpayer money.

THE BIG PICTURE

Conceivably, the funding used to address merit pay could be used to address the real concerns with education. Perhaps this money could be used to focus on the intrinsic motivations of teachers. Improved work environment, increased professionalism within education, and teacher value are a few suggestions. Teachers should be proud of their chosen profession. It should be an honor to educate the future of the United States. Finland and Korea were ranked at the top for child literacy by the Organisation for Economic Co-operation and Development (OECD). Finland does not pay its teachers more than the United States does; however, becoming employed as a teacher in Finland is highly competitive. The teaching profession is revered and highly desired. One distinct difference between the United States and Finland is that Finland has social health care and low poverty. Students entering the school system are more prepared before they walk in the door balanced with the comparably aged U.S. child.

In all likelihood, the concerns with the U.S. education system are really more associated with our general societal issues. High poverty and inequitable education systems are more likely the reasons our education system is struggling. Merit pay bares an eerie similarity to other education "reforms" that essentially throw money at the problem expecting it to then go away. That solution has not worked in the past, and there is no reason it should work now.

Improving education is going to take more effort, thought, and ingenuity. Education is not a private sector system. Instead of looking toward the private sector, policymakers need to look abroad. What are our national rivals doing? This examination needs to go beyond the education system and look at government structures and incentive programs. These nations are successful because of multiple influences beyond education policies. If the United States wants to improve education, the policy innovations need to reach beyond the

Department of Education. Our economic viability and sustainability depend on innovative policy approaches that reach beyond simple reward systems based on extrinsic awards. National success will require work, focus, and bipartisan collaborations in multiple facets of the governmental structure. Education is complex, and many variables influence student achievement. This is not the time to look for magic pills or quick fixes; this is a time for intense collaboration, compromise, and practical, honest reflection regarding the direction this country is heading in and the direction in which we would like to go.

FURTHER READINGS AND RESOURCES

Belfield, C. R., & Heywood, J. S. (2008). Performance pay for teachers: Determinants and consequences. *Economics of Education Review, 27*(3), 243–252.

Caillier, J. (2010). Paying teachers according to student achievement: Questions regarding pay-for-performance models in public education. *The Clearing House, 83,* 58–61.

Center for Teaching Quality. (2008). *Performance pay for teachers: Designing a system that students deserve.* Retrieved from http://www.teacherleaders.org/sites/default/files/TS2008_0.pdf

Glazerman, S., & Seifullah, A. (2010). *An evaluation of the Teacher Advancement Program (TAP) in Chicago: Year two impact report.* Washington, DC: Mathematica Policy Research.

Hunter, R. C. (2010). Merit or performance-based pay: A look at teacher compensation. *School Business Affairs, 76*(2), 22–24.

Mendes, E. (2010, August 25). *U.S. parents want teachers paid on quality, outcomes.* Retrieved June 23, 2011, from http://www.gallup.com/poll/142664/parents-teachers-paid-quality-student-outcomes.aspx

Moran, M. (2010). *Teacher performance pay alone does not raise student test scores—New Vanderbilt study finds.* Retrieved from http://www.peabody.vanderbilt.edu/ncpi_point_findings.xml

Podgursky, M., & Springer, M. G. (2007a). Credentials versus performance: Review of teacher performance pay research. *Peabody Journal of Education, 82*(4), 551–573.

Podgursky, M., & Springer, M. (2007b). Teacher performance pay: A review. *Journal of Policy Analysis and Management, 26*(4), 909–949.

Rockoff, J. E., & Speroni, C. (2009). Subjective and objective evaluations of teacher effectiveness. *The American Economic Review, 100*(2), 261–266.

Solmon, L. C., & Podgursky, M. (2000). *The pros and cons of performance-based compensation.* Santa Monica, CA: Milken Family Foundation. Retrieved June 23, 2011, from http://web.missouri.edu/podgurskym/articles/files/Pros_cons.pdf

Springer, M. G., Ballou, D., Hamilton, L., Le, V., Lockwood, J. R., McCaffrey, D., et al. (2010). *Teacher pay for performance: Experimental evidence from the Project on*

Incentives in Teaching. Nashville, TN: National Center on Performance Incentives at Vanderbilt University. Retrieved from http://www.performanceincentives.org/data/files/pages/POINT%20REPORT_9.21.10.pdf

U.S. Department of Education. (2010). *Teacher Incentive Fund.* Retrieved from http://www2.ed.gov/programs/teacherincentive/index.html

COURT CASES AND STATUTES

American Recovery and Reinvestment Act (ARRA) of 2009, Pub. L. 111-5, 123 Stat. 115.

No Child Left Behind Act of 2001, 20 U.S.C. §§ 6301 *et seq.*

9

Should state courts adjudicate challenges to public schools' financing systems?

POINT: William S. Koski, *Stanford University*
COUNTERPOINT: R. Craig Wood, *University of Florida*

OVERVIEW

The focus of this chapter is on whether courts should review the constitutionality of a state's education finance system. In other words, are those claims justiciable, that is, can they be decided by a court? As the essays in the chapter point out, in the past several decades, courts in many states have been asked to strike down school finance schemes as unconstitutional and to order state legislators to craft more equitable means of paying for public education. At the heart of the question is a debate about whether courts should intervene in decisions about how states finance public schools, or leave it to state legislative and executive branches to determine.

Regardless of the specific issues raised by plaintiffs, a recurring question in school finance litigation is whether the courts should even consider a claim that a state's educational finance system violates the state constitution. Stated another way, do such claims meet the constitutional requirements for justiciability? For the past 150 years, courts have refused to resolve certain "political questions" because the resolution of those questions was beyond judicial competence. In many states, the judiciary has determined that the constitutionality of the school finance system is incapable of judicial resolution. Other courts have said that concerns about separation of powers preclude judges from second-guessing legislative judgments. However, most courts have determined that school finance claims are justiciable.

As has been pointed out in many essays in this volume, education is not a fundamental right under the U.S. Constitution. Even so, every state constitution has a provision mandating, at a minimum, that the state provide a system of free public schools. Moreover, the U.S. Supreme Court has recognized, "Education is perhaps the most important function of state and local governments," and "It is doubtful that any child may reasonably be expected to succeed in life if he is denied the opportunity of an education" (*Brown v. Board of Education,* 1954, p. 493). Further, the Court has stressed "the importance of education in maintaining our basic institutions . . ." (*Plyler v. Doe,* 1982, p. 221). Thus, free public education must be regarded as a U.S. state constitutional value.

Despite free public education for all being a state constitutional value, U.S. public schools remain ravaged by vast savage inequalities that lead to failure of the public schools. Moreover, because the failure of the public schools is particularly clear in our cities, the consequences of that failure are felt most among minority students.

Although local school districts receive funds from both federal and state sources, all local school districts, except those in Hawaii, raise much of the money necessary for operations through a percentage tax, with the rate set by the local residents, on the value of the real property in the district. Differences in rates and in the value of real property result in vast disparities such that some districts have trouble providing even the basics, whereas others are able to offer superior opportunities. Given the probable relationship between expenditures and the quality of the education received by the students, disparities in funding lead to disparities in educational achievement. Although the states' legislatures and executives have tried to correct this financial inequality, many disparities remain.

Given the obvious conflict between the constitutional value of free public education for all and the funding disparities created by the state school finance systems, courts have been asked to intervene and vindicate the constitutional value of free public education for all by declaring that current systems of financing the schools are unconstitutional. Indeed, as the essays in this chapter emphasize, during the last 4 decades, the high court of virtually every state has wrestled with the question of whether the state's school financing system is constitutional.

School finance litigation has relied on two distinct litigation approaches. First, there are "equity suits," in which the plaintiffs assert that all children are entitled to have the same amount of money spent on their education or that children are entitled to equal educational opportunities. In effect, the plaintiffs believe that more money means a better education, and they have little or no tolerance for any differences in money or opportunities. In an equity suit, the plaintiffs rely on clauses that guarantee state equality and argue that disparities in funding violate the fundamental right to education. The equity suits tended to be the dominant legal theory during the 1970s and 1980s.

Second, there are "adequacy suits" in which the plaintiffs argue that all children are entitled to an education of at least a certain quality, and that more money is necessary to bring the worst school districts up to the minimum level mandated by the state constitution. The emphasis is on differences in the quality of education delivered rather than on the resources available to the districts. The systems are struck down not because some districts have more money than others, but because the quality of education in some schools, not necessarily the poorest in financial terms, is inadequate. In an adequacy suit, the plaintiffs assert that the state constitution establishes a particular level of quality and that the schools do not measure up to that standard. The plaintiffs assume that the reason for this failure is inadequate funds. Although many contemporary cases contain equity suit arguments, the adequacy suit has been the dominant strategy of the 1990s and the early 21st century.

Summary of the Debate

William S. Koski, a law professor at Stanford University and a leading school finance advocate, answers the question in this debate in the affirmative—the claims are justiciable. He makes two points. First, state supreme courts have the authority and a constitutional obligation to enforce state education articles that ensure children equal and adequate access to educational resources and that courts as institutions are uniquely suited to play an effective role in the school finance policy-making process. Second, the four common objections to judicial policy making are misplaced. The issue is not whether courts ought to be involved with ensuring that state legislatures comply with their constitutional duties to provide equal and adequate educational resources. Rather, the issue is to determine the appropriate role for courts and the conditions under which courts efficaciously intervene in school funding.

R. Craig Wood, a professor at the University of Florida and one of the nation's leading experts on school finance litigation, responds to the question in the negative. He raises five points. First, state constitutions are fundamentally different from the national constitution. For example, state constitutions typically authorize the state to do anything that is not explicitly prohibited, but the U.S. Constitution authorizes the federal government to exercise only those powers explicitly stated in the text. Consequently, it is inappropriate to use federal interpretative methods when construing state constitutions. Second, state judiciaries are more limited than the federal courts. Thus, it is inappropriate for state judges to second-guess legislative judgments. Third, the terms used in the state constitutions—terms such as *thorough* or *efficient*—are vague and amorphous. They do not lend themselves to precise legislative or judicial definitions. Fourth, to the extent that there are differences in educational quality between school districts, those differences may be the result of nonfinancial factors. In other words, money cannot be blamed for everything. Finally, school finance litigation essentially represents a dispute over policy choices. The plaintiffs do not like the policy choices made by the legislature and are asking the courts to correct those choices. Such judicial policy making is inappropriate.

William E. Thro
Christopher Newport University

POINT: William S. Koski
Stanford University

When the U.S. Supreme Court rejected a challenge to the Texas public school finance system under the U.S. Constitution in *San Antonio Independent School District v. Rodriguez* (1973), school finance litigation shifted to state courts. Relying on state constitutional "education articles," state supreme courts of late have been willing, more often than not, to strike down state school finance schemes and demand that the state legislatures reform their school finance policies to honor the constitutional rights of children. This judicial willingness to review the political branches' school finance policies has rekindled debates from the federal desegregation era regarding "judicial activism" in educational policy making, as court critics deride the "imperialist" judiciary's intervention in educational policy making. Those critics frequently contend that judicial intervention in school finance policy making violates separation of powers principles and thrusts courts into the complex terrain of educational policy and practice where judges have neither the expertise nor resources to be successful.

This point essay argues that those judicial activism objections are outdated and misplaced. This essay first argues that state supreme courts have the authority and have the constitutional obligation to enforce state education articles that ensure children equal and adequate access to educational resources and that courts as institutions are uniquely suited to play an effective role in the school finance policy-making process. The essay then addresses four common objections to judicial policy making. Indeed, rather than posing the outdated question of *whether* courts ought to be involved with ensuring that state legislatures comply with their constitutional duties to provide equal and adequate educational resources, the better question is *what is the appropriate role for courts and under what conditions can courts efficaciously intervene in school funding?*

WHY COURTS MUST INTERVENE

Too often those who challenge dysfunctional and insufficient school finance systems are left in the defensive posture of responding to state executives and legislatures, not to mention critics and pundits, who argue that courts should not be permitted to veto school finance legislation. This section argues that it is proper and necessary for courts to do so because state constitutions enshrine children's rights to equal and adequate educational opportunities, because legislatures suffer gridlock and cannot be relied on to protect minority rights, and because courts as institutions possess certain advantages over the political branches in the school finance reform process.

The State Constitutional Right to an Education

In our federalist system of government, the U.S. Constitution is said to place "negative restraints" on the actions of the government, preventing it from legislating without clear authorization and from transgressing the rights of individuals. By contrast, state constitutions are said to provide "positive rights" to citizens, placing affirmative obligations on state legislatures and executives to advance the purposes of those rights. Among those positive rights is the right to what might be described as "equality of educational opportunity," an "adequate" education, or a "meaningful" education. Irrespective of the specific articulation of the educational right to be found in state constitutions, all state constitutions (except Mississippi) contain a provision requiring the state to establish an educational system that ensures that all children receive that constitutional right. Whether it is described in the constitution as a "thorough and efficient" education, "adequate" education, or "system of common schools," the legislature must affirmatively establish an educational system—and a school finance regime to support that system—that fulfils the constitutional duty.

But the state's duty to provide a constitutional school finance system is not unfettered. Since the landmark decision in *Marbury v. Madison* (1803), it has been recognized in the United States that because "It is emphatically the province and duty of the [the judicial branch] to say what the law is" and because "the Constitution is superior to any ordinary act of the Legislature," any legislation or government action that runs afoul of the judiciary's interpretation of the Constitution cannot stand. This fundamental principle of judicial review requires state supreme courts to review the constitutionality of educational systems and corresponding school finance schemes pursuant to the state's education article. As the Arkansas Supreme Court put it, "This Court's refusal to review school funding under our state constitution would be a complete abrogation of our judicial responsibility and would work a severe disservice to the people of this state" (*Lake View School District No. 25 v. Huckabee*, 2002, p. 507).

The Failure of Educational Politics and Policy Making

The judicial duty to enforce children's state constitutional right to an education becomes even more pressing when one considers that many state legislatures have failed to ensure that all children receive equal and adequate educational opportunities. This failure may not be malevolent; rather, it is the predictable outcome of institutions that must respond to majoritarian electoral politics and interest group pressure. Although many state court judges are elected, they are nonetheless relatively sheltered from political pressures and can therefore make decisions that are not compelled by the political pressures the legislature faces. In the realm of school finance policy, this political independence manifests itself in two specific ways: breaking the gridlock of the legislature and protecting the rights of individuals and political minorities.

Political Gridlock and Educational Finance Reform

In the wake of the landmark *Rose v. Council for Better Education* (1989) decision, in which the Kentucky Supreme Court struck down the commonwealth's entire system of public schooling, the legislature quickly overhauled its entire educational finance and service-delivery system. One prominent explanation for the prompt and effective action of the legislature is that the court's decision provided the necessary political "cover" to allow such dramatic reform, increase education funding, and even increase taxes. Stated differently, the courts facilitated a result that many legislators sought, but would not pursue, fearing punishment at the ballot box.

This type of political gridlock is not unusual. There are other examples of state legislatures that recognize the need for funding reform but are hampered by institutional rules that stymie reform (such as the local property tax limitations and supermajority voting rules in California); the inability to maintain focus on long-term, complex finance reform resulting from institutional constraints (such as legislative term limits or part-time legislatures); or fear of interest group or voter reprisal. Put simply, the relatively politically independent courts are able to act where institutional gridlock blocks what is widely regarded as necessary reform.

Protection of Individual and Minority Rights in Majoritarian Politics

Although some scholars have characterized judicial review over legislative action as the "countermajoritarian difficulty" in which unelected judges essentially veto the actions of elected public officials, there is a powerful strand of legal and political theory that argues it is the judiciary's province and duty to ensure that minority rights are protected in the face of majority politics that might systematically disadvantage those minorities. Historically, state school finance schemes that rely on local control for school funding and thereby privilege those who live in high property wealth communities were protected in statehouses by powerful suburban majorities. Left without an effective political voice, low income and minority communities could not persuade legislatures to undertake equity-minded school finance reform. Thus, in fulfilling their constitutional duty to interpret and enforce the constitutional right to an education, courts in many school finance litigations are playing their constitutionally appropriate role of protecting minority rights against majority interests.

The Advantages of Judicial Policy Making in School Finance

Beyond the political malfunctioning of the legislature in many states that confounds effective, adequate, and equitable school funding, courts possess distinct advantages, allowing courts to play an effective role in the school finance policy-making process.

Judicial Analysis and Decision Making

Although some may criticize the adversarial process of the U.S. justice system as producing a distorted version of the truth, in the context of educational finance, the procedures for managing evidence and the methods of analysis employed by courts may lead to effective review of school finance policy and even effective design of policy reforms, at least compared with dysfunctional legislative processes. In a typical school finance trial, the judge will hear partisan evidence from both sides, often consisting of complex financial data, expert opinion, and real-world experiences from students, teachers, and administrators. Though judges possess *ex ante* no specific expertise in school finance policy, by the end of such lengthy evidentiary presentations, they will have developed expertise. More important, the parties will have refined and honed their evidentiary presentations to address difficult school finance policy questions. Contrast this process with that of the hurly-burly of state legislatures in which often inexperienced and perhaps term-limited legislators and their overworked staffers do not have the time to consider difficult questions with the same attention.

Then, at the close of the evidentiary presentations, the requirement that judges articulate legal principles and factual findings in reasoned opinions compels judges to decide cases in a rational and analytic manner. Contrast this process of reasoning and decision making with the "sausage making" of the legislative process in which political expediency and concerns apart from sound policy may drive decision making. Although one could not argue that judges are immune from irrational decision making based in prejudice or emotion, the process of judicial decision making is designed to ameliorate those effects. Hence, it is not uncommon to see robustly reasoned, hundred-plus-page decisions supporting judicial findings of liability in school finance cases.

Staying Power

School finance reform is a long-term, dynamic process. Rarely is it possible to quickly marshal large quantities of data, develop sound theories for reform, draft detailed legislation, and begin the process of implementation and evaluation. Given the short attention span of state legislatures that are forced to deal with the latest policy crisis, courts appear to provide the type of staying power required of such long-term school reform. Many judges are life tenured, many more serve lengthy terms, and nearly all are insulated from frequent turnover (though there are exceptions), so they are better able to persevere in the reform process.

CRITIQUE OF THE STANDARD OBJECTIONS TO JUDICIAL INTERVENTION

Turning from the affirmative case for a judicial role in reviewing school finance policy, this section addresses four (sometimes overlapping) objections to judicial intervention.

Judicial intervention does not run afoul of the separation of powers principle. High school civics classes teach us that, in our tripartite government, the legislative branch passes laws, the executive branch implements the laws, and the judicial branch interprets the laws. The difficulty, of course, is that the functioning of our modern complex government is not so neat because executive agencies routinely develop regulations with the force of law, the legislature conducts inquiries and hearings that appear judicial in nature, and courts invalidate legislation and executive actions on constitutional grounds. Yet states routinely object to school finance lawsuits on the grounds that "separation of powers" (or "political question" or "justiciability") principles bar judicial review of school finance policies.

Notwithstanding, approximately three quarters of the state supreme courts that have considered this question reject those objections. Although separation of powers concerns should counsel courts to provide some deference to legislative decisions in school finance policy making, most courts have held that such concerns do not prevent review of the constitutionality of state school finance schemes pursuant to constitutional requirements. Separation of powers is a flexible constraint that only makes sense in light of past practices and some principled theory of democratic governance, so there can be no outright bar on school finance litigation without such prior precedent or accepted political theory of governance that rarely exists.

Courts can find and apply judicially manageable standards. Because state education articles are written in sometimes vague and even arcane language, court critics argue that judges cannot find and apply sound standards for a "thorough and efficient" or "adequate" education. Such conceptual indeterminacy can stymie judicial intervention because reform proceeds without coherence or clear objectives. Yet the judicially manageable standards objection has also been rejected by most state supreme courts because courts are quite comfortable with interpreting often vague constitutional language, developing standards for constitutional compliance, and analyzing complex evidence to determine whether the state has complied with those standards. In traditional equity-minded school finance litigation, courts have relied on varying theories of equality of educational opportunity ranging from strict horizontal equality (treating all students and districts alike), vertical equity (treating unlike students differently, i.e., providing more to those students who need additional resources), and fiscal neutrality (permitting inequality, so long as such inequality is not based on arbitrary characteristics such as school district wealth). In modern adequacy litigations, some courts have followed the lead of the *Rose* court and articulated specific qualitative standards for adequacy, others have looked to state educational content standards (which delineate what all children should know and be able to do) for guidance, but others have simply relied on broad concepts such as the ability to compete in the modern economy and engage in civic life. Whatever the specific formulation, the critics' fear of an unmoored legislature unable to respond to vague judicial edicts or the greater concern of legislatures simply ignoring those edicts have not been realized because legislatures for the most part have responded to judicial orders to reform school finance without widespread backlash.

Courts can play a role in the design and implementation of school finance policy. There can be no doubt that generalist judges alone lack the subject matter expertise to devise educational policies that will enhance educational opportunities for disadvantaged children. Moreover, cloistered so far from the school and classroom, judges likely lack the knowledge to understand how street-level bureaucrats such as school administrators and classroom teachers will respond to judicial mandates in their own contexts. The result may be either outright disregard for unpopular and unworkable judicial reforms or perverse and unintended consequences when compliance-minded teachers and administrators hew too closely to ill-designed policies.

But courts in school finance litigation do not act alone to develop and implement remedial reforms. When plaintiffs prevail in school finance lawsuits, rarely—if ever—does the court single-handedly command a specific remedy. Rather, the court most often sends the matter back to the legislature with specific, though broad, parameters for constitutional compliance. Although some have complained about this use of the "judicial veto," such a remedial process demonstrates appropriate judicial modesty and deference to the complexities and trade-offs necessary for developing school finance policies. Even when courts become more involved with the remedial phase, many have developed processes and organizations to both formulate and administer complex reform decrees. Courts can employ numerous administrative structures to monitor and enforce those decrees, including monitoring committees that may include party representatives, magistrates and masters who may be charged with resolving disputes or tweaking remedial schemes, and monitors who evaluate progress toward compliance with those decrees. Put simply, courts do not go it alone at the remedial phase; rather, they engage in a dialogue with relevant stakeholders, including the political branches, to develop constitutional school finance schemes.

Judicial intervention has been efficacious. That court-driven school finance reform does not work is also raised as an objection to judicial intervention. The glib response is to say that courts are at least no less effective than legislatures who preside over dysfunctional and inadequate school finance systems. A more considered response, however, is that the determination of whether court-driven school finance reform works is a difficult theoretical and empirical matter. How is success measured? Student achievement? Attainment? Are schools receiving more funding? Is money more equitably distributed among schools? Equally difficult methodological questions must be addressed to determine the causal effects of judicial intervention while controlling for the effects of other school reforms, student demographics and demographic changes, and other intervening factors. Given the multifarious factors that influence student outcomes, isolating the effects of judicial intervention is a daunting task.

That said, researchers who have addressed this issue have reached some consensus on a number of issues and continue to disagree on others. A large body of research on equity finance litigation seems to suggest that successful equity lawsuits generally increased overall equity in school finance, increased the funding for the most disadvantaged schools, and created greater centralization of funding at the state level. Little is known about the effects those lawsuits had on student achievement. Research into modern adequacy litigation is much more hotly contested with some researchers presenting data that such lawsuits have had little (or even negative) effects on student outcomes, but others pointing to contradictory evidence of success in raising student outcomes.

What can be said, however, is that in nearly all states in which plaintiffs have prevailed, state legislatures have reformed educational funding systems with at least the goal of improving the adequacy or equity of school funding. Wasn't that the immediate goal of such lawsuits anyway? More important, more recent school finance litigation recognizes that money alone is unlikely to improve student performance unless other reforms, such as accountability and teacher policy reforms, accompany such increased funding. What was once a simple battle over dollars has become a much more nuanced conversation about school finance reform coupled with effective school reform.

A MODEST, APPROPRIATE, AND EFFECTIVE ROLE FOR THE COURTS IN SCHOOL FINANCE POLICY MAKING

Courts have become part of the modern, complex systems that govern our civic and social institutions, and litigants from the political left and the right now freely turn to courts to reform those institutions. It can hardly be said that abstract concepts of separation of powers can or should bar judicial intervention. Rather, the more nuanced approach would be to understand the circumstances under which the courts can play an effective role in correcting political malfunction and reforming the policies and practices of the executive and legislative branches. Nowhere is this more evident than in modern school finance litigation where courts are engaged in a productive dialogue with the political branches to work toward what all agree is the common goal— improved educational performance for all of our children and closing the gaps between those who have suffered disadvantages and those who have not. That is an appropriate, modest, and effective role for judges.

COUNTERPOINT: R. Craig Wood
University of Florida

E very state legislature uses an education finance distribution formula that specifies how the state distributes funds to public school districts. The state education finance distribution formula also controls, in some manner, the amount and manner of local taxation for the support of public elementary and secondary education throughout a given state. The state education finance distribution formula is the manner by which a state legislature operationalizes the state constitutional requirement regarding public education. The goal of every state education finance distribution formula is to provide elementary and secondary education for the residents of the state in an equitable and adequate fashion. This opportunity is provided without geographical, cultural, social, or economic differences among the children of the state. The state legislature does so in combination with school districts. Generally, local school districts are creatures of the state legislature and operate within strictly defined statutes as to operations, taxation, and expenditures.

The financing of public elementary and secondary education varies among the 50 states in many significant ways. Each state education finance distribution formula reflects an array of economic and political philosophies, organizational arrangements, and fundamental financial goals and theories.

In recent years, state legislatures have faced numerous challenges to the state education finance distribution formula over arguments that the formula is not compatible with the state constitutional education clause. These challenges, although historically based on theories of education finance equity, have in recent years moved toward a theory of education finance adequacy. Thus, the arguments have to some extent shifted from measuring whether poor and wealthy public school districts have the same fiscal resources and expenditures to whether all school districts can meet state achievement standards and whether public school districts with greater concentrations of high need students should have a given level of funding to reach these achievement levels. Thus, it is argued that in schools serving high need students, the fiscal resources should be significantly greater compared with other schools serving students who are achieving state standards.

In essence, the movement reflects a political shift toward attempting to use the state courts to enforce a sociopolitical-economic interpretation of what plaintiffs perceive how society should be. This concept is fraught with peril and reflects political and social philosophy rather than sound state constitutional interpretation.

MEASURING EDUCATIONAL ADEQUACY

A great deal of education finance literature examines the various models of measuring education finance adequacy. The models range from evidence-based models, professional judgment models, production or cost production models, and successful schools models. More rigorous studies use all four methodologies to produce a range of targeted expenditures. Numerous studies have been conducted in a variety of states over the years. The various models have strengths and weaknesses and have been conducted with various levels of validity. The concept of measuring educational adequacy continues to evolve and provide information for the parties to engage in better informed decisions. Nonetheless, these adequacy studies cannot produce exact empirical evidence regarding what a state legislature should spend to produce an adequate education for all children within a state. To assume that these studies can do so is a misunderstanding of this area of education finance research. Additionally, one has to be cautious because such studies are often funded by advocacy organizations whose sole mission is to increase public spending on education to benefit a given constituency. Thus, in many instances, these studies are actually political approaches to answering political questions disguised as scholarly education finance research. Lori Rosen Benton (2008) has examined every education finance adequacy study to date and characterized approximately half of all studies as being conducted or sponsored by some type of advocacy organization.

ROLE OF STATE CONSTITUTIONS

It must be clearly understood that state constitutions were designed to be significantly different from the U.S. Constitution. State constitutions were designed for different purposes than those of the U.S. Constitution. The controlling doctrines of the federal judiciary do not necessarily apply to state judiciaries. State supreme courts were designed to engage in a variety of activities that are different from the federal judiciary. Judicial review is generally limited to whether the actions of the legislature are consistent with the state constitution and whether those legislative actions fail to meet a state constitution standard.

When this concept is applied to the funding of public elementary and secondary education, state constitutional clauses vary significantly in wording, scope, and specific detail. Many state constitutional mandates are without definition and are clearly aspirational, reflecting goals developed by the original founders of the state (Wood, 2007).

In addition to this significant difference, the concept of justiciability must be understood for its application in this arena. That is, what is the function of the judiciary? Is it to view a state constitution with respect to its literal meaning or a contemporary interpretation? Thus, the role of a given state supreme court is often ill defined and not understood even by the judiciary itself. That is, the doctrine of what is to be justiciable is interwoven among a host of often self-assumed assumptions. Although the U.S. Supreme Court in *Marbury v. Madison* (1803) clearly assumed the authority to review the actions of the other branches of the federal government, this concept has been noted to be somewhat of a "deviant" one within a democracy. That is to say, whenever one branch in reality becomes superior to another branch, the system as described in the *Federalist Papers* becomes somewhat distorted in its results.

Political questions provide a clear illustration of the question of what is judicable. Political questions, which vary from state to state and among local communities, raise issues that the courts are not qualified to address within our form of government. The issue, of course, is the definition of a political question. Notwithstanding this observation, the amount of taxation, the ability to tax, and for what public purposes clearly lie within the sole purview of a state legislature. Although the separation of powers doctrine is certainly open to question, there can be no question that the state legislature is the sole arbiter of taxation that is, by its very nature, a political question.

Each state constitutional challenge concerning educational financing must be understood within the context of the actual language of the state constitution and the actual operation of the education finance distribution formula. Thus, each challenge becomes extraordinarily complex because of political, social, and economic interests within a given state.

Although numerous courts have addressed these issues over time, various results have occurred. Some courts have noted that it is not proper for the judiciary to overrule the legislature absent actual conflict with the state constitution. Other courts have ruled exactly opposite given similar issues. How can similar issues before different state supreme courts, with almost identical constitutional mandates, result in totally different rulings? This can only be explained by the concept of judicial philosophy. The concept of judicial restraint versus that of judicial activism is the only concept that offers a useful model of explanation. Thus, the model is one of individual court interpretation and view as opposed to a judicial standard or level by which state public policymakers can use. Unfortunately, the model is highly idiosyncratic, reflecting the judicial philosophies of the courts. In reality, models should have predictive validity.

By definition, the plaintiffs cannot define *adequacy* in terms of any universal standard, establish the standards by which the term would be measured, or argue that the state must provide an education at a given level of quality. With rare exceptions, state constitutions do not establish an individual right to education. Courts and many commentators are often confused by these basic concepts.

RULINGS IN STATE COURTS

It is also important to understand that although language in a state constitution may define a high standard, the courts do not necessarily hold the system to be unconstitutional if the legislature has failed to pass legislation to meet these standards. Despite language calling for an "efficient system of high quality public educational institutions and services," as well as language calling for education as a "fundamental goal," the Illinois Supreme Court declined to address these issues, stating, "It would be a transparent conceit to suggest that whatever standards of quality courts might develop would actually be derived from the constitution." The court went on to note a significant distinction between an educational right and an educational goal. The court specifically stated that the state constitutional language was a "purely hortatory statement of principle" (*Committee for Educational Rights v. Edgar,* 1996).

The opposite end of the judicial spectrum is illustrated by the supreme court of Vermont in *Brigham v. State* (1997). The Vermont constitution contained a specific phrase regarding public education, stating, "A competent number of schools ought to be maintained in each town unless the general assembly permits other provisions for the convenient instruction of youth." The court interpreted this phrase to direct the state legislature to "make educational opportunity available on substantially equal terms," and directed the lower court to maintain jurisdiction "until valid legislation is enacted and in effect" (*Brigham v. State,* 1997). In interpreting this phrase, the Vermont Supreme Court went far beyond the words of the state constitution. The plaintiffs had not alleged that the system of public education in the state of Vermont was inadequate. Neither did the plaintiffs argue that the educational system failed to provide basic educational services. Based on the stated constitutional mandate, the state supreme court dismissed the state's education finance distribution formula. The constitutional mandate regarding the "competent number of schools" is clearly stated. To direct the state legislature to create a new state education finance distribution formula is, at best, beyond the intent of the constitution, and, at worst, a clear and creative action beyond the bounds of the state constitution itself. In reaching its decision, the court never defined the term *adequacy* or how the actual constitutional mandate was to be operationalized by the state legislature via a state education finance distribution formula.

CRITIQUE OF CASES ALLEGING INEQUALITY IN FUNDING

Often plaintiffs argue that expenditures are not equal because vast expenditure ranges exist. At least in certain instances, it appears that the plaintiffs purposefully overlook the undeniable fact that many school districts fail to levy the maximum tax rates and thus take in less revenue. Or, in a few states, the school board must present its budget to another agency, for example, the county commissioners or the city council. Often, this party controls the local tax rate and thus local revenues. In certain instances, if the plaintiffs were to have an argument, it would be against the county commissioners or city council rather than the state legislature. Or, one could argue that the argument is *with* the legislature, not in terms of the state education finance distribution formula, but rather the role of the county or city commissioners. This approach also is problematic because often such provisions are found within the state constitution, and thus the arguments become complex and difficult for the plaintiffs. In summation, at least in a few instances, the plaintiffs are not really pursuing the correct party to alleviate their concerns.

Often, plaintiffs argue that achievement variations among and between school districts reveal vast differences. Thus, they argue that the state constitutional phrases dictate that achievement must reach a given level, or at least, the plaintiff school districts' test scores are below a given level. The difficulty of this is obvious: Even when student population data are controlled, achievement varies among school districts. The plaintiffs then argue that the only solution is to allocate more funds to the school districts in which students are not achieving. That is to say, when students of low socioeconomic status are measured by achievement, some school districts achieve standards but others do not. This is true even when school districts are expending similar amounts on per pupil instruction.

Yet, it is argued, low achievement is somehow solely the result of the state legislature's education finance distribution formula. In this instance, certain school districts, with the same fiscal resources as the nonachieving school districts are meeting state mandated achievement levels despite serving the same socioeconomic status students. In this instance, no rational remedy is available to the courts and no remedy is offered by the plaintiffs other than to increase state and local funds to certain school districts that are unable to reach state achievement levels despite the same fiscal resources as other school districts.

Since *San Antonio Independent School District v. Rodriguez* (1973), plaintiffs in a variety of challenges across the nation have presented numerous theories and arguments. When the plaintiffs can cite an obvious standard that is clearly articulated in the state constitution and school districts are unable to meet a minimal standard because of the actions of the state legislature, an argument can be made. It is important to understand that the plaintiffs must prove that the state education finance distribution formula prevents them from meeting the state constitutional mandate. In many instances, if not most, the plaintiffs are in reality unable to show how the state education finance distribution formula conflicts with the state constitutional mandate. Generally, the judicial result favors the plaintiffs only when the court takes an activist role, a role that it assumes on its own terms, rather than exercising restraint.

Ultimately, state supreme courts must decide state by state the acceptable expenditure differences and cost points for educating different children across a given state in each and every school district. Needless to say, this task is daunting, and one could easily observe that the realm of education finance research is pushing the limits of the known methodologies and abilities to produce usable research for state and local policymakers. In doing so, a court must venture forth into the realm of educational policy and administration, which is outside of its duty and expertise. For example, on occasion a court is called on to define a "basic education." Is a "basic education" an entry-level job or one that is highly technical in nature? The answer to this simplistic question is highly profound and highly expensive for the public treasury and the fiscal costs to every taxpayer in the state. Additionally, this question often calls on the court to make judgments beyond the state constitutional mandate.

The plaintiff claims are often presented as attempting to ignore education finance research and to present their perception of what education finance should be. That is, their value system somehow becomes the vehicle by which they wish to have the courts implement their views of society. The courts are being asked to essentially resolve issues that are clearly of a political nature.

Plaintiffs seek more funds while preserving the status quo regarding school organizations, union contracts, and structures. That is, plaintiffs are adamantly opposed to the remedy that would create fewer districts, via consolidation and other services. The concept of having literally more than a thousand school districts within a given state, some of which serve very few students, whereas others are huge government bureaucracies, is by definition inefficient.

Thus, in many instances, state supreme courts are creating constitutional standards beyond those that are articulated within state constitutions. The court then stresses the primacy of public elementary and secondary education over other state concerns, despite the vast array of public needs addressed by the constitution itself as well as contemporary political will and desire.

THE POLITICAL NATURE OF COURT INTERVENTION

In essence, courts in every state intervene in state finance decisions for a variety of reasons. State courts are often overwhelmed with these exceedingly complex state constitutional challenges. The cases are highly charged, are highly political, and exhibit conflict between the various political forces that exist within every state. The questions are complex and not easily resolvable, and remedies are complex and difficult to implement. The courts are being thrust into the role in a political-social-economic debate that takes place without clear and concise state constitutional standards. Often, the plaintiffs' arguments are based on what they believe society should do to meet their personal views. Often these views are simply absent any rigorous scientific evidence as exhibited by education finance research data that would assist the courts in reaching their conclusions.

In essence, the plaintiffs are attempting to implement their political and social quests via the courts while ignoring state legislatures. The state legislature reflects the commonweal; it is the marketplace of the political capital of supply and demand, and the ultimate authority on political questions. Thus, the question and the issues reflect various judicial theories, special interest groups, and what has been referred to as legal and political theater.

FURTHER READINGS AND RESOURCES

Benton, L. R. (2008). *Examination and application of the education adequacy models and studies to the State of Florida.* Unpublished doctoral dissertation, University of Florida, Gainesville, FL.

Hanushek E. A., & Lindseth, A. A. (2009). *Schoolhouses, courthouses, and statehouses: Solving the funding-achievement puzzle in America's public schools.* Princeton, NJ: Princeton University Press.

Koski, W. S., & Hahnel, J. (2008). The past, present, and possible futures of educational finance reform litigation. In H. F. Ladd & E. B. Fiske (Eds.), *Handbook of research in education finance and policy* (pp. 42–60). New York: Routledge.

Liebman, J. S., & Sabel, C. (2003). A public laboratory Dewey barely imagined: The emerging model of school governance and legal reform. *New York University Review of Law and Social Change, 28,* 183–304.

Madison, J. (1788). Federalist No. 48. In A. Hamilton, J. Madison, & J. Jay. *The federalist papers.* Retrieved from http://thomas.loc.gov/home/histdox/fedpapers.html

Rebell, M. A. (2009). *Courts and kids: Pursuing educational equity through the state courts.* Chicago: University of Chicago Press.

Reed, D. (2001). *On equal terms: The constitutional politics of educational opportunity.* Princeton, NJ: Princeton University Press.

Wood, R. C. (2007). *Educational finance law: Constitutional challenges to state aid plans—An analysis of strategies* (3rd ed.). Dayton, OH: Education Law Association.

Wood, R. C. (2009–2010). Justiciability, adequacy, advocacy, and the "American Dream." *Kentucky Law Review, 98*(4), 739–787.

COURT CASES AND STATUTES

Brigham v. State, 166 Vt. 246, 692 A.2d 384 (1997).

Brown v. Board of Education, 347 U.S. 483 (1954).

Committee for Educational Rights v. Edgar, 672 N.E.2d 1178 (Ill. 1996).

Lake View School District No. 25 v. Huckabee, 91 S.W.3d 472 (2002).

Marbury v. Madison, 5 U.S. 137 (1803).

Plyler v. Doe, 457 U.S. 202 (1982).

Rose v. Council for Better Education, 790 S.W.2d 186 (Ky. 1989).

San Antonio Independent School District v. Rodriguez, 411 U.S. 1 (1973).

10

Do state constitutional provisions concerning education establish a judicially enforceable standard?

POINT: Luke M. Cornelius, *University of North Florida*

COUNTERPOINT: Scott R. Bauries, *University of Kentucky*

OVERVIEW

As Luke M. Cornelius observes in his essay, the question posed for this chapter is primarily an academic one inasmuch as decades of judicial precedent that are situated on both sides of the analysis speak to the justiciability of education clauses embedded in state constitutions. Nonetheless, this question continues to vex legislators and courts, and to provoke debate among legal scholars. The two essays presented here are evidence of the passions and intellect that are aroused by the principle of justiciability and its applicability to the provisions for education as articulated in each state's constitution.

A review of more than 2 centuries of U.S. jurisprudence and legal theory suggests that it is the duty and accepted practice of courts to interpret the language of the constitution over which it has jurisdiction. The federal courts manage the meaning of the U.S. Constitution, and state courts decipher their own constitutional documents. What is equally evident from this review is that interpretation of constitutional language is neither a precise science nor a well-crafted art.

However, courts have established legal principles that guide interpretation. Courts are careful to assume that legislatures are acting in the best interest of their constituencies. Courts seek to understand the intent of those who wrote the constitution and its amendments. They rely on the plain meaning of the language, but they may have to contextualize meaning if the terms are open to multiple definitions.

The application of these principles over time does result in elasticity in meaning, which is troubling for many legal theorists and jurists. If one follows the evolving application of the federal General Welfare Clause or interstate Commerce Clause in federal jurisprudence, one can find multiple examples of how the U.S. Supreme Court has agreed or disagreed with congressional attempts to apply the same constitutional authority to a variety of legislative endeavors.

For example, take the meaning of *commerce* within the context of the Commerce Clause in the U.S. Constitution. Chief Justice John Marshall, in *Gibbons v. Ogden* (1824), declined to limit the meaning of *commerce* to trade or commercial activity. He wrote that its application was for the "advancement of society, labor, transportation, intelligence, care, and various mediums of exchange."

Of course, this is exactly what opponents of school funding litigation fear. They are concerned that the interpretation and application of the constitutional provisions for education are subject to judicial whim. They assert that judicial intervention removes constitutional duties regarding public education from the political process, one in which legislators debate, reach consensus, and then codify the parameters of a system they deem appropriate for the state and in keeping with the constitutional provisions. Furthermore, the political process, through state elections, holds legislators accountable if the citizenry perceives that what they have accomplished is inadequate.

Some jurists agree with this appraisal, and, for this reason, have refused plaintiffs' relief by directing them to express their concerns about the equity and adequacy of school funding, or of the state system of public education as a whole, through the political process. These jurists argue that the legislature, not the court, determines the responsibility or duty that the education clauses place on them. The state legislature defines and constructs a system of public education and determines how and at what cost it will be funded. If citizens are not satisfied with the legislature's handling or funding of public education, then the solution is at the ballot box.

Other courts have been satisfied to conclude that the constitutional provisions for education are merely aspirational and require no action from the court. They contend that legislators should regard the constitutional provisions as indicators of what they should desire to accomplish in maintaining and funding a system of public schools.

The tension that arises from these multiple perspectives is healthy. It stimulates meaningful debate and substantial research to investigate whether court activity related to public school funding, desegregation, and other education imperatives has had a positive effect on student achievement and graduation rates. That is, after all, the focus of our interest in the topic, the academic success of our citizen children.

Summary of the Debate

Luke M. Cornelius, an associate professor at the University of North Florida, maintains that education clauses in state constitutions are judicially enforceable by virtue of the fact that plaintiffs have sought and won relief in school finance litigation in roughly half of the states. He asserts, "A judicially enforceable standard is established as a matter of law when a state court of competent jurisdiction assumes jurisdiction of a school finance program and then passes judgment about that program's fidelity to constitutional provisions and interpretations."

Cornelius also questions the logic of making any education clause immune from judicial scrutiny out of hand, given the important role public education plays in the health and welfare of citizens and government alike. Likewise, he does not accept the proposition that courts are ineffectual interpreters of constitutional intent:

> The *Rose* precedent strongly suggests that whether courts can or should define what an adequate or equitable education should be, they are certainly competent to determine when that education clearly and obviously fails to meet any reasonable definition of state constitutional language.

He further argues that there are instances in which a state court has had to protect the expressed wishes of the people—educational provisions that were introduced into the constitution by referendum—when the legislature attempted to ignore or to act contrarily to the mandate.

Opposing Cornelius's position, Scott R. Bauries, an assistant professor of law at the University of Kentucky Law School, disagrees that years of funding litigation have resolved the question of justiciability. He argues that much of the language of education clauses is vague, making its interpretation untenable and beyond the capacity of the court:

> From the standpoint of justiciability, the problem with these terms is that they have no generally accepted meaning and that any judicial interpretation of such terms must therefore inherently be made ad hoc and based on the subjective impressions and policy preferences of the judges, rather than on legal principle.

Bauries also argues that education clauses impose an affirmative duty on the legislature. This means that the legislature should enact laws to create a benefit, in this instance, a system of public education. When a court opines that what the state has created is insufficient, then it is implicitly—or in some instances, explicitly—crafting the remedy by directing the legislature to do more. This invites accusations from lawmakers and legal scholars that the separation of powers doctrine has been breached.

The one result all sides of the debate can agree on is that the states must provide a system of education in which all students will be prepared for the contemporary workforce and for responsible citizenship. Whether the court has a role to play to that end remains unsettled.

Jennifer A. Sughrue
Old Dominion University

POINT: Luke M. Cornelius
University of North Florida

Perhaps the simplest and best evidence that state constitutions do create a judicially enforceable educational standard is that the state courts of no less than half of the states have found in favor of plaintiffs and against state legislatures in school finance cases during the past 4 decades. It is essential to remember that questions such as justiciability remain, ultimately, the province of 50 independent state judiciaries. Although finance experts and law professors may debate legal theories of school finance litigation, a judicially enforceable standard is established as a matter of law when a state court of competent jurisdiction assumes jurisdiction of a school finance program and then passes judgment about that program's fidelity to constitutional provisions and interpretations. After more than 4 decades of school finance litigation, the enforceability of state constitutional provisions should be beyond debate as a practical matter. This is not to suggest by any means that all states and their courts have either accepted this proposition or actually upheld challenges to their specific funding systems. But it is a simple fact that in more than two dozen states, ranging from California to New Jersey and Ohio to Kentucky, the justiciability of legislative school funding programs is, at best, an academic question.

As a preliminary matter, there is in this debate an inherent suggestion that because of questions of both justiciability and manageability, judicial review simply cannot apply to school funding statutes. This is not merely a constitutionally dubious proposition, but as a matter of policy, it also raises troubling concerns. Education is not merely a state prerogative, but regardless of specific constitutional language, it is in nearly all states the most significant of state functions. State funding for education usually constitutes the single largest share of a state's annual budget, ranging from a third to more than half of all state expenditures. To suggest that state funding of public schools is not an appropriate subject for judicial review is to suggest eliminating the judicial element of a state's constitutional system of checks and balances with regard to the state's most substantial annual fiscal enactment, to say nothing of abrogating the enforcement of constitutional rights for potentially millions of citizens.

Here again, exempting school finance from litigation would appear opposite of the general purpose of state courts in interpreting their respective constitutions. State constitutions are both more expansive and specific than the U.S. Constitution. State constitutions contain provisions requiring the creation and support of everything from specific colleges and schools to the preservation of forests and other natural resources. If the argument that state education clauses are nonjusticiable is correct, then so too must be numerous other provisions calling for the creation and maintenance of many other agencies, institutions, and funded programs. By contrast, it is more generally true that where state constitutions confer certain rights and privileges to their citizens, those citizens, whether as beneficiaries, taxpayers, or simply residents, may avail themselves of the courts to enforce these rights. To accept the counterargument is to essentially confer on the legislature the sole authority to interpret the language of constitutional provisions that affect schools and public education. At a minimum, such an interpretation raises serious concerns about the separation of powers doctrine by transferring primacy in judicial review from the judiciary to the legislature. To be certain, state constitutions generally require judicial deference to legislative enactments. But deference does not equate to a complete abdication of judicial oversight or the transference of constitutional interpretation to legislative bodies.

In a more detailed analysis, state school finance litigation depends on three essential variables: equal protection clauses, education clauses, and the legal history and judicial culture of each state. All state constitutions provide some measure of equal protection of their laws to their citizens similar to those provided in the Fourteenth Amendment, although the specific provisions and nomenclature of these provisions do vary considerably. These clauses were essential in the early finance litigation cases. As discussed by William E. Thro (1990), school finance has evolved in several phases or "waves" since 1960. The first of these waves saw a reliance on the Fourteenth Amendment's Equal Protection Clause. This wave was effectively terminated in 1973 by the U.S. Supreme Court's ruling in *San Antonio Independent School District v. Rodriguez*, in which the Court held that the Fourteenth Amendment was inapplicable to state school funding because education was not an enumerated or fundamental federal constitutional right. However, far from ending the application of the equal protection doctrine to school finance, commonly referred to as "equity" litigation, the effect of the *San Antonio* ruling was to create a second wave of litigation based on state equal protection provisions. For unlike in the U.S. Constitution, education is an enumerated and fundamental right in the state constitutions, thus invoking whatever equal protections might also be contained in those state constitutions.

The classic example of this legal principle can be found in the classic precedents of the *Serrano v. Priest* litigation. In 1971, the California Supreme Court struck down the state's school funding system on Fourteenth Amendment grounds. The system in question had been challenged as being inequitable both to school children and taxpayers because citizens in one Los Angeles district were required to pay more than twice the tax rate of those in a more affluent neighboring community, and yet their children still received less than half the per pupil funding of their neighbors. This ruling, since referred to as *Serrano I,* was overturned by the *San Antonio* decision. However, in 1976 the California Supreme Court, in *Serrano II,* affirmed its original decision while substituting state constitutional protections for equity and equality for the now inapplicable federal ones. Subsequent second wave equity litigation confirmed that state equal protection clauses provided manageable standards for determining whether state funding schemes provided for equitable treatment of students, school districts, and taxpayers.

In 1989, a third wave of school finance litigation was inaugurated with rulings declaring school finance systems to be inadequate according to state constitution education clauses, beginning with the groundbreaking litigation in Kentucky in the *Rose v. Council for Better Education. Rose* represents a classic precedent for the enforceability of state education clauses. The Kentucky constitution provided for an "efficient" system of state schools. In making their rulings, neither the trial judge nor the Kentucky Supreme Court sought to impose his or its own system of school finance on the commonwealth. Rather, they examined 177 school districts and found such pervasive inequalities and disparities that they declared the system to be clearly neither uniform nor efficient. The *Rose* precedent strongly suggests that whether courts can or should define what an adequate or equitable education should be, they are certainly competent to determine when that education clearly and obviously fails to meet any reasonable definition of state constitutional language. Hailed as an exemplar simultaneously of both judicial intervention and restraint, the decision in *Rose* operated effectively to provide judicial notice to the state legislature that it had failed to meet its constitutional obligation and resulted in a significant reform of school financing in Kentucky by the legislature.

Despite *Rose,* and subsequent successful third wave litigation, the suggestion is still made that state constitution education clauses are too vague or subjective to be adjudicated by state courts. Additionally, even if such disputes can be adequately litigated, the assertion is made that courts cannot establish or maintain a manageable judicial standard over such complex litigation. Yet recent legal history suggests both of these theories are invalid. To be certain, school finance litigation falls under the category of extremely complex litigation. The decision by many state supreme courts to open their education clauses to litigation has led in many cases to intricate and highly technical trials, ongoing court oversight and jurisdiction, and even decades of serial lawsuits. Nonetheless, the successful legal invocation of the specific language of state education clauses for 4 decades indicates that individual state courts have overcome this presumption. Indeed, it can be easily asserted that the definition and interpretation of constitutional language is the proper and essential work of the courts. U.S. courts are called on every day to interpret and apply the meanings of words such as *adequate, good faith, probable,* and the oft-debated *reasonable.* Accordingly, is it any less reasonable to submit to judicial review terms such as *uniform, efficient, thorough, adequate, high quality,* or *paramount?*

Erica Grubb (1974) and Gershon Ratner (1985) have suggested that such terms can be effectively defined and applied, and they have even suggested that state education clauses can be categorized by their language and effect. Category I clauses are those that simply mandate the creation of a system of schools with no mention of quality or specific form. Category II clauses are those that set some conditional level of quality or provision, such as "uniform schools" on a funding system. A Category III is proposed where school systems might be defined by achieving a specific purpose or outcome. Category IV clauses establish some explicit language that adds a qualitative imperative to the clause, such as making public education a "paramount" or "fundamental" function of the state. It can be suggested that state courts presiding over this last category of education clauses are implicitly charged with the responsibility to remind legislatures of their constitutional duty to provide for the schools above all other priorities. Furthermore, an additional category of education clauses explicitly authorizes their legislatures to solely define measures of educational adequacy. States such as Virginia and Mississippi are examples of such constitutional language, and noticeably, neither has seen successful litigation against their plans. However, these state education clauses offer further proof that if other states truly did not wish their legislative enactments regarding school finance to be subject to judicial review, they would or could adopt similar prohibitory constitutional language.

The importance of language in the interpretation of state education clauses cannot be underestimated or ignored in school finance litigation. Although some may argue that such clauses are too opaque or vague for judicial interpretation, the same can be said for many other routinely litigated constitutional clauses. Again, more than a dozen state high courts have risen to the challenge of both interpreting and enforcing such constitutional phrases. Perhaps the clearest example of the applicability of education clauses comes from the most recent challenge to the school finance system in Florida. In 1996, the Florida Supreme Court upheld the dismissal of an adequacy suit based on an education clause that mandated "adequate provision shall be made by law for a uniform . . . system of free public schools. . . ." In response to this ruling, the voters of the state in 1998 amended the education clause to read, in significant part, "The education of children is a fundamental value of the people of the State of Florida. It is, therefore, a paramount duty of the state to make adequate provision for the education of all children residing within its borders."

In 2009, a new adequacy suit was filed based on this new constitutional provision. *Citizens for Strong Schools v. Florida State Board of Education* has not yet been adjudicated on its merits and, therefore, may or may not represent a successful challenge to the Florida school funding system. However, in 2010, a state court rejected the state's motion for summary judgment based on previous state school finance rulings that had referenced the earlier education clause. In rejecting this motion, the state court found that to accept the state's arguments of legislative immunity and a lack of justiciable standards would in effect constitute a "nullity" of the voters' amendment of the education clause. The court then went on to conclude that the new clause provided sufficient language to render it both justiciable and also to provide a judicially discoverable and manageable standard of review. In so ruling, the court rejected the state's attempt to maintain an exclusive legislative prerogative over school funding and, in the process, rejected the legislature's effort to subordinate the constitutional will of the voters to its own interpretations.

Additionally, there is the consideration of establishing a judicially discoverable and manageable standard. To be certain, analyzing, to say nothing of establishing, school funding programs represents a daunting challenge for any jurist or tribunal. And yet, the courts are increasingly challenged by ever more complex and technical legal disputes, often in the form of mass class actions or fundamental questions of constitutional law. And in most of these challenges, they are able to discern and apply a justiciable standard. Nor are school finance disputes so abstract or arcane to defy judicial discovery and interpretation. In many recent cases, such as those in New York and Ohio, courts have been able to determine with great accuracy fiscal and program deficiencies such as inadequate classroom materials, insufficient media resources, and unmet capital needs. Even in the more difficult areas of educational curricular and program quality, courts can increasingly rely on well-established and reliable methods of fiscal analysis such as "costing-out" studies. Indeed, even many forward-looking legislatures and state education agencies have begun to use such techniques even in the absence of litigation. It is therefore insincere to argue that courts cannot, at a bare minimum, make constitutionally and educationally appropriate determinations when confronted with decrepit school facilities or a lack of current text materials.

The *Citizens for Strong Schools* litigation presents an unusually clear demonstration of the importance of language in determining the justiciability of state education clauses. In 1998, the voters of the state, perhaps without fully appreciating the legal change they were enacting, essentially converted Florida from a Category II to a Category IV state. In the process, voters also clearly instructed the state's courts as to both their authority and appropriate standard to review the legislature's educational plans and enactments. Although other states may lack such a clear evolution of legal standards to evaluate their education clauses, the Florida litigation nonetheless demonstrates the range of possible responses to either adequacy or equity litigation.

It is not within the scope of this essay to fully survey the jurisprudence of all 50 states. Yet, if there is truth in the assertion that each state represents, within the constraints of the federal system, an independent and sovereign legal and political entity, then it stands to reason that each state can and has evolved its own unique state legal system, replete with its own specific interpretations of constitutional language, case law, and precedents. It is therefore, not particularly surprising to find that even between states with similar constitutional language, including equal protection clauses and phrases such as "uniform and efficient," that considerable differences can exist in justiciability and interpretation between them. Although the similarities in equal protection and, to a lesser extent, education clauses may lend themselves to informed debates about judicial standards and justiciability in general, such discussions are subject to preemption as soon as an actual court, and especially a state's high court, decides that in its application of local rules and precedent, it will, in fact, exercise jurisdiction in a school funding dispute.

It is undeniable that in well over a dozen states the courts have, in fact, refused to exercise such jurisdiction in school finance questions, based on a variety of grounds including deferring to the legislature on grounds such as legislative immunity, judicial deference, political questions, or a finding that no judicially determinable standard of review can be found. But it is also unquestionable that in even more jurisdictions, state courts have found a constitutional basis for not merely adjudicating these disputes but, in certain cases, even imposing specific remedies in response to legislative intransigence. It certainly can, and should, be debated whether such judicial interventions in legislative functions are appropriate. But in the face of more than 40 years of litigation and judicial intervention in school finance, it would appear the question of whether state constitutional provisions create a judicially enforceable education standard has been answered at least partially in the affirmative—by the state courts themselves.

COUNTERPOINT: Scott R. Bauries
University of Kentucky

This essay takes the position that the best answer to the question is "No." Since 1973, when the U.S. Supreme Court decided in *San Antonio Independent School District v. Rodriguez* that educational funding decisions made at the state level do not violate the U.S. Constitution where these decisions create educational funding inequities based on wealth, litigation regarding school finance has occurred almost entirely in state courts. In these state court cases, parties have principally relied on the provisions of state constitutions.

Like the United States, each state has its own constitution, and each state constitution contains a provision requiring the state legislature to establish and fund a state educational system. The existence of this basic duty is uncontroversial, but a significant debate exists about a related question—whether state constitutional education provisions contain requirements that courts are able to apply to either strike down or uphold legislative school funding statutes when they are challenged in court. This debate exists against a backdrop defined by the legal concept of "justiciability"—the constitutional and prudential ability of a court to render a principled and legally binding decision on the merits of a case. Justiciability has many facets, most of which are beyond the scope of this essay, but one facet directly related to the question posed earlier is the well-known requirement that, for a court to exercise its adjudicatory function, it must be able to base its ultimate decision on "judicially discoverable and manageable standards."

This facet of justiciability doctrine is central to school finance litigation. Consider the text of a few representative state constitutional education provisions. Kentucky's constitution states that its legislature "shall, by *appropriate* legislation, provide for an *efficient* system of *common* schools." Georgia's makes the "provision of an *adequate* education" the "*primary* obligation" of its legislature. New Jersey's requires its legislature to establish a "*thorough* and *efficient*" education system. Florida's makes it "*a paramount* duty of the state to make *adequate* provision . . . for a *uniform, efficient, safe, secure,* and *high-quality* system of free public schools." New Hampshire's imposes on its legislature "the duty" to "*cherish* the interest of literature and the sciences." A cursory glance at these varying standards leads one to wonder whether they state requirements or goals. The provisions use words such as *cherish, thorough, common, efficient, adequate,* and *appropriate* to define the duties imposed, yet the constitutions in which these provisions are found contain no definitions of such vague terms.

From the standpoint of justiciability, the problem with these terms is that they have no generally accepted meaning and that any judicial interpretation of such terms must therefore inherently be made ad hoc and based on the subjective impressions and policy preferences of the judges, rather than on legal principle. For example, no guiding principle exists to allow a court to know when a piece of state legislation placed before it makes "adequate provision" for a school system. In operationalizing such provisions in school finance litigation, courts essentially have to decide whether the funding of a school system, the programs of a school system, or both meet a vague standard of *adequacy* or *sufficiency,* terms on which reasonable people will always disagree.

This problem of vagueness, standing alone, might be surmountable. As scholars such as Michael Rebell (2007) have pointed out, after all, the federal courts have managed to provide sufficient content to the similarly vague Due Process Clause of the Fourteenth Amendment. However, even accepting this disputed claim, another problem—this one unique to state constitutions—compounds the more universal problem of vagueness. This is the problem of affirmative constitutional legislative duties and their correlatives, affirmative constitutional individual rights. The rights contained in the U.S. Constitution are uniformly what scholars would term *negative rights.* That is, they are rights to be free from affirmative governmental action. For example, the Due Process Clause discussed previously provides an individual with the right to be free from governmental deprivations of the individual's life, liberty, or property unless the individual is first afforded sufficient procedural protections—usually interpreted as notice and an opportunity for a hearing.

The education provisions of state constitutions instead provide for an affirmative duty that the state legislature *must perform*—the legislature must set up, fund, and maintain some kind of education system in the state. Several state courts have read these provisions to provide each individual school child of the state with a right to receive state-provided education. As Frank Cross (2001) has aptly explained, the easiest way to see the difference between these affirmative education provisions and negative provisions such as the Due Process Clause, for example, is to imagine a world with no government. In such a world, it would be impossible for anyone ever to suffer the violation of a negative right because there would be no government to take action to violate the right. In contrast, in such a world, an ostensible affirmative right to state-provided education would always be violated because there would not be a government to provide education.

In the context of *negative* rights and legislative prohibitions, when courts interpret vague terms, the courts establish limits on the extent or reach of otherwise permissible governmental actions. Importantly, a court that finds a violation of a negative right may remedy that violation by prohibiting the enforcement of the legislation that causes it. After such a ruling, the legislature remains free to legislate or not legislate, with the only limit being that it may not validly enact legislation like the legislation that the court has invalidated. Because the courts' role in such cases only extends to invalidating existing legislative enactments, their action in defining vague terms do not cause the courts to intrude significantly on the legislative function of actual lawmaking.

In the context of *affirmative* duties and rights, a judicial decision invalidating legislation determines that whatever the legislature has done has not gone far enough. A court adjudicating a challenge based on the content of an affirmative duty may not simply decide whether the challenged statute meets that duty or not. Rather, the court must in some way convince the legislature to enact new legislation that does meet the duty (or fix the existing legislation similarly). In such cases, courts are placed in the unique position of mandating, or at least encouraging, the making of beneficial law—a position very different from that of prohibiting the making of harmful law. This unique position causes courts, through their interpretations of vague constitutional terms, to define the legislative agenda, and thus to intrude significantly on the core legislative function of lawmaking.

Taken together, then, the vagueness of state constitutional education provisions and the affirmative nature of the duties these provisions impose present an intractable problem of institutional conflict. When asked to provide content for these vaguely stated duties, the judiciary is placed into the role of a general supervisor of legislative activity—what some courts have termed a *super-legislature.* This is because, in applying state constitutional text to school finance litigation, the judiciary must pass judgment whether enough funding has been provided and, accordingly, whether legislative priorities have been allocated properly and whether sufficient revenues have been raised through taxation—all classic legislative functions. Further, the affirmative nature of the education duties means that, once the judiciary has passed judgment on these matters, two practical options exist.

The court can, of course, choose to issue an explicit order requiring the legislature to enact a specific piece of legislation complying with its duty. However, this choice requires the court to pass judgment on legislative policy choices and places the court into the position of making those choices. Alternatively, the court can require the legislature to determine again for itself how much funding to allocate to education, much as it already has under the now-invalidated law. However, the only information that the legislature would have this time around that it did not possess when it enacted the initial law is the knowledge that the initial law is unconstitutional. Thus, if the legislature's new effort also falls short of fulfilling the affirmative constitutional standard, the process might come to resemble a legislative-judicial game of "hot and cold" until the legislature finally arrives at a funding number that the judiciary deems acceptable. Public policy was not meant to be made in such ways.

Recognizing these problems, scholars such as William E. Thro (1989) have argued that the content of a state education provision need not be judicially determined in isolation. Instead, a court may approach its state constitution comparatively and make a general determination whether the state constitution imposes a more or less demanding duty on the state legislature than the duty imposed by other state constitutions. Where such a determination is made, the court may allow for more legislative guidance by giving the legislature a set of comparator states and those states' funding levels on which to gauge whether proposed funding levels are within an acceptable range.

This comparative approach to state constitutional interpretation has many adherents, but it presents interesting dilemmas of its own. The very idea that the constitution of one sovereign entity can be interpreted by reference to the content of the law under the constitution of a different and coequal sovereign entity is highly controversial. This controversy appears in contemporary debates about the use of the principles of international or foreign law in interpreting the federal constitutional right to be free from cruel and unusual punishment. To make the comparative interpretive method the foundation of state constitutional jurisprudence on affirmative education duties accordingly may create its own institutional legitimacy problems for state courts. Even if not, though, the idea that the generosity or stinginess of a state's courts or legislature might contribute to the content of a provision of the foundational constitutional law of a neighboring state seems to fly in the face of the familiar conception of the 50 states as coequal and sovereign entities.

Another answer to the institutional conflict dilemma, first proposed by Molly McUsic (1991) and later refined by others such as Thro, is to allow the judiciary to interpret vague state constitutional provisions but require such interpretation to draw its content from state legislative acts imposing learning achievement standards. The theory supporting this approach is that where the judiciary makes an essentially unguided attempt to interpret the vague, quality-based terms of a state constitution, it is vulnerable to the charge of "judicial activism" in the form of substituting its own subjective judgments in place of the legislature's. In contrast, where the judiciary draws its own interpretation from what can be characterized as the legislature's own interpretation of the extent of its duty, then the court can be seen as merely legally operationalizing the legislature's decision.

Two significant problems exist with this approach. The first is that it puts the cart before the horse to hold that even an otherwise valid legislative action can provide the content of a provision of the state constitution. A constitution—if it is to be called a constitution—ought to be the fundamental, stable law of the land, and the validity of legislative acts ought to be judged based on this fundamental law—not the other way around. A constitution imposes boundaries within which governmental power may be exercised, and where political actors seek to alter these boundaries, they must seek the consent of the people, whether through the amendment process or a full-blown constitutional convention. A mere legislative act to establish a set of content standards that the state seeks to have its citizens achieve during their schooling cannot legitimately form the meaning of a constitutional provision any more than a judge's or governor's whim can form such meaning.

Further, allowing a legislative act to provide the content of the state constitution leaves two equally distressing possibilities. Either the legislature on one specific day when the content standards are adopted is allowed to bind all future legislatures to its conception of what the education duty requires, or each successive legislature may define the content standards up or down based on political whim or will in each legislative session. Neither of these practical effects is desirable from a constitutional perspective. The former effectively amends the state constitution to enshrine one legislature's interpretation of it as fundamental law, and the latter allows for the very meaning of the constitution to shift with the winds of political change.

A second problem exists with the legislative reference approach. The approach itself results from a flawed assumption of what state content standards are. The assumption underlying the legislative reference approach is that state content standards are always minimum standards of achievement—and thus appropriate to adopt as a constitutional "floor" for funding. However, this assumption is provably false. Many—perhaps most—states have drafted their content standards not as minimum standards, but as ongoing goals and targets for instruction. To make these "stretch goals" the minimum *floor* of the constitutional education funding duty, therefore, would place an impossible burden on state legislatures and would undoubtedly incentivize massive legislative reductions in the rigor of state learning targets—a result that few policymakers would prefer. Based on the arguments summarized previously, the newest thinking on the justiciability of the terms of state constitutional education provisions would approach each such provision as a mandate to legislate nonarbitrarily in pursuit of educating the state's people. That is, each provision is reducible to a broad command that the legislature pass funding statutes rationally directed at achieving the goals set forth in the provision (adequacy, high quality, efficiency, etc.). Accordingly, courts should focus their inquiries on whether the legislature has deliberated and has acted rationally in enacting education policy. Courts should avoid deciding whether the resulting legislation actually achieves the stated constitutional goals because this determination requires the courts to define the goals, and thereby to define the legislative agenda. In the rare event that a legislature has acted arbitrarily, courts are well equipped to invalidate the resulting legislation, step back, and allow the legislative process to work properly on its own. This approach would allow courts to fulfill their role to check legislative power without substituting their own subjective policy preferences for those of the elected state legislature.

Further Readings and Resources

Bauries, S. R. (2010). Is there an elephant in the room? Judicial review of educational adequacy and the separation of powers in state constitutions. *Alabama Law Review, 61*, 703–772.

Bauries, S. R. (2011). State constitutions and individual rights: Conceptual convergence in school finance litigation. *George Mason Law Review, 18*, 301–366.

Cross, F. (2001). The error of positive rights. *UCLA Law Review, 48*, 857–924.

Grubb, E. B. (1974). Breaking the language barrier: The right to bilingual education. *Harvard Civil Rights–Civil Liberties Law Review, 9*, 52–94.

McUsic, M. (1991). The use of education clauses in school finance reform litigation. *Harvard Journal on Legislation, 28*, 307–340.

Ratner, G. (1985). A new legal duty for urban public schools: Effective education in basic skills. *Texas Law Review, 63*, 777–816.

Rebell, M. A. (2007). What are the limits and possibilities of legal remedies? Poverty, "meaningful" educational opportunity, and the necessary role of the courts. *North Carolina Law Review, 85*(5), 1467.

Thro, W. E. (1989). To render them safe: The analysis of state constitutional provisions in public school finance reform litigation. *Virginia Law Review, 75*(8), 1639–1679.

Thro, W. E. (1990). The third wave: The implications of the Montana, Kentucky, and Texas decisions for the future of public school finance reform litigation. *Journal of Law & Education, 19*, 219.

Thro, W. E. (1991). The implications of *Coalition for Equitable School Funding v. State* for the future of public school finance reform litigation. *Education Law Reporter, 69*, 1009–1022.

Thro, W. E., & Wood, R. C. (2010). The constitutional text matters: Reflections on recent school finance cases. *Education Law Reporter, 251*, 520.

West, M. R., & Peterson, P. E. (Eds.). (2007). *School money trials.* New York: Brookings Institution Press.

Wood, R. C. (1996). *Educational finance law: Constitutional challenges to state aid plans—An analysis of strategies* (2nd ed.). Dayton, OH: Education Law Association.

Wood, R. C. (2007). *Educational finance law: Constitutional challenges to state aid plans—An analysis of strategies* (3rd ed.). Dayton, OH: Education Law Association.

Court Cases and Statutes

Campaign for Fiscal Equity, 769 N.Y.S.2d 106 (N.Y. 2003).

Citizens for Strong Schools, Inc. v. Florida State Board of Education, Case No. 09-CA-4534 (Fla. Cir. Ct. 2010).

DeRolph v. State, 93 Ohio St.3d 309 (2001), 754 N.E.2d 1184 (Ohio 2001) [DeRolph III].

Gibbons v. Ogden, 22 U.S. 1 (1824).

Rose v. Council for Better Education, 790 S.W.2d 186 (Ky. 1989).

San Antonio Independent School District v. Rodriguez, 411 U.S. 1 (1973).

Serrano v. Priest, 5 Cal. 3d 584 (1971), 96 Cal. Rptr. 601 (Cal. 1971) [Serrano I].

Serrano v. Priest, 18 Cal. 3d 728 (1976), 135 Cal. Rptr. 345 (Cal. 1976) [Serrano II].

11

Should the courts ensure that student expenditures are substantially equal (the equity theory of school finance litigation)?

POINT: Robert J. Safransky, *Nova Southeastern University*

COUNTERPOINT: R. Craig Wood, *University of Florida*

OVERVIEW

Distinguishing between what is equitable and what is equal and how these two concepts interact in school finance may be the best way to situate the question posed for this chapter. *Equitable* is defined as what is fair or just. As a social justice principle, being equitable requires authorities to distribute government-issued benefits and burdens to citizens based on morally relevant differences, such as need, merit, and capacity. In other words, distribution is proportional, not equal, when there are meaningful differences among members of the population. *Equal* means the same shares for all. It requires that all be treated in the same way and have the same opportunities. No individual or group may be denied a state benefit available to others and must share in the burdens, as well. Access must be open to all regardless of differences among individuals.

To fund education equitably requires the state to determine the expense of educating each child based on a number of cost factors, such as grade level, student–teacher ratios, and other programmatic inputs. If the analysis goes no further, then it is presumed that all children are alike in regard to their educational context. Per pupil expenditures for elementary school children, for example, would be equal across the state. This is referred to as *horizontal equity.* "Likes cases" are treated alike.

However, there is another tier to equity funding. The state also should consider costs that are unique to groups of children who require additional support so that they can overcome barriers to educational opportunity, with respect to such factors as English language proficiency, special needs, and poverty, or who have exceptional capabilities that require a more challenging curriculum. Many states construct funding formulas that account for these differences by weighting per pupil expenditures. An additional per pupil amount is allocated based on the number of students in each category, for example, English language learners, and each category has its own per pupil value. Per pupil allocations to individual school districts will be unequal because the districts are educating students with differing capacities and needs. This is referred to as *vertical equity.* "Unlike cases" are not treated alike.

Based on these explanations, it may seem a simple matter for the state to adjust per pupil funding and distribute the funds accordingly to ensure that *all* students have an equal educational opportunity through the public schools, regardless of who they are and where they live in the state. However, this is a fallacious assumption.

Although the state determines the basic programmatic and infrastructural design of the system of public education and calculates education funding accordingly, it does not prohibit local education agencies (LEAs, school districts) from aspiring to do more, to prepare students to contribute to the sustainability or improvement of the region in which they live and may intend to stay. An LEA may exceed the minimum per pupil expenditure to fund the educational programs it believes best serve the community's interests. However, not all school districts are created equal.

To generate additional funds, as well as their portion of the per pupil expenditure that is required by the state, school districts rely on their taxable wealth, which is usually a function of property values. Property values vastly differ across regions within a state, and, therefore, so does the ability of individual school districts to generate additional revenues for education (leeway funds). Poorer districts, those with less taxable wealth, must tax at a higher rate to generate the same amount of revenue as a wealthier district generates. This seems counterintuitive to notions of equity and equality.

The debate begins on this point. The authors argue the merits and shortcomings of requiring equalization of education funding in response to concerns that the relative taxable wealth of individual school districts should not be the primary determinant in educational programming.

Summary of the Debate

Robert J. Safransky, an adjunct professor with Nova Southeastern University, employs constitutional arguments to underpin his assertion that per pupil expenditures should be equal across the state and within each school district. He reasons that each state's constitution, through its provisions for public education, places an affirmative duty on the legislature to provide for a system of public schools that affords all students an equal educational opportunity. Disparate funding at the local level undermines the constitutional intent that all children receive equal educational opportunity; he alleges it is their right.

He also asserts that state equal protection guarantees require equalization in education funding. He considers disparities in funding based on local wealth as arbitrary and irrational, and therefore, a violation of equal protection of a constitutional right.

R. Craig Wood, a professor at the University of Florida, argues that local control is essential for building educational opportunity on the foundation that the state provides. To require LEAs to limit their spending to a state-determined per pupil expenditure would result in discouraging "initiative, higher education standards, and experimentation."

Wood also worries that stifling educational innovation or otherwise restraining educational opportunity by limiting funding at the local level might well result in wealthier families seeking alternative educational venues for their children, such as private academies. He suggests that this defeats one of the historical and philosophical purposes of public education—to bring children from across society's spectrum together for a common purpose, to study and learn together, which in turn results in understanding and tolerating differences among groups of people.

Among other points, Wood also warns that there is no linear relationship between the amount of investment and student achievement. He notes, "The concept of educational productivity is vast and remains unclear." It may not be wise to attach equalization of funding to the goal of increasing student achievement.

Of course, one could argue that the problem is not one of equalization, but of the state determining the correct funding level to meet political expectations with respect to increasing graduation rates and preparing students for postsecondary education. Perhaps the problem is that governments at all levels set their sights too low. If state funding were adequate to produce the innovation and opportunities we all claim we want for all children, then wealthy families would have no excuse for leaving public schools, and the state's neediest students would have the support and educational opportunities they deserve. Then perhaps the sound bite "a world-class education" would carry some hope and meaning.

Jennifer A. Sughrue
Old Dominion University

POINT: Robert J. Safransky
Nova Southeastern University

The expenditure of taxpayer dollars on public education has resulted in long and contentious debates from the very beginning of public education in the United States. The Old Deluder Satan Act of 1647, enacted by early Puritans in the Massachusetts Bay Colony, required the townspeople to fund the education of the town's youth. Specifically, the law required towns that had at least 50 but no more than 99 households to provide instruction in reading and writing to children within the town. Larger towns—those that had 100 households or more—were required to establish grammar schools whose goal was to prepare children for the universities. A main purpose of the law, from which its name derives, was to battle Satan's attempts to keep people ignorant of the scriptures.

Although the Massachusetts statute mandated the establishment of schools, it did not make attendance compulsory. Children's attendance was strictly up to parental discretion. For the most part children attended school for only a few weeks during the winter, studied in poorly outfitted premises, and were instructed by untrained teachers. The first compulsory school laws were not passed until 1853 and 1854 when Massachusetts and New York, respectively, enacted such statutes at the urging of social reformers. Publicly funded schools began to emerge in the 19th century when legislation was passed in several states to require school attendance and provide for tax-supported schools. These early schools, especially those in rural areas, were supported largely through a combination of property taxes and tuition paid by parents.

The differences of opinion in the provision of public education funding reached the U.S. Supreme Court in 1859 in *Springfield Township v. Quick*. The dispute involved the use of funds from Section 16 of the land grant of the Northwest Ordinances of 1785 and 1787. The Supreme Court held that the state legislature had the power to raise and expend tax revenues and that the Supreme Court should not be "called on to interfere with the power exercised by the State legislature." This closing line would establish the precedent that the U.S. Supreme Court did not want to rule on state education finance cases.

The public schools in the U.S. have experienced major discrepancies in their funding levels, which has led to the failure of many. Further, many of the failing public schools are located in cities, serving a predominantly minority student population. In spite of several lawsuits aimed at correcting the funding disparities, they still exist.

Local school districts, except those in Hawaii, obtain much of their revenue from a percentage tax placed on the value of the real property in the district. These revenues are supplemented with federal and state funds. Even so, due to the differences in rates and in the value of real property from one locale to another, reliance on property taxes results in vast disparities in funding schools. Consequently, some districts find it impossible to provide even the basics, while others, in more affluent areas, are able to offer superior educational services. Since there is a likely relationship between the amount of money spent and the quality of the education received by the students, such funding disparities frequently result in disparities in educational achievement. In fact, because the disparities in local funding have become so pronounced in many areas, it is unlikely that states today would initiate such a system for financing their public schools. While many state legislatures and governors, in some cases under court order, have implemented various ways to correct this financial inequality, disparities continue.

With the apparent variance between the constitutional value of free public education for all students and the funding disparities that exist as a result of the states' school finance systems, it was inevitable that courts would be asked to intervene to support the constitutional value of a free public education for all students by finding that current school finance systems are unconstitutional. Thus, over the last 40 or so years, the highest courts in almost every state have dealt with the issue of the constitutionality of the respective states' school financing systems.

This school finance litigation has been based on two divergent legal theories. On the one hand, there have been so-called equity suits, in which the plaintiffs claimed that all students are entitled to have the same amount of money spent on their educations or, in the alternative, that they are entitled to equal educational opportunities. In essence, the plaintiffs' argument is based on the premise that more money equals a better education, and proponents of this line of reasoning have little or no tolerance for any differences in funding and/or educational opportunities. Basically, in an equity suit, the plaintiffs, relying on equality guarantee clauses in their state constitutions, contend that education is a fundamental right or that the finance system in question is irrational.

On the other hand, are the so-called adequacy suits in which the plaintiffs argue that all students are entitled to an education that meets a given minimal quality level and that more funds are needed to bring the worst school districts up to the minimum level required by the state constitution. The emphasis in these suits is on differences in the quality of education provided as opposed to the resources available to the districts. In this type of litigation, the education systems are not struck down because some districts have more money than others but, rather, because the quality of education in some schools, but not necessarily the poorest schools, is not adequate. In an adequacy suit, the plaintiffs claim that the state constitution establishes a particular quality criterion and that the schools do not meet that standard. Even so, the plaintiffs presume that the the failure is due to inadequate funding.

HISTORY OF SCHOOL FINANCE LITIGATION

School finance litigation has come in three cycles. The first cycle began in the late 1960s and lasted until the Supreme Court's 1973 decision in *San Antonio Independent School District v. Rodriguez*. In this litigation, which was essentially an equity suit, the plaintiffs based their arguments on the federal equal protection clause. Similarly, during the second cycle, which began with the New Jersey Supreme Court's decision in *Robinson v. Cahill* (1973) and continued until 1989, the emphasis was on adequacy suits. However, since *Rodriguez* had foreclosed reliance on the federal constitution, the plaintiffs were forced to make their cases on the basis of state constitutional provisions, particularly education clauses. Plaintiffs were successful in Arkansas, California, Connecticut, New Jersey, Washington, West Virginia, and Wyoming, but the overwhelming majority of the decisions were handed down in favor of the states. In contrast, the third cycle, which began with plaintiffs' victories in Montana, Kentucky, and Texas in 1989 and continues today, has been marked by fundamental differences. First, rather than emphasizing equality of expenditures, the plaintiffs in many of these cases argued that all students are entitled to an education that meets minimum quality standards and that more funding is needed to bring the worst school districts up to the minimum level required by the state education clauses, with the emphasis being placed on the differences in the quality of the education delivered instead of the resources available to the districts.

Second, rather than basing their claims on the state equal protection clauses, the focus of the litigation before 1989, the new wave of litigation was based exclusively on the respective state constitutions' education clauses. To the extent that the interpretation of the education clauses had fewer implications for other areas of the law, this shift in strategy appears to provide plaintiffs with a better chance of a favorable outcome. As a result, if the plaintiffs can prove that some schools are below the constitutional standard and that this deficiency is due to inadequate resources, it is more likely that the plaintiffs will prevail.

Finally, the courts seem more willing to take control of the finance systems. For example, Kentucky's highest court struck down the finance system as well as all statutes related to the public schools and ordered the legislature to design a new system. Similarly, when the Texas Legislature attempted to correct that state's finance system, the state's highest court ruled that the remedy was inadequate and ordered the legislature to try again (*Edgewood Independent School District v. Kirby*, 1991). The future of school finance reform litigation may well rest on an emphasis on quality of education rather than on equality of funding.

ARGUMENTS FOR APPLYING EQUITY THEORY TO SCHOOL FUNDING

Although there are two different theories of school finance litigation, this essay focuses on the equity theory. Put another way, should courts mandate that expenditures are equal or nearly equal?

Quite simply, the courts should mandate equal educational expenditures. This is so for two reasons. First, as a matter of state constitutional law, education in most states is a fundamental right. Although education is not a fundamental right under the U.S. Constitution, every state constitution has a provision mandating, at a minimum, that the state provide a system of free public schools. Moreover, the U.S. Supreme Court has recognized, "Education is perhaps the most important function of state and local governments" because "it is doubtful that any child may reasonably be expected to succeed in life if he is denied the opportunity of an education" (*Brown v. Board of Education*, 1954, p. 493). Indeed, the Court has stressed "the importance of education in maintaining our basic institutions . . ." (*Plyler v. Doe*, 1982, p. 221). Thus, free public education must be regarded as a fundamental right. Assuming that education is a fundamental right, then the state cannot maintain a system where some schools have inadequate funding.

Second, regardless of whether education is a fundamental right, a school finance system that permits vast disparities in funding violates state equal protection clauses because it irrationally creates a social injustice. To explain, as Scott R. Bauries (2010b) demonstrates, education clauses actually are limits on legislative power. In the absence of an education clause, state legislatures would have absolute discretion to create a public school system or to decline to create a public school system. An education clause limits that discretion—state legislatures may not decline to have a public school system. By limiting legislative discretion, the state constitution education clauses effectively compel the legislature to perform an affirmative act—establishing a school finance system. Thus, judicial review in school finance litigation becomes a question of whether the legislature has violated the limits established by the Constitution. As

William E. Thro (2010b) explains, this inquiry necessarily focuses on the face of the statute alone; there is no need to consider evidence. If the judiciary is limited to the face of the statute and cannot consider evidence outside the statute, then the inquiry becomes whether the legislative action is arbitrary. This is consistent with Bauries' concept, "A state education clause, if it is to be enforced as a legislative disability, should be read to disable only legislative action which is arbitrary in its pursuit of the broadly universal goal of a system that adequately educates the people" (Bauries, 2011, p. 364). Thus, the question becomes whether a school finance system that has unequal funding is in fact arbitrary.

Although both Bauries and Thro believe a system with unequal funding is not arbitrary, this writer disagrees. If the legislature knowingly permits a system where educational expenditures are not equal, then the legislature has acted arbitrarily and, thus, has violated both the both the education clause and the equal protection clause in the state constitution.

COUNTERPOINT: R. Craig Wood
University of Florida

The concept of equal expenditures among school districts across a state is one that is found throughout the study of education finance. It is a concept that the vast majority of educational finance researchers and policymakers would reasonably accept. That is, the wealth of the state as a whole should be the guiding fundamental value behind the quality of a child's education, rather than a given school district's wealth, which may be limited or vast. The production of human capital is a worthwhile activity of society as a whole, not that of just a given community. Actually, one can easily observe that the wealth of a state as a whole would benefit society in a more resourceful manner than would the given wealth of a local community. Nevertheless, this concept of equal expenditure has severe limitations. The nature of government and its actions always creates levels of inefficiencies and inabilities as it attempts to respond to local changing needs and aspirations. Whatever the definition of *local control* may be within society; it will always be diminished when a state legislature controls the expenditures of school districts.

The concept of mandating equal student expenditures seems to be most reasonable to many in the general public as well as to many public policymakers. These education finance observations seem to be reasonably well-established goals within many states. Notwithstanding these observations, the actual policy leaves much to be desired and essentially, at least in many instances, creates a system of minimal financial effort by every level of government. Additionally, this policy may actually lower the ambitions of individuals and communities to the lowest common level of desire and sacrifice, resulting in a decrease in the willingness of individuals and communities to commit financial resources to public education. In this manner, the state is forced to make up the difference because there is no local incentive to do anything else. As a result, serious public education finance policy questions must be addressed. Are local school districts permitted to have tax rates less than a given maximum? Does the legislature oversee the assessments of all property within each school district? Does the legislature want to become the final arbitrator of all educational and financial decisions regarding public elementary and secondary education?

These highly centralized decision-making policies tend to discourage initiative, higher educational standards, and experimentation. Further, in many instances, public education is lowered to the lowest common level of desire, which influences wealthier individuals to remove their children from the public schools and abandon the public purpose for which schools were founded. As a result, over time, in many urban areas, wealthier parents, or those who tend to choose higher quality education exercise this decision by abandoning the public schools. Thus, over time, such state imposed polices produce the exact opposite of the intended goals.

When all individuals benefit from a public education, then by definition, society as a whole benefits. Proponents of these one-size-fits-all policies and those who adhere to equal expenditures notions essentially ignore the benefits that accrue to the individual—that is, who benefits from an expenditure or a receipt of a good or service? In education, individuals clearly benefit first, and the initial impact is always to the individual. There can be no debate about this activity. The proponents of this one-size-fits-all notion clearly concentrate on the benefits to society. The notions of societal benefits are ones that must be classified as spillovers. Thus, the proponents of equality are ignoring the primary benefit and focusing on the secondary benefit. Such focus will always be limited and at the expense of individuals and ultimately damage the society as a whole. Our society is based on maximizing the ability of all individuals to be productive citizens and thus, by way of spillover, create a more productive nation.

In essence, to take equity to an absolute level would damage the society the concept purports to enhance. That is, those with money will undoubtedly leave for greater educational opportunities for their children in the face of the inevitable decline of quality given the limited fiscal resources of the public treasury. Those with less educational opportunities are forced to stay in a system that will ultimately produce less, demand less, and spend more. Thus, in the name of equity, society will unknowingly create a subpar system of low expectations and low performance for those who are forced to stay.

Although no serious research shows a negative association with public educational investments, one should also note the lack of a linear relationship. Public education is a significant socioeconomic investment for society. Regardless of the investment, one cannot assume a direct association between the investment and educational achievement. The concept of educational productivity is vast and remains unclear. Nonetheless, the examination of the relationship between resources and achievement yields, at best, unclear observations. What can be said, without reservation, is that the same amount of moneys expended for all children is neither wise nor productive as an investment. That is, are the absolute equal expenditure proponents advocating the elimination of enhanced expenditures for children with mental and physical disabilities?

That is to say, the proponents of equity often define *equity* in the most simplistic terms regarding horizontal equity. That is, expenditures must be reasonably equal for all students. This concept of horizontal equity, though useful, does not address the issue of student needs, student abilities, or student achievement.

Every state legislature has an education finance distribution formula by which it distributes state revenues and allows for local taxes, in some manner, to finance public elementary and secondary education. Every state education finance distribution formula has its strengths and weaknesses. State education finance distribution formulas vary in content and scope as well as philosophical intent. No state has a perfectly equitable education finance distribution formula because the definition of *equity* continues to expand as well as face political and social interpretations within our society. Defining an equitable resource distribution cannot be based on simply an analysis of equal pupil expenditures. Generally, the proponents of absolute equity reflect their lack of education finance knowledge and research by simply stating that the range of expenditures varies from a certain point to another. It is entirely possible that a given education finance distribution formula allows significant expenditures for special education categories, children who live in poverty, children from the poorest communities of the state, and so on. The proponents wish to have absolute equity. Yet, the vast majority of state education finance distribution formulas reflect a variety of legitimate vertical equity adjustments for a variety of student needs. Each vertical equity adjustment designed to serve underachieving populations will, by necessity, create a greater degree of variance within a state education finance distribution formula (Wood, 2007).

Thus, the proponents argue for greater equity which, given their definition, can only be achieved by actually taking moneys away from some children to give more moneys to other children. Thus, the proponents of equity are actually arguing for blind equality (Thompson & Wood, 1994).

If adequacy were the concept of having enough resources to attempt to reach a given achievement level, then equity is the concept of a fair and just method of distributing fiscal resources among the children of a given state. Apparently lost on the proponents of equity is the concept that a truly equitable system does not mean the same fiscal expenditures for each child. Equity must entail a more sophisticated concept of meeting the needs of different children in different fashions. Thus, if a state education finance distribution formula were to adjust for a variety of elements, then expenditures would vary greatly among school districts.

If resources were substantially equal, then the poorest of a given society would not be advantaged. Given the reality of limited state and local fiscal resources, every community will suffer from a lack of fiscal resources. Concerns regarding equity have historically produced uneven results. Concerns continue to be presented regarding what constitutes the equitable treatment of individuals or groups. These questions are often unanswerable within our society because fiscal resources will always be finite and state legislatures must constantly settle for something less than fully satisfactory in terms of political, economic, and social solutions. In essence, one could observe that every state legislature is the market place for competing social, economic, and political interests regarding the funding of public elementary and secondary education.

The definitions and concerns within constitutional challenges have changed from state to state as well as year to year, producing confusing definitions, illusive searches, and often illusive solutions. Courts are often forced to make choices within limited resources, constitutional limitations, and less than ideal public policy solutions.

When the issues of taxpayer equity are examined in light of these solutions, the solutions themselves become even more problematic. That is, poor individuals live in wealthy school districts and wealthy individuals live in poor school districts. The complete reliance on assessed valuations may not actually represent the ability of a given school district to pay the appropriate share. The point is that in many school districts, throughout the nation, the local school board has chosen less than the maximum tax rate in generating its local fiscal share to further complicate the fact that the reliance on assessed valuations does not represent the ability of a school district to pay.

In that several states do not have a state income tax, as prohibited by the state constitution, no income data exist on a school district basis, and no ability to tax individuals who may have greater wealth exists within these states. Thus, regardless of the revenue source—that is, the property tax, sales tax, or income tax—all have limitations within state constitutional restrictions. Additionally, many states have state constitutional prohibitions against state imposed property tax levies, and other similar restrictions in various forms exist, making the concept even more difficult to operationalize.

Additionally, virtually every school district in the United States operates within carefully constructed state statutes involving the ability to set millage rates, budgets, and expenditures. School districts in a few states are created by constitutional actions and thus operate in conjunction with the state legislature. The point of this discussion is that ultimately the taxpayers of a given state pay for all services regardless of the nature of the activity. Each taxpayer has a different ability to pay for services, and pursuant to state statutes, state and local governments tax a variety of fiscal resources. It is also critical to note that the state education finance distribution formula operates within the revenue structure of the state. The state education finance distribution formula does not create the revenue structure; it is operationalized within the revenue structure that is created by the state legislature. Every school district has a different capacity for generating revenue within a given state.

Thus, the operative question becomes one of examining whether the courts have the ability to determine the actual tax capacity of each school district, the ability to pay for each educational service, and the various issues of groups and individuals on both the educational side of the discussion as well as the taxpayers throughout the state. How a court can make this determination beyond the expertise and wisdom of a given state legislature is fundamentally unanswered by the proponents of this equity concept.

State constitutions, as well as state legislatures, vary greatly in the philosophy of funding public elementary and secondary education. One of the most fundamental concepts is the nature of what level of government sets the primary taxing rates regarding the funding of public education. If the state legislature assumes this role, then a variety of minimum foundation programs emerge from this concept. If, however, the primary tax rate is set by the local school district then the educational finance distribution formula may reflect a percentage equalization formula, a guaranteed tax base formula, a guaranteed tax yield formula, or some form of a power equalization formula. Additionally, there are education finance distribution formulas that reflect combinations for foundation and guaranteed tax base concepts, foundation and guaranteed tax yield combinations, foundation and flat grants, as well as percentage equalization and flat grant combinations.

Regardless of the education finance distribution formula model, state legislatures have made vertical adjustments as well as categorical adjustments based on a host of variables including compensatory education, special education, bilingual education, poverty weights, density and scarcity factors, enrollment declines or increases, and weights for various grades and organizational structures.

If the courts are fundamentally interested in equity, then education finance definitions and measurements must be applied to the public policy question. Simply looking at the range, which is quite common, is misguided, and education finance researchers would reject such a simplistic concept. When those in our society state that expenditures should be essentially equal they are actually displaying a lack of knowledge and understanding of education finance research—that is, they either reject or have no knowledge of measures such as the restricted range, the federal range ratio, the standard deviation, the variance, the coefficient of variation, the McLoone Index, the Gini coefficient, and overall observations regarding the wealth neutrality tax yield of the state education finance distribution formula.

If the courts were to determine the exact amounts to be expended for children, one could safely note that the courts have expanded beyond the capacity of education finance research. If the courts were to determine the exact capacity of each individual or community to pay for the same educational services without sensitivity for different children with different needs in seeking perfect equity, then society has actually abandoned the concept of equity in its very pursuit.

Assessing if a state financial aid distribution formula is equitable would require various vertical adjustments reflecting various need equalization factors or cost equalization factors. Need equalization factors generally reflect such things as bilingual and special education. Cost equalization factors generally reflect some form of adjustment for market differences and economies of scale regarding the price of education among various school districts of a given state. Additionally, the most common method of formula adjustment demonstrates a variety of weights reflecting the costs of delivering services to different student populations.

Thus, those who advocate equal expenditures must decide what they are seeking as a public policy. The public policy issue is so profoundly broad and complex as to suggest that only absolute income equality and other more insightful political and economic solutions are the real goals in order to reach socioeconomic opportunity.

FURTHER READINGS AND RESOURCES

Bauries, S. R. (2010a). Forward: Rights, remedies, and *Rose*. *Kentucky Law Journal*, *98*(4), 703–716.

Bauries, S. R. (2010b). Is there an elephant in the room? Judicial review of educational adequacy and the separation of powers in state constitutions. *Alabama Law Review, 61*(4), 701–772.

Bauries, S. R. (2011). State constitutions and individual rights: Conceptual convergence in school finance litigation. *George Mason Law Review, 18*(2), 301–386.

Johnson, A. (1979). State court intervention in school finance reform. *Cleveland State Law Review, 28,* 325–357.

Thompson, D. C., & Wood, R. C. (1994). *Fiscal leadership for schools.* New York: Longman.

Thro, W. E. (1989). To render them safe: The analysis of state constitutional provisions in public school finance litigation. *Virginia Law Review, 75*(8), 1639–1679.

Thro, W. E. (1990). The third wave: The impact of the Montana, Kentucky, and Texas decisions on the future of public school finance reform litigation. *Journal of Law and Education, 19*(2), 219–250.

Thro, W. E. (1993). The role of language of the state education clauses in school finance litigation. *Education Law Reporter, 79,* 19–31.

Thro, W. E. (1994). Judicial analysis during the third wave of school finance litigation: The Massachusetts decision as a model. *Boston College Law Review, 35*(3), 597–617.

Thro, W. E. (1998). A new approach to state constitutional analysis in school finance litigation. *Journal of Law and Politics, 14*(3), 525–554.

Thro, W. E. (2010a). Judicial humility: The enduring legacy of *Rose v. Council for Better Education. Kentucky Law Journal, 98*(4), 717–738.

Thro, W. E. (2010b). Rosenkranz's constitutional subjects and school finance litigation. *Education Law Reporter, 260,* 1–24.

Wood, R. C. (2007). *Educational finance law: Constitutional challenges to state aid plans—An analysis of strategies* (3rd ed.). Dayton, OH: Education Law Association.

COURT CASES AND STATUTES

Brown v. Board of Education, 347 U.S. 483 (1954).

Edgewood Independent School District v. Kirby, 804 S.W.2d 491 (Tex. 1991).

Plyler v. Doe, 457 U.S. 202 (1982).

Robinson v. Cahill, 62 N.J. 473 (1973), 303 A.2d 273 (N.J. 1973).

Rose v. Council for Better Education, 790 S.W.2d 186 (Ky. 1989).

San Antonio Independent School District v. Rodriguez, 411 U.S. 1 (1973).

Springfield Township v. Quick, 63 U.S. 56 (1859).

Should the courts ensure that every school district has sufficient funds to provide a quality education (the adequacy theory of school finance litigation)?

POINT: Barbara M. De Luca, *University of Dayton*

COUNTERPOINT: R. Craig Wood, *University of Florida*

OVERVIEW

Equal protection, equity, and adequacy have been the primary theories under-girding state and federal litigation that has targeted public school funding for a number of decades. Early in the history of funding litigation, plaintiffs filed equal protection claims and applied for relief in federal courts, alleging that insufficient state funding and the overreliance on local taxes resulted in a disparate impact on children in poorer regions. By virtue of where they lived, children were being denied the educational opportunities afforded their peers who lived in wealthier districts. The U.S. Supreme Court put an end to this legal strategy by reminding plaintiffs that the U.S. Constitution was silent on the issue of education, and, therefore, education was not a fundamental right on which federal equal protection claims could rest.

Following this, equal protection challenges were submitted to state courts by plaintiffs who argued that state funding formulas that placed a heavy funding burden on localities created inequitable educational opportunities for students. That is, the amount of taxable wealth in the district in which a student resided determined whether the locality would be able to cover the cost differential between what the state provided and the actual expense of educating a child. Wealthier districts were in the enviable position of being able to tax at a lower rate yet generate considerably more revenue and, therefore, could provide something more than the basic infrastructure and programming that the state was willing to finance. Likewise, plaintiffs charged that significant differences in taxable wealth also diminished or enhanced a school district's ability to fund programmatic and service provisions for students with diverse challenges related to English language acquisition, disabilities, or poverty.

Challenges based on adequacy emerged with a series of state supreme court decisions in Texas, Montana, and, most notably, Kentucky, in 1989. The Kentucky Supreme Court stunned defendants and others following state trends in school funding litigation by declaring that the funding mechanism was unconstitutional and that the entire system of public education in Kentucky was "constitutionally deficient." The court ordered the state legislature to start over and to construct and fund a system of education that prepared students for work and for citizenship. The court went so far as to provide a list of elements that would characterize an "efficient system of common schools." This decision was and continues to be decried by many who contend that the court exceeded its authority when it went beyond its duty of determining the constitutionality of the state funding formula by mandating the remedy, as well.

It is not uncommon today for plaintiffs to challenge state funding of public education and to prepare for and advise the court on the matter of the remedy. Funding cases in New Jersey and New York evince this approach. Decades of court appearances have been required as plaintiffs and defendants argue the drawbacks or merits of the legislature's attempts to comply with court orders. The underlying question, however, is whether the court has the expertise, the data, or the authority to structure a remedy such as determining the adequacy of or ensuring the allocation of funding across and within school districts.

Summary of the Debate

It has long been recognized that two of the primary duties of the state courts are to interpret the language of state constitutions and to determine the constitutionality of state statutory law. The authors here seek to demonstrate the fairness or the folly of a state court going beyond determining whether the state funding formula is constitutional, by virtue of the interpretation of the constitution, and advising the state about the level of funding needed to provide an adequate education or whether the districts have that funding available to them.

In this instance, the court is asked first to decipher the intended meaning of education codes and of education clauses in the state constitution. If a court renders a decision that the state's funding scheme violates the state's constitution, then the second question becomes whether the court should ensure that each school district has the funds needed to provide a quality education.

These two questions are perhaps the heart of the debate. Barbara M. De Luca, an associate professor at the University of Dayton, asserts that although no definitive studies can correlate successful litigation to improved educational outcomes, the alternative—an end to adequacy litigation—is not the answer. The court is a part of the system of checks and balances that underpins the creation of a triad model of government structure (executive, legislative, and judicial). It provides one avenue for those who feel they are being harmed by the actions of one or the other two branches of government in some legally definable manner. Plaintiffs pursuing adequacy cases are intent on holding the state responsible for providing an education that prepares their children for a productive and satisfying future.

R. Craig Wood, a professor at the University of Florida, asserts that the courts are ill prepared to address the complexities of adequacy in education. The existing methodologies employed by expert witnesses are flawed or for other reasons are limited in their ability to determine and correct inadequacy. He also asserts that the legislature—not the courts—has the constitutional prerogative to define and fund an adequate education.

On the one hand, plaintiffs are most often disenfranchised families who reside in poor urban centers or rural communities where there is minimum taxable wealth and who can ill afford high tax rates to provide for the public education system their children need and deserve. They argue that a political solution is not accessible to them. In other words, it is unrealistic to direct these families and others like them to vote for change if they are unhappy with the manner in which the legislature is funding education. They need the support of the court to apply sufficient pressure on the state legislature to adequately fund education. It is equally impractical to simply direct the legislature to do "something" to resolve the funding problem. This often results in decades of lengthy and expensive litigation as legislators tweak education codes and twist funding formulas, often to deflate the plaintiffs' resolve.

On the other hand are the defendants, who are the state legislature, governor, state board of education, or state superintendent of public instruction. They assert that it is within the constitutional purview of the legislature, with input from the governor and other state authorities, to determine the nature and scope of the state's public education system and to assign the per pupil value to that system. The defendants also aver that it is their sole legal responsibility to determine to what extent localities will contribute to the operating budget. They complain that the court is actively engaging in promoting a legislative agenda if it either calculates the value of an adequate education or gauges whether school districts have adequate funds to cover the expense. The defendants argue they were elected by their constituents to legislate and that the court may not usurp their authority to do so.

As pressures build on state and local budgets because of lower revenues and greater demands from increasingly diverse groups, the court plays an important role in meting out justice on behalf of those who do not have the political or fiscal resources that buy them a place at the table. Also, it is short-sighted to disregard the importance of adequately funding public education; to ignore the problem is to invite increased social and economic costs. If state legislatures do not want interference from the courts, then it behooves them to act responsibly and ethically in discharging their duties in providing for an adequate and equitable system of education.

Jennifer A. Sughrue
Old Dominion University

POINT: Barbara M. De Luca
University of Dayton

Although the quality of elementary and secondary education has been a public concern throughout history, the impetus behind the modern-day quality movement was the 1957 Soviet Union launch of Sputnik, the first space satellite. The United States considered this a national insult, a serious threat to national security, and certainly a national embarrassment because the Soviet Union obviously had the intellectual and physical capacity to beat us into space. Since then, much federal legislation has been passed to advance national defense efforts as well as improve national productivity. This myriad of laws began with the 1958 National Defense of Education Act to promote the study of mathematics, science, and modern foreign languages to improve national defense, and includes the 1965 Elementary and Secondary Education Act, which was intended to improve national productivity and morphed into the No Child Left Behind Act of 2001, a comprehensive reauthorization of the Elementary and Secondary Education Act. Though the ultimate goal is not the improvement of education, because public education is not in the purview of the federal government, improving the quality of education is the effect. Improving education quality is simply another way to express the need for adequacy in education.

Although federal laws regarding education exist to promote national security and productivity, public education is actually a state responsibility. There is no mention of public education in the federal constitution. Every state has its own mandates regarding the provision of public education within its boundaries. However, the specificity of the constitutional mandate regarding education varies from state to state. Some state constitutional education mandates are vague. For example, the Mississippi constitution, Article 8, Section 201, says nothing remotely related to adequacy: "The Legislature shall, by general law, provide for the establishment, maintenance and support of free public schools upon such conditions and limitations as the Legislature may prescribe." Some are a bit less vague, but still leave considerable room for individual interpretation. For example, one could infer that the Ohio constitution (Article 6, §2) suggests a possible concern for adequacy in its mandate for a "thorough and efficient system of common schools throughout the state." This lack of specificity and clarity is a major reason the courts have been involved in the effort to define and promote adequacy in elementary and secondary public school education.

More than 40 legal cases rooted in adequacy issues were filed between 1973 and 2002, but not until *Rose v. Council for Better Education* in Kentucky in 1989 were adequacy cases actually recognized as such. This is considered the beginning of the third wave of education legal cases, known as the adequacy wave. Since 1989, states involved in adequacy court cases have seen a variety of outcomes, some in which the claims of inadequacy are upheld, some defeated, and some dismissed. Some experts who follow the legal course of education lawsuits suggest that the third wave of education finance lawsuits has run its course. Actually, there is a long way to go in meeting state adequacy requirements, and the courts can play a major role in this effort.

CURRENT ISSUES

Adequacy court cases have run into several problems recently, but that does not mean the end has come for litigation. One of the problems with seeking adequacy in education through the courts lies in defining it. Just as education clauses in state constitutions vary considerably, so do the definitions used as the basis for litigation. An additional problem is rooted in the separation of powers, that is, the line between the responsibility of the judicial branch and the legislative branch. Courts are concerned about potential accusations that they are making law rather than interpreting it. One more problem to be addressed here is the funding angle. Although plaintiffs often claimed that a state's education funding system was inadequate, more recently they have argued instead that the funds are not being used where they are most needed for school systems to ensure that students achieve at an adequate level. Another argument used for suggesting that adequacy cases should not be taken to the courts is that they are expensive. Opponents of continuing the court battles contend that a great deal of money has been spent litigating these cases, money that could better be spent elsewhere. Finally, opponents of continuing the adequacy battle in the courts claim that student achievement has not substantially improved since the cases began in the 1970s.

The overarching issue is that these problems do not occur in isolation of each other; they are intricately entwined in nearly every legal case. The contention here is that the courts are still a vital part of the process for ensuring adequacy in public elementary and secondary education, but the plaintiffs must reframe their cases in a way that truly addresses the adequacy of the education system, not the adequacy of the funding allocations.

IMPROVED ACADEMIC ACHIEVEMENT

Some proponents of keeping adequacy cases out of the courts believe too much money is spent on legal remedies and that there is little evidence that the quality of education improves as a result of a successful lawsuit. According to the National Center for Education Statistics (NCES), the average scale score in mathematics on the National Assessment of Educational Progress for eighth graders in public schools in Kentucky increased from 257 in 1990 (the year immediately following the court's ruling for the plaintiffs in *Rose*) to 274 by 2005 (U.S. Department of Education, n.d.). Of course, there is no evidence that this increase was caused by the court decision, but there is, likewise, no evidence to the contrary. Average scores in other states increased, some more and some less than Kentucky and, in some cases, there is no consistent pattern in the change of average scores for this 15-year period. The point is that it is difficult to say that there is no evidence of academic improvement as the result of adequacy legal cases.

Those with the greatest academic needs, according to many plaintiffs, include minorities. Although there is no doubt that minority students are not achieving at levels equal to nonminority students in many parts of the country, particularly urban areas, the Condition of Education 2010 report from NCES indicates that dropout rates of 16- through 24-year-olds for whites went from 11.4% in 1980 to 8% in 2008, a decrease of 29.8%. For the same period, the dropout rate for blacks went from 19.1% to 9.9%, a decrease of 48.2%. Again, these decreases cannot necessarily be attributed to adequacy litigation, but they do indicate substantial improvements and suggest something is working. Rather than giving up on existing work, U.S. children would be better served by moving forward and perfecting the efforts currently in process.

COSTS VERSUS COSTS

If adequacy litigation ends, the financial consequences could be grave. As the numbers cited previously indicate, something is "working." To stop now would trigger severe financial consequences. There is a rather common saying: Good education is costly, but poor education is even costlier. Consider the costs that will increase if states are not required to ensure adequacy in their public education systems: public assistance (welfare, as some people refer to it) because more people will be unemployable; criminal justice because statistics show that as education decreases, criminal activity increases; and health care because lower income people are generally uninsured and use public health care. Consider the lost revenue in decreased income tax dollars because poor education generally results in lower-paying jobs (or unemployment) and thus fewer tax dollars will be paid. Economic losses include decreased national income and decreased investment dollars as lower personal income results in decreased savings. Researchers who have calculated dollar values for these increases and decreases suggest that the cost of not providing an adequate education to elementary and secondary school students is two to three times higher than the cost of providing it.

Researchers have had a more difficult time putting a dollar value on other losses, such as opportunities lost because our best and brightest are not given adequate education to succeed. Remember 1957 and Sputnik.

TIME IS UP

Those who contend that adequacy legal cases have run their course and that it is time to solve the poor student achievement problems in other ways need only look at the length of time it took to seriously address education equity issues. The first case considered to address equity, *Serrano v. Priest*, was in California in 1971 and was followed immediately by *Robinson v. Cahill* in New Jersey in 1973. Some even contend that the equity movement goes back to *Brown v. Board of Education* in 1954. As this piece is written, it is 2011, 57 years after *Brown* and 40 years after *Serrano*. If one size fit all or if it were easy to achieve equity in school finance, states could simply add up all the money they have for education and divide it by the number of students. Every student would get an equal amount of the pie. However, all cases are not the same, and the task is not an easy one. It has been only 22 years since the first adequacy court case. Recall that the plaintiffs initially lost the equity case in *San Antonio Independent School District v. Rodriguez* in 1973. If advocates of equal public education for all had grown discouraged at that point, none of the subsequent equity cases would have occurred, and state education systems, though still imperfect, would not be as equitable as they are today.

Opponents of courts ensuring that every school district has sufficient funds to provide a quality education must be patient, whereas advocates need to refocus their positions. Rather than arguing in terms of inadequate funding, they must focus on inadequate education. Although the two concepts are not necessarily mutually exclusive, the courts have tired, both literally and figuratively, of the funding bent. Weariness has set in, and they have shown serious concern about separation of powers.

In the first *DeRolph v. State of Ohio* decision (1997), the court found that the funding formula of the foundation program used at that time had no relationship to the actual cost of educating a student. It took three more *DeRolph* decisions (2000, 2001, 2002) and until school year 2009–2010 for the state to implement a new funding formula. Ohio developed an evidence-based model, one of the various adequacy funding models recommended by school finance professionals, for funding adequate education systems in its 600+ school districts. The problem was that parts of the model were unfunded because of lack of state money, and some poor-achieving urban districts ended up with less money than they received with the old foundation funding model. This is only one example to illustrate that it takes time to "get it right."

STEPPING ON TOES

Weariness has set in, and courts and legislators have shown serious concern about separation of powers. Careful review of the *Rose* case in Kentucky and *DeRolph IV* (2002) in Ohio provides a clear indication of this anxiety. The findings in the *Rose* case were nearly nullified because of claims that the courts were stepping over the bounds of interpretation and into the legislative realm of making law. The final *DeRolph* decision brought with it a reprimand by the court that it would no longer be involved in the case, claiming that it was not the court's job, but rather that of the legislators, to structure an adequate system. With this understanding, future adequacy court cases must focus on education outcomes. If the focus is finance, it must be restricted to funding systems, not funding allocations. At the same time, however, measures must be put in place to ensure that money is available (unlike the Ohio situation described earlier) and that state school systems are accountable for allocating the money to ensure an adequate education for all students.

Rather than using financial data alone, plaintiffs would do well to use over-all student test scores, graduation rates, and dropout rates as well as data for individual subgroups to show inadequacies. These data have been used successfully to show that more money is needed to educate students in urban districts and minorities in other districts to the same level of adequacy as suburban, rural, and nonminority students. The courts would then be within their jurisdiction to interpret the data within the context of education mandates of state constitutions. The cases would not be a matter of creating law, but rather interpreting it.

A MATTER OF DEFINITION

Opponents of continued litigation to ensure sufficient funds for a quality education contend that the courts can do only so much. Courts are not prepared to evaluate a system in which standardized and state assessments do not test the state-established standards, or the standards are ambiguous, or there is no consistency between classroom teacher-made assessments and standardized and state assessments. It is not even clear that the plaintiffs are equipped to do this. Because of this lack of understanding of all the issues, most adequacy claims are reduced to arguing that there are insufficient funds to provide an adequate education, and again, the courts have become reluctant to favor finance cases. Although this is not an easy problem to work out, the solution could be in the definition of *adequacy.*

Although many definitions of *adequacy* have been proffered, the one that encompasses all components is found in a finance textbook, *School Finance: A Policy Perspective* by Allan Odden and Lawrence Picus (2000):

> The provision of a set of strategies, programs, curriculum, and instruction, with appropriate adjustments for special-needs students, districts, and schools, and their full financing, that is sufficient to provide all students an equal opportunity to learn to high performance standards. (p. 75)

This definition encompasses nearly all the bases on which adequacy cases have been filed. It addresses the needs of disadvantaged or at-risk students—including minorities and those with special needs—who have not benefited from the standards era of education. Several adequacy legal cases addressing a gap in achievement between these students and the more advantaged ones have been filed with the claim that adequacy had not been met because there was insufficient money to meet their needs. Other adequacy cases have been filed on the basis of there being inadequate facilities or equipment, again because of insufficient funds, for students to succeed academically. Finally, legal cases have been filed because of lack of adequate programs and curricular offerings to meet the needs of students in particular school districts.

One of the most recent cases, *Robles-Wong et al. v. State of California,* filed May 2010, is based on the plaintiff's contention that the California funding system is not related in any way to the cost of education and because of this, the state is not fulfilling its constitutional obligation as stated in Article 9 of the state constitution. The plaintiffs contend that the funding does not provide for a "system" of schools as mandated and furthermore, the money is not allocated in a manner consistent with Article 16, which states that of all state financial obligations, education must be the first to be funded. The problem the courts face is clear in this recently filed case. The courts are faced with the obligation to reconcile constitutional clauses regarding education with the actual meaning of adequacy, to which, in many cases, they are not privy, primarily because there is no "real" meaning. Again, however, this does not mean that the courts should not continue to make inroads into trying to ensure that every school district has sufficient funds to provide a quality education.

In a 1996 decision in the Florida case *Coalition for Adequacy and Fairness in School Funding v. Chiles* to challenge the state's system of funding, the Florida Supreme Court expressed great concern about separation of powers, claiming that there was no standard to use to determine whether the state failed to fund to adequacy. The court implied that the legislators must establish a standard that could be used to judge the system's adequacy. Subsequently, in 1998, the voters approved a substantially strengthened education clause (Article 9):

> It is, therefore, a paramount duty of the state to make adequate provision for the education of all children residing within its borders. Adequate provision shall be made by law for a uniform, efficient, safe, secure, and high quality system of free public schools that allows students to obtain a high quality education and for the establishment, maintenance, and operation of institutions of higher learning and other public education programs that the needs of the people may require.

Subsequent paragraphs mandate that funding be provided to maintain specified class sizes and to provide preschool. This is considered one of the strongest education mandates in the nation.

Clarifying language in state constitutions along with educating all parties involved in education litigation regarding the meaning of adequacy could minimize some of the problems encountered by litigants and the courts and lead to more productive findings for increased education quality.

CONCLUSION

Certainly, courts must continue to ensure that every school district has sufficient funds to provide a quality education. Clearly, it is each state's responsibility to grant such an education. However, it has become increasingly difficult to provide high levels of education because of intervening social, economic, and political factors. The courts as well as the litigants must find a way to circumvent these complications and do their jobs.

COUNTERPOINT: R. Craig Wood
University of Florida

The question of whether the state should ensure that school districts have sufficient funds to provide a quality education is one that permeates many public education policy discussions. Taken without an understanding of public education finance theory and practice, the answer would be an obvious one in the affirmative. Upon closer examination and understanding, the answer becomes increasingly complicated and raises many public education finance issues. For example, why is it that certain students in certain school districts do not achieve well on standardized tests, but similar students in similar school districts do well on the same tests with similar spending patterns? Why is it that in certain school districts, children do not reach achievement levels and yet the local school board refuses to maximize local tax rates as allowed by statute? Why is it that despite overwhelming evidence of the need for reorganization, many school districts are organized as highly inefficient units? Why is it that in many school districts the costs of personnel and benefits are comparatively high relative to other school districts with similar fiscal resources? Under the rubric of "adequacy," such questions are troubling and largely unexamined by those who advocate such social and educational policy absent education finance data.

In many instances, state courts have been called on to determine whether the applicable education finance distribution formula meets the required state constitutional mandate. The actual education finance distribution formula, as well as the state constitutional mandate, varies from state to state. Within the last several years, state courts have been asked to determine whether the education finance distribution formula is "inadequate" and thus unconstitutional. The difficulty is found in attempting to determine, in a judicial manner, whether the education finance distribution formula is adequate or inadequate.

There are two main arguments against relying on the courts to determine the constitutionality of a given state education finance distribution formula. The first issue reflects the undeniable fact that the question, and thus the answer, is essentially a political one, which is not appropriate for the courts to decide (Thro & Wood, 2010). Regardless of the applicable state constitutional mandate, only the state legislature may decide such questions. A great deal has been written regarding this point, demonstrating that the courts should not delve into this area, given that it is largely beyond the knowledge and skills of the court (Dayton & Wood, 2007). The second point is that adequacy studies, in general, are unable to determine what an adequate education is within a state and thus cannot determine the cost of providing an adequate education in every school district, in every school, and to each student within a given state.

Adequacy studies, when done well, may help inform a state legislature in terms of the range of spending that might improve a given education finance distribution formula for selected school districts and selected schools. Essentially, the proponents of these adequacy constitutional challenges have confused equal opportunity with equal achievement. This essay focuses on the second point in that one must understand the strengths and weaknesses of the various adequacy models to understand the limitations of each. The limitations are so pervasive that adequacy studies should not be the basis for a state supreme court to declare an education finance distribution formula unconstitutional.

TYPES OF ADEQUACY STUDIES

The literature concerning state adequacy studies is growing over time as education finance researchers continue to examine and refine education finance studies. However, the actual examination of these documents is scarce, and objective analysis is almost unheard of within the literature. In some instances, the actual studies are unattainable. Nearly all commentators have either a self-interest or a social and political perspective that prevents objective analysis regarding the public policy issues under examination. Of the studies done to date, many reflect advocacy groups, and thus, one has to examine the validity of their claims. Additionally, many are based solely on small, nonscientific, selected professional judgment panels. With rare exceptions, professional judgment panels will always produce the highest cost estimates compared with the other models (Wood, 2004).

The concept of adequacy, as it is presently used for the purposes of challenging a state education finance distribution formula, is deeply flawed for several educational finance research reasons. As these court cases have evolved, state legislatures are beginning to grasp the conceptual and technical arguments against these elusive and aspirational concepts.

Essentially, the adequacy argument states that the state aid distribution formula is fiscally and thus educationally inadequate. The adequacy proponents argue that even if a state aid distribution formula were to allocate funds in an equitable manner, but such funds were unable to meet various educational and achievement standards, such a distribution formula would be by definition inadequate. The question becomes whether the education finance distribution formula then violates the applicable constitutional and statutory obligations of the state. Plaintiffs do not satisfactorily address the specific question of why some school districts are unable to reach certain levels of student achievement when other school districts, serving the same populations and receiving the same moneys, are able to do so under the same education finance distribution formula. The answer to this conundrum lies in the research methodology on which the adequacy concept is based (Wood, 2009a).

Various state legislatures have unwittingly established standards by which many plaintiff groups are able to question and attempt to quantitatively establish noncompliance via the state education finance distribution formula. In the movement toward greater educational accountability and raising academic standards for the public schools, the legislature has, unsuspectingly, defined an adequate education by statute. Thus, when school districts are unable to meet those stated standards because of fiscal constraints as placed on them by various constitutional tax limitations and statutory and economic realities, the plaintiffs argue for relief. The relief sought is to declare the state education finance distribution formula unconstitutional while ordering the state legislature to fund to a given level with little, or no, greater fiscal effort by local school districts. Often, this is further compounded because the state legislature is at its maximum tax ability while observing constitutional limitations regarding operating the state with a balanced budget. Thus, the court is called into judging which constitutional standard must be met by the legislature (Wood, 2009a).

Generally, the plaintiffs are not challenging the equity of the distribution formula in the conventional sense. That is, the most recent arguments have centered not on whether wealthy and poor school districts have roughly the same amount of revenue per pupil, but whether, in general, there is enough funding to achieve state achievement standards, and further, whether school districts with higher concentrations of high need students have sufficient additional funding to achieve these standards. In many instances, plaintiffs link insufficient overall funding, or insufficient additional support, primarily in poor urban schools, to insufficient student outcomes occurring disproportionately in those same schools. The plaintiffs argue that by virtue of the fact that certain groups of children are underachieving on these state imposed achievement standards, the education finance distribution formula is, by definition, inadequate, at least for these groups of children. Interestingly, the question remains the same when achievement varies among school districts even though per pupil expenditures may be remarkably similar within a given state (Wood, 2009a).

Also, increasingly, various groups ranging from state legislatures themselves to a variety of advocacy groups have attempted to determine the adequacy of public education. An overview of these adequacy studies reveals that an increase of approximately 30% to 50% of expenditures would be necessary to meet the adequacy targets of the plaintiffs (Wood, 2009a).

THE MEASUREMENT OF EDUCATIONAL ADEQUACY

According to R. Craig Wood and Associates (2007), determining educational adequacy is determined primarily by using one or a combination of the four following approaches:

- Evidence-based model
- Professional judgment model

- Production/cost production model

- Successful schools model

The evidence-based model is essentially built on the approach of what educational strategies and concepts appear to be the most successful in improving achievement in the elementary and secondary schools. Because the bulk of these studies are virtually impossible to cost out, it cannot be determined whether a strategy might be generalizable to other states. Nonetheless, the mainstream of professional opinion supports certain programs, for example, full-day kindergarten and pilot programs, as reasonable and cost-effective mechanisms for state legislatures to explore. Evidence-based analysis requires a specific empirical research basis for recommended resource configurations. Evidence-based models do not, however, require rigorous meta-analysis of all available studies on each possible intervention. Nor does application of evidence-based cost analysis require that the interventions in question be evaluated with respect to specific, policy-relevant outcome measures. Thus, various studies purport to be evidence-based and yet use various standards of what are chosen for this standard, and how they are selected.

The professional judgment model concept varies greatly from small nonscientifically selected panels to more robust statewide surveys. A few studies have actually surveyed every building principal to estimate the adequacy levels of various prototype schools (Wood & Associates, 2005a). In this manner, different sized schools and organizational variables may be estimated (Wood & Rolle, 2007).

The production/cost production model essentially creates a regression equation consisting of a host of variables to create a curve of best fit. The cost of education variables such as poverty, language proficiency, and disabilities as well as competitive wages and issues of scale may be addressed. Increasingly common among recent analyses of educational adequacy are statistical methods that may be used to estimate either (a) the quantities and qualities of educational resources associated with higher or improved educational outcomes or (b) the costs associated with achieving a specific set of outcomes, in different school districts, serving different student populations. The first of these methods is known as the education production function and the second is known as the education cost function.

The successful schools model essentially uses performance measures reflecting schools and districts that are successful by a state's criteria while accounting for student needs and demographics to establish a benchmark for what all schools should spend. The model determines a targeted expenditure equal to what successful schools and districts are achieving in a state. Successful schools studies use outcome data on measures such as attendance and dropout rates and student test scores to identify that set of schools or school districts in a state that meet a chosen standard of success.

Using the exact same data from a given state, the four models will produce a wide array of adequacy targets. The models will yield, from the highest to the lowest adequacy target, in the following order: professional judgment model, production/cost production model, successful schools model, and the evidence-based model.

Unfortunately, a major shortcoming of both professional judgment and evidence-based models is that these studies appear to be poor estimators of the actual costs of educating children. Professional judgment models suffer from significant reliability and validity issues whereas evidence-based models often draw assumptions based on studies with limited or no generalizability (Wood & Associates, 2005a; Wood & Associates, 2007).

Thus, the adequacy concept is useful in developing better informed decisions, only if all four models are used at the same time to offer a range of data to a state legislature. Unfortunately, few state adequacy studies engage in the four models. Typically, they use one or two of these models. Thus, the typical adequacy suit is severely limited by its design limitations.

CONCLUSION

Adequacy is defined differently by plaintiffs in different states. It is critical to understand a fundamental flaw in the concept of adequacy within the education finance equity literature. That is, if equity were judged to have been met; then, by definition, all school districts would either be adequate or inadequate. Statistical measures determine whether fiscal equity has been met for the state, not for isolated, individual school districts that might be statistical outliers. Education finance formulas adjust for these within separate categories. If it were determined that fiscal equity existed by the traditional measures used in such studies, then the plaintiffs' burden changes significantly in explaining why the plaintiffs' districts are offering an inadequate education. For example, if expenditures were remarkably the same, that is, within a narrow range and exhibited a high level of horizontal equity as reflected in the variance, the McLoone Index, the coefficient of variation, and the Gini coefficient, then equity as defined by these statistical measures would have been met. Plaintiffs' explanations must be drawn toward issues of student achievement (Wood, 2009a).

Making student achievement the primary variable on which the adequacy claims are made presents a conundrum for the courts when the argument is examined and analyzed. If equity were statistically present, and assuming that a given set of state standards have even a modest degree of discrimination, then the result will always be that some students will not meet the prescribed state standards. Given the undeniable fact that a bell curve of student abilities exists, and assuming that the state standard actually measures some degree of achievement, then some students will fail. Conversely, assuming that the state standards are at best minimalistic, then the vast majority of students may meet the state standard with a high passage rate regardless of the existence of the bell curve of individual abilities. The concept of 100% passage based on a state standard is, at best, questionable, and in actuality, not possible if state standards were indeed meaningful (Wood, 2009a).

That is, often the examination reveals a setting in which statistically similar school districts serving statistically similar students produce significantly differing results within a state that exhibits a high degree of statistical education finance equity. That is, some school districts pass the state standards, but other school districts do not even though they have similar access to revenues and have similar expenditures.

Given these realities and given the highly political nature of adequacy claims, several state courts reflect a manipulation of precedent and text to fit a desired result. The difficulty with these views is obvious; the answers are often preordained based on the political, social, and economic views of the court. That is, it is only an answer if the court ordains what the answer should be absent the constraints of the state constitution and the privilege of the people as represented in the state legislature (Wood & Lange, 2006).

The dilemma for the various state courts is overwhelming on any examination. It is perhaps one thing to assert the role of the court into a political, social, and economic discussion absent specific constitutional language. Most adequacy studies are interwoven with political appeal but lacking scientific justification. Thus, at least in some instances, absent what we know to exist in society, advocacy groups will construct what they wish to exist in society (Wood, 2009b).

Moreover, focusing on the amount of money available may be misleading. As a broad generalization, education finance formulas consist of a state and local fiscal share. Generally, the state share reflects state income tax revenues or sales tax revenues whereas the local share generally consists of property tax revenues. In periods of economic recession, state legislatures have less revenue because of declining income and sales receipts. Generally, property taxes reflect assessed valuations that are lower than retail. Commonly, property assessments tend to be relatively stable over short periods and thus the local property tax levies remain consistent. Thus, the formula reflects different revenue streams regardless of the economic conditions at a given point in time. Accordingly, in these types of formulas, in periods of economic recessions, the state revenues will decrease while local revenues will remain relatively stable. In other words, a period of economic contraction or slow growth results in less money from the state government (Wood, Thro, & Escue, 2010). Thus, these economic cycles cannot be viewed as a state legislature failing to fund public education at an adequate level. Furthermore, adequacy studies may help inform a legislature, but they are not capable of determining a level of adequate education for the state legislature or the courts of a given state.

FURTHER READINGS AND RESOURCES

Belfield, C. R., & Levin, H. M. (Eds.). (2007). *The price we pay: Economic and social consequences of inadequate education.* Washington, DC: Brookings Institution Press.

Dayton, J., & Wood, R. C. (2007, November 29). School funding litigation: Scanning the event horizon. *Education Law Reporter, 224*(1), 1–19.

Hanushek, E. A. (2006). *Courting failure: How school finance lawsuits exploit judges' good intentions and harm our children.* Stanford, CA: Education Next Books.

Kauffman, A. H. (2004). Equity and adequacy concepts as considered in school finance court cases. *IDRA Newsletter.* Retrieved July 18, 2011, from http://www.idra.org/ IDRA_Newsletter/March_2004_Self_-_Renewing_Schools_Early_Childhood_ Education/Equity_and_Adequacy_Concepts_as_Considered_in_School_Finance_ Court_Cases

Odden, A., & Picus, L. (2000). *School finance: A policy perspective* (2nd ed.). New York: McGraw-Hill.

Springer, M. G., Liu, K., & Guthrie, J. W. (2009). The impact of school finance litigation on resource distribution: A comparison of court-mandated equity and adequacy reforms. *Education Economics, 17*(4), 421–444.

Thro, W. E., & Wood, R. C. (2010). The constitutional text matters: Reflections on recent school finance cases. *Education Law Reporter, 251*(2), 510–532.

U.S. Department of Education, National Center for Education Statistics. (n.d.). *Table 15. National Assessment of Educational Progress (NAEP) mathematics scores, by age and selected student characteristics: Various years, 1973 to 2004.* Retrieved from http://nces.ed.gov/programs/youthindicators/Indicators.asp?PubPageNumber=15 &ShowTablePage=TablesHTML/15.asp

Walker, E. M. (2005). *Educational adequacy and the courts.* Santa Barbara, CA: ABC-CLIO.

West, M. R., & Peterson, P. E. (Eds.). (2007). *School money trials: The legal pursuit of educational adequacy.* Washington, DC: Brookings Institution Press.

Wood, R. C. (2004, Fall). An examination and analysis of the equity and adequacy concepts of constitutional challenges to state education finance distribution formulas (Education Funding at the Crossroads Conference). *University of Arkansas at Little Rock Law Review, 27*(1), 125–168.

Wood, R. C. (2009a). Justiciability, adequacy, advocacy, and the "American dream." *Kentucky Law Journal, 98*(4), 739–787.

Wood, R. C. (2009b, October). Rose *at 20: The past and future of school finance litigation.* Paper presented at the Education Law Association meeting, Louisville, KY.

Wood, R. C., & Associates. (2005a). *Determining the costs of providing an adequate education in the state of Montana* (Quality Schools Interim Committee and the Montana State Legislature). Gainsville, FL: Author.

Wood, R. C., & Associates. (2005b). *Financing Missouri's public elementary & secondary schools: Final report* (Missouri Joint Interim Committee on Education of the Missouri General Assembly). Gainsville, FL: Author.

Wood, R. C., & Associates. (2007). *State of Rhode Island education adequacy study* (Joint Committee to Establish a Permanent Education Foundation Aid Formula for Rhode Island). Gainsville, FL: Author.

Wood, R. C., & Lange, G. (2006). The justiciability doctrine and selected state education finance constitutional challenges. *Journal of Education Finance, 32*(1), 1–21.

Wood, R. C., & Rolle, R. A. (2007, Fall). Improving "adequacy" concepts in education finance: A heuristic examination of the professional judgment research protocol. *Educational Considerations, 35*(1), 51–55.

Wood, R. C., Thro, W. E., & Escue, C. P. (2010, November). *Recent developments in school finance litigation.* Paper presented at the annual meeting of Education Law Association, Vancouver, BC, Canada.

COURT CASES AND STATUTES

Brown v. Board of Education, 347 U.S. 483 (1954).

Coalition for Adequacy and Fairness in School Funding v. Chiles, 680 So.2d 400 (Fla. 1996).

DeRolph v. State, 78 Ohio St.3d 193 (1997), 677 N.E.2d 733 (Ohio 1997) [DeRolph I].

DeRolph v. State, 89 Ohio St.3d 1 (2000), 728 N.E.2d 993 [DeRolph II].

DeRolph v. State, 93 Ohio St.3d 309 (2001), 754 N.E.2d 1184 (Ohio 2001) [DeRolph III].

DeRolph v. State, 97 Ohio St.3d 434 (2002), 780 N.E.2d 529 (Ohio 2002) [DeRolph IV].

Elementary and Secondary Education Act of 1965, 20 U.S.C. §§ 6301 *et seq.*

National Defense of Education Act of 1958, 20 U.S.C. §§ 401 *et seq.*

No Child Left Behind Act of 2001, 20 U.S.C. §§ 6301 *et seq.*

Robinson v. Cahill, 62 N.J. 473 (1973), 303 A.2d 273 (N.J. 1973).

Robles-Wong et al. v. State of California, unpublished (2010).

Rose v. Council for Better Education, 790 S.W.2d 186 (Ky. 1989).

San Antonio Independent School District v. Rodriguez, 411 U.S. 1 (1973).

Serrano v. Priest, 5 Cal. 3d 584 (1971), 96 Cal. Rptr. 601 (Cal. 1971) [Serrano I].

Should students pay additional fees to participate in extracurricular activities such as athletics or band?

POINT: Robert J. Safransky, *Nova Southeastern University*

COUNTERPOINT: Steven K. Million, *Nova Southeastern University*

OVERVIEW

Every state constitution mandates the establishment of a system of *free* public schools and, in many states, specifies a level of quality. Yet, such constitutional commands necessarily beg the question of what constitutes a "free" public education. Certainly, basic courses in reading, composition, mathematics, and science must be free, but what about other educational opportunities such as extracurricular activities? Must they also be provided for free?

On the one hand, extracurricular activities often are an important part of the educational process. Extracurricular activities teach important lessons regarding teamwork, self-discipline, hard work, courage, determination, dealing with adversity, working for long-term goals, and so on. Those lessons can be more critical to success in our society than some of the skills that students learn in the basic curriculum. Indeed, the Duke of Wellington purportedly said that the Battle of Waterloo was won on the playing fields of Eton.

Even so, if athletics and band are not part of the educational curriculum, then why are the schools spending thousands of dollars employing coaches and band teachers as well as constructing facilities? If the purpose of these activities is to entertain the community rather than education, then such activities are incompatible with the core mission of public schools. On the other hand, extracurricular activities—particularly sports and band—involve only a small portion of the student body and require enormous additional expenditures. Only a dozen male students may play varsity basketball even though several hundred males attend the school. Band or chorus inevitably involves less than 10% of the student body. Why should the school pay all or even most of the costs of an activity that benefits only a few?

The current financial crisis, which began in 2007, has hit school districts particularly hard. Most districts have been forced to lay off teachers and other staff, eliminate programs such as summer school, reduce building maintenance, and cut textbook accounts. The net result is that class sizes are larger, remedial programs are not available to students who need them, necessary repairs are not being done, and curricular updates are being postponed. Hawaii even went so far as to furlough teachers on several Fridays, shortening the school year by 17 days (Osborne & Russo, 2011).

To offset the loss in revenues and save programs from the chopping block, many school districts have instituted fees for student participation in extracurricular activities. Generally, fees are based on the costs of the program. Waivers are often given to low income students, and caps are sometimes set on the amount of fees one family will be charged in a school year. Although most states do not allow schools to charge for core curriculum courses, many allow schools to charge for extracurricular activities, supplemental materials, and even electives (Simon, 2011).

Summary of the Debate

This debate asks whether students should pay additional fees to participate in educational activities, such as athletics and band, that are extracurricular in nature.

Robert J. Safransky, a professor at Nova Southeastern University in Florida and a former school administrator, takes the affirmative view. He makes several points. Safransky points out that school districts have limited resources and simply cannot fund every activity that is desirable. Although extracurricular activities teach some invaluable life lessons, these lessons traditionally have not been part of the school curriculum. Furthermore, the costs of extracurricular activities, particularly athletics, are simply staggering. The few students who participate should bear at least some of the costs. Moreover, every dollar spent on extracurricular activities represents a dollar that is not spent on normal academic programs. The lessons learned may be important, but they are not more important than the general academic programs. Safransky also argues that middle-class and affluent students can easily afford to pay the additional fees, although Safransky acknowledges that it may be necessary to make special arrangements for poor students or to use fund-raising activities. Last, he notes that the number of students who have the desire and the ability to participate in extracurricular activities is relatively low. Resources should not be diverted from the general programs to benefit only a few.

Steven K. Million, who is also a professor at Nova Southeastern University in Florida, takes the negative view. In his view, the real issue is not determining whether additional fees are necessary, but defining the objectives of the public educational system. Million presents three main arguments. First, Western culture traditionally has offered a broad-based educational approach. It is not enough to be technically proficient in core subjects. Rather, those who were considered educated had a deep knowledge and appreciation of art, literature, music, and even sports. Indeed, the ancient Greeks, Protestant reformers of the 16th century, and early architects of the U.S. educational system all viewed artistic and physical pursuits as among the goals of education. Second, extracurricular activities teach valuable life skills—attributes that any society wants to encourage. Third, extracurricular activities have been particularly beneficial to the poor and those from ethnic minority groups. Imposing fees will limit their participation and may cause them to leave school entirely.

Additionally, Million contends that our society has decided that all citizens must support the education of all students. There is no need to abandon that commitment. Although current revenue may be insufficient, he suggests that taxes be raised or that noncurriculum services be cut.

William E. Thro
Christopher Newport University

POINT: Robert J. Safransky
Nova Southeastern University

The idea that public education should be free is a principle that has its roots in the theories and beliefs of public educators, such as Horace Mann of Massachusetts and Henry Barnard of Connecticut, beginning in the 1840s. The goal of free public education was by and large accomplished for elementary schools students by the end of the 19th century. Mandatory high school attendance laws were enacted by many states during the latter part of the 19th century with the last state to pass a mandatory high school attendance law being Alaska in 1929. The proponents of free public education theorized that the country would benefit if all students, regardless of parental economic status, could attend school and develop their mental capacities, which would prepare them for more education or to enter the work force.

In our current downsized economy, schools have been finding it more difficult, if not impossible, to meet their operating costs as both salaries and the costs of goods and materials have increased. Furthermore, in most jurisdictions, schools have been faced with a loss of revenue as states and local communities have been unable to raise sufficient funds through taxation to fully support the public schools. Most schools have been financially strapped for several years to the point that there is nowhere else to cut. Consequently, many school systems have instituted fee structures for participation in extracurricular activities to help defray the costs of providing programs such as sports, band, clubs, and other worthwhile, but not essential activities. Many districts have even begun to assess fees for transportation. Charging fees for such activities, it has been argued, prevents the elimination of these activities and helps preserve essentials, such as reasonable class sizes. Further, the pressure to add to school districts' current academic and extracurricular offerings to meet the various needs of diverse populations adds to the need to charge fees to support such programs (Valente, 1986).

Given that education is largely a function of state governments, legal controversies regarding charging fees for students to participate in extracurricular activities, as are most educational finance issues, would be settled by state courts according to state constitutional and statutory provisions. Christine Kiracofe (2010) notes that despite constitutional provisions in a majority of states calling for free public schools, many school boards have found it necessary to charge fees for certain activities to help cover their costs. She stresses that although charging tuition would, with limited exceptions, almost certainly be struck down by courts, school districts do have some degree of latitude when it comes to charging fees.

The answer to the question regarding whether students should pay fees to participate in extracurricular activities is a resounding "Yes!" Although many may initially question the rationale for such a response, when it is fully delineated, most will also agree that in our current economic climate, charging students fees to participate in extracurricular activities is fair and is an economic necessity. The rationale for this point of view is that most people have unlimited wants but limited resources, and the same is true of schools and school systems. The very name *extracurricular* should sound a warning bell as schools consider the costs to an individual school or the school system of offering such activities. The term *extracurricular* is derived from two Latin words; *extra,* which means "on the outside" or "beyond," and *curriculum,* which means "a race ground or course." Thus, activities that may be common to most school districts, such as athletic teams, drama clubs, debate societies, and bands, are outside of the school's normal curriculum. When the advocates of free public education spread their vision of how a free public education would benefit the individual child and then the country as a whole, they neither mentioned nor contemplated extracurricular activities as being financed by property taxes or other local and state forms of taxation.

The original concept of a public school was that the students therein would learn the basic essentials of reading, writing, and arithmetic. When the basic skills were learned, the students would begin studying the classics in their original Latin or Greek, which meant that the students had to learn Latin and Greek. To prepare for dealing with life's problems, students were expected to read and learn about how the Greek and Roman philosophers dealt with problems in their time and to study many other subjects. There were no school-sponsored athletics or bands in those days because the emphasis was on learning and studying the classic subjects. As years went on, additional essential courses such as science and history were added to the general curriculum.

One can easily question the wisdom of expending public funds on items such as equipment, fields, coaches, locker rooms, transportation, and athletic association fees. The costs just for coaching stipends in many large school systems can approach one million dollars. The costs for other extracurricular personnel reach into the tens and hundreds of thousands of dollars. The costs for additional items such as athletic fields and courts, weight lifting rooms, locker rooms, player equipment and uniforms, licensed athletic trainers, transportation to and from games for athletic teams and bands, band instruments, band technology equipment, band uniforms, music, practice rooms, membership fees for high school athletic associations and state music associations, along with necessities such as hiring of police officers for security for games may be found in capital outlay budgets or in the operating budgets of most school systems. Taxpayers foot the bills for the initial cost of these physical facilities and their continuous upkeep when the money might better be spent on the academic programs in the districts' schools.

Requiring participants in these nonessential extracurricular activities to pay to play will reduce the costs of these programs so that more funds may be directed to the essential academic programs. It is reasonable to ask whether and how students can afford to pay for the extracurricular activities. The answer is that most students or their parents seem to have the necessary funds to buy many other nonessential items such as designer clothes, the latest electronic gadgets and technology, movie tickets, and so on. The funds now spent on these nonessential items could be redirected to pay for participation in extracurricular activities if the students feel that such participation is a higher priority. Asking students and their parents to prioritize their wants and spend their funds first on those that are top priority is not unreasonable. After all, that is what school districts routinely do when it comes to spending their scarce funds.

Thus, school systems should start requiring students who want to participate in extracurricular activities to pay a reasonable fee for each activity. If students can find the funds to purchase other nonessential items, certainly they can find the funds to help finance the extracurricular programs at their schools if they want to participate.

Unfortunately, many students and parents honestly cannot afford to pay participation in extracurricular activities, even when the fees are reasonable. School systems must make accommodations so that no student is denied the opportunity to participate in extracurricular activities because of an inability to pay. In such situations, many school systems that charge fees have placed caps on the amount any one student or family is required to pay in a school year, regardless of the number of children in a family or the number of activities a child participates in. Other districts have established payment plans whereby the fees can be spread out over several months rather than having to be paid all at once. In extreme cases, fees should be waived entirely.

The fees structure should be based on the cost of the activity itself. For example, an individual sport's coaching and other costs should be divided proportionately among the number of players who ordinarily play the sport. Thus, the fees for participation in more costly activities should be higher so that those who participate in low cost activities are not subsidizing high cost programs.

Parents can also defray the costs of extracurricular activities by forming and joining organizations such as booster clubs whose purpose is to raise funds for the school system's extracurricular programs. This type of activity generates revenue for the programs and has the added benefit of getting parents involved in a positive way. Fund-raising events sponsored by booster clubs can generate significant funds for the extracurricular programs.

School systems need to first fund their basic academic programs so that their students receive a quality education. This has to be their top priority. Athletic and other extracurricular programs may be considered equally important by some members of the community who feel that they deserve to be supported by taxes levied on all. However, participation in extracurricular activities is not required, and not all students participate in such programs. Some students may not have the interest in or the physical attributes needed for most activities offered at the school. Some students choose not to participate because they are more interested in improving their academic skills. Others have obligations such as working after school to help support their families that may prevent participation. There are also a number of students who have no desire to participate in any school-sponsored extracurricular activities because they have other interests and hobbies that they feel merit their time and energy after school. When students choose not to participate in school-sponsored extracurricular activities, perhaps their parents should be eligible for a proportionate refund of their taxes because they are not participating in the athletic programs. Why should the parents of nonparticipating students pay more taxes to subsidize students who have chosen to participate? Is this not unfair taxation?

In a case from higher education, *Board of Regents of the University of Wisconsin System v. Southworth* (2000), the U.S. Supreme Court held that a university was within its right to charge students fees for extracurricular activities because it had charged student fees from its beginning as a university. Would not this decision apply to fees for extracurricular activities at the secondary school level? Thus far, as noted by Kiracofe (2010), only California has struck down charging fees for extracurricular activities, concluding in *Hartzell v. Connell* (1984) that extracurricular activities are an integral part of public education. Courts in other states, Kiracofe observes, have allowed fees for supplementary supplies and materials (*Sneed v. Greensboro*, 1980), elective classes (*Norton v. Board of Education*, 1976), and extracurricular activities (*Attorney General v. East Jackson Public Schools*, 1985).

There will be challenges to a district's right to charge fees to students to participate in extracurricular activities. As with all other matters, the school board must prepare to meet these challenges before they are raised by outside bodies. The board and school officials must inform parents, students, faculty, staff, the community, and the media that because of budget shortfalls, the only feasible way for a district to offer extracurricular activities and to support the academic programs is to have a set fee for each participant in each extracurricular activity. These fees should not be unreasonable but should cover the cost of each program. If a school system wants to offer these extracurricular activities for its students, but faces budget shortfalls and cannot adequately fund all of its academic and extracurricular offerings, it may be able to offer nonessential extra programs only when students pay a participation fee. Some parties will resent this policy; however, if it is clearly presented as a positive action by the school system that enables it to operate as efficiently as possible by charging those who want to participate in the extracurricular activities a fee, parents and students will buy into such a policy.

COUNTERPOINT: Steven K. Million
Nova Southeastern University

Asking students or parents to pay fees to participate in athletics, band, chorus, art and other nonacademic school experiences is a far more complex issue than it may at first seem. The real debate is, or should be, less about charging add-on fees than about the fundamental objectives of U.S. education and what it means to be well educated. Understanding the problems involved with assessing special charges, also known as pay-to-play fees, will suggest that they are a bad idea, inconsistent with both the historical expectations of whole child development and a violation of long-standing agreements between school leaders and U.S. taxpayers.

In the recent past, extracurricular activities were fully funded by most of the nation's public schools. Participation in athletics, music, art, and similar fields of study were available to thousands of youngsters who encountered these subjects for the first time at school. The arguments for providing extracurricular activities grew from the belief that schools should go beyond instruction in mathematics, science, social science, and language arts. Most everyone agreed that preparing students in these academic subjects was essential, but doing so was only part of the more complex challenge of developing all of a child's potential. Few credible thinkers argued for a world populated by mathematicians, scientists, or other academics who knew nothing of literature, music, art, or sport. Instead, schools were expected to liberally prepare students to think rationally within the bounds of contemporary knowledge, maintain healthy bodies, and grow in appreciation of music, art, and other life enrichments. This concept of whole child preparation was deeply rooted in the cultural experience of the Western world.

HISTORICAL FOUNDATION

In ancient Greece, the Athenians encouraged boys and a few girls, both rich and poor, to attend private schools. Tuition was charged, but it was affordable for even the poorest of children. Beginning at age 6, Athenians learned reading, writing, counting, and literature. In recognition of the varied benefits of developing all of a child's capabilities, youngsters also studied calisthenics, games, and sports such as running, wrestling, and discus and javelin throwing. To these intellectual and physical subjects, Athenian educators added the refined arts of singing and lyre playing. Their purpose, as explained by Aristotle, was to develop citizens complete in mind, body, and aesthetic spirit, in the belief that persons so educated would become community leaders with gentle, civilized natures capable of advancing Athenian social, political, and cultural life. The persuasive power of this educational philosophy influences Western pedagogical thinking to the present day.

During the 16th century, European social and religious reformers, including Martin Luther, devoted considerable thought to why children should be educated, what they should learn, and how communities should finance schools. Luther believed that all children must learn a classical curriculum in preparation for reading and understanding the Bible, living healthy lives, and comprehending the beauty of God's creation. He believed in developing young minds, bodies, and aesthetic aptitudes with a robust focus on each child's search for God. This religious imperative caused him to worry that the expenses associated with schooling might prevent all but the wealthiest youngsters from attending school. This was a perplexing problem for Luther because he believed that all children possessed souls, and reading and understanding the Bible were prerequisites to obtaining personal salvation. Because all souls deserved saving, he appealed to community leaders to fund education and, thereby, promote both civil advancement and the furtherance of divine will. Luther encouraged temporal leaders throughout his native Germany to meet their civil and religious obligations by establishing and maintaining schools. He contended that this was essential because all children, rich and poor, required access to community schools capable of improving their minds, bodies, and aesthetic awareness. For municipal leaders to do less was to risk complicity in the loss of community benefit and spiritual salvation. Luther's view of community schools featuring comprehensive curricula profoundly influenced educational thought throughout Europe and the United States.

Nineteenth-century U.S. educators such as Horace Mann endorsed Luther's ideas, believing that schooling must be available to all children regardless of social position or financial circumstances. Mann and his contemporaries saw prosperity and social progress as tied to participation in free, community-sponsored schools. Writing in the *Common School Journal* (1841), Mann argued that it was in society's self-interest to be taxed in support of public education because both society and business stood to gain from a well-educated citizenry. He reasoned that social and commercial progress required the academic, physical, and aesthetic development of every child. In 1852, his leadership led to adoption of the nation's first compulsory school attendance law in Massachusetts and a statewide comprehensive curriculum, extending academic, athletic, and aesthetic experiences to thousands of youngsters.

The tenets of Western education suggest that it is wrong to think of music, athletics, art, and other such activities as "extracurricular." Participation in these activities teaches teamwork, problem solving, courage, hard work, determination, dedication, and other desirable knowledge, skills, and dispositions. Such experiences are critical to social and intellectual maturation as well as civic advancement. Teaching these attributes is precisely what schools should be doing. In 2005, the College Board (Everson & Millsap, 2005) pointed to research indicating that students enrolled in art classes often do better in school and on standardized tests than do students who do not study art. Learning about art helps students recognize patterns and discriminate among similar and diverse concepts while challenging their minds to think in creative ways. Just as one cannot remove sections of track without derailing a train, one cannot do away with vital elements of a comprehensive curriculum without limiting the intellectual, physical, or aesthetic development of children. To allow such curricular deletions is to limit child growth and the individual and cumulative contributions these youngsters may make to the fund of human experience.

It is worthwhile to consider just how many U.S. musicians, athletes, artists, and others first encountered their areas of expertise in U.S. schools. How many would have pursued greatness had they been faced with pay-to-play fees or the stigma of seeking financial assistance? Those who suggest that making financial assistance available to poor children will solve the special fee predicament fail to grasp the importance of pride in many school-aged youngsters. Young people often view the risk of being labeled *underprivileged* as sufficient grounds to avoid seeking or accepting needed school services.

Regrettably, the same youngsters who stand to suffer most from a limited curriculum may be the ones most negatively affected by pay-to-play fees. Many such youngsters come from homes where academic and other experiences are limited, making these encounters all the more important within the schooling experience. The majority of such young people live in urban and rural settings where the availability of broad educational experiences pale in comparison with those offered by many affluent suburban schools. Ethnicity, language skills, disabilities, and other factors further menace student access to comprehensive curricula. It is reasonable to argue that the well-being of a democratic society depends partly on student access to free, comprehensive curricular experiences.

The pay-to-play fees debate does not justify limiting access to nonacademic topics. History argues for developing the whole child and points to community benefits growing from liberally prepared citizens. Centuries of experience demand the full funding of these activities because they are essential to the development of youth and because communities stand to forfeit the benefits of cultivated minds, healthy bodies, and inspired, creative, and determined spirits.

A TAXPAYER COMPACT

Like the civic leaders to whom Martin Luther appealed, U.S. taxpayers agreed decades ago to pay taxes in support of public schooling. The promise of a well-educated populace was sufficient motivation for most taxpayers who believed that public schools would provide a steady supply of competent employees, thoughtful consumers, and informed voters. The use of *ad valorem* (assessed value of property) and sales taxes in support of public education, although variable across states, created an informal compact between public school leaders and taxpayers. At the core of the compact was an agreement that paying taxes satisfied a citizen's obligation to the public schools. It would have been unthinkable until recently to ask for more.

Revenue raised through taxes was expected to cover the costs of operating local schools and, when funding was seen as no longer adequate, school leaders could request an increase in the tax burden through special tax elections. When tangential financial needs arose such as travel funding for band trips, yearbook production, or such matters, additional funding could be raised through voluntary, one-time activities such as bake sales, car washes, advertising in school-sponsored publications, and so on. Those who wanted to contribute in this way could do so, but those who did not found comfort in the knowledge that through paying their taxes, they had met their obligation to public schools. This compact was widely accepted by those with family members attending the public schools, those with no school-age relatives, and even those who elected to send their children to private and parochial schools. The taxpayer compact has well served U.S. education and should not be set aside because of current economic challenges.

TOWARD A SOLUTION

The resolution of this problem is not the imposition of fees on students and their families, but rather the courage of school leaders to seek increases in tax levies or the reallocation of current school resources, directing more money to nonacademic school activities. The basic nature of humans has not changed since the ancient Athenians prepared youngsters intellectually, physically, and aesthetically. Neither have there been fundamental changes in the community imperative to support education as advanced by Luther, Mann, and others. When contemporary public figures struggle to provide funding for comprehensive curricular experiences, they would do well to consider the challenges Luther and Mann faced in their times. What is needed is a recommitment to U.S. educational ideals. Leaders must put the interests of U.S. youth before political timidity or economic helplessness. Surely the current U.S. school funding dilemma is not the first to challenge U.S. creativity and ingenuity.

Beyond the historical arguments cited earlier, pay-to-play assessments are internally contradictive. Those who advance the need for fees argue that funds to support nonacademic activities are simply unavailable. In the next breath, they propose that these experiences are so vital to a good education that students (or parents) should pay for them. As with all such quandaries, proponents cannot have it both ways. If they believe schools should provide instruction exclusively in academic subjects, then let them make the argument for setting aside hundreds of years of comprehensive curricular practice. Alternatively, if they are willing to acknowledge the value of intellectual, physical, and aesthetic education, then, as a matter of conscience, they must find ways to fund these activities. Declaring defeat and resorting to special fees smacks of political expediency compounded by pedagogical deceit. The observer may question how leaders can recommend special fees for nonacademic experiences even when they owe some part of their own successes to the activities they now seem unwilling to fund.

DOING THE RIGHT THING

In resolving this problem, school leaders should be guided by the old adage, "Where there is a will, there is a way." Increasing tax levies is an option in many jurisdictions. In this economy, taxpayers may be little inclined to vote for tax increases, but the case for a comprehensive curriculum and its benefits should be made to voters. In addition, interest rates on borrowed money are at record lows, making this an ideal time to undertake expenditures. Local and state governments also can be approached about increasing school funding, paying for unfunded or underfunded government mandates, or redistributing existing funding so that all children have an opportunity to be well educated. Other options include reductions in nonessential services unrelated to curricula, delaying planned capital improvements, state adoption of innovative funding methods, expansion of school and business partnerships expressly in support of nonacademic subjects, use of discretionary funds to support nonacademic experiences, grant writing, or the formation of special commercial agreements earmarked for nonacademic purposes. History has created a mandate for providing physical and aesthetic learning opportunities propelling students beyond the boundaries of purely academic studies. It is essential that young people have access to these experiences and that schools eliminate special fees that can reduce student participation and diminish the value of schooling.

FURTHER READINGS AND RESOURCES

Aristotle. (1984). *The Athenian constitution* (P. J. Rhodes, Trans.). New York: Penguin Classics. (Original work published in 350 BC)

Brandt, W., & Lehman, H. (Eds.). (1962). *Luther's works* (Vol. 45, pp. 340–378). Philadelphia: Muhlenberg Press.

Everson, H. T., & Millsap, R. E. (2005). *Everyone gains: Extracurricular activities in high school and higher SAT scores* (Report No. 2005-2). New York: College Entrance Examination Board.

Jacobs, C. M. (1967). *Luther's works* (Vol. 46, pp. 209–258). Philadelphia: Fortress Press.

Kiracofe, C. (2010). Isn't school supposed to be free? An analysis of state constitutional language and school fees. *Education Law Reporter, 253*, 1–16.

Mann, H. (1841). *Common School Journal. Fifth annual report.* (Reprinted by General Books, 2009). Available from http://general-books.net

Osborne, A. G., & Russo, C. J. (2011). Teacher furloughs and the IDEA: An emerging issue? *School Business Affairs, 77*(2), 34–36.

Simon, S. (2011, May 25). Public schools charge kids for basics, frills. *The Wall Street Journal.* Retrieved from http://online.wsj.com/article/SB10001424052748703864204576313572363698678.html

Valente, W. (1986). Legal limitations on public school fees. *Education Law Reporter, 29*, 483–489.

COURT CASES AND STATUTES

Attorney General v. East Jackson Public Schools, 372 N.W.2d 638 (Mich. Ct. App. 1985).

Board of Regents of the University of Wisconsin System v. Southworth, 529 U.S. 217 (2000).

Hartzell v. Connell, 35 Cal. 3d 899 (1984), 679 P.2d 35 (Cal. 1984).

Norton v. Board of Education, 553 P.2d 1277 (N.M. 1976).

Sneed v. Greensboro, 264 S.E.2d 106 (N.C. 1980).

Should school districts charge additional fees for academic programs such as advanced placement classes?

POINT: Robert J. Safransky, *Nova Southeastern University*
COUNTERPOINT: Christine Kiracofe, *Northern Illinois University*

OVERVIEW

Newspaper headlines and articles everywhere provide numerous examples of the toll the current financial crisis and consequent cuts in local and state budgets, have taken on schools. These cuts, combined with increased costs, have substantially reduced the buying power of school districts so that they are being asked to do more with less. Even with funds provided to states by the federal government under legislation such as the American Recovery and Reinvestment Act of 2009, which specifically targeted education, most schools are struggling to provide essential services, and many have been forced to provide only a bare-bones educational program without any so-called frills. Many school districts have been forced to cut teaching positions and eliminate nonessential programs. To offset the loss in revenue, school boards across the country have begun charging fees for extracurricular activities, transportation, and even electives. Without these fee schedules, many of the programs typically offered in U.S. schools might be eliminated for lack of revenue. The people of the United States expect that public education will be free. Indeed, every state constitution contains a provision mandating the establishment of a public system. In many states, the provision explicitly demands that the education be free. Yet, such constitutional commands necessarily beg the question of what constitutes a "free" public education. Certainly, basic courses in reading, composition, mathematics, and science must be free, but what about other specialized educational opportunities such as advanced placement (AP) or International Baccalaureate (IB) classes? Under these programs, academically gifted high school students are able to take courses that are equivalent to undergraduate college courses. Participating colleges often grant credit to students who have successfully completed these courses and scored sufficiently high on qualifying exams. It can be costly to provide these intensive courses, which usually are taken by limited numbers of students. Must they also be provided for free?

On the one hand, AP courses and IB programs (offering a rigorous academic curriculum) are an integral part of the curriculum for gifted students. Just as the parents of special education students do not have to pay for the enormously expensive educational services that are provided to children with disabilities, the parents of gifted students should not have to pay for the specialized educational services that are available to them. Moreover, AP and IB programs often serve as a means of promoting social mobility. They allow children from poor or lower-middle-class households to obtain the equivalent of a private school education, and they increase the likelihood that those students will attend and, ultimately, graduate from college. The possibility of such movement up the socioeconomic ladder is a deeply held value of U.S. society and is one core purpose of the public schools.

On the other hand, these specialized classes involve only a small portion of the student body and require enormous additional expenditures. An AP class may have only 10 students, whereas a regular class may have 25. IB programs require additional teacher training and, in some instances, may require the school to restructure the curriculum sequence. In those districts where such specialized programs are offered only at one particular school—the normal practice for the IB programs—the school district may well incur additional transportation costs. Moreover, students who complete AP or IB classes generally may receive college credit. A student with an IB diploma or numerous AP classes may be able to complete a 4-year degree in only 3 years. There is an obvious financial benefit to having a year or more of college credit. Those who receive such an enormous financial benefit should pay for the benefit. The costs of the AP tests or the IB tests are minimal in comparison with the cost of a year of college.

Summary of the Debate

This debate asks whether students should pay additional fees to participate in specialized programs such as AP or IB classes.

Robert J. Safransky, a professor at Nova Southeastern University in Florida and a former school administrator, takes the affirmative view. He makes three points. First, the costs of these programs are enormous. Given that school districts have limited resources and given that state law imposes restrictions on class size, districts simply cannot afford to pay all the costs of a specialized class that benefits only a few students. Second, if students and their families are forced to pay at least some of the costs, students are more likely to value the classes and put additional efforts into succeeding. He uses the analogy of students who have to work to finance a portion of their college educations. Third, Safransky argues that providing such specialized programs for free will lead to an increased demand for the specialized programs, thus creating an additional financial burden for schools. He concludes that people expect to pay more for quality and that the extra costs of these quality programs will provide lifelong results for the students.

Christine Kiracofe, a professor at Northern Illinois University, takes the negative view. She makes five arguments. First, it is essential that the United States have a college-educated workforce, and programs such as AP and IB are essential to preparing the best and the brightest for college. Second, the plain language of the state constitutions seems to preclude charging students to take classes that are part of the curriculum. Third, imposing fees on students' families inevitably will cause some students not to take the advanced classes. Fourth, although the costs of such programs are significant, the total costs are minimal in comparison with overall school budgets. Finally, Kiracofe points out, because these advanced programs actually reduce the amount of time students spend in college, there is a positive fiscal impact on state budgets. She feels that the dividends states and local communities receive, both fiscal and societal, more than pay for the modest financial investment expended by local school districts in AP and IB programs.

William E. Thro
Christopher Newport University

POINT: Robert J. Safransky
Nova Southeastern University

The College Board offers 37 advanced placement (AP) courses to high school students. The courses cover almost every academic subject from art to world history, and even include courses on topics such as Virgil. The courses are intensive and require students to devote much time and effort on them to be successful. The teachers assigned to instruct these classes are usually experienced educators who possess master's degrees in the particular discipline taught. Students must take a final exam administered by the College Board and score 3.0 or better to earn college credit for the class. These AP classes enhance the educational opportunities available to gifted students, but should they be provided without cost to students or their parents?

The concept of school districts charging students who wish to enrich their high school experience and prepare for college is repugnant to some members of the public, educators, parents, and students. School boards are proud to tell parents, students, and accrediting agencies that AP courses are available to their students. However, not all the high schools within a district may be able to offer the same number and type of AP classes, and not all districts will have readily available all the AP classes that would benefit the students within the district. Nor do all districts readily have available the number of teachers—let alone qualified teachers—to offer a good variety of AP classes. Further, smaller districts may not have sufficient student enrollment for each class. Many districts struggle to procure the textbooks and other specialized learning materials needed for the total AP enrollment.

School districts throughout the country are struggling to implement other federal and state mandates. For example, in keeping with a constitutional amendment passed in Florida in 2002, the student enrollment in a class cannot exceed 25. Schools in Florida have spent more than $16 billion for operating costs and more than $2.5 billion in outlay costs to build additional classrooms to comply with the class size amendment. The taxpayers are shouldering significant costs to put into effect the reduced class size amendment specifying that there must be a maximum of 25 students in a high school class. What happens if the enrollment reaches 26 students? In the case of AP classes, should one student be removed from the class, or should another AP class be formed to accommodate that student? A discussion of legislated maximum class sizes is relevant to the topic of fees for programs such as AP courses because these programs require classrooms, textbooks, and teachers that otherwise might be used for a regular class of 25 students.

The enrollment for individual AP courses will determine how many AP courses an AP teacher will be scheduled to teach during a semester. If course enrollment drops for the second semester, as it may because students can and do change their minds regarding which classes they wish to take, the AP teacher might have to teach another regular class, as most school systems require teachers to teach six of seven periods per day. Student enrollment in a non-required class will depend on the reputation of the teacher among students and the students' willingness to sign up for the class. Some teachers have their classes overenrolled because of student perceptions that the class will provide a fruitful learning experience or that they will earn a good grade.

The topic of grades brings up another point about AP classes—a student who earns an A in an AP class may also earn an additional quality point, so what would normally be worth four points for an A grade would then be worth five points and would thus raise the student's standing on the grade point average list. Grade point averages are used to determine class rankings of students for valedictorian and salutatorian honors. Thus, because AP students have the opportunity to gain additional quality points, thereby enhancing their class standing, assessing fees for AP courses is not unreasonable. Students and their parents are paying for an added benefit.

AP classes often use textbooks that differ from those used in a regular high school class such as a U.S. history class. Thus, the school district must purchase a limited number of advanced level textbooks that will be used by the students in the AP classes but not in other classes. This adds to the overall costs of the school.

STATE POLICIES ON ADVANCED PLACEMENT FEES

Although policies vary among states, Florida provides an example of a state that encourages school boards to offer AP courses. The Florida Education Finance Plan (FEFP) for the 2010–2011 school year provided certain incentives for school districts to offer AP classes. These incentives included the district's earning an additional 16 full-time equivalent (FTE) if a student scored a 3.0 on an AP examination. When students earn a grade of 3.0 or better on an AP exam, the teacher receives a bonus of $50 per student up to a maximum bonus of $2,000. A teacher in an underachieving school that offers AP classes may earn a bonus of $500 if a student earns a grade of 3.0 or better on an AP exam. Even though school districts receive financial incentives for offering AP classes, these incentives are not sufficient to completely offset the added costs to the district of maintaining an AP program. Charging fees for participation in AP courses can help further fund such electives.

The question of whether students should pay fees for AP classes is no longer a rhetorical one because Indiana has established the precedent that it will charge high school students a fee for taking AP classes and earning credits that can be used for college credit. Indiana University High School offers online AP classes for $132 per high school credit. It also charges other fees and charges for textbooks. The school is accredited, and students will have their earned credits accepted by other schools and universities. Conversely, the American Civil Liberties Union (ACLU) filed a lawsuit in California alleging that 35 school districts were charging students fees for activities such as participation in sports or taking tests for AP classes. The suit maintained that the state is to provide a free public education (Dillon, 2010). The ACLU reached a settlement agreement with the state that establishes a monitoring system to make sure that school districts do not illegally charge fees (ACLU of Southern California, 2010).

School districts currently are charging fees for a variety of programs and offerings. The San Diego Unified School District's parent website lists questions and answers about fees. The list contains 20 items or areas for which the schools may collect fees. For example, the district has established a fee of $340 for a student to be transported to school. A second child from the family gets a reduced rate. Students with disabilities and students on the free and reduced lunch list are not charged a fee. If students are routinely being charged for services that are connected, but not an integral part of basic education, such as transportation to school, it is not unreasonable to charge them for participating in an AP program that can easily be defined as a program that goes beyond the realm of a basic education.

ARGUMENTS FOR CHARGING AP FEES
Savings on College Tuition

By the same token, other states should adopt similar policies of having students and parents pay for the advanced classes, given that such classes will save the parents money in the future when their students enter college. Many colleges will accept enough of the AP classes to equal a full year's credit so students who have taken AP courses may only have to pay for 3 years of college. Thus, the fees students and parents pay for AP courses translate to significant savings in college tuition later. The savings more than offset the fees charged for AP classes. The fees paid by parents for AP classes are a good investment when viewed in terms of the eventual cost savings.

Lessons and Life Skills Students Learn by Paying Fees

A further argument supporting AP and similar fees can be made when students themselves are asked to contribute toward such fees. In a column titled "For

College, I'll Pay Half, Kids Pay Half," Mitch Anthony (2010), founder of Financial Life Planning Institute, explained why he required his children to pay for a share of their college costs. Anthony has four children, three of whom have finished college and one of whom is still in high school. The children who have finished college have ended with no debt because Anthony agreed to pay half of their education but required them to pay the other half, and the children took jobs before and during their college attendance to earn money to pay for their educations. Anthony said, "But we have learned that our plan has encouraged our kids to develop a good work ethic, to remain focused on courses that will be valuable to their lives and to be more prepared when they enter college to know why they are there."

Anthony has summed up the argument for why students should pay for their AP classes. If they have to pay for it, these classes will have more value for them. They will have to learn how to get a job, how to keep a job, and how to save and wisely invest the money that they earn. They will also learn that they must use their time wisely so that they can master their subjects and still have time for jobs and other student activities.

Do parents want their children to grow up with values and life skills that will make it possible for them to be successful? If so, then children should pay for part of their educations so that they know that there is a cost and someone must pay it. If more students learned that they have unlimited wants but limited means to satisfy those wants, they, their parents, and our school systems, states, and the national government would be fiscally solvent.

Another issue regarding students not earning money to pay for their tuition may prevail in a number of households. Some parents who are able to pay for their children's education will not require their children to contribute to these costs. Does this give students more time to study and to become involved in school activities? Does this give students more time to party and to be student protesters? Or does this give students an opportunity to learn how to live off their parents even though they are now legally adults? Some will argue that not requiring students to pay for educational costs inappropriately prolongs childhood and delays children's maturation into adulthood. The prolongation of childhood does take place and this will have some effects on society, but that is an issue for another debate.

Social Impact of Not Charging AP Fees

The U.S. Supreme Court decisions involving racial segregation and student rights during the 1960s and 1970s have had a great impact on public schools and have led to changes regarding race and ethnicity and to better treatment of students with disabilities. The federal government has enacted various laws, rules, and regulations regarding the education of students who meet the criteria established by the Individuals with Disabilities Education Act (IDEA) and Section 504, Rehabilitation Act. These students are entitled to a free appropriate public education (FAPE). Although the federal laws do not included gifted students, some states have passed their own statutes, modeled after the IDEA, granting similar rights to students classified as gifted. These laws could present an interesting challenge for a school or school system if it adopted the policy of requiring students to pay for the AP classes. The requirement that gifted students be given a free and appropriate education could be interpreted to imply that the school system could not charge the parents for their children's AP classes. In addition, more parents might seek to have their children tested to determine if they meet the gifted student guidelines and merit placement in the gifted program and AP classes. Gifted students and their parents would win because they would not have to pay for AP classes. Schools would also win if they received additional funds as a result of the FTE funding formula as applied to AP classes. However, these benefits for individual parents and students and for the school could be seen as an unfair cost imposed on those whose children are not eligible to participate in AP programs.

CONCLUSION

Some people believe that students are entitled to an excellent education and that the state should provide it. Others hold that public schools should provide a basic education and that an excellent education may be obtained from private schools. Although some people will always be looking for someone else to pay for their education, other people believe that the parents and students need to pay a portion of the costs of the education. In summary, the argument for students to pay for AP classes can be concluded with the reminder that people expect to pay more for quality in products, services, and residences. The extra funds expended on a quality AP program will produce lifelong results for the students, parents, schools, and society.

COUNTERPOINT: Christine Kiracofe
Northern Illinois University

Statesman Adlai Stevenson famously remarked that the "most American thing about America is the free common school system." Unlike many countries in which K–12 education is an expensive privilege reserved for the wealthy, all U.S. children are provided with at least 12 years of basic educational services. Compulsory attendance statutes specifically require all students of set ages to receive public, private, or home instruction. Child labor laws help ensure that educational opportunities are not just available, but are accessed by each and every U.S. child. It follows, then, that U.S. children aren't simply provided the opportunity to go to school; they are legally required to do so.

The U.S. investment in education is based on a deeply held belief that education provides benefits to the individual and to society as a whole. Societal benefits arise from an individual's K–12 education and from an individual's college education. College graduates often enjoy numerous benefits over their nondegreed peers. As a group, college graduates make significantly more money than nongraduates make, enjoy better health, have healthier children, experience lower overall early mortality rates, and are less likely to exhibit prejudice. College graduates also make a significant positive contribution to economic growth. As a group, they enjoy greater workplace productivity and flexibility, have lower health care costs, contribute to local economies through greater consumption of goods and services, and are better prepared to assist their children with their educational pursuits. If the United States is to reap the economic and societal rewards of a college-educated workforce, it is essential that public K–12 schools adequately prepare students to be successful in their postsecondary educational studies. Advanced placement (AP) courses and exams are a cost-effective way to provide precollege students with the skills to be academically successful in college. School districts should not charge additional fees for academic programs such as AP classes.

STATE CONSTITUTIONS AND FREE PUBLIC SCHOOLS

Although states may disagree about the specific scope of a proper public education, all 50 states have incorporated some type of education clause into their constitutions. Of the 50 state constitutions, 31 mandate that education should be provided to children in the state free of charge. This "free schools" constitutional language varies widely in breadth. For example, Article VIII of the Connecticut constitution states simply, "There shall always be free public elementary and secondary schools in the state." The free schools language included in Article IX of the North Carolina constitution is much more specific, mandating, "The General Assembly shall provide by taxation and otherwise for a general and uniform system of free public schools, which shall be maintained at least nine months in every year, and wherein equal opportunities shall be provided for all students." Although it would seem that students in states with free schools constitutional language could not be required to pay school-related fees, this isn't the case. Many students in these states are routinely assessed fees, sometimes with the blessing of state courts. Although courts have interpreted free schools language differently from state to state, the spirit of this language is inescapable. The majority of state legislatures intended to provide for a free public education for the children in their states.

In many states, a specific school-related fee is constitutionally impermissible if the fee is determined to be equivalent to the charging of tuition. For example, charging a fee for extracurricular athletics might be okay, but charging a fee for classroom instruction would likely not be acceptable. When AP courses are offered as part of a school's general curriculum, it would likely be unconstitutional in many states to charge a fee simply to take the course. A more difficult question is whether schools may charge students a fee to cover the costs associated with taking an AP exam, which is usually optional for students enrolled in AP courses.

ADVANCED PLACEMENT EXAM FEES: WHO PAYS?

The organization that administers AP testing, the College Board, currently charges $87 per AP test. This fee includes an $8 rebate for the school to cover test administration expenses. Students who are eligible for free or reduced-price lunches are entitled to a reduced AP exam fee of $57. This reduced rate is achieved by the College Board's reduction of the testing fee by $22 and by the testing schools foregoing their $8 rebate. However, nearly all states provide additional financial assistance for students eligible for free or reduced-price lunches, which brings the cost of taking an AP test to $0. Students from families who are not eligible for free or reduced-price lunches, however, are often required to pay the full $87 for each AP exam they take. Although fee proponents have suggested that the AP test fee of $87 is a fairly insignificant cost for middle- and upper-class families, testing fees become quite significant when a student takes multiple AP exams. For example, a student taking six AP exams would be required to pay $522 in testing fees. This is likely an amount that most families would find to be significant. The poorest families are usually eligible for fee waivers, but lower-middle-class families generally are not. For families in this socioeconomic stratus, $522 could well be 2 months' worth of car payments. Passing AP exam fees on to students can have a negative effect on whether families elect to enroll their students in these courses or, if enrolled, whether a student elects to take the AP exam.

COMPARISON OF AP EXAM COSTS WITH OTHER INVESTMENTS IN K–12 EDUCATION

The United States has committed a great deal of money to public K–12 education, especially in comparison with other first world nations. A 2010 report from the U.S. Department of Education's National Center for Education Statistics shows that in the 2007–2008 school year, the school districts in the United States spent an average of $10,297 to educate a public school student. This figure is 41% higher than the $7,283 spent, on average, by comparison nations in the Organisation for Economic Co-operation and Development (OECD). In fact, of the 30 member nations that make up the OECD, only three spend more money per pupil for public K–12 education: Luxembourg ($15,440), Norway ($10,448), and Switzerland ($11,129) (OECD, 2009). When it comes to postsecondary public education spending, the United States ranks first, spending $25,109 per student. This figure is more than double the OECD average of $12,336. Given these statistics, there is no question that the United States chooses to invest significant financial resources in educational opportunities for students both at the K–12 and at the postsecondary level.

Spending patterns can be seen as evidence of what is important to a nation. The United States clearly values postsecondary educational opportunities for its citizens. According to a 2010 report issued by the College Board, the same organization overseeing AP exams, in 2007 40.4% of all 25- to 34-year-old Americans had earned an associate's degree or higher (Lee & Rawls, 2010). Internationally, 11 countries have higher percentages of college graduates in the 25 to 34 age range; the top 3 countries producing college graduates are Canada, Korea, and Russia, which have more than 55% of their population holding a college degree. In response to these data, the College Board Commission on Access, Admissions and Success in Higher Education, in 2008, set a goal to increase the percentage of U.S. 25- to 34-year-olds who are college graduates to 55% by 2025. This challenge has been echoed and supported by President Barack Obama who has set a goal for the United States of having the highest proportion of college graduates of any country in the world by the year 2020. Encouraging AP exam participation is a relatively low cost way to help meet these goals. To this end, eliminating student fees for taking AP exams makes sense.

One common reason schools require students to pay AP exam fees is that school district budgets are often tight. AP courses are often viewed as "extras." However, given that U.S. school districts spend an average of more than $10,000 per year educating a K–12 student (with some districts almost doubling this amount), the financial burden to a school district of paying an additional $79 for an AP exam fee is a minimal expense. Even in cases where students might be taking multiple AP exams, the cost to the district or state of covering the testing fees is small in comparison with the overall investment in students' education. Additionally, fee waiver programs at the federal level and in most states ensure that students eligible for free or reduced-price lunches are able to take the exams fee-free. Thus, districts would not need to absorb the cost of testing fees for this group of students. It is also important to note that school districts always bear the cost of paying for AP instruction. AP fees do not cover anything but testing costs. Teachers assigned to teach AP courses are funded by taxpayer-supported local school districts. Thus, when school districts elect to offer an AP course, they are electing to invest in advanced educational opportunities for their students. Given that AP courses often have a much lower than normal teacher–student ratio, the investment in teacher salary alone for an AP course represents a significant financial investment by school districts. It is counterintuitive, then, for a school district to provide classroom space, hire a teacher, offer material support in the form of teaching aids, photocopies, and so on, and then fail to pay the final $79 needed by AP students to take the AP exam. One would have to suppose that districts operating in such a manner hypothesize that the benefit to students is the AP course, and not necessarily the exam. However, research suggests that although AP courses benefit students' later academic pursuits, they receive greater benefits from taking both the course and the exam.

THE ADVANCED PLACEMENT EXAM MATTERS

Research suggests that students who take AP courses and exams are more likely to graduate from college than are students who take AP courses (but not exams) or students who take neither. Furthermore, students who take both the AP course and exam are more likely to graduate from college within 4 years, putting them into the workforce earlier than their peers who do not graduate within 4 years (Hargrove, Godin, & Dodd, 2008). Research also suggests that the number of AP courses a student takes affects college graduation rates: The more AP courses and exams taken by a student, the more likely he or she is to graduate from college.

FISCAL BENEFITS OF ADVANCED PLACEMENT EXAM PARTICIPATION

Students who participate in both AP courses and exams experience significant personal financial benefits. On an individual level, families benefit from reduced tuition costs when students are able to graduate from college within 4 (instead of

4½ or 5) years. If these financial benefits were all personal, it might be more difficult to argue that schools should bear the cost of AP exam fees. However, research demonstrates that both states and local communities benefit from students who take AP exams. States benefit from reduced time-to-graduation when students are able to graduate from state-supported institutions more quickly. Individual tuition costs rarely cover the full cost of an education at a state college or university. The state government (or local government, in the case of community colleges) frequently funds a percentage of students' educational expenses at these institutions. State funds expended on a student's education are reduced when the student graduates early. Additionally, states and localities benefit when AP students graduate from college and enter the workplace earlier, contributing to local economies both through consumerism and the payment of taxes while their non-AP peers are often still enrolled in college (if they enrolled in college at all). It is thus not surprising that research suggests that school district investment in AP exam fees may actually result in a net fiscal benefit for states and localities. Indeed, one state is putting this into practice.

On July 13, 2010, Maryland Governor Martin O'Malley announced the "AP Access and Success" initiative. This program will provide state funds to cover the cost of AP exams for all Maryland students. The estimated annual cost to Maryland to cover all AP student fees is somewhere between $3.0 million and $7.5 million. However, the governor's proposal indicates that the AP Access and Success plan "is projected to reduce the number of students requiring [postsecondary] developmental education, resulting in a reduction in cost to the state" (O'Malley, 2010). Remedial or developmental education classes taught by community colleges and 4-year universities cost Maryland an estimated $25 million to $30 million annually. At the family level, increased AP course and exam participation can also yield significant fiscal benefits. The O'Malley plan notes that AP students are more likely to finish college, and to do so within 4 years. Considering that each additional year of college (at a public institution) is estimated to cost students and their families between $8,000 and $19,000, the AP Access and Success plan would also result in a significant financial benefit for parents of AP students (O'Malley, 2010). Thus, under the AP Access and Success plan, the state of Maryland could realize a net financial benefit of millions of dollars each year in addition to the tens of thousands of dollars individual families could save in tuition costs.

CONCLUSION

Student participation in AP courses and exams benefits individual students and society as a whole. Students who have taken AP exams are more likely to attend and graduate from college. This is exactly the outcome that the College Board

Commission on Access, Admissions and Success in Higher Education and President Obama are working toward. Given that AP exam fees are a relatively minor cost compared with the overall investment in a student's education, it only makes sense for schools to cover the cost of AP fees and not pass them along to students and their families. Eliminating AP exam fees for students also ensures that students will not be dissuaded from taking multiple AP courses simply because their families are unable or unwilling to pay testing fees.

School districts should pay AP exam fees for all students. Although exam fees may be cost prohibitive for individual families, the amount is relatively minor for school districts. More importantly, the dividends that states and local communities receive, both fiscal and societal, more than pay for the modest financial investment expended by local school districts.

FURTHER READINGS AND RESOURCES

American Civil Liberties Union of Southern California. (2010, December 9). *ACLU California affiliates announce major settlement in school fees case.* Retrieved from http://www.aclu-sc.org/releases/view/103057

Anthony, M. (2010, September 7). For college, I'll pay half, kids pay half. *St. Petersburg Times*, p. 11A.

Dillon, S. (2010, September 10). Public schools face lawsuits over fees. *The New York Times.* Retrieved September 10, 2010, from http://www.nytimes.com/2010/09/10/education/10education.html?_r=1

Florida Department of Education. (n.d.). *Class size reduction amendment.* Retrieved September 7, 2010, from http://www.fldoe.org/classsize

Florida Department of Education. (2010). *Funding for Florida school districts, 2010–2011.* Retrieved August 10, 2011, from http://www.fldoe.org/fefp/pdf/fefpdist.pdf

Hargrove, L., Godin, D., & Dodd, B. (2008). *College outcomes comparisons by AP and non-AP high school experiences* (College Board Rep. No. 2008-3). New York: The College Board.

Indiana University High School: http://iuhighschool.iu.edu/index

Kiracofe, C. (2010). Isn't school supposed to be free? An analysis of state constitutional language and school fees. *West's Education Law Reporter, 253,* 1–16.

Lee, J. M., & Rawls, A. (2010). *The college completion agenda: 2010 progress report.* Retrieved September 12, 2010, from http://completionagenda.collegeboard.org/sites/default/files/reports_pdf/Progress_Report_2010.pdf

O'Malley, M. (2010). *AP Access and Success plan expands opportunity for MD students.* Retrieved September 8, 2010, from http://www.martinomalley.com/blog/category/C54

Organisation for Economic Co-operation and Development (OECD), Center for Educational Research and Innovation. (2009). *Education at a glance, 2009: OECD indicators* (Tables B1.1a, B1.2, B2.1, and X2.1). Paris: OECD.

San Diego Unified School District parent website: http://www.sandi.net/parents/site/
default.asp

U.S. Department of Education, National Center for Education Statistics. (2010).
*Current expenditures per pupil in fall enrollment in public elementary and secondary
schools: Selected years, 1961–62 through 2007–08.* Retrieved from http://nces.ed.gov/
fastfacts/display.asp?id=66

COURT CASES AND STATUTES

American Recovery and Reinvestment Act (ARRA) of 2009, Pub. L. 111-5, 123 Stat. 115.

Individuals with Disabilities Education Act (IDEA) of 1990, 20 U.S.C. §§ 1400 *et seq.*

15

Should the state give vouchers to poor students to allow them to attend private schools?

POINT: Christine Kiracofe, *Northern Illinois University*
COUNTERPOINT: Lenford C. Sutton, *Alabama State University*

OVERVIEW

Although education is not a fundamental right under the U.S. Constitution (*San Antonio Independent School District v. Rodriguez,* 1973, p. 33), each state constitution has a provision mandating, at a minimum, that the state provide a system of free public schools. Moreover, the U.S. Supreme Court has recognized, "Education is perhaps the most important function of state and local governments" because "it is doubtful that any child may reasonably be expected to succeed in life if he is denied the opportunity of an education" (*Brown v. Board of Education,* 1954, p. 493). Indeed, the Court has stressed "the importance of education in maintaining our basic institutions . . ." *Plyler v. Doe,* 1982, p. 221). Thus, free public education must be regarded as a U.S. constitutional value.

Despite free public education for all being a constitutional value, U.S. public schools remain ravaged by "savage inequalities" that lead to failure of the public schools. Indeed,

> There are very few people who have the temerity to stand up and say that the public school system is doing a good job of educating its students. Virtually everyone who comments on education, be they defenders or enemies of the establishment, agrees that the system is in dire need of reformation. (Peyser, 1994, p. 626)

More than 20 years ago, the National Commission on Excellence in Education noted, "The educational foundations of our society are being threatened by a rising tide of mediocrity" (1983, p. 5). The threat to the republic identified by the commission included (1) low performance of U.S. students on international comparisons of student achievement, (2) a finding that 23 million U.S. adults were functionally illiterate, (3) evidence that functional illiteracy among minority youth was as high as 40%, and (4) statistics demonstrating that average achievement of high school seniors on standardized tests was lower than in 1957, when the Soviet Union launched Sputnik I (National Commission on Excellence in Education, 1983, p. 8). The commission's members cited failures in the content of educational offerings and the quality of instruction and concluded that the decline in educational performance had resulted largely from the way education in the United States was being conducted (National Commission on Excellence in Education, 1983, pp. 22–23).

Moreover, because the failure of the public schools is particularly clear in our cities, (Pixley, 1998, pp. 26–27), the consequences of that failure are felt most among minority students. Almost 30 years ago, one scholar observed, "The gap in educational achievement between black and white students was so great that it threatened to defeat any other attempts to narrow the economic differences separating blacks and whites" (Murray, 1984, p. 105). Indeed, the most recent data suggests that minority students' mastery of basic skills is less than half of that of their white counterparts (Bolick, 1998, p. 36). One scholar has observed that black males fare most poorly under the current conditions faced by most urban schools that experience problems with dropout rates higher than 50%, rampant truancy, students struggling to attain basic literacy, and school buildings being in poor condition (Barnes, 1997).

Given this crisis in urban education, particularly among students of color, it is not surprising that some would propose revolutionary reforms. Perhaps the most controversial reform is a school choice or voucher program. In a voucher program, the parents of poor children are given a specific amount of money to spend on their child's education. The money can be spent at any public school or at any private school, including religious schools, that meets certain standards. Although the voucher amount may not cover all of the tuition and fees associated with attending a private school, it does cover a substantial part of the costs. Thus, instead of paying several thousand dollars for their children to attend a private school, the parents may only pay a few hundred. The net effect is to allow some poor children to attend private schools, which are often educationally superior and safer than the public schools. To the extent that private schools have a religious focus, a school choice system makes benefits for the religious school and makes it easier for parents to send their children to religious schools.

Not surprisingly, opponents of voucher systems as well as those who believe in the strict separation of church and state have questioned the constitutionality of using religious schools in a school choice program. In 2002, the U.S. Supreme Court found that a school choice program that included religious schools did not violate the federal Establishment Clause (*Zelman v. Simmons-Harris,* 2002). However, there may be instances where state constitutional provisions preclude the participation of religious schools.

Constitutional issues aside, there remains a profound policy debate about whether school choice programs are a good idea. Proponents of vouchers argue that urban schools are failing and that there is a moral, if not constitutional, obligation to allow children to pursue opportunities that are more likely to educate them. Moreover, forcing schools to compete with each other for students likely will cause all schools—both public and private—to improve. Conversely, opponents of school choice programs argue that vouchers undermine the public schools. Resources that would normally be spent on public schools are diverted to private schools. Moreover, children who do not wish to attend a religious school may have little or no choice. Furthermore, the solution to failing urban schools is to reform them, not to abandon them in favor of private, often religious, institutions that are not fully accountable to the public.

Summary of the Debate

This debate asks whether the states should create school choice systems to allow poor students to escape failing schools.

Christine Kiracofe, a professor of education at Northern Illinois University, takes the affirmative view, supporting school choice programs. She makes four arguments. First, voucher systems give meaningful choices to poor families. Second, school choice is cost effective. In most instances, the amount of the voucher is less than the cost of educating a child in the public schools. Third, contrary to the assertions of some school choice opponents, vouchers do not allow only the best students to escape. Rather, children with significant educational risk factors are frequently the beneficiaries. Fourth and perhaps most significantly, school choice programs actually result in better educational achievement for the students who participate.

Lenford C. Sutton, a professor of education at Alabama State University, takes the negative position, opposing voucher systems. He makes five points. First, there is a lack of sound social science research demonstrating that vouchers lead to improved student outcomes. Existing studies tend to be flawed in that the studies do not account for selection bias. Second, given the current and long-term economic prospects, scarce financial resources should not be diverted to private schools. Third, the net effect of school choice programs is to divide the community along religious and racial lines. Vouchers will lead to religious and racial segregation at a time when our nation needs to unite and embrace its diversity. Fourth, based on the experience of urban areas that underwent mandatory bussing to achieve desegregation, relocating poor students to new schools will not lead to better student achievement. Fifth, allowing religious schools to participate in school choice programs, though constitutional, will lead to religious divisiveness.

William E. Thro
Christopher Newport University

POINT: Christine Kiracofe
Northern Illinois University

In 2002, the U.S. Supreme Court addressed the issue of public school vouchers in *Zelman v. Simmons-Harris*. At issue in this case was a voucher program in the Cleveland City School District that provided students from poor families with a voucher worth more than $2,250 a year. Parents of eligible children could use this money to pay for a seat at any participating school, public or private. As might be expected, the vast majority of schools that agreed to accept vouchers were private schools. Of the participating private schools, 82% had some sort of religious affiliation, and 96% of voucher students ultimately enrolled in these religiously affiliated schools. Opponents of Cleveland's voucher program argued that the Establishment Clause of the First Amendment of the U.S. Constitution prohibited a "pass through" of public moneys to the religious schools. However, the U.S. Supreme Court disagreed and upheld the Cleveland voucher program as constitutional.

Should states give vouchers to poor students to allow them to attend private schools? Yes—but not just because they are constitutional. For poor families, voucher programs such as the one used in Cleveland provide opportunities that would not otherwise be available to them, and at *less* cost per pupil. Additionally, research suggests that voucher students perform at least as well, if not better than, their public school counterparts and that parents of voucher students experience empowerment and increased levels of engagement with their children's education.

VOUCHER PROGRAMS GIVE POOR FAMILIES CHOICES

Debates about voucher programs are often couched in a larger discussion of "school choice" options. Opponents often characterize voucher programs as a money grab for the rich—a legal way of having the state foot the bill for rich families' private school tuition payments. This couldn't be farther from the truth. Nearly all major voucher programs employ means testing, ensuring that only the poorest families are eligible to receive vouchers. Furthermore, the amount of money provided by a voucher is no more (and often significantly less) than per pupil spending in the public schools. Voucher programs will never pay enough for a child to attend an elite prep school, for example. However, vouchers do even the playing field for poorer families by providing schooling options that would otherwise not be available to them.

School choice options do not always take the form of a voucher. Middle- and upper-class families have been "choosing" their children's schools for decades by electing to move into (and out of) school districts based on their perceived quality. Realtors know that public school quality is a major attraction to a geographical area for young families. Families often limit home searches to homes within highly ranked school districts. As a result, homes in the best school districts often cost significantly more than similarly sized homes located in weaker school districts cost. Middle- and upper-class families who can afford to move often flee underperforming urban school districts in search of better educational opportunities for their children. This has resulted in demographic shifts in many large urban areas of the United States. "Voting with one's feet," as this phenomenon has been called, is often not possible for poorer families who cannot afford the inflated housing prices in better school districts. As middle- and upper-class families leave urban districts, poor families are left behind. Even more troubling is that because socioeconomic status and race are often tightly linked, school districts not only become socioeconomically segregated, but become racially segregated as well.

Urban flight has left the Cleveland City School District with a disproportionately high percentage of low income and minority students. Indeed, the demographics of the Cleveland public schools do not reflect Ohio as a whole, nor do they even reflect the greater Cleveland metropolitan area. Middle- and upper-class families have been "voting with their feet" and moving into the suburbs for decades. Those families left behind, often unable to afford to move to a better school district, had a lot to be concerned about. The U.S. Supreme Court decision in *Zelman* (2002) outlined the unacceptable performance of the district's schools, noting

> The district had failed to meet any of the 18 state standards for minimal acceptable performance. Only 1 in 10 ninth graders could pass a basic proficiency examination, and students at all levels performed at a dismal rate compared with students in other Ohio public schools. More than two-thirds of high school students either dropped or failed out before graduation. Of those students who managed to reach their senior year, one of every four still failed to graduate. Of those students who did graduate, few could read, write, or compute at levels comparable to their counterparts in other cities. (p. 644)

Chief Justice William Rehnquist, writing for the majority in *Zelman,* observed, "Few of these [voucher] families enjoy the means to send their children to any school other than an inner-city public school" (p. 644). Thus, without a voucher, children from poor families were relegated to schools where they had a 10% chance of passing a basic proficiency examination in the ninth grade, and a dismal one-in-four chance of graduating from high school. Sadly, Cleveland public schools are not unique in their academic challenges and dismal performance. Many urban school districts have similar—and in some cases, worse—educational outcomes.

The dismal performance of urban districts like Cleveland is unconscionable. Any private institution that fails to adequately serve 90% of its customers would quickly go out of business; customers would simply go elsewhere. This is exactly what middle- and upper-class "customers" have been doing for years. However, poor children have no exodus options. The system has failed them and, without the options afforded by vouchers, they have simply nowhere else to go. Voucher programs are one way of evening the playing field and providing options for poor families in these failing school districts.

VOUCHER PROGRAMS ARE COST-EFFECTIVE

If the $2,250 available to students in the Cleveland voucher program sounds a bit low, that's because it is. In 2002, the year *Zelman* was decided by the Court, Ohio spent an average of $8,100 to educate a child enrolled in one of the state's public schools. In fact, the $2,250 figure was significantly lower than the per pupil average of each of the 50 states that year. This figure does not reflect the actual cost of educating a student from the Cleveland public schools. Actually, most private schools that accept vouchers (in Cleveland and elsewhere) take students at a significant financial loss. And, because private schools cannot afford to operate at a loss, the majority of voucher receiving schools need alternate sources of income. Religiously affiliated schools rely on private money in the form of charitable donations or other forms of support from the religious organizations they are affiliated with to cover the difference. The perception that religiously affiliated schools have a net financial benefit from voucher programs is simply not true.

As pointed out in the majority opinion in *Zelman*, parents, too, had a financial disincentive to select religiously affiliated schools. Students who elected to stay at community schools received twice the funding allotted for voucher students, and those electing to attend one of Cleveland's magnet schools received three times the voucher funding. Yet the vast majority of parents still opted to select the underfunded private school vouchers. It is important to note that, on the whole, voucher families pay property taxes at the same rates as other families in the district. Thus, two neighbors could pay the same amount of money in property taxes, but the state would spend different amounts on the education of their children. For example, assume that families A and B both live in the same neighborhood, in similar-sized houses, and both pay about $4,000 in annual property taxes. Family A elects to send its child to a magnet school and Family B elects to take a voucher for its child. Under the Cleveland plan outlined in *Zelman,* the state would spend $2,250 to educate the child from Family B opting for the voucher option. However, three times that amount—$6,750—would be spent to educate the child from Family A at the public magnet school.

Although Cleveland is one of the more dramatic examples, the overall fiscal benefit of voucher programs to public school districts is not unique. A 2007 study reviewing financial impacts of vouchers on public school districts showed that voucher programs have saved public school districts an average of $1,000,000 each, with only two exceptions. Even then, the two voucher programs that didn't save the district any money were fiscally neutral, not costing the districts any more than they would have otherwise spent to educate the voucher students in public school classrooms (Aud, 2007).

Vouchers make sense from a fiscal point of view. The programs transfer part of the financial burden of educating public school children from cash-strapped state governments to private organizations while maintaining the level of property tax revenues.

SKIMMING?

Opponents argue that voucher programs "skim off" the best students in a school, leaving the most educationally needy students behind. However, the converse is actually true. Voucher programs target and generally serve students with significant educational risk factors and needs.

Researchers have long argued that poverty is one of the most devastating educational risk factors. Children from low income families are more likely to perform poorly on standardized tests and to have trouble behaviorally, they often drop out of school, and they have greater incidences of both physical and emotional disease (Moore, Redd, Burkhauser, Mbwana, & Collins, 2009). The majority of voucher programs employ means testing to make sure that they are helping the districts' poorest students. Means testing ensures that voucher programs assist this at-risk subgroup.

As a group, students from poor families generally cost more to educate than their middle- and upper-class peers cost. Part of the cost differential is because children living in poverty are more likely to be diagnosed with special needs. Children with special needs require additional educational supports and services that can be pricey. Private schools accepting vouchers have been widely criticized for limiting the number of special needs students they can serve. For example, a small private school accepting voucher students may specify that it is unable to accept students with special needs. Although these limitations have often been characterized as discriminatory in intent, the real reason for the limitations is usually pragmatic. The school simply may not have a trained special education teacher necessary to fully meet the needs of voucher students requiring special education services.

There is an incredible financial disincentive for private schools to serve special education students. When a special education student receives services in a public school under the Individuals with Disabilities Education Act (IDEA), the district is eligible for federal reimbursement for some of the services the district provides. Even in cases where students are traditionally enrolled in private schools (i.e., not via a voucher program), eligible students may be entitled to federally funded special education services. However, when a private school accepts students through a voucher program, it is ineligible for federal reimbursement for special education services provided. Thus, private schools accepting voucher students with special needs incur an additional financial liability: Vouchers rarely cover the cost of a basic education, and they never cover the cost of the education of a student with special needs. Given this incredible financial disincentive for private schools to accept voucher students with special needs, one might assume that few private schools would accept their vouchers. However, this isn't the case. A 2008 meta-analysis by researcher Patrick Wolf found that nearly one third (30%) of all voucher students have a "diagnosed disability that affects them educationally" (p. 420). (Fourteen percent of students, nationally, are similarly diagnosed.)

VOUCHER PROGRAMS IMPROVE STUDENT ACHIEVEMENT AND PARENTAL SATISFACTION

Increased choice, cost effectiveness, and inclusivity are significant advantages of voucher programs. However, of primary concern is whether children and families actually benefit from voucher programs. Although voucher impact research is complex and often hotly debated, "nine of the ten gold standard evaluations of voucher programs have reported positive and statistically significant achievement impacts for all or at least some subgroup of voucher recipients" (Wolf, 2008, p. 443). Research does not suggest that voucher students always outperform their counterparts in the public schools. Just as there are good and bad public schools, there are good and bad private schools that accept voucher students. However, the net benefit to voucher students is positive.

Interestingly, voucher programs benefit voucher recipients and appear to benefit the public schools they leave. Research on Milwaukee's voucher program indicates that there is a positive correlation between the number of participating private schools and standardized test performance of students remaining in the public schools (Chakrabarti, 2008; Greene & Marsh, 2009). Thus, voucher programs do not hurt students who elect to remain in the public schools, they actually appear to help them.

Although educational performance outcomes are important, voucher programs provide other benefits that are not as easy to measure. In addition to test performance increases, voucher research studies also suggest that parental satisfaction with their child's school is significantly and positively affected by voucher programs (Wolf, 2008). This is no minor outcome when considering the vast amounts of research suggesting that parents' engagement and participation in their children's education is critical in ensuring student success.

CONCLUSION

Voucher programs empower low income families to make some of the same school choices that middle- and upper-class families have been making for decades. These programs also result in positive outcomes for both voucher-receiving students and those students remaining in the public schools alike. Voucher programs benefit communities by shifting some of the financial burden of educating students from failing schools to private organizations while maintaining property tax revenues. Simply put, voucher students do at least as well as their public school counterparts, voucher programs cost communities less money, and they result in parents who are empowered and satisfied with their child's school. Academic performances of students remaining in the public schools are positively affected, and at-risk students are served. Voucher programs make sense and should be encouraged.

COUNTERPOINT: Lenford C. Sutton
Alabama State University

One of the most contentious issues in U.S. educational reform is the public debate concerning government support of school vouchers and tax credits in elementary and secondary education. Voucher advocates have long believed that public schools have little interest in significant education reform that diminishes their monopolistic position in the public education enterprise, effectuating a system of escalating costs, inefficiencies, and unacceptable student performance. In addition, voucher advocates claim that in a nation historically devoted to free enterprise and equal education opportunity, the expansion of school choice opportunities is a natural progression. Conversely, voucher opponents posit that vouchers are unconstitutional and redirect valuable resources away from schools serving students with the greatest need to further the individual interest of a small segment of the population; opponents also view voucher policy as a highly divisive approach that fosters government entanglement with churches and serves as a catalyst for the resegregation of public schools, further exacerbating educational inequality.

Even though rivals in the voucher debate have made assertions about the effect of school vouchers in U.S. school enterprise, there exists little credible evidence to support claims by those who support or oppose education vouchers for private school enrollment. Notably absent from the debate are declarative statements and sound research studies that connect school affiliation and superior student outcomes in a manner that accounts for inherent selection bias, a problem encountered when performing research in the behavioral sciences. Instead, the discourse pertaining to school vouchers is filled with political talking points concerning the age-old argument about the role of government and its relationship to the rights of families and the appropriate level of regulation applied to the private sector of the economy. Nonetheless, the current debate concerning school vouchers is a small departure from previous points of contention in that nearly a decade has passed since the U.S. Supreme Court in *Zelman v. Simmons-Harris* (2002) held that the federal Establishment Clause was not a barrier to school voucher expansion. Today, the most credible opposition to state provision of vouchers to enable poor children to attend private schools is also found in legal rulings and political conflicts that have historically separated the educational interests of children along racial, religious, and ethnic lines.

LEGAL OBSTACLES TO VOUCHER PROGRAMS

Today, credible legal grounds for opposing vouchers can be found in many state constitutions. The high court's decision in *Zelman* is the seminal case in support of voucher expansion; however, the accelerated production of new voucher programs has not materialized as expected in response to the decision. One of the primary reasons for the limited expansion in voucher programs since *Zelman* is the legal provision in at least 39 state constitutions and the District of Columbia that prohibits the use of public money in support of any religious organization. In addition, 15 state constitutions contain "uniformity" provisions that threaten voucher expansion (Sutton & King, 2011). For example, a few years after *Zelman*, the Florida State Supreme Court struck down the nation's first statewide voucher program with its ruling in *Holmes v. Bush* (2006). Florida statutes require its legislature to provide "a uniform, efficient, safe, secure and high quality system of free public schools that allows students to obtain a high quality education" (Florida Constitution, Article IX, §1). For that reason, the state court ruled that the statewide voucher program contravened the state education uniformity laws primarily because it allowed some children to receive a publicly funded education through an alternative system of private schools that are not subject to the uniformity requirement of the public system.

DAMAGE TO THE U.S. ECONOMY

To explain why states should not provide vouchers to poor students for attendance in private school, especially in 2010, one only has to consider the state of the national economy and its impact on state resources. Even a novice economist should understand that when there is a severe downturn in the economy, exploratory spending of state resources is a risky proposition. In the aftermath of the collapse of the housing industry and financial services markets, fiscal realities should be a dominant driver of education policy and respective spending. When state financial coffers have a surplus, it is certainly reasonable to expect state lawmakers to leverage the state's funding authority to secure a larger return on private sector investment in the public education enterprise; conversely, it is also rational to expect frugality in periods of severe revenue shortages. Moreover, the long-term outlook of the U.S. economy should give pause to all lawmakers who might consider risky spending of taxpayer moneys to fund school voucher programs while taking away funds from public schools already in dire need of additional resources.

Concerns about the national debt, energy costs, trade imbalances with China, retiring baby boomers, escalating health care costs, and the potential collapse of global markets such as that of Greece has unleashed an enormous amount of fear and uncertainty about the long-term condition of the U.S. economy. Consequently, if the correct mix of spending cuts and tax increases is not applied to bolster the long-term prospects of the national economy, then states can surely expect to experience sustained levels of high unemployment and revenue shortfalls. This possibility should give pause to all lawmakers who might consider any experimental measure that would change current public school funding levels, especially school vouchers for children to attend private schools. Voucher advocates suggest that such publicly funded programs provide governments an opportunity to use the private sector of the economy for expanded vouchers programs that would create competition through public pressure, eliminate bureaucratic waste, and lower education costs. Should policymakers laud school reform efforts in a Race to the Lowest Cost of education, or should they be more committed to education reforms that provide students with high quality educational opportunities and outcomes? The ill effects of the worst economic decline since the 1930s, together with the residual effects of the global financial crisis, seem to have served as a pretext for policymakers and school officials to implement radical school reforms—reforms designed to increase the role of the private sector and destroy long-held traditions related to public school offerings.

VOLATILE POLITICAL CLIMATE

For nearly 60 years, public school advocates have used school desegregation and education finance litigation in an attempt to permanently unify the education interests of all children in public education and to address educational inequities therein. However, efforts to divide the interests of children in the United States through voucher programs initiated more than 150 years ago appear to be on the rise against the backdrop of the current U.S. economy and looming financial crisis. For example, in response to the nonrenewal of State Fiscal Stabilization Funds (SFSF) from the federal government, Florida Governor Rick Scott has proposed a plan to cut $1.75 billion from public education but to expand vouchers by redirecting 85% of the per pupil education costs to parents who choose to participate in the program. The money would be diverted into personal education savings accounts that could be used by parents to purchase tutoring services, pay college costs, and enroll in private or virtual school education programs. There is ample need for restraint by Florida policymakers if they are to avoid political overreach on the school voucher issue.

First, the radical expansion of school vouchers in the Sunshine State may serve as the catalyst for a constitutional challenge to the state's existing voucher plans, the McKay Scholarship for students with special needs and the Florida Tax Credit Scholarship that provides scholarships for children living in poverty; both currently have voter support. In 2006, the Florida Supreme Court ruled that the Opportunity Scholarship Program (OSP) violated the state constitution's education clause, which calls for "uniform, efficient, safe, secure and [a] high quality system of public schools." The court said the OSP illegally diverted public dollars into a separate and private system that competed with public schools. To date neither of the current Florida voucher programs has faced a legal challenge; however, if Governor Scott were to transfer a significant portion of public dollars to the private sector, teacher unions and civic organizations would invoke both "uniformity" and "no aid" constitutional language to eliminate all voucher programs in the state of Florida.

Second, voucher advocates who seem to be deeply convinced that private enterprise will flourish only when the size of the federal government and its regulatory elements are significantly reduced should heed the lessons learned from the banking crisis of 2008. Voucher advocates preach about the lack of accountability in the public school "monopoly" while romanticizing the infusion of public dollars into private education markets that are not subject to government regulation and accountability. One has only to ask the millions of foreclosed homeowners about the net effect of unregulated markets and the way in which public incentives morph into unintended consequences of self-serving practices. A lack of regulation in education will surely cloud the principal–agent relationship associated with funding and educating children.

FUTILITY OF RELOCATING STUDENTS

School voucher provisions, which are attempts to geographically reposition poor and minority children to other learning communities, are not new methods for reforming public education. Nearly 14 years after the U.S. Supreme Court declared segregated schools unconstitutional in the decision of *Brown v. Board of Education* (1954), the Court implemented a forced bussing program in the Charlotte-Mecklenburg public school system that removed numerous students from their residential schools (*Swann v. Charlotte-Mecklenburg Board of Education*, 1971). At that time, the Court believed that such a plan would lead to more integrated schools and create increased educational opportunities for all students. Nevertheless, 4 decades of forced bussing have not produced evidence of improvement within the U.S. education enterprise, and the idea that relocating poor students to so-called better schools enhances student learning has not come to fruition.

Moreover, parents of poor minority children have second-guessed the wisdom that bussing and relocating children have done a great deal to provide quality educational outcomes for their children. A generation of parents from minority and impoverished communities revile decades of funding disparities within their public schools but also embrace the nostalgia of community schools that placed parents in direct partnership with the local schools. However, if vouchers were provided for poor students to attend private schools away from their residential communities, many parents would probably remain excluded from the education of their children. Moreover, parents from impoverished communities may have extended work hours that make it more difficult for parents to participate in school activities in support of their children's education. In sum, the expansion of voucher programs for poor students will only exacerbate the same barriers that limit the full and active participation of parents in the education of their children. An unregulated expansion of voucher programs for poor children to attend private schools will incentivize private schools to select from the most talented students for admission and leave the public schools with the task of serving the hardest-to-educate children. Schools that serve the most talented students will be geographically positioned near affluent residential areas, effectively subsidizing the ability of more wealthy parents to fully participate in the school culture, but residents from poor communities whose children attend these same schools will be required to exert greater efforts to be involved in their children's education.

When placed in a historical context, the rapid expansion of voucher programs has a sordid history in contemporary U.S. society. The reality is that the popularity of vouchers for private education consumption only emerged in the wake of *Brown v. Board of Education,* when southern states used them as a tool to nullify and circumvent the equal protection guarantees under the Fourteenth Amendment. The clearest example of this political maneuver was the Virginia state legislature's enactment of laws that permitted the closing of public schools and the opening of private segregated academies in its local school districts. For that reason, a group of parents within the Prince Edward County Schools formed charter schools intended for white children only, and the governing school board awarded publicly funded vouchers and tax credits to fund these segregated schools—effectively evading the federal equal protection guarantees for all children in the state of Virginia. Voucher expansion goals amid research that provides little clarity about the effect of voucher plans on student achievement raise questions concerning other political goals that may be contravening the fundamental goal of having an educated citizenry, something essential to our cultural longevity.

RELIGIOUS SLIPPERY SLOPE

Questions regarding the separation of church and state have been controversial, and for several years, the issue of providing vouchers for students who attend religious schools has been the focus of much debate. One has to wonder, however, what direction this discussion will take in the future. The recent controversy over the building of an Islamic mosque on private property near Ground Zero in New York City serves as an example of the public's strong feelings toward religion and highlights the importance of the principles of separation of church and state. School choice expansion through voucher programs may develop unprecedented intensity as one of the most contentious educational reforms in the U.S. educational enterprise. In the aftermath of 9/11, does the United States have the resolve to secure the progeny of *Zelman* for parents who may opt to enroll their children in sectarian schools affiliated with Islamic mosques? Clearly, the question of its federal constitutionality is settled law; however, the political climate in the United States post–9/11 may once again challenge our nation's ability to remain true to our founding principles of liberty and justice for all, especially when confronted with fear. In the dissenting opinion in *Zelman,* Justice David Souter described the "divisiveness" created by the majority's disposition and urged state and federal lawmakers to act to minimize the eminent threat to viable public schooling.

> The applicability of the Establishment Clause to public funding of benefits to religious schools was settled in *Everson v. Board of Ed. of Ewing,* 330 U.S. 1 (1947), which inaugurated the modern era of establishment doctrine. The Court stated the principle in words from which there was no dissent:
>
>> No tax in any amount, large or small, can be levied to support any religious activities or institutions, whatever they may be called, or whatever form they may adopt to teach or practice religion.

Also dissenting in *Zelman,* Justice John Paul Stevens surmised,

> I am convinced that the Court's decision is profoundly misguided. Admittedly, in reaching that conclusion I have been influenced by my understanding of the impact of religious strife on the decisions of our forbears to migrate to this continent, and on the decisions of neighbors in the Balkans, Northern Ireland, and the Middle East to mistrust one another. Whenever we remove a brick from the wall that was designed to separate religion and government, we increase the risk of religious strife and weaken the foundation of our democracy.

Before the election cycle of 2010, there was little evidence to support Justice Stevens's forecast of religious discord in U.S. society; however, if vouchers were provided for attendance at Islamic private schools in the United States with teachers similar to imams in Saudi Arabia, there would certainly be a hue and cry from community groups. More importantly, the thought of publicly funding vouchers for attendance at schools that question the legitimacy of Israel under international law or support the sexual mutilation of school-age children would surely lead to even more religious confrontation, immense public concern, and validate the fears of the dissenting justices in *Zelman*.

There appears to be political consensus concerning the shortcomings of the educational enterprise in the United States, and policymakers and education pundits will serve our children well if they unite around education policy designed to connect the educational interests of all school-age children.

FURTHER READINGS AND RESOURCES

Aud, S. (2007). *Education by the numbers: The fiscal effect of school choice programs, 1990–2006.* Indianapolis, IN: Friedman Foundation for Educational Choice. Retrieved August 31, 2010, from http://64.71.179.146/downloadFile.do?id=243

Barnes, R. D. (1997). Black America and school choice: Charting a new course. *Yale Law Journal, 106*(8), 2375–2409.

Bolick, C. (1998). *Transformation: The promise and politics of empowerment.* Oakland, CA: ICS Press.

Chakrabarti, R. (2008). Can increasing private school participation and monetary loss in a voucher program affect public school performance? Evidence from Milwaukee. *Journal of Public Economics, 92,* 1371–1393.

Greene, J. P., & Marsh, R. H. (2009). *The effect of Milwaukee's parental choice program on student achievement in Milwaukee public schools.* Fayetteville: University of Arkansas, School Choice Demonstration Project.

Jorgenson, L. (1987). *The state and the non-public school, 1825–1925.* Columbia: University of Missouri Press.

Moore, K. A., Redd, Z., Burkhauser, M., Mbwana, K., & Collins, A. (2009). *Children in poverty: Trends, consequences, and policy options* (Child Trends Research Brief, Publication #2009-11). Washington, DC: Child Trends.

Murray, C. (1984). *Losing ground.* New York: Basic Books.

The National Commission on Excellence in Education. (1983). *A nation at risk: The imperative for educational reform.* Washington, DC: Author. Retrieved from http://www2.ed.gov/pubs/NatAtRisk/index.html

Peyser, J. A. (1994). School choice: When, not if. *Boston College Law Review, 35*(3), 619–661.

Pixley, C. J. (1998). The next frontier of school finance reform: A policy and constitutional analysis of school choice litigation. *Journal of Legislation, 24,* 21, 26–27.

Sutton, L. C., & King, R. (2011). School vouchers in a climate of change. *Journal of Education Finance, 36*(3), 244–267.

Wolf, P. (2008). School voucher programs: What the research says about parental school choice. *Brigham Young University Law Review, 2008*(2), 415–446.

Court Cases and Statutes

American Recovery and Reinvestment Act of 2009, Pub. L. 111–5, 123 Stat. 115.

Brown v. Board of Education, 347 U.S. 483 (1954).

Everson v. Board of Education, 330 U.S. 1 (1947).

Florida Constitution, Article IX, Education, Section I Public Education (1968).

Holmes v. Bush, 919 So.2d 392 (2006).

Individuals with Disabilities Education Act (IDEA) of 1990, 20 U.S.C. §§ 1400 *et seq.*

Plyler v. Doe, 457 U.S. 202 (1982).

San Antonio Independent School District v. Rodriguez, 411 U.S. 1 (1973).

Swann v. Charlotte-Mecklenburg Board of Education, 402 U.S. 1 (1971).

Zelman v. Simmons-Harris, 536 U.S. 639 (2002).

16

Should the state give tax credits to parents who pay for their children to attend private schools?

POINT: Korrin M. Ziswiler, *University of Dayton*
COUNTERPOINT: Barbara M. De Luca, *University of Dayton*

OVERVIEW

Education tax credits are a diverse set of policies administered by states to allow taxpayers to receive tax credits or tax deductions to offset qualified expenses of attending a private school or for contributions to corporations that sponsor scholarships for private school students. As of 2011 seven states offer one or both of these policy alternatives, most having been initiated since 2006. These policies are essentially incentives managed through the state tax system for the support of nonpublic schools. To satisfy the public school constituencies, some states' policies also include tax credits for certain qualified expenses for attending public schools as well.

Proponents of these initiatives are frequently aligned with school choice advocacy groups that advance the claim that public schools are failing to meet the needs of many children whose needs can be met by private schools, charter schools, or homeschooling; the purpose of the tax credits is to allow parents educational choice. However, most economists argue that the purpose of the tax credits is to lower the price of a private school education. Once the cost of attending private school is lowered, then it follows that there will be a greater demand for private schools and a decreased demand for public education.

The tax credit statutes in the states differ in important ways, making it difficult to make many generalizations about them. For example,

- Is the policy a tax credit or a tax deduction? Tax credits pay above and beyond an individual's tax liability with the excess refunded to the taxpayer. Those individuals with income but no state tax liability will not be able to benefit from a tax deduction.

- Who is the target group for the tax credit? Is the credit only available to parents of children currently enrolled in private schools or can any state taxpayer (individual or corporate) apply for the tax credit? If the target group is limited exclusively to parents of currently enrolled children, then is it plausible to assume that the goal is indeed parental choice of educational institution—fair and simple? If at the other extreme, the target group is all taxpayers (some of whom are not parents of children enrolled in private schools), then it might be assumed that the policy goal is broader than parental educational choice. Rather, the policy goal may be to incentivize the large-scale enrollment of children in the private schools.

- What are *qualified expenses* for the state's policy? The term *qualified expenses* by definition varies by state. A *qualified expense* includes tuition in most states, but additionally may cover extracurricular activities, tutoring, music lessons, academic summer camps, renting of band instruments, and personal computer hardware and software (subject to dollar limits) depending on the state.

In the point essay, Korrin M. Ziswiler argues that the state should provide education tax credits to allow parents to exercise their right to school choice in the education of their children. She suggests that parents constrained by inadequate finances do not possess choice and that tax credits would advance that possibility for well-informed buyers. Her discussion draws on analysis from Milton Friedman to advance the position that difference between using government as a funder but not as an end provider of services, and connects these ideas to what she characterizes as current inefficiencies of government monopolies. She argues that the lack of competition in the public school system has "failed to produce significant results" and that tax credit programs would inspire competition between educational providers. Next, she argues that tax credits advocate choice that will enable parents to exercise their democratic right in choosing a school for their child and will advance the goal of educational equality because children from middle and lower classes will be able to attend schools with upper-class children. Finally, Ziswiler presents the argument that tax credits save the state money because students are no longer in public education where the state per pupil contribution to education is higher than the tax credit.

In the counterpoint essay, Barbara M. De Luca argues that education tax credits are only one of many recent options for parents to "opt out . . . of the public school system altogether, in favor of private schools." She states that there is little evidence that introducing competition into the public school system increases academic achievement. Next, De Luca addresses the fallacies in the popular belief that only those families that can afford to pay to move into a better neighborhood (and therefore can exercise choice) have an equal opportunity for a high quality education.

There is a serious debate about whether the state revenue that is used for the tax credit is "government money" or not. Proponents of tax credits will advance the claim that the funds never were government funds, so that the funds can be legally used to support religious schools. However, De Luca disagrees with this reasoning and takes the view that the funds are government funds and that use of the tax credits for religious schools is indeed not an innocuous event. Finally, this issue would not be complete without a delineation of how the simplistic application of public goods versus private goods depends not on how these entities are funded, but rather on their degree of rivalry and excludability. De Luca concludes that tax credits that allow students to opt out of the public schools would exacerbate the very problems they are attempting to solve.

Lisa G. Driscoll
University of North Carolina at Charlotte

POINT: Korrin M. Ziswiler
University of Dayton

At the base of this argument for tax credits is the idea of parental choice (or school choice)—the right of parents to choose the schools they feel will best meet their children's educational needs. As funding for public schooling continues to be cut by state and federal governments, the cost to educate children adequately continues to increase, and the quality of education offered by public schooling continues to be questioned. The decision to exercise school choice can be shaped by numerous factors such as religious beliefs, whether a child is gifted or has special needs, a school's inadequate past performance, lack of funding for public schools, or a higher caliber of education provided by private schools. Unfortunately, choosing which school their children attend—referred to interchangeably as parental or school choice—is not an option for many families whose inadequate financial resources limit their ability to exercise this right by choosing the school that they believe would best fit their concept of the ideal educational experience for their children. This essay explains private school tax credits and asserts their importance in allowing parents to exercise school choice in the education of their children.

TAX CREDIT PROGRAMS: A FOUNDATION

As public schools continue to fall short in meeting the array of educational demands of the diverse U.S. student population, many citizens are searching for alternate options to provide their children with a quality education. The United States, unlike many other Western democracies, does not generally provide federal funding for private schools to which parents send their children, except for a small number of voucher and tax credit programs in certain states. Charter schools exist as a publicly funded option to traditional private schools, but most are not more successful in providing a better education than their public school counterparts are. Furthermore, even though charter schools are constrained by fewer government mandates, public funding usually comes with some level of government control. Private school tax credit programs differ from state to state depending on the policy established by the state legislature. Typically, tax credit programs function in one of two ways. The first way allows any parents who send their children to a private school to deduct tuition or expenses related to attendance at private schools directly from their income taxes—a dollar-for-dollar forgiveness of taxes owed to the government. This type of private school tax credit will be the basis for arguments that follow because the majority of private school tax credits allow deductions based on tuition expenses. Most programs have a ceiling on the amount that can be deducted; it varies from $500 to about $2,500 per pupil attending private school. For example, according to the Minnesota Department of Revenue, the state of Minnesota offers a tuition tax credit of $1,625 for children in Grades K to 6 and $2,500 for students in Grades 7 to 12. Although these tax credits help reduce the cost of private school tuition, by no means do they cover the entire cost of attending a private school. In these situations, parents must make tuition payment to the school of their choice a priority in their household spending, and in many cases, they are making sacrifices to allow their children to follow the educational path the parents believe is best.

The second way in which educational tax credits contribute to school choice is by creating scholarship funds for students whose families cannot bear the financial burden of attending private school. These scholarship funds differ in each state, but generally, businesses and individuals can earn tax credits, ranging from $500 to $1,000, for donating funds to private institutions for use in their scholarship programs. This type of tax credit program is specifically geared at enabling children and young adults whose families are under or slightly above the poverty line to attend private schools, which in many cases offer educational opportunities superior to those available in public schools. As statistics from the National Center for Education Statistics from 2008 show, the average parochial school tuition is approximately $6,000, and the average private school costs approximately $8,500 per year, per child (U.S. Department of Education). Since programs giving tax credits for private schools still require parents to pay a significant portion of the tuition owed, parental decisions to exercise this option will be carefully made by well-informed buyers. The following sections will outline the major points that support the argument for tuition tax credits for private school education costs.

FREE MARKETS, COMPETITION, AND UPWARD SOCIAL MOBILITY

In his book *Capitalism and Freedom* (1962), Milton Friedman, a noted economist famous for his staunch support of free market economies, states that though government should finance such public goods as education, it does not have to be the end provider of such services. To build on Friedman's premise, most people can agree that all citizens should have equal access to a high quality education and that education is a public good—like national defense or public law enforcement—that benefits all members of society. However, there has been a lack of discussion concerning how revenues from this tax-supported public good can be most efficiently used and disseminated. The government has created other social programs, such as health care and food stamps, for which it does not provide the end product. To this end, why should government-run public schools be the only option funded with educational tax dollars?

Tax credit programs for private school costs would facilitate parental choice, increasing the competition between educational providers and spurring change in ways that reforms have failed to produce significant results in the past. The increase in demand for private schools would inevitably increase the number of private schools, create a competitive educational environment, and keep tuition costs reasonably low. Currently, local public schools possess somewhat of a monopoly in the educational sector in that they are the only available "free" option. Public schools far outspend their private counterparts partly because of bloated administrative costs and increasing teachers' salaries. In this large, centralized bureaucracy with its centralized decision making and multiple layers of administrative hierarchy, incentives for teaching staff are rarely (if ever) tied to performance, and public schools are painfully slow in responding to market needs and growing internal problems. In defense of public school employees, the restrictive control placed on local schools by federal and state governments makes it difficult for leadership to respond quickly and limits the ability of public schools to provide innovative programming and to have the adaptability that would advance the organization. As the costs of the public education system continue to increase, the quality of the education provided has not—another negative side effect of the ability of these institutions to control the whole education "market." Frustratingly, citizens must pay for the public education system even if they are dissatisfied with the product being produced, and as a result, there is little pressure for school systems to undergo overhauling change processes. With increased competition, schools not meeting standards would be forced out of the market if competitors were offering consumers another high quality, cost-comparative option. Increasing the ability to exercise school choice would raise the quality of educational programming and reduce the debilitating bureaucracy that diminishes the capacity for these institutions to be responsive to changes in the environment and in public demand.

Another argument in support of private school tax credits concerns the upward social mobility of the lower economic class and the avoidance of downward social mobility for the middle class. As the gap between the middle class and upper class continues to steadily increase, in many cases tax credits could make private schools affordable for lower- and middle-class families and thus enable them to exercise their school choice rights. Education has often been the tool used to combat poverty in the Unites States particularly during economic readjustment and turmoil. For example, during the Industrial Revolution, the middle class used education to keep from sliding backward into the lower economic class and to better prepare children for the changing job market. Similarly today, the middle class, a socioeconomic sector of society that in recent economic times has been financially squeezed, is desperately searching for a way to better prepare children for future opportunities.

This being said, the argument for tax credits is not an argument for a shift toward socialism in the United States. There is no redistribution of wealth from the affluent to the needy; the private school tax credit is one that can be universally applied to private school expenses incurred by all families regardless of family income. Providing tax credits to assist with private school tuition costs opens avenues to children of all classes by making the educational experience that parents feel will best affect their children's future more affordable. The pull between individual rights and public rights (which belong to all citizens but are controlled and disseminated by the government) is at the heart of the debate over private education tax credits, in that education is both a private good (valuable to parents and children) and a public good (valuable to society). School choice policies such as tax credits support the idea that education is a private good as much as it is a public one, in that they help individuals gain a competitive advantage in their quest for future economic stability and social standing.

ABILITY TO EXERCISE CHOICE

The first argument in support of these tax credit programs revolves around the concepts of democracy, equality, and choice. Tax credits would allow those in the middle and lower classes to exercise their democratic right to choose the school that supports their moral or educational goals for their children, a right that can only be exercised if one can afford it. Upper-class families have the disposable income to make any educational choice possible. For example, recent presidents and wealthy diplomats have sent their children to a prestigious private school in Washington, D.C., with a tuition of approximately $32,000 a year per child (not including textbooks and transportation). Although most of the parents in this country cannot afford to spend this much on their children's education, all families should be able to choose the school that would best suit their children's needs; upper-class families already have the means to make any choice possible.

Although tax credits do not compensate for the entire amount of private school tuition in many cases, it is a step in the direction of attempting to extend educational choice to middle and lower socioeconomic families. Currently, those who send their children to private schools are paying twice to educate their children: once through tax dollars that support local public schools that their children do not attend, and second in paying the private school tuition. This significant amount of tuition severely strains the finances of the average family, especially during times of economic recession when education is most relied on to improve the quality of life. Private school tax credit programs allow for the deduction of a portion of this expense, so they offer some relief for parents who are paying for an educational service they are not consuming.

Although there are arguments concerning increased academic performance of children attending private schools, statistics show that private school students score significantly better on the National Assessment of Educational Progress (NAEP) test, an assessment periodically given by the National Center for Education Statistics to evaluate student knowledge and aptitude in all subjects. Private schools offer differentiated curricula; student self-selection (increased dedication); small, tight-knit communities; and stimulating learning environments, all of which can benefit a spectrum of students from those with developmental issues to those who test as academically gifted. Studies also show that school choice programs, tax credits being one component of this category, increase parental involvement, which has a positive effect on student achievement. Tax credits would enable parents to send their children to private and parochial schools that they might not be able to afford without assistance, and they would provide the students with a more personalized educational curriculum, smaller class sizes, more advanced placement courses, higher graduation standards, and a safer learning environment (e.g., there are fewer instances of hate crimes, brutality, and bullying, and fewer substance abuse issues) that would give them a leg up in getting into better colleges. This access to better education could provide children with better opportunities and brighter futures.

REDUCTION OF THE OVERALL EXPENSE OF STATE GOVERNMENTS

Taxes collected for the purposes of schooling are intended for the betterment of all children, so why should these taxes benefit only those who attend public school? The cost of educating children in the public education system continues to soar, but negligible gains are being made relative to performance indicators. In some urban areas, high educational challenge factors (factors that contribute to increasing the cost of education) have raised the cost of education to $6,000 to $10,000 per pupil. Since private school tax credit programs will lower the cost of tuition, they not only will save money for those parents who already send their children to private schools but will also motivate more parents to choose alternate schooling options, thereby reducing state expenditures on education. As more students leave public schools to attend private ones, the per pupil education expenditures of each state will be reduced. In essence, when a child leaves the school system, the state no longer pays the cost to educate him or her, but it still receives tax dollars from parent's property taxes and income taxes. These excess funds can be reinvested in public education, used for other initiatives, or returned to the taxpayers. Studies completed to analyze projections of national savings from tax credit programs show that although savings would occur in all states, the most significant benefit would be realized by states with sizable urban areas where per pupil expenses are the highest and there is great demand for private education because of underperforming public schools. Although tax credits would cost the government tax revenue, it would reduce the burden of the states' education costs, which now consist of about 90% of the money spent on primary and secondary education.

ISSUES OF CONCERN

Although private school tax credit programs have a multitude of benefits, improper use of such policies could negate the gains made. Should the government impose increased requirements on private school tax credit plans, the benefits of exercising school choice could be severely limited. For example, giving tax credits only to parents of children enrolled in "preferred" schools would inevitably lead to state or federal requirements on curricula and functioning of private schools. In addition, the entrance of more for-profit private schools to meet the increased demand for alternate K–12 educational options brings about a completely new set of issues to debate. In most arguments for school choice, proponents are supporting nonprofit private or religiously affiliated schools, but the shift to a more market-based competitive educational setting would undoubtedly lead to schools aimed at making a financial profit. In the end, parents have to make responsible, carefully planned decisions about how to best educate their children.

STRATIFICATION, DIVERSITY, AND SKIMMING

Many opponents of private school tax credits assert that such programs will increase the separation of the student population by socioeconomic status.

This increase in inequality, they claim, would occur because even with tax credits, not all families could afford to send their children to private schools. Critics of tax credit programs contend that those families who could flee public schools would do so, decreasing school diversity. These assumptions are fundamentally flawed. Most public schools lack a diverse student population because of closed enrollment policies that assign students to a school on the basis of geographic location, which is mainly determined by the costs of living in neighborhoods. As a result of such policies, high-performing public schools mostly serve upper- to middle-class students living in prosperous neighborhoods. Empirical evidence shows that there is a correlation between income and race; public schools themselves suffer from stratification based mainly on wealth. In contrast, private schools have open enrollment policies, accepting students from all neighborhoods. Although tuition expenses may impede students in lower socioeconomic classes from freely entering private schools, tax credits, scholarships created by the credits, and scholarships given by the schools themselves are awarded to children from lower income families to make attendance possible.

Along these same lines, opponents of private school tax credits stress the harmful effects of private schools "skimming" the best students from public schools, weakening the ability of students to model and learn from high-performing peers. This may already be occurring as students choose to attend magnet schools or charter schools, both of which are public schooling options. The moral question is whether these high-performing students should be held back for the purpose of educating their peers. Public schools should not rely on high-performing students to give educational advantages to other students. Furthermore, if some high-performing students left the public system, it would free up time and resources for middle- and lower-performing students.

SEPARATION OF CHURCH AND STATE

Some oppose private school tax credits because they believe that allowing government money to flow to parochial schools is unconstitutional. This "no money flow" argument is intended to stem government funding of religious causes that not all Americans support; however, there are instances when such funding is already given and is not deemed unconstitutional. For example, the GI Bill offers government funding for higher education to veterans who can choose any higher education institution, religious or otherwise. Because funding in this case is not considered unconstitutional, the argument concerning money flow seems to be one conditionally applied to the case of tax credits. It is true that the majority of people who currently send their children to private schools do so to educate their children at faith-based schools that align with their moral and religious beliefs. Some argue that when parents cannot send their children to a faith-based school because of the cost, their rights as citizens are infringed upon because they are being forced to have their children educated in a system that promotes a belief system contradictory to their own.

COUNTERPOINT: Barbara M. De Luca
University of Dayton

Back in the 1700s, when Benjamin Franklin, George Washington, and Thomas Jefferson, among others, sanctioned public education, their goals were both political and moral. To maintain the democracy, our forefathers contended that the populace must be able to read, write, add, and subtract. To read the Bible, people must be able to read. Fast forward to the 21st century, and recognize the same goals reiterated in the No Child Left Behind Act of 2001, the imperative to teach students reading, writing, and mathematics. By many people's standards, the public school system in this country has failed to meet these goals. Achievement levels of urban school students, particularly minority students, lag behind the levels of their suburban white counterparts. The same gap exists with graduation and dropout rates. These discrepancies have created the impetus behind the current education choice movement in public education.

School choice is not a new concept in this country. The concept of the voucher system was introduced back in the 1700s by Adam Smith when he suggested that parents should be given the money to pay teachers appropriately for educating their children. Since then, many school choice provisions have surfaced. The Supreme Court's finding in *Brown v. Board of Education* in 1954 clearly allowed for choice by ruling that no student could be denied the admission to a school on the grounds of race. Magnet schools were an option after desegregation in the 1960s and 1970s, and vouchers remain a viable option in a few communities in the first decade of the 21st century. The most prevalent option available to all public school students is a charter school. Although the concept of charter schools began in the 1970s, it did not take hold until the 1990s, first in Minnesota (1991) and soon after in California (1992). Most recently, provisions of the No Child Left Behind law, as well as some state laws, allow parents with children in failing public schools to opt out of their assigned public school and out of the public school system altogether, in favor of private schools. One of the most recent options being discussed is tax credits.

EDUCATION TAX CREDITS

Although the education tax credit programs in place at the end of the first decade of the 21st century all differed in one way or another, at least seven states allowed some form of education tax credit for public elementary or secondary school students. Iowa enacted tax credits for education as early as 1987. Arizona and Minnesota followed suit 10 years later in 1997. Florida, Pennsylvania, Rhode Island, and Georgia had tax credit legislation by 2008, and Iowa expanded its program in 2006.

Education tax credits allow the taxpayer to subtract some or all expenses associated with educating a child at a private elementary or secondary school, from the taxes owed at the state level. Several different iterations of tax credits currently exist. There are personal income tax credits for the tuition, or, in some states, other education expenses. Some states cap this amount, but others do not. Some states allow credits in an amount greater than the taxes owed, reimbursing the taxpayer for the difference, and some allow the credit for no more than the value of the tax owed, whether or not that amount meets the state cap or the individual need. In some states, only individual taxpayers with dependents transferring from public to private school are eligible, but in others, anyone is eligible for the tax credit as long as the individual owes state taxes and the credit dollars are donated to a nonprofit organization established to fund private school educations for public school students.

In both Arizona and Florida, corporate tax credits are allowed. Florida does not have individual tax credits, only corporate ones. In each state, corporations are permitted to take advantage of education tax credits by donating the tax credit to a nonprofit corporation specifically established to fund, either partially or completely, a private school education for elementary and secondary students opting out of the public system. Generally, the tax credits are dollar-for-dollar up to a specific cap, although corporations in Pennsylvania only get a credit for 90 cents on the dollar. Caps are applied in a variety of ways. Some states cap the amount of the donation from any one corporation, and some cap the total amount of corporate donations, essentially capping the amount of money lost by the state. The private, nonprofit organizations receiving the tax credit dollars are responsible for distributing the money to individual families for their students to attend private elementary or secondary schools.

MARKET-BASED EDUCATION POLICY

Promoters of education tax credits contend that they are but one of several ways to impose competition on a public education system that otherwise more closely resembles a monopoly. Traditionally defined, a monopoly is a market in which there is only one seller. In the case of public schools, although there are many districts in a state and each district might interpret state regulations slightly differently, in reality, there is only one provider/seller, the state government. The problem with monopolies is that there is no competition, and when there is no competition, there is no incentive to adjust, change, or, in the case of public schools, improve. Some believe that education tax credits allowing students to attend private schools that accept the credits will induce public schools to improve their academic programs to improve student academic achievement, thus retaining students who might otherwise use tax credit money to attend private, more academically successful, schools.

There is little evidence that imposing competition will improve the quality of education provided by the public school system. The first publicly funded voucher program of modern times began during the 1990–1991 school year. If one looks at programs that provide vouchers funded with state money to students for attending private elementary and secondary schools, evidence indicates that parents are happier with the new school, but there is little to support that academic achievement improved in the public schools affected by the loss of students because of voucher programs.

The charter school movement is another example of an effort to infuse competition into an otherwise monopolistic system. The first charter school law passed in Minnesota in 1991; at the beginning of the 2010–2011 school year, approximately 5,400 charter schools were operating in 40 states and Washington, D.C. The evidence of improved academic achievement in a traditional public school district subsequent to losing many students to local charter schools is inconclusive at best. Early research found no impact on student achievement for traditional public school students.

In other words, the data do not show that creating competition for the traditional public school systems improves the quality of education they provide. More recent research indicates that there is a small positive impact on achievement for students remaining in traditional districts affected by charter schools.

The small positive impact on the traditional public school system as a result of the two major choice models currently in place seems even smaller when we consider that there have been 20 years since their inception to make a difference. There is little evidence that education tax credits will contribute to improved student achievement in traditional public schools to a greater degree than have vouchers or charter schools. However, there is even less evidence that tax credits will do greater harm by attracting "the cream of the crop" to private schools. It simply is not clear that the existence of tax credits will substantially improve or harm the state systems currently in existence because of the threat of competition.

RELATIONSHIP BETWEEN CHOICE AND EQUITY

Promoters of education choice contend that tuition tax credits will result in greater equity in the elementary and secondary education system. That is, the money garnered from tuition tax credits will allow parents of students in failing schools to pay for education at better quality schools than the ones their children are currently attending. Without tuition tax credits, only those families who can afford to move into a successful school district or to send their children to private schools have choices. Because of this, all children do not have an equal opportunity to receive a high quality education. Therefore, as the argument goes, lack of choice in education translates into lack of equity.

There are a couple of problems with this line of thought. First, most states that support tuition tax credits cap the dollar value of the credit. In some states, the cap decreases as income increases; in others, it is fixed at all income levels. This cap is not high enough to pay the full tuition amount at most private schools.

Tuition tax credits in some states are refundable but are nonrefundable in other states. A nonrefundable credit can reduce the taxpayer's tax liability to zero, but not below, whether or not the value of the taxes owed is more or less than the tuition tax credit cap. In contrast, a refundable tax credit reduces the tax liability to zero and provides any additional money for which the taxpayer is eligible, because of the tax credit cap, in the form of a check from the state. According to the Tax Foundation, using numbers from the Internal Revenue Service, the average income tax burden of households in the bottom 20% income category was $171 compared with $1,431 in the second lowest income bracket in 2004. The burden increased to $3,720 for the third 20%, $7,973 for the fourth 20%, and jumped to $29,257 for households in the top 20% income category. This means that with a nonrefundable system, households in the lowest income bracket would receive, on average, a tax credit of $171. The value of this tax credit would not be great enough to pay tuition at any private school, leaving the poorest students from a socioeconomic standpoint in the poorest schools from an academic standpoint.

If $7,973—the average tax burden for households in the fourth 20%—were permitted as a tax credit, it is unlikely it would be enough money to pay tuition at most private schools for one year. The point here is that even if tuition tax credits are authorized by law, it is not likely that the value of the credit would pay for full tuition at a private school or be enough money for a family to move to a school district with high academic credentials. If the tax credit does not cover the tuition, it is unlikely that many households living in urban districts with academically poor schools would be financially able to supplement the credit to pay tuition. However, those in households in the upper income brackets would likely be able to afford to add the money to that needed to send their dependents to academically better schools. Without tax credits, the poor have little choice, but it is not clear that tax credits would give them any greater choice. Tuition tax credits for elementary and secondary schools would not increase education equity by providing greater opportunities for low income children in academically poor schools.

CHURCH–STATE ISSUE

Choice advocates go to great lengths to deny that vouchers allowing children to transfer from public to private schools violate the Establishment Clause. The 1947 ruling in *Everson v. Board of Education* supported their claim, as the U.S. Supreme Court determined that it was not a violation of this clause for parents of children attending parochial schools to be reimbursed for bus transportation. Many subsequent cases testing the constitutionality of vouchers (including *Lemon v. Kurtzman,* 1971 and *Zelman v. Simmons-Harris,* 2002) have been used to defend spending public money for private (usually religious) education. The defense is that the money is not going directly to the religious education institution but, rather, to the parents of the children. However, the impact of voucher programs is that the money *is* going to educate students in religious schools. Education tax credit proponents follow this argument through and contend that there is no reason to believe that tuition tax credits that allow students to transfer from public to private religious schools are a violation of the First Amendment's separation of church and state doctrine. In his book, *NeoVouchers: The Emergence of Tuition Tax Credits for Private Schooling* (2008), Kevin Welner calls tax credits "neovouchers" because they are the newest strategy for channeling public money into private schools, most of which are religious. Promoters of such policies argue that the credits do not have to go to private religious schools. The problem is that the data show that most voucher money does go to private religious schools, and there is no reason to believe that tax credit money will not be routed in the same direction. The limited data available on the use of tax credit money confirm this. Clearly, public money is being used for private religious education.

Supposedly, the law does not allow the money to be used for any nonsecular purpose. The problem is, it is nearly impossible to distinguish between secular and nonsecular purposes in this context. Tax credit money in some states that currently allow the practice is specifically designed to pay tuition. Sure, the money cannot be used to teach religion. But, is it "excessive entanglement" to hire a history teacher who also teaches one religion class? Furthermore, it seems impossible to measure the entanglement if tax credit money is used, for example, to buy new tables in the cafeteria, and the money originally set aside for the tables is used to buy new religion books. In other words, tax credit money can supplant money for secular uses, and the money it supplants can be used for nonsecular purposes. This manipulation of money creates a serious dilemma with respect to separation of church and state.

Promoters of tuition tax credits claim that the money being used really is not government money nor is it technically a government expenditure; therefore, there is no issue with the Establishment Clause or any problem with excessive entanglement. Because the government never had the money, it is not government money, and as such, the government could not spend it; therefore, the credit is not a government expenditure. Consequently, the government is not involved with funding religious schools. The operative word here is *technically*. In economic terms, technically, it is not an expenditure; however, the intent of the credit is certainly to promote private schools, most of which are religious. In reality, the government is supporting religious schools.

Another justification for spending government money for private schooling is that much of the money really comes from corporations, not the government. Individual taxpayers get the credit and donate the credit to a nonprofit corporation specifically established to fund a private school education as described earlier. In this way, advocates claim, government money is not going directly to the private school; it is going to the corporation. Similar to the expenditure argument just posed, the intent of the credit is to fund private, generally religious, education. This is another case of the government funding religious schools.

PUBLIC VERSUS PRIVATE GOODS

Although choice advocates would argue this point, public schools are public goods and private schools are private goods. A public good is one that is nonrivalrous, that is, its consumption or use by one person does not reduce the availability of the good to others, and non-excludable, meaning that it is difficult if not impossible to exclude anyone from using it. The most common example of a public good is national defense. Public goods exist for several reasons, particularly because of their non-excludability; if they were paid for individually, some people would not pay but would still enjoy the benefits of the good offered—again, consider national defense. These are goods that benefit everyone because they are available to everyone.

Private goods, on the other hand, are goods from which nonpayers can be excluded. One consumer's use of a private good benefits that user only, not the greater public (although this could be argued a little in the case of such things as antiperspirants and soap). In addition, if one person consumes a good—an omelet, for instance—another person cannot consume that same omelet; a rivalry exists for that one omelet. Private goods are rivalrous.

Students of economics are often taught that public schools are not public goods and private schools are not private goods because the distinction is not based on how they are funded, but rather on the characteristics of nonrivalry and excludability. Even if this is the case, it does not mean that public schools are not public goods and private schools are not private goods. Public schools are non-excludable and nonrivalrous, but private schools are both excludable and rivalrous. There is little doubt of this.

No one can be excluded from a public school, except when he or she is expelled for an egregious violation of the rules. Public elementary and secondary schools are nonrivalrous. That is, one student attending public school in the fourth grade does not prevent another student from attending fourth grade at the same school. This is not the case with private elementary and secondary schools. Anyone who does not meet the school's admission criteria will not be enrolled in the school. Furthermore, it is quite possible that when the private school is "filled to capacity," students will be assigned to a waiting list, indicative of a rivalrous situation. When the capacity of a public school is exceeded, however, class sizes are usually increased beyond the desired levels.

Public goods are often funded with public money, that is, tax revenue, whereas private goods are often paid for with private money. The argument often posited in favor of using public money for a good is that providing the good benefits others—in some cases, many others. These benefits are called positive externalities. Two positive externalities of public education are lower community crime rates and higher levels of living because of well-educated citizens. Some would contend, and rightly so, that these would exist with private education as well. This is true, but the point of public education is that everyone gets educated at a level that will provide these benefits. If this is not happening in the public school system, paid for with public money, then something must be done with the public system.

Education tax credits that would allow students to opt out of the public system are not the answer. They are the equivalent of letting anyone carve a new road wherever a driver wants to because there are terrible potholes in the public road provided with tax money. The solution, of course, would be to fix the damaged road, not to create more roads.

CONCLUSION

In summary, for the many reasons identified previously as well as others there was no space to discuss, no, the state should not give tax credits to parents who pay for their children to attend private schools.

FURTHER READINGS AND RESOURCES

Catterall, J. S., & Levin, H. M. (1982). Public and private schools: Evidence on tuition tax credits. *Sociology of Education, 55,* 144–151.

Choice in education: Are tuition tax credits the answer? (1982). *IFG Policy Notes, 3*(1), 1–4.

Chubb, J. E., & Moe, T. M. (1990). *Politics, markets, and America's schools.* Washington, DC: Brookings Institution.

Flowers, M. R. (1988). Tuition tax credits and the public schools. *National Tax Journal 41*(1), 87–96.

Friedman, M. (1962). *Capitalism and freedom.* Chicago: University of Chicago Press.

Glazer, N. (1982, October 22). *The future under tuition tax credits.* Paper presented at the Tuition Tax Credit Seminar, Washington, DC.

Hakim, S., Seidenstat, P., & Bowman, G. W. (Eds.). (1994). *Privatizing education and educational choice.* Westport, CT: Praeger.

Hansen, K. H. (1980). *Tuition tax credits: Current status and policy issues.* Portland, OR: Northwest Regional Educational Laboratory.

Labaree, D. F. (1997). Public goods, private goods: The American struggle over educational goals. *American Educational Research Journal, 34*(1), 39–81.

Merrifield, J. (2001). *The school choice wars.* Lanham, MD: Scarecrow Press.

U.S. Department of Education, National Center for Education Statistics. *Table 63. Private elementary and secondary enrollment, number of schools, and average tuition, by school level, orientations and tuition: 1999–2000, 2003–04, and 2007–08.* Retrieved from http://nces.ed.gov/programs/digest/d10/tables/dt10_063.asp

Welner, K. (2008). *NeoVouchers: The emergence of tuition tax credits for private schooling.* Lanham, MD: Rowman & Littlefield.

COURT CASES AND STATUTES

Brown v. Board of Education, 347 U.S. 483 (1954).

Everson v. Board of Education, 330 U.S. 1 (1947).

Lemon v. Kurtzman, 403 U.S. 602 (1971).

No Child Left Behind Act of 2001, 20 U.S.C. §§ 6301 *et seq.*

Zelman v. Simmons-Harris, 536 U.S. 639 (2002).

Should the state create and fund charter schools that are not subject to the same standards and requirements as traditional schools?

POINT: Lenford C. Sutton, *Alabama State University*
COUNTERPOINT: Betty Cox, *University of Tennessee at Martin*

OVERVIEW

One of the most revolutionary—and controversial—educational reforms of the last 20 years is the creation of charter schools. Charter schools are public schools, but they have substantially more autonomy than the typical public school has. Rather than being run by the school district's central administration and being accountable to the local school board, charter schools are run by a school-based governing board. More importantly, charter schools are exempt from many, if not most, of the regulations that apply to the typical public school. Consequently, charter schools may pursue a different curriculum than the rest of the school district. Similarly, teachers at charter schools may have different salary schedules or professional qualifications than those in the regular public schools have. Perhaps most significantly, the role of parents in school decision making is substantially higher than at the general public schools.

Since Minnesota enacted the first charter school law in 1991, most of the states have followed suit. However, the states vary greatly in how charter schools are created and in the accountability mechanism. In some states, such as Virginia, charter schools are rare and do not play a significant role in education. In other states, such as Colorado, charter schools have become viable competitors to the traditional public schools. Parents have a meaningful choice between the charter school and the regular school.

Essentially, charter schools represent an experiment in educational reform. Not surprisingly, some charter schools are enormously effective, but others have struggled and performed worse than the traditional public schools. The uneven quality of charter schools has only increased the controversy over their existence. Quite simply, many feel that resources should not be diverted to experiments that fail. Moreover, because charter schools operate outside of normal union work rules, teachers generally are somewhat skeptical of charter schools. Finally, in communities where there is a history of unconstitutional racial discrimination, charter schools seem to be reminiscent of the private, all-white academies that characterized the era of massive resistance to desegregation.

Summary of the Debate

This debate asks whether the states should establish charter schools. In general, those who favor charter schools tend to distrust the existing educational establishment and oppose the traditional union work rules. The public schools are broken, and charters offer one solution that may help. Conversely, those who oppose charter schools tend to be staunch defenders of the existing educational status quo and generally favor protections for teachers. The public schools face many problems, and resources should not be diverted for projects that benefit only a few children. Moreover, the infusion of business for-profit management practices—which is a common characteristic of charter schools—is inappropriate for public education.

Lenford C. Sutton, a professor of education at Alabama State University, takes the affirmative view favoring charter schools. He makes three points. First, the evidence indicates that, overall, charter schools have had a positive impact on student performance. Second, charter schools bring together teachers, parents, and administrators and unite them in a common goal. Such a development, particularly the involvement of parents, is essential to bettering education. Third, charter schools have made significant innovations in how teachers relate to each other and to their students. In addition, Sutton notes that charter schools often produce better results with less money and have made significant strides in reducing inequality. If the public schools are to be a force for social mobility and if education is to be reformed to confront the global challenges of the 21st century, charter schools can play a vital role in the process.

Betty Cox, a professor of education at the University of Tennessee at Martin, takes the negative view—opposing charter schools. She makes four arguments. First, greater autonomy has not led to greater accountability. To the contrary, fewer accountability standards are applied to charter schools. Because charter schools receive public funds, they should not be exempted from the regulatory standards applicable to traditional public schools. Indeed, there have been several cases of fraud and abuse involving charter schools. Second, evidence indicates that the management of charter schools is ineffective. The managers are either incapable or unwilling to take the necessary steps for prudent management. Third, charter schools' record with respect to student achievement is, at best, mixed or incomplete. Indeed, in some instances, it is impossible to know whether the charter school is performing or not performing. Fourth, charter schools have disproportionate political influence, which makes accountability and oversight more difficult.

William E. Thro
Christopher Newport University

POINT: Lenford C. Sutton
Alabama State University

Charter schools are publicly funded alternative institutions designed to provide parents with a school choice option. To date, the majority of charter schools are independent of local school systems in that they have been given flexibility to work without teacher union work rules and given the power to hire and fire school personnel. In addition, charter schools also have the autonomy to control their own budgets and, more importantly, parents, students, and teachers have the freedom to organize around a common education theme or teaching methodology.

Nearly 2 decades after the establishment of the first charter school in Minnesota, 40 states have enacted statutory provisions and established more than 4,000 charter schools serving more than 1.2 million public school children (Education Commission of the States, n.d.). Nevertheless, charter schools remain one of the most contentious issues in the public discourse concerning comprehensive reform of the education enterprise. Charter school opponents have long believed that learning institutions that adopt business principles may eventually succumb to the uncertainty of market forces and shut down, effectively minimizing continuous learning for a number of students. Similarly, opponents assert that the infusion of for-profit management companies to lead school improvement efforts may result in decision making that occurs far away from the actual school and that ignores the culture of the learning organization. The opposition has also expressed concerns about the critical tension between the government's goal of securing accurate student accountability measures and the relaxed regulations required to unleash market forces, which may make it even more difficult to determine what actually works to help improve student performance. In addition, those who oppose the proliferation of charter schools fear that it may lead to resegregated schools and a diminished quality of learning opportunities afforded students with limited English proficiency and students with special needs (Education Commission of the States, n.d). This point essay specifically articulates why states should create and fund charter schools that operate under standards different from those required of traditional schools.

IMPROVED STUDENT PERFORMANCE

First, a body of empirical evidence suggests charter schools have had significantly positive results for their students. An evaluation of charter schools in

New York City revealed that students accepted into charter school through a lottery system performed better than did their peers who lost the lottery and remained in traditional public schools (Hoxby, Murarka, & Kang, 2009). Another study revealed that middle school students enrolled in Florida charter schools, who also enrolled in charter high schools were more likely to enroll in postsecondary education than were their peers who returned to traditional high school settings because no charter high schools were available for them (Sass, 2006). Additional research concluded that students enrolled by lottery at independently operated charter schools in Boston performed significantly better than did students who lost the lottery and remained in traditional schools. In addition, the same study found that students enrolled by lottery in schools under union influence received no significant change in their performance (Abdulkadiroglu et al., 2009).

Not surprisingly, charter school opponents have criticized the study for its short-term comparisons, the absence of vetting by independent scholars, and its political intentions (Carnoy, Jacobsen, Mishel, & Rothstein, 2005). All serious researchers acknowledge the difficulty of variable isolation in behavioral sciences; however, the degree to which differentiated charter schools, in the studies mentioned, affect student learning should compel traditional schools to improve the performance of their schools—especially if they intend to compete for students and the dollars tied to their enrollment. A study conducted in 49 school districts in 2001 found that each made significant changes to its curriculum and operations in response to the presence of charter schools within its district (RPP International, 2001).

BUILDING A LEARNING COMMUNITY

Second, the self-selection and commitment of charter school participants provide a great opportunity to establish cooperation, unity, and common purpose within a newly formed learning community. Since their inception, charter schools have been designed to join like-minded founders who are afforded the opportunity to adopt and design a governance infrastructure that supports the mission and objectives of the school (Budde, 1988). The spirit of cooperation among charter schools is primarily reinforced by the coalition of willing students and parents who freely exercise their individual "choice" of learning environments. A comprehensive study reported a difference between groups of parents who opted out of traditional schools and chose charter schools for their children, on the one hand, and those who opted out but chose private schools, on the other hand. Parents who selected charter school settings were more likely to have learned about the charter school from its own literature and advertisement, whereas parents who chose private settings were more likely to learn about their school selection through families and friends. Furthermore, charter school parents were more likely to cite academic reasons as the main factor in selecting schools, but private school parents were nearly twice as likely to focus on school culture and student population when selecting their schools (Teske & Reichardt, 2006). Accordingly, one must conclude that most charter school parents who searched for alternatives to traditional public schools were serious about finding schools with an academic focus that would meet the needs of their children, as opposed to finding a systematic method to segregate their children from others who are different. That kind of commitment and focus among parents is much needed for strong school improvement efforts, and charter school settings, free of antiquated regulations, are the perfect environments for sustaining parental enthusiasm and support for the school's mission.

EMPLOYMENT PRACTICES

Third, charter schools are empowered to innovate and explore best practices when they are liberated from union regulations. For example, a number of studies of charter schools have chronicled a laundry list of reforms that would not be possible if the schools agreed to collaborate with teacher unions. These studies revealed that charter schools (a) use performance pay in lieu of single salary schedules and rewards for years of experience and graduate credit hours, (b) are able to hire uncertified teachers, (c) provide pay incentives to attract high need teachers in math and science, and (d) have teacher turnover rates greater than those in traditional public schools, allowing charter schools to build stronger faculties. On the other hand, if charter schools are unionized, then they will not be able to retain the human resource policies necessary for the schools to succeed. As a former school administrator, this writer can recall many instances in which new teachers fully committed to the goals of the organization were pushed aside and relegated to the least desirable teaching assignments as part of their induction into a traditional public school. It certainly would have been nice to channel their exuberance and enthusiasm to children and classes commensurate with their readiness before it was suppressed by collegial rites of passage within the school. Regulated charter schools provide these kinds of leadership opportunities.

FINANCING OF CHARTER SCHOOLS

Now this point essay will turn to making the case for why states should finance charter schools that operate under standards different than those required of traditional schools, which requires a discussion in an appropriate context.

Historically, fiscal support for public education in the United States has largely been a local enterprise; however, the specter of the spread of communism throughout the height of the cold war with the Soviet Union in tandem with the space race served as incentive for increased state and federal government involvement in public education (Spring, 2004). For that reason, many scholars have come to believe government may have overreached into local school matters and subsequently suppressed the organizational flexibility necessary to meet the individual needs of students. Forty years of civil challenges to state school funding plans have resulted in persistent disparities in public school revenues nationwide. School finance scholars predict these funding disparities will continue well into the future, primarily because local control is still a major determinant of school funding (Ritchey, 2000). In effect, wealthy districts with higher assessed values, in tandem with low tax efforts, retain advantages over areas with lower assessed values tasked with generating similar revenue levels but with higher tax efforts. Even more obvious is that students from the poorest communities, often black and Hispanics, continue to have the least amount of financial resources available in their respective learning communities (Books, 1999).

Currently, charter schools are funded like traditional public schools because they receive revenue from private donors, local school districts, state legislatures, and the federal government; however, they are not allowed to raise local taxes or receive state or local funding for school facilities. Until there is a body of research suggesting that bricks, mortar, and infrastructure significantly affect student performance, dollars for charter school facilities should remain as is. However, a long-term analysis of productivity in California charter schools found that even though charter schools received less funding per pupil than traditional public schools received, student productivity was similar in both school settings. Thus, the principal investigators of the study proclaimed that California charter schools were providing payers with "more bang for their buck" than traditional public schools were (Center on Educational Governance, 2007, p. 6). The private–public partnership configuration of charter schools provides a tremendous opportunity to enhance educational equity, provide nonpunitive school choice, and provide the type of deregulated environment needed to encourage risk taking and instructional innovation that works for students; not surprisingly, the usual points of contention regarding school reform are a real threat.

CHARTER SCHOOLS AND SOCIAL EQUALITY

Horace Mann believed "common schools" would be the "great equalizer" and the obvious method for eliminating poverty. An educated citizenry would be empowered to develop "new treasures of natural and material wealth." He also believed education was the key to uplifting the moral climate of the nation as a whole and ultimately served as a "common good" to all citizens of our nation (Cremin, 1957). Today, many state legislatures advocate egalitarianism in their constitutional provisions for public education, yet there remains a clear need to restructure schools to equip them to address the differentiated needs of each student.

Support for the state creation and funding of charter schools that are regulated differently than traditional public schools should not be examined in the context of any political ideology. Rather the creation of charter schools should be viewed as one of the strongest means to facilitate a fundamental restructuring of schooling. Since U.S. schools were declared at risk nearly 30 years ago, students, parents, and teachers have wanted schools to look the same as they did for the previous generation of students. Moreover, a large portion of the public believes that schools are fine the way they are and that those who can actually make a difference—students and teachers—have not put forth the effort needed to enhance student performance. After decades of legislative changes to the education enterprise and political skirmishes about the appropriate role of government in public education, the public perception of public schools is no better than it was 3 decades ago. To alter this perception, expanded school choice should be considered as one method of restructuring, but not as a silver bullet cloaked in an attempt to politically influence the electorate. Policymakers must embrace the idea that school choice is needed, but they should not pretend that the quality of life for children can be improved by schools alone. Reforms in child care, health care, housing standards, social welfare, and job training for the 21st century must become realities before the lives of children can be substantially enhanced through schools.

SCHOOL CHOICE

In 2002, school choice was expanded when the U.S. Supreme Court declared public funding of religious education acceptable, finding that it did not violate the Establishment Clause of the First Amendment (*Zelman v. Simmons-Harris,* 2002). In the aftermath of the decision, conservative coalitions have embraced the decision as a victory for more parental control over education, but they seem unable to demonstrate a nexus between their legal victory and instructional innovations that move student performance. Conversely, liberal coalitions continue to criticize the judicial activism as the hallmark of both the Rehnquist and Roberts Courts, but they seem unwilling to demand structural changes in public education that would reduce dissatisfaction with public education. The major change needed in the current discourse around school choice is that public school advocates should embrace the winds of political change ushered in by the historic 2008 presidential election and an ecumenical coalition calling for comprehensive school reform. This phenomenon, along with the financial incentive for education reform provided by the Obama administration's Race to the Top program, signals a bipartisan platform for school reform that insists public schools must change; charter schools provide such an opportunity.

Charter schools will allow schools to go in and out of business based on their performance. However, if they are held to the same standards as public schools and if unions are allowed to have great influence, then new and perhaps more appropriate human resources (teacher and administrators) will not be available to implement changes needed for the survival of charter schools. Less state regulation for charter schools can provide an opportunity for the marketplace to reward excellent schools and minimize the number of bad schools, but it is important not to run the risk of abandoning those students whose parents are not actively searching in the education marketplace. Charter schools should not be used for political gain, to enhance individual financial positions, to assist advantaged students alone, or to isolate children on the basis of factors such as socioeconomic class or race/ethnicity. Rather, charter schools should be used to benefit all school-age children in the United States by providing an option to traditional public schools.

The author of the counterpoint essay has eloquently focused on the fringe elements of the charter school movement to substantiate the reinforcement of the public school hegemony that has existed for decades. The author's mere implication that charter schools free of government regulation would initiate an influx of lower-quality teachers is the classic case of an advocate's use of a straw man to strike fear in the minds of parents who may embrace charter school options. Sure, some charter schools have come under scrutiny and have eventually closed because of fraud and mismanagement of school funding; however, when such problems are identified at a school, it is quickly shut down, as it should be, in keeping with free market principles. About 8% of charter schools have been shut down for these reasons thus far; but such problems also occur in public schools. How many public schools have been closed down for similar violations? When such indiscretions occur within the regulated public school system, individual school leaders are often replaced by others who continue with the same problematic business structure, and the system is treated as the holy grail of education—free from scrutiny and immune from systemic reforms. Calls for complete uniformity between public school and charter schools only perpetuate the status quo, offering little incentive or even the capacity for schools to provide innovative pedagogy. Furthermore, if there were truly an advocacy for uniformity among charter and public schools, then my colleague would surely embrace the allocation of the 20% start-up costs charged to charter schools by state lawmakers; an expenditure that would be dead on arrival in the midst of the current financial crisis. Be careful what you ask taxpayers to support! The idea that increased regulations for charter schools will provide more information to help parents evaluate school performance severely underestimates the ability of parents to determine when schools are meeting the needs of their children. Lastly, education that is grounded in behavioral science research has always and will continue to struggle with its ability to minimize error and isolate attribution for variables that enhance student learning. Any attempts by my counterpart to claim that charter schools have promised any level of certainty for student outcomes knowing there are many variables, both internal and external, that contribute to student learning are, at a minimum, inaccurate.

COUNTERPOINT: Betty Cox
University of Tennessee at Martin

The charter school movement originated with the purpose of affording schools the opportunity for innovation coupled with freedom from regulation. In theory, in exchange for autonomy, charter schools would be held accountable for student results, thus producing a more effective educational environment than have traditional schools. Despite the original intent and exemption from various standards and regulations, the record of charter schools is marred by uncertainty about their quality and viability.

Charter schools are public schools created by state law to provide parents and students with an alternative to traditional public schools. They do not charge tuition and are generally open to all children in the school district in which they are located. Designated as schools "that have no rules," state legislatures define their form and structure, and charter schools are established and maintained at public expense.

As public schools, charter schools receive per pupil funding comparable with that of other public schools. Although the revenue primarily derives from state and local funding, eligible charter schools may receive federal dollars through formula subsidies as well as discretionary grant funding for planning, start-up, and implementation costs. As a result, traditional schools lose financial support once charter schools emerge within their district and accept students and the funding attached to them.

By its definition, the U.S. Department of Education exempts charter schools from state or local rules that inhibit the flexible operation and management of public schools. Even though charter schools are bound by some mandates that generally apply to all public schools, such as the No Child Left Behind Act of 2001 (NCLB), the common theme running throughout state laws is that charter schools are not subject to the same restrictions and are not held to standards equivalent to those governing traditional public schools.

The flexibility of charter school laws varies considerably among states, but most do not require charter schools to comply with a variety of conventional public school requirements. Depending on the independence granted in state provisions, charter schools may not be expressly compelled to hire certified teachers, use core curricula, contract for services, or adhere to common practices of teacher compensation, collective bargaining, and teacher termination procedures. Further, these schools can determine the length and number of instructional days and are often released from basic reporting obligations of other public schools. The result is that charter school operators enjoy the freedom to make their own decisions on numerous matters.

Despite this freedom, it is impossible to read charter school research without concluding that the free market proponents who initially promoted the notion have succeeded only in achieving a deregulatory reform instead of an innovative approach to public education. The political ideology that supports the concept opposes government control as antithetical to good practice and fails to recognize that autonomy alone does not guarantee success. To the contrary, schools' compliance with educational requirements advances responsible practice by fulfilling their responsibilities to the public and strengthening accountability. Moreover, equitable regulation will not infringe on the autonomy of charter schools but will produce advantages for schools, students, parents, taxpayers, and policymakers.

ACCOUNTABILITY AND TAXPAYER FRAUD

Compelling reasons exist for changing the current landscape and subjecting charter schools to the same standards and requirements as traditional schools. To begin with, the vision of charter schools is premised on an autonomy-for-accountability exchange that has not materialized. Actually, the claims of de facto equity and greater accountability are mere illusions. The available evidence shows that charter schools are not held to a higher level of accountability than traditional schools in student academic achievement or fiscal stewardship. Rather, charter schools are mired in diminished accountability pursuant to the public funds expended; the result is tremendous latitude for individual schools with limited knowledge of which programs succeed and which fail. Requiring charter schools to adhere to the same constraints as conventional schools will provide some rational method of assessment to hold them accountable in ways that regular public schools are, rather than making their survival simply a matter of popularity.

Another obvious reason for requiring charter schools to meet the same conditions as traditional schools is that they are public institutions predominantly funded at taxpayers' expense. Common sense alone suggests that it is not prudent to allow a system to be unregulated when it uses public dollars. Additional regulation is requisite to ensuring that taxpayer dollars are not wasted through fraud, incompetence, or mismanagement because such exploits have occurred in charter schools. For example, Edutrain Charter School in Los Angeles lost its charter in 1994 after audits disclosed financial mismanagement and the use of school funds for personal expenses. The circumstances surrounding the closure of 60 California charter schools operated by California Charter Academy (CCA), the largest charter school operator in the state, further illustrates the risks. In this case, the CCA founder and a city councilman were indicted in 2007 on 117 counts stemming from the misappropriation of $23 million in taxpayer funds to pay for items including personal watercraft and trips to the Disneyland Hotel Spa. Likewise, a school in Phoenix, Arizona, Citizen 2000, closed in 2001 after administrators inflated enrollment estimates, resulting in insufficient state aid and ultimate bankruptcy. When the school's students returned to public schools, their academic credits failed to transfer, and some had to repeat entire semesters. Granted, these occurrences may be uncommon; nevertheless, they still highlight the potential for fiscal irresponsibility. Frequently, operators of charter schools are educators who lack business and financial acumen. With the prospect of such adverse effects, additional regulation of charter schools can be viewed in proper perspective.

AUTHORIZERS OF CHARTER SCHOOLS

Overwhelming data exist concerning the ineffectiveness of charter schools. Various entities are authorized to grant charters. Depending on state law, the state board of education, local school districts, or a special agency established for that purpose are delegated the authority of issuing charters. These entities are charged with approving charter schools, monitoring their compliance with applicable laws and regulations, and evaluating their progress, yet state legislation has afforded little guidance as to how such authorizers should approach these responsibilities. Furthermore, findings demonstrate that the actual role of oversight has been minimal. A report contracted by the U.S. Department of Education and authored by Kara Finnigan et al. (2004) found that authorizers experienced difficulty effectively overseeing charter school operations and progress toward meeting charter goals because of competing duties and a lack of capacity and access to organizational resources such as facilities and staff. In this same regard, another researcher, Rebecca Gau (2006), determined that nearly half of all authorizers she surveyed engaged in the activity only halfheartedly, thus disregarding the importance of oversight of their schools. Pursuant to these findings, authorizers are failing to serve as the regulatory control device that holds charter schools accountable, and they incur no real consequence for the poor management.

Likewise, there is no consistent system for monitoring corrective action from these schools, thereby preventing authorizers from holding them liable through nonrenewal or revocation of their charters. To a large degree, the fault does not lie with the authorizers; rather, the primary cause for this failure is ambiguous legislation. Statutory provisions that grant charter schools autonomy omit the terms of accountability and liability. Consequently, few charters specify performance measurements or minimum performance standards and those that do are unclear or unquantifiable. Such incongruity of purpose makes for incoherent accountability policies, producing a lack of authority to implement sanctions if problems or noncompliance are detected. Thus, for the majority of charter schools, liability has not occurred. Not surprisingly, Lee Anderson et al. (2003) found that charters have only been revoked by 8% of authorizers; other studies indicate no occasion where a charter was revoked or not renewed because the school failed to meet its charter goals. Exacerbating the situation is that authorizers often lack the necessary political clout to revoke a charter.

EDUCATION MANAGEMENT ORGANIZATIONS

Additional justification for subjecting charter schools to the same standards and requirements as traditional schools is the problematic role that education management organizations (EMOs) assume. These entities constitute for-profit businesses and are approved by laws in a number of states to operate charter schools. As determined by Amy Stuart Wells (2002), 10% to 20% of all charter schools nationwide are run by EMOs; a similar report issued by Western Michigan University established that 72% of Michigan charter schools contract with a for-profit firm (Horn & Miron, 2000). EMOs' corporate agenda is making profit for their shareholders, a system subject to profit motives and shareholder pressure. For-profit relationships foster exploitation and mismanagement at public expense as EMOs cut costs and quality in imperceptible ways. In public education, money counts and diverting money from public schools is counterintuitive.

DATA AND RESEARCH ON CHARTER SCHOOLS

If there is any doubt that congruity of obligation with respect to charter schools is clearly necessary, one has only to consider student achievement to resolve the matter. Despite the resounding argument that charter schools freed from regulation will produce better educational environments, when the overall scores on standard assessments of charter school students are compared with those of their peers in traditional public schools, the former perform only similarly or even slightly worse than the latter. Moreover, in view of the aforementioned limitations relative to oversight by authorizers, charter schools are not being held more accountable for academic outcomes than other public schools, which is perhaps the most pervasive theme in the research.

Reflecting the laissez-faire approach to charter schools accountability, current practices thwart the gathering and dissemination of consistent and valid data concerning charter schools. Although the first charter school opened more than a decade ago, we still know comparatively little about these schools; information generated has been suspect and often ambiguous and is literally missing from a large percentage of the nation's charter schools. For example, in reporting on education in Arizona, Alex Molnar and Jamie Joanou (2005) found a lack of available information concerning that state's charter schools on basic facts including the following: the number of charter schools, their average size, the number of public school students attending these schools, the ethnic composition of the student populations, the number of charter school teachers, and the number of charter school administrators. Furthermore, the scant existing charter school studies use different methodologies and present mixed results. If this information deficit continues, it will remain difficult to gauge charter schools' performance and make rational policy decisions. Standard reporting requirements across all public schools would yield a core of meaningful, comparative information and provide more streamlined, nuanced data than the present system.

Similarly, more transparent data are a must. As with traditional schools, states should make available cumulative facts on every charter school with the individual school report cards for all public schools pursuant to NCLB mandates. In this manner, the public, who is paying the bills for public schools, could compare the demographics and performance of each school in the state. Unequivocally, the scrutiny afforded in a transparent structure positions policymakers to ensure high quality for each and every public school.

Subjecting charter schools to the same standards and requirements as traditional schools offers a variety of benefits. Reporting requirements ensure policy continuity and create more reliable relationships between schools and public authorities. Additionally, standards give a metric against which every school's performance is judged, which is especially significant given the previously described examples of mismanagement and criticisms of ill-defined accountability procedures; thus, rendering equitable treatment common to all schools. Creating more regulations is not antithetical to the charter school movement because the experience thus far has demonstrated pitfalls endangering the viability and sustainability of charter schools.

In addition, under the present system, it is often impossible for parents and other members of the public to determine how well a charter school is performing or whether the school has faced compliance issues. Increased regulation would ensure more consistent information and serve as a valuable tool to inform the public and to help charter schools improve. Communities would be better able to judge schools and decide, based on consistent requirements and standards, which schools offer the best education. By eliminating the existing fragmented system, charter schools could accomplish the necessary educational outcomes and better realize their goals.

CHARTER SCHOOLS AND POLITICAL INFLUENCE

A further benefit of imposing traditional requirements and standards on charter schools is to mitigate the political influence associated with these types of entities. The decision to revoke or not renew a charter can be difficult for authorizers because of staunch parental and community support; despite shortcomings, these schools have remained open as a result of external pressure. At the other extreme, school boards reluctant to issue charters may be pressured to do so because of political connections. As publicly funded institutions, politics are inherent; nevertheless, quality data garnered from uniform procedures can counter political manipulation and influence in the decision-making process.

TRENDS AND FUTURE DIRECTIONS

Moreover, the trend for demanding standardized requirements and standards for charter schools already exists because of several factors. First, in response to audit findings and widespread criticism of charters, states have revised many of their operational procedures. For example, in recent years, Florida passed legislation requiring charter schools to conform to express education cost accounting and reporting practices, whereas Idaho passed legislation requiring all those who have access to children in a public school setting, including employees of charter schools, to undergo a criminal background check. Second, the mandates of NCLB defined charter accountability equable with mainstream public schools, thus shifting accountability to a more bureaucratic model. Lastly, charter schools are implicitly subject to the restrictive rules and regulations governing state and federal categorical programs, such as Title I, and other, extensively regulated programs such as special education.

Imposing traditional requirements and standards on charter schools will not severely infringe on the opportunity for innovation. Public schools have always found ways to create unique curricula and governance structures even given heavy regulation. Akin to conventional schools, charter school teachers retain flexibility in their choice of instructional approaches, and schools maintain latitude through programmatic emphases. Moreover, countless studies report that the majority of charter schools have not instituted innovation to teaching and learning; their approaches to teaching and learning are indistinguishable from their conventional counterparts. It is further noteworthy that the relatively few innovative programs found in charter schools, such as the Montessori curriculum, are available in a number of traditional public schools.

In sum, the state should not create and fund charter schools that are not subject to the same standards and requirements as traditional schools. The increased parameters are not so cumbersome as to impose an unwarranted burden or a counterproductive force to the reform effort; rather such measures create a more responsible approach to school improvement. The vital public interest to be served by education in all public schools unquestionably justifies maintaining a uniform governance system.

FURTHER READINGS AND RESOURCES

Abdulkadiroglu, A., Angrist, J., Cohodes, S., Dynarski, S., Fullerton, J., Kane, T., & Pathak, P. (2009). *Informing the debate: Comparing Boston's charter, pilot, and traditional schools* (Understanding Boston Series). Boston: Boston Foundation.

Anderson, L., Finnigan, K., Price, T., Adelman, N., Cotton, L., & Donnelly, M. B. (2003, April). *Multiple perspectives on charter school accountability: Research findings from charter schools and charter school authorizers.* Paper presented at the meeting of the American Educational Research Association, Chicago, IL.

Books, S. (1999). School funding: Justice v. equity. *Equity & Excellence in Education, 32*(3), 53–58.

Budde, R. (1988). *Education by charter: Restructuring school districts. Key to long-term continuing improvement in American education.* Andover, MA: Regional Laboratory for Educational Improvement of the Northeast and Islands.

Carnoy, M., Jacobsen, R., Mishel, L., & Rothstein, R. (2005). *The charter school dust-up: Examining the evidence on enrollment and achievement.* New York: Teachers College Press.

Center on Educational Governance. (2007). *Charter school indicators* (CSI-USC 2007). Los Angeles: University of Southern California.

Cremin, L. A. (1957). *The republic and the school: Horace Mann on the education of free men.* New York: Teachers College Press.

Education Commission of the States. (n.d.). *Charter schools.* Retrieved June 22, 2011, from http://www.ecs.org/html/issue.asp?issueid=20

Finnigan, K., Adelman, N., Anderson, L., Cotton, L., Donnelly, M. B., & Price, T. (2004). *Evaluation of the public charter schools program: Final report.* Jessup, MD: U.S. Department of Education.

Gau, R. (2006). *Trends in charter school authorizing.* Washington, DC: Thomas B. Fordham Institute.

Horn, J., & Miron, G. (2000). *An evaluation of the Michigan charter school initiative: Performance, accountability, and impact.* Kalamazoo: Western Michigan University.

Hoxby, C., Murarka, S., & Kang, J. (2009). *How New York City's charter schools affect achievement* (August 2009 Report. Second report in series). Cambridge, MA: New York City Charter Schools Evaluation Project.

Molnar, A., & Joanou, J. (2005). *The condition of pre–K–12 education in Arizona: 2005.* Tempe, AZ: Education Policy Studies Laboratory.

Ritchey, D. (2000). Disparities in public school finance support. *School Business Affairs, 66*(9), 29–30, 32–36.

RPP International. (2001). *Challenge and opportunity. The impact of charter schools on school districts.* Washington, DC: Office of Educational Research and Improvement, U.S. Department of Education.

Sass, T. (2006). Charter schools and student achievement in Florida. *Education Finance and School Policy, 1*(1), 91–122.

Spring, J. (2004). *The American school 1642–2004* (6th ed.). New York: McGraw-Hill.

Teske, P., & Reichardt, R. (2006). Doing their homework: How charter school parents make their choices. In R. J. Lake & P. T. Hill (Eds.), *Hope, fears, reality: A balanced look at American charter schools in 2006* (pp. 1–9). Seattle: Nation Charter School Research Project Center on Reinventing Public Education, Daniel J. Evans School of Public Affairs, University of Washington.

Wells, A. S. (Ed.). (2002). *Where charter school policy fails: The problems of accountability and equity.* New York: Teachers College Press.

Court Cases and Statutes

No Child Left Behind Act of 2001, 20 U.S.C. §§ 6301 *et seq.*
Zelman v. Simmons-Harris, 536 U.S. 639 (2002).

Should students be required to engage in fund-raising activities as a condition of participating in certain activities or events?

POINT: Robert J. Safransky, *Nova Southeastern University*

COUNTERPOINT: Dana K. Bagwell, *D'Youville College*

OVERVIEW

Americans expect that education in the public schools will be free. In fact, the constitutions of most states mandate the establishment of a free public school system. Even so, in our current economic environment, school districts have only limited budgets and frequently do not have sufficient funds to pay for educational field trips, musical and theatrical productions, or athletics. As other essays in this volume have shown, many school districts are charging fees for students to participate in extracurricular activities. As an alternative means of financing the costs, schools or parent groups often engage in various fund-raising pursuits to finance these activities. Indeed, in some instances, school districts have even resorted to fund-raising to cover the costs of the basic curriculum. Inevitably, some parents and students do more than others do to raise money. This begs the question of whether students should be required to engage in such fund-raising as a condition of participating in activities such as sports, clubs, extracurricular programs, and field trips.

The practice of schools using fund-raising programs to generate additional revenue is not a new phenomenon. For many years, schools have sold tickets to sporting events and concerts to help defray the costs of these programs.

Parent organizations and booster clubs have often raised moneys by selling products, such as candy bars or wrapping paper, and holding events, such as fall fairs or auctions, to provide extra items for classrooms, sponsor field trips, and support enrichment programs, or to supplement the schools' sports and extracurricular activities programs. Although school-related organizations often develop and organize their own fund-raising events, many others rely on commercial businesses that specialize in fund-raising. Fund-raising has become a big business, with more than 1,200 companies now being listed in an online directory, the All Fundraising Companies Directory. In the past, students were not routinely required to take part in fund-raising activities to participate in the programs such activities supported. With schools increasingly mandating such participation, the question in this debate is whether student participation in fund-raising should be obligatory.

On the one hand, proponents of requiring participation in fund-raising efforts insist that it is only fair that those who benefit from the programs should do something—however minimal—to assist in defraying the costs. Additionally, given that these specialized activities involve only a small portion of the student body, proponents state that it is unreasonable to ask that the school board provide a complete subsidy. Furthermore, it can be argued that the very process of fund-raising can teach valuable lessons for life such as hard work, dealing with customers, the importance of record keeping, and so forth.

On the other hand, those who are opposed to mandated participation in fund-raising point out that there is a state constitutional obligation to provide a free public education. Assuming that all of these activities are important parts of the educational process, then logically they should be provided for free and, at minimum, no one should be required to engage in fund-raising as a prerequisite for participating in a school activity. If these activities are not part of the educational process, then one may question why the schools are promoting these activities in the first place. Moreover, there are compelling reasons why students or their parents do not wish to participate in fund-raising. For example, some students and parents may have religious or moral objections to staffing the bingo hall to support the band. Other parents may be in a position—such as that of an elected official or a judge—where engaging in fund-raising activities is prohibited. Similarly, assisting the local school district in raising money may undermine the parents' responsibility to raise money for another charity or organization.

Summary of the Debate

Robert J. Safransky, a former school administrator who is currently a professor at Nova Southeastern University in Florida, takes the affirmative view in this debate. In arguing that students should be required to support fund-raising efforts that pay for activities in which they participate, Safransky makes three points. First, he contends that requiring students to fund-raise ensures that no student receives the benefit of the activity without contributing to its success. Second, from his own experience, Safransky notes that participation in fund-raising builds a sense of teamwork and community. Third, he feels that involvement in fund-raising activities builds character and teaches important life skills. In conclusion, Safransky acknowledges that there are legitimate concerns about mandatory participation in fund-raising but feels that they are outweighed by the many educational advantages of having students participating in fund-raising.

Dana K. Bagwell of D'Youville College in Buffalo, New York, takes the negative view. First, Bagwell is concerned that fund-raising that involves junk food, such as selling candy or cookies, has the indirect effect of promoting unhealthy eating and, thus, contributes to long-term health problems. Second is that despite enormous amounts of money raised, the overall quality of the schools has not improved. Moreover, the private companies that are profiting from fund-raising activities are not always local businesses, but distant national concerns. Third, there is evidence that the fund-raising efforts do not necessarily result in greater money for schools. This is particularly true when one considers the true costs of doing the fund-raising. Indeed, it may be more effective to simply ask for a single yearly donation. In sum, Bagwell states that fund-raising does not work and arguably causes more harm than good.

William E. Thro
Christopher Newport University

POINT: Robert J. Safransky
Nova Southeastern University

In the current economic climate, many schools have turned to fund-raising as a means of supporting extracurricular activities or to provide the school with extras that cannot be purchased through the school's budget. Private and public schools hold a variety of fund-raising activities to obtain the moneys needed for the financial support of student activities. Fund-raising projects may range from cake sales to selling tickets for school-sponsored events. A number of commercial companies specialize in school fund-raising promotions. Typically, these outfits supply the schools with products for students to sell with the schools earning a profit from every product sold. Students are often provided with incentives, in the form of prizes, for selling the merchandise.

In an era when fund-raising has become commonplace in schools, students are often required to support the fund-raising efforts to participate in the activity or event financed through the fund-raising project. The student activities supported through fund-raising efforts may be curricular-related activities such as attending field trips, participating in the band or chorus, buying sheet music or uniforms for a band or chorus, purchasing production rights for a copyrighted play, or procuring additional equipment for classrooms or science labs. Fund-raising projects also may support cocurricular or extracurricular activities such as athletic teams or cheerleader squads, performing arts programs, chess clubs, student councils, or intramural sports. The list of activities could go on and on but covers a wide range of school-sponsored activities at all educational levels. However, financing these myriad activities often requires individuals who will raise the funds to purchase the goods and objects for the participants to sell because the school budget in the current downsized economy is often insufficient to support these types of activities.

Funds can be raised to supplement school budgets in a number of ways. One possibility that is common, but controversial, is to require students to support and participate in fund-raising projects to sustain the activities and events in which they wish to participate. Schools and school-related groups, such as booster clubs and parent–teacher organizations, throughout the country currently engage in a variety of fund-raising efforts to provide for activities and experiences that could not take place without this external funding. Many of these fund-raising projects are designed to foster school spirit and teamwork in addition to raising much-needed moneys. Students and the school community work together toward a common goal, and this shared activity helps build school spirit, establish school traditions, and set high expectations for excellent performance in academics and athletics. This essay provides a rationale to support the contention that students should be required to participate in fund-raising activities as a condition of participating in activities or events financed through the fund-raising effort. First, however, the essay will address the issue of how to involve the students in fund-raising activities as well as the policies and procedures involved with fund-raising and the appropriate procedures for accounting for funds each day during the fund-raising activity.

ORGANIZING FUND-RAISING ACTIVITIES

The first step in organizing a fund-raising activity is for the sponsor to meet with school officials to learn what fund-raisers are approved by the school board for schools and to identify the procedures to be followed in the collection of funds and delivery of goods. The sponsor must understand and be aware of all of the school district's mandated procedures, and, in turn, must adequately inform parents and students of the measures to be followed. This process should ensure that everyone is aware of all proper procedures and will follow them. If the participants are not aware of the procedures and trained in how to implement them, and if proper accounting measures are not followed, fund-raising dollars may disappear into the wrong pockets with disastrous results.

The second step is to clearly identify and delineate the purpose of the fund-raising project. As part of this process, school officials need to explain what the funds will be used for and how this will enhance the school's overall program. Reasonable goals must be set to obtain the cooperation and support of all stakeholders.

The third, and perhaps most difficult, step is to inform the parents and students that all students who are members of the particular group that will benefit from this fund-raising activity will be required to participate in the fund-raising as a condition of participating in the activity. School officials must take a positive approach in presenting this requirement to both students and parents. The sponsor should meet with the students before the fund-raising activity begins to emphasize that everyone is being asked to participate in this activity because everyone will benefit when the fund-raising goal is reached. The sponsor must emphasize the importance of teamwork by informing the students that all teams, if they want to be winners, need to have all team members supporting and working toward the achievement of the teams' goals. Thus, the sponsor needs to emphasize that all participants have to do their part by setting time aside and making an effort to make the fund-raising project a success.

REASONS FOR PARTICIPATION IN FUND-RAISING

The requirement that students participate in a fund-raising project may be abhorrent to many people, and some school systems may even have policies prohibiting mandatory participation in the fund-raising activities. However, there are many educational reasons why students should be required to participate in the school's fund-raising projects. The rationale for requiring all students to participate in fund-raising can be expressed with a number of basic questions. How do we develop and build a cohesive community if some do not want to participate but want to gain the benefits of the community activity? Some students will ask why freeloaders get to participate in the activity or event that was made possible by other people's hard work. Why are schools developing the concept that the students are owed something just because they are students? Why should a school develop in students the wrong attitude and expectation that the students will receive rewards without working for them?

Competition and Character Building

Most students are aware of the size of their school and the number of students enrolled, but some students are not involved in school activities because they do not feel that their participation is needed to make the school activities or events successful. When the school has a fund-raising activity that will benefit the whole school and there is competition among the various participating groups, the fund-raising activity will be more successful because students will want their class or group to win the competition and be recognized as the winners. Students will and do respond to challenges to reach new heights if they believe that they can be successful. The students will become involved in the activity and want to do as much as they can to make it possible for their class to win the fund-raising contest.

Involving students in fund-raising activities is a way to build their character and prepare them to achieve success as adults. There is competition in the adult world among companies, entrepreneurs, athletic teams, and nations. One of the best examples of this adult competition occurs internationally: Why do we have the Olympic Games every 4 years? Why do athletes train for 4 years to win their country's tryouts so that they can be members of the country's Olympic teams? Why do nations compete to be chosen as the site for the Olympics? Why do they compete against each other to win medals? Why did the president of the United States travel to Copenhagen to the International Olympic Committee meeting in 2009 in an effort to have the 2016 Olympics in Chicago? It seems that within each human being there is the desire to compete with other human beings and to win that competition.

This willingness to compete and to achieve is a character trait that should be encouraged and supported throughout all the school years so that the students will achieve academically and athletically. They will know that they have the will and determination to make time in their daily schedules to do what is needed to learn the subjects and to reach new academic heights. In the same way that people who want a physically fit body find the time to do exercises each day and eat a healthy diet, then students who want to do well should find the time and energy to participate in the school fund-raising activities. These positive character traits can be developed and nurtured by requiring students to participate in various fund-raising activities at their schools.

Developing People Skills

The students who participate in these mandatory fund-raising activities should recognize that they will develop some people skills that they can use now and in the future. The ability to meet a stranger and present oneself and the item being sold to convince the stranger to spend some money to purchase a good or ticket is a skill that will help a person be successful throughout life. A person must be able to sell her or his ideas to other people so those people will be willing to follow her or him. Vince Lombardi gave a speech titled "What It Takes to Be Number One" that, although originally delivered in the context of sports, applies equally to students' participating in a school fund-raising campaign:

> Every time a football player goes to ply his trade he's got to play from the ground up—from the soles of his feet right up to his head. Every inch of him has to play. Some guys play with their heads. That's O.K. You've got to be smart to be number one in any business. But more importantly, you've got to play with your heart, with every fiber of your body. If you're lucky enough to find a guy with a lot of head and a lot of heart, he's never going to come off the field second. (Lombardi, 2010)

Running a football team is no different than running any other kind of organization—an army, a political party, or a business. The principles are the same. The object is to win—to beat the other guy. Maybe that sounds hard or cruel. I don't think it is.

If we review what Coach Lombardi has said about being a winner, we note that being a successful football coach should enable a person to be a successful leader in any organization. Companies, businesses, and countries fail in the world of competition, and others rise to take their place. How did they accomplish that? They used their heads, hearts, and bodies to win

Coach Lombardi's closing statement applies to the fund-raising program and to all school activities:

> It is a reality of life that men are competitive and the most competitive games draw the most competitive men. That's why they are there—to compete. The object is to win fairly, squarely, by the rules—but to win. (Lombardi, 2010)

We want our students to be winners now and in the future. Thus, by requiring them to be active participants in the fund-raising program they are building the abilities, approaches, and attitudes that will see them successful if they put everything they have into it.

CONCLUSION

Every student must participate in the fund-raising program because it benefits every person at the school now and into the future. If we do not require total participation, we will end up with a few people doing the work and the others wanting to benefit from the work of others. That freeloader philosophy of life does not work in athletics or business, and it surely will not work in a school. Educators must realize that they must remind their students that success comes before work only in the dictionary. Thus, if students work and work hard, they will be successful and the school program or event will be successful.

Some may argue that there are negative consequences to having students participate in fund-raising activities. Among the top arguments are that having students sell items such as candy bars only contributes to the obesity epidemic in this country and that it is inherently unfair to use children to raise funds for education. Although the obesity epidemic is undeniable, there is no evidence to support the contention that it is fueled by school fund-raising projects. Students who are obese did not get that way simply by eating candy bars from a school's fund-raising project. Further, although legitimate differences of opinion may exist about whether students should be used to raise funds for education, we must remember that this debate is about raising funds for extracurricular activities. Children (and adults) are often asked, and required, to contribute to the support of groups they belong to, such as Scouts, youth sports, church groups, and social organizations, by actively taking part in fund-raising activities. Why should they not help to pay for their own extracurricular activities in school?

COUNTERPOINT: Dana K. Bagwell
D'Youville College

More than $2.3 trillion in financial aid has been given to the world's poorest countries during the last 50 years; yet, 30,000 children across the globe continue to die *daily* from extreme poverty. Even though billions of dollars continue to be spent on the worldwide AIDS epidemic, more than 2 million individuals were infected with HIV in 2009 and almost as many died from the virus. Although international fund-raising efforts obtained more than $5 billion in aid for the Haiti earthquake reconstruction effort in 2010, less than 2% of the rubble has been removed and little was rebuilt in the 9 months following the event. Surely education in the United States is immune from such disparities between a mass outlay of funds and corresponding lackluster progress? It is easy, if cynical, to dismiss the lack of real progress in worldwide poverty reduction and in reducing the AIDS epidemic—the world's poor lack the skills and means to draw substantial media attention to their plight. However, the K–12 educational system in the United States encompasses about 48 million students—students whose parents are better educated than any previous generation, and who are not reticent about speaking their mind and being partners in their child's education. This parental investment in education is the reason why so many schools engage in fund-raising: Parents are a captive audience. And, parents respond in droves to fund-raisers convinced that moneys raised enrich their children's education, but are the outcomes justifying the amount of fund-raisers? Three implicit presuppositions underwrite the argument for mandating fund-raising. First is the assumption that the fund-raising status quo produces no unintended side effects. Second is the assumption that the experiential knowledge gained from fund-raising will augment education outcomes. Third is the assumption that more fund-raising will produce more money. These three assumptions guide this examination of why fund-raising should *not* be required as a condition of participation in certain activities or events.

Before we examine whether these underlying assumptions support mandating fund-raising, much less whether current fund-raising is even working, let us quickly examine why schools bother with the expense and hassle of fund-raising to begin with. Although exact numbers on fund-raising totals are unobtainable, the first of many problems with mandating fund-raising, most estimates are in the $1 billion to $2 billion range—aggregate each year. Schools report that fund-raising supports the purchase of educational products, for example, books and computers, and tangentially related educational activities, for example, playgrounds, field trips, and so on. A nationwide survey of school principals revealed that 3% of schools have between 10 and 15 fund-raisers each school year, which equals about one every other week; a full 20% of surveyed schools average a fund-raiser every month. Schools rely on this yearly influx of money; 94% of principals said fund-raising supplements the moneys received from state and federal agencies. If donations from philanthropic organizations such as the Gates Foundation, and smaller, more local donations, not to mention in-kind donations, are included, the *extra* money pumped into the national K–12 educational system yearly is likely more than $20 billion. Notwithstanding the total spent on education at more than $2.3 trillion (2007–2008), what is the tangible return on such an enormous yearly investment? Further, what are students getting out of the considerable amount spent on education, and is requiring students to raise more money really the answer? Unfortunately, the outlook is not promising.

ASSUMPTION 1: FUND-RAISERS AND THE STATUS QUO

The dangers of fund-raising extend beyond the eager child knocking on the door of the stranger at the end of the block, although, such scenarios warrant significant concern. Often the biggest danger of fund-raising is the content of fund-raisers itself. A recent scientific article in the *Archives of Pediatrics and Adolescent Medicine* (Kubik, Lytle, & Story, 2005) found a 0.10 unit increase in body mass index (BMI) for each food practice permitted in schools (such as fund-raising involving food) excluding meals. Most schools have numerous fund-raisers throughout the year, and unfortunately, schools largely sell junk food, an alarming fact especially given that fund-raising often begins in kindergarten. A survey from the Association of Fund-Raising Distributors & Suppliers (AFRDS, n.d.) indicated that the most popular K–12 fund-raising items are food items for baking, such as cookie dough. Current estimates of childhood obesity are projected to cost the United States $254 billion. Making fund-raising mandatory, when the fund-raising activities involve food, will only increase the scope of this public health problem. Further, beyond the traditional side effects of obesity—for example, heart failure—emerging research indicates that thinking, memory, and other cognitive skills decrease with such extreme weight gain. Data from the National Association of Elementary School Principals and the AFRDS indicate that, apart from the most popular item of cookie dough, most fund-raisers involve other unhealthy food: box tops (sugary cereals), candy bars, bake sales, and confections. Even the long-standing collection of high-sodium canned soup labels is potentially counterproductive in the long run. A 2009 article in the *American Journal of Health Promotion* reports that decreasing sodium intake to the *maximum* daily dose would save about $50 billion annually by decreasing health care costs and increasing quality of life (Dall et al., 2009). The irony is that increasing quality of life is one of the reported goals of fund-raising. Schools frequently boast of their fund-raising success via the amount of money collected; yet, the immediate and long-term cost in decreased health and child safety, potential for impaired cognition (e.g., increased forgetfulness), and overall cost to society, such as rising health care premiums, far outweigh any transient benefit from that fifth-grade field trip to the zoo. Furthermore, a 2011 report by the Centers for Disease Control indicates this childhood upswing in obesity rates continues into adulthood where the number of obese adults has doubled in recent decades—childhood rates have tripled. At the least, school fund-raising cannot continue along this same path; the health of our children and our nation is at stake. If schools continue to sponsor, or worse mandate, fund-raising activities that involve selling food, particularly unhealthy food, they must be curtailed.

ASSUMPTION 2: FUND-RAISING INCREASES EDUCATION OUTCOMES

Proponents of mandatory fund-raising will undoubtedly cite the volume of money raised (average estimates range between $10,000 and $25,000 per school each year) as evidence that fund-raising should not only continue but expand. As already shown, fund-raising content is contributing to the nation's obesity epidemic, but what has all this money done for educational outcomes? Schools assert that fund-raising results in a better education for students, but do we have empirical proof in student outcomes to support such a claim? Although a direct correlation cannot be made, despite the amount of money schools raise each year, the number of college freshman enrolled in remedial courses is at an all time high. The Strong American Schools campaign released a report in 2008 showing the overall cost of providing remedial classes to incoming high school graduates in public universities exceeds $2 billion. Students and their families paid out of pocket, on average, $786 million to colleges to shore up this gap, where high schools failed to educate students adequately. Remedial classes typically do not count toward a college diploma, therefore such unfortunate necessities require additional moneys from parents and taxpayers. Some may think this problem is relegated to lower-performing students; however, the overwhelming majority of those taking remedial courses had a 3.0 GPA or higher in high school. Further, an estimated 60% of community college students require remedial classes—a fact made more disturbing by the fact that community colleges *expect* incoming freshman to begin at a lower level and adjust first-year classes accordingly. Far too many of these remedial students read and perform arithmetic at an alarmingly low elementary-to-middle school level. Is this what our bake sale goods are buying? School fund-raising contributes to unhealthy lifestyles, and there is no empirical evidence that it helps prepare students for the basic college courses. What then, are all these fund-raising dollars doing for education? The point essay contends that there are educational reasons for requiring students to participate in fund-raising activities. However, evidence is lacking that participating in fund-raising activities improves students' academic success. If fund-raisers do not help students as individuals, do they instead raise the quality of education for the school or district?

There is no denying that schools are strapped for funds. One teacher in Wisconsin offers extra credit to students who bring their own tissues to class; in 2009, a Detroit school asked for toilet paper and light bulb donations. Federal funding for education is at a historic low, accounting for inflation. However, desperation does not always breed the best solutions. For example, one Texas school proposed a "slave for a day" auction, and newspapers, blogs, and PTA meetings across the nation are littered with similar fund-raising horror stories.

Present-day fund-raising lacks real community connections as well. Businesses that provide schools with free glossy catalogs for school fund-raisers are often out-of-state shell corporations importing goods from China; therefore, there is no opportunity for improved school-to-community relations. Fund-raisers often purchase a product, whereas partnering with local businesses and community leaders fosters a symbiotic relationship. Research has shown that strong ties between schools and communities reduce adolescent crime and vandalism, reduce school absenteeism, and strengthen the general education environment of the school—all positive outcomes that are presently much needed. Instead, the disconnect among schools, the community, students, and parents has produced an additional cost that has been labeled *fund-raising fatigue.*

ASSUMPTION 3: MORE FUND-RAISING EQUALS MORE MONEY

In the Labels for Education program, parents must purchase more than 13,000 cans of soup, spending more than $20,000, to earn enough points for one computer. Even the ubiquitous bake sales require parents to purchase goods, prepare and cook the items, and then supply their children with funds to purchase the items at school—to say nothing of the greenhouse gases involved in transport and oven operation. There is an inherent law of diminishing returns with stacking fund-raiser on top of fund-raiser—to say nothing of student participation in nonschool fund-raisers such as Girl Scout cookie sales. In fact, the survey of principals mentioned earlier indicated that a full 64% would end fund-raising entirely if they could. Further, parents already complain about the amount of pandering their kids do and subsequently they give less and less throughout the year. Furthermore, there is no evidence that more fund-raisers would even produce more money.

Unfortunately, the return on investment for fund-raisers often leaves parents in the negative, and schools do not come out much better. Businesses that supply fund-raising products to schools often price according to quantity purchased. The more products the school purchases, typically sold in cases rather than individually wrapped items, the higher the potential profit margin. Unsold items are often not returnable, and schools are left absorbing the costs of the unsold items. Using data from one business that sells fund-raising products to schools as an example: To reach a 50% profit margin, schools would need to sell around 200 cases, or 1,200 individual containers at $13.50 each; profit margins drop precipitously with each product not sold, reducing the profit margin to 30% or lower (Top School Fundraisers, n.d.). Profit margin assumes that no cost is incurred by the school to hold the fund-raiser, and these calculations do not factor in the health and safety costs associated with fund-raising.

What if, in lieu of multiple fund-raisers, schools offered parents and teachers the option of a single yearly donation? Several nonprofit organizations offer their consumers this option, in lieu of an extended telethon drive, with good success. Assuming that each school has an average of 516 students and each school currently raises an average of $17,500 per school via fund-raising, a rudimentary cost–benefit analysis is possible. If each student's parent donated $100, about 56 cents each day, the school would have approximately $51,600, perhaps more. School personnel who say they are overwhelmingly tired of fund-raisers, would likely donate $10 to $20 themselves to "buy back" time otherwise spent on fund-raising activities. If each teacher gave $10 per year, the average school with 37 teachers would bring the yearly donation to almost $52,000 per school—almost three times the amount fund-raising garners. These donation levels are quite realistic; teachers often spend $10 or more of their own money on classroom materials. The $100 parental donation is not a stretch either. If schools have a fund-raiser every month, as many schools already do, and cookie dough or a similar treat sells for around $12 each month for a 9-month school year, parents are already spending more than $100. Students and parents who cannot afford 56 cents per day can volunteer or provide other in-kind donations, and schools and the community can work together to find other creative solutions that benefit everyone.

CONCLUSION AND FUTURE DIRECTIONS

The failures of school fund-raising and its unintended effects on education notwithstanding, an all-out ban on fund-raising is no more realistic than mandating fund-raising for club participation. As it stands, fund-raising is making our children fat, fund-raising is not contributing to education in any meaningful way, and fund-raising is already in danger of tapping the available wells of contributions dry. Given the arrant failure of school fund-raising to produce a meaningful contribution to educational outcomes, it is difficult to accept the proposition that fund-raising become mandatory for group participation. Students today are under an unprecedented amount of pressure with standardized testing and grade scales that exceed a 4.0 average. Further, colleges are becoming more competitive, driving many students to squeeze in extracurricular activities and volunteer at multiple organizations all to gain a competitive edge in an increasingly uncertain world. How will adding another burden help?

What is clear, however, is the urgent need for scholars, school districts, policymakers, and—yes—even advocates for mandating fund-raising, to work together to research and implement proven outcome-based solutions. Such partnerships should move away from the out-of-area confectionary dealer and embrace local organizations, businesses, and academia. Under these new guidelines, fund-raising could be couched in terms of a loan; the payment on that loan is high school graduates that are 100% prepared to enter the workforce or college and will already possess strong community ties. Who knows, such a learning environment might produce the next leader of the World Bank who could figure out how to slow global poverty without wasting another $2.3 trillion.

FURTHER READINGS AND RESOURCES

All Fundraising Companies Directory: http://www.fundraisingweb.org

Association of Fund-Raising Distributors & Suppliers (AFRDS). (n.d.). *Survey confirms product sales outperform other school fundraisers.* Retrieved from http://www.afrds.org/news_20071112.html

A.W.R.S.D. Fund Raising Regulations: http://www.awrsd.org/Forms/FundRaisingForms.pdf

Centers for Disease Control and Prevention. (2011). *CDC grand rounds: Childhood obesity in the United States.* Retrieved from http://www.cdc.gov/mmwr/preview/ mmwrhtml/mm6002a2.htm?s_cid=mm6002a2_w

Dall, T. M., Fulgoni, V. L., Zhang, Y., Reimers, K. J., Packard, P. T., & Astwood, J. D. (2009). Potential health benefits and medical cost savings from calorie, sodium, and saturated fat reductions in the American diet. *American Journal of Health Promotion, 23*(6), 412–422.

Davis, G. (2010, January). *Making school-community ties elementary in federal way.* Retrieved from http://www.publicbroadcasting.net/kplu/news.newsmain/article/0/ 1/1691017/KPLU.Local.News/Making.School-Community.Ties.Elementary.in. Federal.Way

Hess, F. M. (2005). *With the best of intentions: How philanthropy is reshaping K–12 education.* Cambridge, MA: Harvard Education Press.

Hoffman, N., Vargas, J., Venezia, A., & Miller, M. S. (2007). *Minding the gap: Why integrating high school with college makes sense and how to do it.* Cambridge, MA: Harvard Education Press.

Kubik, M. Y., Lytle, L. A., & Story, M. (2005). Schoolwide food practices are associated with body mass index in middle school students. *Archives of Pediatrics and Adolescent Medicine, 159,* 1111–1114.

Lombardi, V. (2010). *What it takes to be number one.* Retrieved December 22, 2010, from http://www.vincelombardi.com/number-one.html

Simonsen, K. (2009, January 5). *Mandated community service: A needed part of the modern curriculum.* Retrieved December 22, 2010, from http://www.associatedcontent .com/article/1339807/mandated_community_service_a_needed.html?cat=4

Top School Fundraisers: http://topschoolfundraisers.com/gourmet-cookie-dough-fundraising.html

Volunteer Canada. (2006). *Volunteering and mandatory community service: Choice—initiative—coercion—obligation.* Retrieved December 22, 2010, from http://www .energizeinc.com/art/documents/MCSDP_ENG.pdf

INDEX

Note: Bolded numbers refer to volume numbers in the Debating Issues in American Education series.